THE DEVIL IS A

Edited by Leo Madigan

CM0092008S5

To the memory of

MONSIGNOR GEORGE ARTHUR TOMLINSON ("TOMMY")
(1906 – 1985)
Priest of the Westminster Diocese
and
Father Douglas Carter
(1905 – 1991)
Priest of the Birmingham Diocese

Ullathorne enthusiasts both.

THE DEVIL IS A JACKASS

being

the dying words of the autobiographer

WILLIAM BERNARD ULLATHORNE

1806–1889

Cabin boy

Benedictine monk

Missionary to penal Australia

Vicar-General in penal Australia

Vicar-Apostolic to the Western and Central Districts of
England and Wales

First Bishop of Birmingham

Titular Archbishop of Cabasa

Edited by
Leo Madigan

Gracewing.

Downside Abbey Publications

First published in 1995 by

Gracewing
Fowler Wright Books
Southern Avenue, Leominster
Herefordshire HR6 0QF

Downside Abbey Publications
Stratton on the Fosse
Bath BA3 4RH

Gracewing Books are distributed

In New Zealand by:
Catholic Supplies Ltd
80 Adelaide Rd
Wellington
New Zealand

In Australia by:
Charles Paine Pty
8 Ferris Street
North Parramatta
NSW 2151 Australia

In the U.S.A. by:
Morehouse Publishing
P.O. Box 1321
Harrisburg
PA 17105
U.S.A.

In Canada by:
Meaking and Associates
Unit 17, 81 Auriga Drive
Nepean, Ontario, KZE 7Y5
Canada

cum permissu

All rights reserved. No part of this publication may be reproduced, stored in a
retrieval system, or transmitted in any form or by any means, electronic,
mechanical, photocopying, recording or otherwise, without the written permission
of the publisher.

Compilation and editorial material © Leo Madigan

*The right of the editor to be identified as the author of this work has been
asserted in accordance with the Copyright, Designs and Patents Act, 1988*

ISBN 0 85244 2513 Gracewing
ISBN 1 89866 3076 Downside Abbey Publications

Cover illustration courtesy of Downside Abbey,
Stratton-on-the-Fosse, Bath
Typesetting by Action Typesetting Limited, Gloucester
Printed by The Cromwell Press, Melksham, Wiltshire

Preface

On any showing William Bernard Ullathorne was a remarkable man and, as Abbot Cuthbert Butler noted in his two volume *Life and Times* so closely was Ullathorne connected with every phase of the history of the English Catholics during the nineteenth century, and so intimate were his relations with the chief actors that it was impossible to write properly of him without including a more general survey of that history, and thus extending the biography to nearly 700 pages.

Not only was his life very influential, it was also extra-ordinarily varied and exciting throughout his first forty years up to his appointment as the first Bishop of Birmingham on the restoration of the English Hierarchy in 1850, the period covered by this autobiography.

Along with Newman and Manning, Ullathorne was un-questionably the most prominent Catholic ecclesiastic in England in the middle years of the nineteenth century, and unlike those two converts from the Church of England, he represented the old Catholic tradition with its solid good sense; and he had indefatigable energy as pastor, leader and teacher.

A selection from the chapter headings of Butler's *Life* gives an indication of the depth and breadth of Ullathorne's significance and influence within the Catholic Church, both in England and in Rome, as well as in social and political affairs in England and Australia: *The Australian Mission; The Convicts; [Parish Priest in] Coventry; Vicar Apostolic [in the Western and Midland Districts]; Bishop of Birmingham; In the Lists at Rome; The Westminster Succession; Ullathorne and Newman; Association for Promoting Unity of Christendom; The Vatican Council; Ullathorne and Manning; Monk; Writer and Teacher* . . .

Ullathorne's life virtually spanned the nineteenth century, being born in 1806 and dying in 1889, and is neatly divided into the two halves represented by the period covered in this auto-biography and his subsequent reign as Bishop of Birmingham. Because of the significance of this latter part of his life, which is very well documented, but perhaps less compelling, it is very valuable to have his own account of the formative years which led up to it. This is further enhanced by the fact that we have the two versions, here collated by Leo Madigan, one written fairly close to the events described and another in old age, looking back with, perhaps, a better perspective but with less lively reactions.

Besides the very significant account of his times in Australia and his adventures all around the world, perhaps the most important section of this book deals with Ullathorne's negotiations in Rome for the restoration of the English Hierarchy, which gets rather scant attention in Butler's *Life*. This gives a very clear indication of the quality of the man, and why he was so important at this crucial period in the history of the Catholic Church in England. We have here a book which has long needed the attention it has now received.

Downside Abbey   Dom Philip Jebb
Epiphany 1995

Bishop William Ullathorne

Introduction

At the time of writing (April 1993) there is a priest, Fr. William Klein S. J., living in the German town of Münster who is 104 years old. He was born on the 24th March 1889, three days after the death of the author of this autobiography (and, incidentally, three months before the death of the Jesuit poet, Gerard Manley Hopkins). I mention this simply to provide a time-bridge with the work. Stark dates — William Bernard Ullathorne 1806 to 1889 — are so impersonal, so icy, as to freeze a reader into indifference.

I recall as a child, in a convent of the Sisters of Mercy in the Wellington diocese of New Zealand, there was a print of the Ullathorne portrait, that appears as the cover to this book, on the classroom wall. I rather liked the face, but the episcopal garb and rigid pose placed the man at several light-years remove from life as we urchins lived it. Even the nuns, despite their veils and gamps and voluminous skirts girdled with rosaries, were human and immediate. I knew nothing about him except his name and the fact that he had ministered in the antipodes in colonial days. So, nearly half a century later, when it was suggested that I collate Ullathorne's autobiographical writings (which I'd never read) the prospect had as much attraction for me as if I'd been asked to catalogue surgical instruments.

Books about Bishops, be they ever so worthy, mostly don't get read because, I suppose, readers are preconditioned to regard them as boring. I was wrong. And I hope you will give William Bernard Ullathorne the chance to prove how wrong I was. If one is still inclined to hold out against Bishops it ought to be said that this volume covers only the first half of his life up to the time when he was created Bishop of Birmingham, though he had been consecrated as the Vicar-Apostolic of the Western District of England & Wales before the Restoration of the Catholic Hierarchy in 1850, which, as he relates, he negotiated in Rome.

At the instigation of Mother Margaret Hallahan he wrote the

story of his life up to this point in the late 1860s (which is referred to in the footnotes as Ms. 1.). It is a lively account from his boyhood in North Yorkshire at the time of Napoleon's domination of Europe, through his early years as a merchant seaman; as an English Benedictine before Catholic emancipation; his appointment as Vicar-General to the Australian penal colony at the age of twenty-six; graphic details of his 'curious and piquant' life there; return to Europe; travel; negotiations in Rome; canvassing for clergy in Ireland; politicing against the penal system; back to Australia where his former Novice Master has been appointed Bishop and where he himself endures a period of trying unpopularity among the settlers, as his lobbying, if effective, would deprive them of the financial benefits of the slave labour they enjoyed in the colony.

He finally leaves Australia – though he himself was not aware that he would never return – on a French ship in November 1840. He visits New Zealand, Chile and Brazil and is soon settled in Coventry where he flourishes as a parish priest. He is active in building a church and establishing a school run by Mother Margaret Hallahan and her companions, whom he forms into an order of Dominicans who still function in Stone in Staffordshire.

He relates how he is created Bishop (titular, of Hetalonia[1]), is appointed Vicar-Apostolic of the Western District, and bases himself in Bristol. He dwells at some length on the markedly stoney opposition he receives from the Prior Park community, which necessitated a journey to Rome to resolve – and even then without any tangible success.

At the request of his fellow Bishops he returns to Rome to represent them on the matter of the Hierarchy, which he successfully negotiates and is created Bishop of Birmingham.

The narrative stops here although, in fact, he was to hold the See for almost forty years, only retiring for the final year of his life to Oscott as titular Archbishop of Cabasa.

In the last years of his life he re-wrote the work (Ms.II in the footnotes) covering the same ground, indeed clearly working from Ms. 1. Presumably he intended to continue the narrative to cover his long episcopacy, but his death prevented this and so we are left with two manuscripts, but differing subtly in style and approach – not to mention handwriting. Ms.II. is blessedly more legible and it is also more succinct, objective and honed. Although Ullathorne had written 'not for publication but for record' he was 'pretty sure it would get out after my time'.

This version was prepared for publication by Mother Drane, the successor of the Mother Imelda of the opening paragraph, who herself succeeded Mother Hallahan, at Stone in 1891. This lady liberally wielded an expunging blue pencil and was not shy about adjusting the text to modify the writer's judgments, or to clothe the naked miscreant being flogged on the beach at Scarborough. She notes in her Preface that, 'a few passages in the Life have, for obvious reasons, been either omitted or briefly summarised, according to what would have been the purpose of the writer'. Her 'few' are modest indeed, and what the 'obvious reasons' are might elude one at this remove of a hundred years.

The 1868 'Life' (Ms.1.) although longer and more discursive is by far the livelier of the two. The manuscript lay in the archives at Stone until it was borrowed by the Anglo-Irish convert Catholic writer, Sir Shane Leslie, who transcribed it in London during the dark winter of 1939–40. In it he found, 'the brave old Archbishop's character a consolation, even a buckler, in days when the devastation of the capital was thought to be immanent.' This was published in 1941 as *From Cabin-boy to Archbishop* of which Leslie wrote, 'It was a thrilling autobiography and worthy of the seemingly sensational title we have given it.'

The title of this volume, too, might be considered in the same light. *The Devil is a Jackass* were not exactly his last words, but were among those uttered on his deathbed. The jackass he was referring to is very likely the Australian kingfisher, the kookaburra, or 'Laughing Jackass' which, as he relates, he encountered in the bush. Its call is said to sound like fiendish laughter. His biographer, Dom Butler, tells us that when he was actually dying at Oscott – on the feast of St. Benedict, March 21st, and what more auspicious day for a Benedictine to pass into the next world? – he said, 'Yes, I see them', presumably the angels, and died with his eyes open. As Leslie comments in his Introduction, 'The beyond held no terrors for him'.

Whether it was the exigencies of war-time, the myopism of an editor or the sheer weight of writing in the days before the computer could act as secretary, Leslie's book is peppered with errors – typographical, spelling, missed words and even lacunae of entire sentences. The book is loyal to the order of the manuscript as it stands, but one cannot believe that the order in which it was written would be the order in which the author himself would have approved publication. For instance, when writing of his experiences in England and Ireland on his first journey back from Australia in 1836, Ullathorne suddenly inserts a chapter of reminiscences of Australian missionary life, followed immediately by another on his ordination in 1831.

In joining the two scripts together to make, I hope, a continuous narrative, I have endeavoured to right these errors and slot chapters into their chronological sequence, without introducing too many mistakes of my own. I have endeavoured to be scrupulously loyal to Ullathorne's own words and, apart from the odd word, very few in number, the text is his. I admit, however, to certain liberties with punctuation and paragraph and chapter division. The Victorians' punctuation was as heavy as their puddings and in many instances I have diluted it to make it more acceptable to contemporary taste. In such a marriage of scripts one must rely solely on one's own judgement and if there be any Catholic historians familiar with the works who are offended by my choices, I beg their indulgence. I am not an historian, or a scholar. I simply wish to introduce a man who has become a friend.

The lengthy business at Prior Park might well be skipped, though it does present some profound interplay of psychology. I get the feeling that the whole incident would make fine theatre in the hands of a skilled dramatist, but a denouement would have to be contrived because as it stands it contains a climax without a resolution − a familiar enough aspect of life, perhaps, but disastrous for the stage.

One matter for slight alarm is that a reader coming to these pages might be left with a prejudice against Prior Park on the strength of the picture Ullathorne paints of it when the singularly unco-operative Dr. Brindle was its Principal. Prior Park is a Catholic College today, but refounded, after closure, by the Christian Brothers and now a lay-run school, it is a very different institution.

Leslie notes that Ullathorne was 'rough and ready of speech' and that 'under his hard crust he hides a grim sense of humour'. I particularly like his cutting Cardinal Manning short by remarking in his archaic Yorkshire accent, 'My dear sir, allow me to say that I taught the catechism with the mitre on me 'ed when you were an 'erectic.' Along with the observation that his treatise on humility was the best book on the subject − true humility, if humility is indeed truth − and scores of like sayings, his clergy were well stocked with verbal illustrations of their original and valiant Bishop.

It is of interest to recall that John Henry Newman spent his Catholic life in Ullathorne's diocese; even when he was created Cardinal-Deacon in 1879 Ullathorne was still his Bishop. In the *Apologia* Newman wrote, 'Did I wish to point out a straightforward Englishman. I should instance the Bishop, who has, to our great benefit for so many years presided over (the Diocese).' In 1850 Newman had dedicated his *Difficulties of Anglicans* to Ullathorne. Thirty six years later Ullathorne dedicated his *Christian Patience* to Newman in the following terms:

To His Eminence,
THE MOST ILLUSTRIOUS AND MOST
REVEREND CARDINAL NEWMAN
MY DEAR LORD CARDINAL: I do not forget that your first public appearance in the Catholic Church was at my consecration to the episcopate; and that, since that time, forty years of our lives have passed, during which you have honoured me with a friendship and confidence which have much enriched my life. Deeply sensible of the incalculable services which you rendered to the Church at large by your writings, to this Diocese of your residence in particular by the high and complete character of your virtues, by your zeal for souls, and by the influence of your presence in the midst of us, I wish to convey to you the expression of my affection, veneration and gratitude, by the dedication of this book to your name. It is the last work of any importance that I shall ever write, and I can only wish that it were more worthy of your patronage.

I am ever, my dear Lord Cardinal,
Your devoted and affectionate servant in Christ,
WILLIAM BERNARD ULLATHORNE
Bishop of Birmingham.
Birmingham,
July 18, 1886.

On August 18th 1887, just after resigning his See, Ullathorne paid his last visit to Newman and thus describes the scene:

I have been visiting Cardinal Newman today. He is much wasted, but very cheerful. Yesterday he went to London to see an occulist. When he tries to read, black specks are before his eyes. But his occulist tells him there is nothing wrong but old age. We had a long and cheery talk, but as I was rising to leave,

*an action of his caused a scene I shall never forget, for its
sublime lesson to myself. He said in low and humble accents,
"My dear Lord, will you do me a great favour?" "What is it?"
I asked. He glided down on his knees, bent down his venerable
head and said, "Give me your blessing." What could I do with
him before me in such a posture? I could not refuse without
giving him great embarrassment. So I laid my hand on his head
and said: "My dear Lord Cardinal, notwithstanding all laws to
the contrary, I pray God to bless you, and that His Holy Spirit
may be full in your heart." As I walked to the door, refusing to
put on his biretta as he went with me, he said: "I have been
indoors all my life, whilst you have battled for the Church in the
world." I felt annihilated in his presence; there is a Saint in that
man!*

Newman died just sixteen months after Ullathorne.

Appended to the present volume, "to redress the egotism of
such a record" as Ullathorne writes in the first paragraph of this
work, and to "give (a) fair and honest representation of that life
which is wholly of the soul" the sermon preached at
Ullathorne's Requiem Mass by his fellow Benedictine and
Bishop, John Cuthbert Hedley, is printed.

My own hope and prayer is that this volume may, in some
little measure, restore a great Englishman to the recognition he
deserves, both among his own countrymen, and among his
spiritual progeny in Australia.

Leo Madigan
Fuzeta, Portugal

Notes

[1]   This see, which has disappeared from recent editions of the *Annuario
Pontificio*, is spelt both Hetalona (*DNB*) and Hetalonia (*Brady* 1877).

Contents

Margaret
of the Mother of God

Foreword to Original Edition

To The Rev Mother Imelda Poole, Second Mother Provincial of the Dominican Congregation of St Catherine of Sienna *sic*.

My dear Mother Imelda — You have asked me so urgently, and that in the days of your great loss and mine, if Mother Margaret's departure to God is not rather a gain, and have asked me separately to write you a sketch of my many-coloured life, that I cannot refuse it to you.

The immediate relations of friendship and of co-operation which reigned between your late venerable foundress and myself for six and twenty years, that is from the date of our first acquaintance, have inspired you with the wish of having some record of one whom God chose as His unworthy instrument to aid and protect the great work of religion and charity, which He called and prepared her to bring into existence.

Two objections to the giving of such a narrative have made me reluctant; one is the egotism of such a record; the other, that the external and visible outlines, which are all that I can touch upon, give no fair representation of that veritable life, which is wholly in the soul, and which, in fact, would be but a long and tedious confession of human infirmities.

Still, as you piously believe that God, in the order of His Providence, destined me, most unworthy though I always knew myself to be, to co-operate in Mother Margaret's work, I will no longer refuse your request. So let me begin.

Chapter One

Birth and Early Recollections

I was born at Pocklington in Yorkshire, on the 7th of May in the year 1806, as the old bible entry used to tell me, at six o'clock in the morning. I was the eldest of ten children. My father was a grocer, draper, spirit merchant etc, in short he did half the business of the town, supplying it with coal before it had a canal and, in the absence of a bank, discounting bills.

His father had descended from gentle birth, but owing to a singular incident, he became a shoemaker, and afterwards a farmer. For his father was a gentleman of landed estate in the West Riding of Yorkshire, which estate he acquired through his marriage with Miss Binks to whom it came as heiress of Mr Binks, who had married Miss More, a lineal descendant of Sir Thomas More[1], the Chancellor and Martyr, and the sister of Mrs Waterton, who is commemorated by her grandson, the late celebrated traveller and naturalist Charles Waterton[2] of Waterton Hall, in his autobiography.

The estate was lost through the insurrection of 1745 in favour of the claims of the Stuarts, after which my grandfather and his brother Francis were taken in charge by Dr. Lawrence, a Catholic physician of York, whose descendants succeeded to an ancient Baronetcy. The two boys, however, were so terrified at the discovery of a skeleton in a cupboard in their bedroom, that they both ran away. My grandfather apprenticed himself to a shoe-maker, his brother fled to London, and there engaged himself to a chemist, and thus the turn in the fortunes of the family was completed. Yet the traditions cherished in the family had the effect, as in similar cases, of sustaining a certain tone and self respect which was not without its influence on mind and manners.

My dear mother was a native of Spilsby in Lincolnshire, of which county her father was Chief Constable. Sir John Franklin, the Arctic navigator,[3] and next-door neighbour in their childhood and youth. She remembered Dr. Banks of Captain Cook's expedition, under whose influence Franklin went to sea.

My father met my mother in London, when they were both engaged in Townshend's great drapery business in Holborn; he converted her to the faith and then married her, after which they commenced business in Pocklington on their own account.

My father, a man of considerable humour and cleverness, used to delight in provoking his Protestant friends by saying that he had married twice though he never had but one wife. Catholics in those days were compelled to go through a Protestant ceremony in order to legalise their Catholic marriage. My father was so popular a character, and my mother, who managed the drapery business, was so much beloved and respected for her kindness, gentleness and good sense, that their children were much noticed and every house was open to them.

I was sent to learn my first letters from a Miss Plummer, the daughter of a Protestant clergyman, who was still living but a few years ago.[4] At home I learned to say my prayers, morning and night, at my mother's knee. Even though she was engaged the long day in business, with the aid of a confidential servant, devoted until old age to the family, she contrived to keep us in good order and discipline.

My imagination as a child was extremely vivid, and communicated a portion of its life and vivacity to all that it looked upon in nature. I can recollect being led by the hand as a little child past a garden in which the snow lay, but the snowdrop and yellow crocus were there in a group, and seemed to me to be mysterious creatures of life that had just come up out of the earth to live in this world. The corn too in the fields seemed to me a great mystery, something inexplicable, and especially when it turned from green to brown, and was gathered into sheaves. It seemed to me as if they had killed the corn to make bread of.

Another childish recollection that set my mind a-wondering was the exercising of the militia on the public green in those warlike times, to see all those red-coated, black-gaitered, beplumed men, moving as if with one soul and one will at the voice of another man with a different shaped hat. Of course our nurse subdued us into good behaviour with the threat that Buonaparte was coming; and I pictured him to my infantile mind as a little man with a great cocked hat, a red coat and a big sword, going in his solitary strength and sternness from house to house and killing all the people. Now and then a sailor would pass through the place, deprived of a leg or an arm, holding in his one hand, or dragging on wheels, a little ship, and singing with brazen lungs about how, 'We Boarded the Frenchman', which led to talk among our elders about the wars, and set the child's mind upon its first wanderings into the great world abroad.

After being first rigged in a suit of cloth, that great transition of childhood, my father took me with him to York, and the walk by his side into the Cathedral gave me an impression of awe and of grandeur, a sense of the power of religion, which to my childish mind was like a revelation and many a long day did my imagination feed itself upon that wonderful recollection. Of course I was told that this marvellous structure was made by Catholics long ago. It did not astonish me, it elevated me and I could write an essay upon the influence which that combination of size, symmetry, grandeur and sublimity produced upon my opening sense.

But the city walls and Clifford's Tower puzzled me completely. Of course, I appealed to my father for information, and he satisfied me in a very simple way. He said, 'If Bounaparte comes, they will get in there and fight him out.' I recall as if it was yesterday the tender tones with which he replied to all my questionings. He seemed to feel all that was passing within me, on that great day in my education.

York Minister was visible as a conspicuous object from a hill near our residence, a spur of the Wolds, though some ten miles distant, so I now could animate that pointed mass of mysterious stone, and could recall its lofty arches, its gorgeous windows, and the figures in their mysterious sleep, of Kings and Bishops, standing in their niches or lying on their tombs. Who can say how much of our future tastes and mental tendencies are unconsciously derived from those earliest impressions made upon us by the greater and more elevating forms of art?

I remember also the impression first made on me by a Greek statue. It was a Flora, standing amongst rich foliage, and it literally dropped honey, for the bees had formed their combs with her wreath. The colourless creature seemed to sleep with open eyes, in her beauty, as she stood, and I suppose it was one of my earliest lessons in mental abstraction, for she seemed to me to be a spirit of a different world from that I lived in, a spirit with whom one could have no communication of speech, though she seemed to think even in her sleep. She simply made me very silent.[5]

But how shall I recall the joys of my first remembered Christmas, joys not of the eye or the palate, but of the imagination? The being awakened at night to listen to the playing and the singing of the waits. Rude strumming they might seem to other ears, but to the child awakened out of sleep, it was little less than celestial harmony. And then the imagination peopled all the heavens with beautiful angels flying so happily amongst the falling flakes of snow, and singing the coming of our little Saviour. And then, next day, came the expected visitor, old Nanny Cabbage, a Protestant woman, going from house to house in her red cloak and black bonnet, producing her little house from under her cloak, with its holly, its two red apples stuck on pegs, and the Child Jesus between them in his cradle as if it had been in Spain or Italy; then, courtesying to the family, she sang the 'Seven Joys of Mary' to the delight of the children − a relic this of Catholic times which I fear has passed away. These things were educating me, if we attend to the sense of the term, far more than Miss Plummer's first lessons in reading and spelling.

We had a little Chapel at Pocklington with its two windows, but recently enlarged, a small priest's house, and a long strip of garden. The priest was Abbé Fidèle, a venerable French emigrant, long remembered there and at York for his piety, simplicity and charity. He used to kneel long before the altar in a Welsh or worsted wig at his prayers, until Miss Constable, the patroness of the mission, arrived in the vestry, which was also his parlour and dining room; then he went there himself to vest, took off his wig, powdered his head, and came in vested for Mass. I was told at a later period that he had four written sermons, and that when he had read the first line of his discourse the little flock knew all the rest by heart. Other French emigrant priests occasionally came and visited our house, and I remember one was Dr. Gilbert, a man of great dignity and bearing, who told dreadful narratives of his escape from the guillotine. He was afterwards raised to an important prelacy in France.

It is very odd that our old nurse who was so fond of us, and had often to hear us say our prayers when our mother was engaged, was a bitter Methodist, and used sometimes to express in our hearing her contempt for priests and 'their trumpery'.

As soon as I was able to read. I got hold of a pictorial book of bible stories, lent me by a Protestant young lady, in which pictures of things were substituted for the words expressing them, amidst the texts. This gave me an early interest in the scripture history, and as I grew a little older I used to read the Book of Genesis and, what delighted me still more, the descriptions in the Book of Revelations in the Bible itself, that is, in the Protestant version, for I do not suppose that my parents then knew that we had a Catholic version in our language.

My father had an intimate friend, a Mr. Holmes, a solicitor, a man of a bright face and who had a cheerful ringing laugh, who was fond of reading good literature aloud. He was quite a character and was passionately fond of the drama. He lent me the *Arabian Nights* and *Gulliver's Travels*, and other books of that stamp which fostered whilst they enlarged the imaginative tendency of my mind.

I was a heavy, clumsy urchin, with what a Protestant clergyman's daughter described as 'large, blobbing eyes', silent when not asked to give an account of what I had been reading, and then always ready to give an account. I cared not for play, and my parents did not know whatever they could make of me. My second brother was quick and agile and this made me look all the more lumpy in the eyes of my neighbours, and awoke many a joke at my expense. But my first great literary rapture was when my father got for me a copy of *Robinson Crusoe*. I never tired of reading it, and of talking of it to everyone who chose to draw me out. I believe it had a great influence in giving me a taste for the sea at a later period; and when in the course of my missionary life I sailed in fine weather past Juan Fernandez, all the dreams of my early life were reawakened.

We could not have been more than seven and eight years old respectively when my father sent me and my next brother Owen to school at the village of Burnby, some two miles or so from our home. The master of the school in that quiet little village was a character, and had a reputation, and my father himself had learnt English grammar under him. We went on the Monday morning and returned on the Saturday afternoon, lodging at the village blacksmith's, whose wife had been my nurse – not the Methodist nurse of the whole family, but another, whose conversion from Church of Englandism with her whole family to Methodism I witnessed, with all the fanatical accompaniments of those times.

We slept in a dark attic under the thatch of their cottage, which only two or three panes of glass ever illuminated. As we sat in the winter evenings by the fire in the brick-floored room which served for kitchen, parlour and hall, we heard a good deal of pious sentiment uttered with an unctuous drawl, much agricultural talk in more vigorous and natural style, and all the gossip and small scandal of the village, of which the blacksmith shop was the focus.

Sometimes we got the privilege of taking a turn at the great bellows; or at hitting the cold chisel with the hammer that cut the glowing horseshoe nail from the cold iron; of which my brother was much fonder than I was. And sometimes we got a half holiday to help plant the family potatoes.

The schoolmaster, I have said, was a character. He was a grave, self-contained man, who when he unbended at the fireside of the farmers could talk of many things, which to them and to us, left the impression of learning beyond our aspirations. He was not only the oracle but the man of business of the village; made up his neighbours' accounts, surveyed their land, at which time we boys were called upon to drag the measuring chains and plant the staffs with their little flags. All the village had been at school to 'the Master', and he lived at all their houses in turn, week and week about. When he came to a house, the blacksmith's amongst the rest, it was a festive time; neighbours looked in in the evening. He had his special armchair, his glass and generally on invitation sang one of his three songs in a grave sweet voice, or, between the puffs of his pipe, told us stories of the wars, or of other men's travels.

We had our annual barring out[6] and our annual school feast, to which the fathers and mothers, the young men and the young women were invited. It was the great event of the year. The school house had mud walls, a thatched roof and a clay floor, but it turned out good accountants and land surveyors.

The 5th of November was a high day for the school. After dinner the pupils got the keys of the church, rang the bells, sported among the pews, and fired off little cannon in the church until twilight came, when they were succeeded by the farm lads and lasses, who carried on saturnalia until late in the night.

Another custom savoured more of the old Catholic times. A funeral was rare, but when it occurred the whole population assembled, sang the psalms in procession to the old chants, and afterwards received a distribution of bread and beer at the house of the deceased.

We were by express arrangement not to learn the Protestant Catechism, but by sitting in the school over our books whilst it was said, we knew it every word by memory.

The 'Master' had more than one stiff bout to conquer my hard stiff pride, in which unfortunately he failed, for the more he thrashed me the more I quietly but desperately stiffened my spirit to endure, and boasted afterwards that he had not conquered.

Still dreamy and clumsy, getting a fair amount of jibes for it, and living in my imagination; I remember going all the way back to school for my task book, and searching about for it, when the Master said, 'What are you looking for?'

'For my book, I fear I have lost it somewhere.'

'What is that under your arm?'

And there sure enough, it had been all the while.

After a certain time we passed from the blacksmith's cottage to lodge at the wheelwright's, whose wife was the daughter of the old village clergyman, and who had a brother who was the clergyman of the neighbouring village. I still bear the marks on my fingers of the chops I got bungling with the great axe in the wheelwright's shop. Here we saw a certain amount of Protestant clerical society from time to time, of the high and dry school, which gave us no idea of there being much religion in it, and which strangely contrasted with the spirit of the good, old, pious and charitable Abbé Fidèle. I remember that when the annual Sacrament Sunday came round, I think on Easter Day, it was preceded by a good deal of talk as an event like that of the annual Christmas party given in the house, but there was no other special preparation. One of the daughters asked her mother, 'Mother, is Jim to go to the Sacrament?'

She replied, 'Oh, no! Jim must not go, he would eat all the Sacrament. You know it is only a little taste!'

Poor Jim was the big apprentice to the wheelwright.

Burnby was a lonely little place; we seldom saw a stranger, and if one rode through it on horseback at rare intervals, he seemed to me to come out of some unknown world, and to pass into another.

Yet a great crisis came upon the village, hitherto so peaceful, and united as one family. A group of Methodists appeared one evening upon the green and began to preach and sing hymns; and amongst the group was an uncle of my own, one who had early left the Faith and become a dissenter, and this reminds me that his mother, my grandmother, was a Protestant. I never knew a man who pulled a longer face than he did, and he turned out very unfortunately. Week after week this group appeared on the green. Sundry convictions of sin and conversion took place; and amongst the rest one that made a great sensation.

It was the case of a particularly steady young man, son of the chief farmer. He got his conviction and some kind of visionary view whilst sitting on a stile, and becoming a Methodist of the Methodists. And when Christmas approached, it was a great subject of discussion in the village circles as to whether he would ever again attend any of the Christmas parties, or, as he sang a good song, would ever sing again, or play at cards. He came to his friends' parties, but did not sing, or play at cards.

At last the blacksmith received the Methodists to preach and pray in his house, which thus became their chapel; but we had already left it for the wheelwright's. From this time the village was divided, and got uncomfortable in its social relations. Its old simplicity was sadly marred by the introductions of this sour principle.

As to the old schoolmaster, I never knew until after years that he was devoid of religion of any kind. I saw him in the year 1850, just before he died, in his decay, and at the interview were also Bishops Briggs, Gillis and Brown,[7] on our way through Pocklington to visit Lord Herries. The poor old man had lost all his savings by the failure of a bank, and was supported by a subscription of his old pupils. I asked him if he had done his best to make his peace with God, and, weeping all the interview, he said that he had done so.

The things I have described were not without their practical influence in opening my intelligence to the then existing state of Protestant and sectarian life. They awakened my curiosity, but certainly presented no attraction to my youthful mind. We had our Sundays at home, but in the weekdays I fear our prayers were short and limited to the Sign of the Cross, the Our Father, Hail Mary and Creed.

Notes

1   Thomas More (1477–1535), was canonised by Pope Pius XI in May 1935.

2   Charles Waterton (1782–1865). His maternal grandmother was seventh in descent from Thomas More. Charles Waterton travelled much in South America, particularly what is now Guyana. His contributions to science were many. He is said to have raised taxidermy from a sorry handicraft to an art. His work was recognised by Darwin and Thackery mentions him in *The Newcomes*. Although Ullathorne calls the house Waterton Hall it was generally known as Walton Hall, near Wakefield. After his many adventures in the jungles of South America Waterton actually met his death in his own park by stumbling over a briar root. His brother met Ullathorne when he arrived in New Zealand. See Chapter 33.

3   Sir John Franklin (1786–1847), whose search for the Northwest Passage on the *Erebus* and *Terror* ended in disaster when the ships were crushed by ice. All concerned perished.

4   This is from Mss.1. Mss.2. reads: . . . who lived to a very advanced age.

5   This statue stood in the grounds of Kilnwick Hall near Pocklington.

6   'Barring out' was a term then in use to indicate the closing of the doors of the school room against a school master. It sounds here as if it was something of a ritual rather than an act of rebellion. At Bromfield in Cumberland it took place at 'dfasting Even', i.e. the three days of carnival before Lent and perhaps this was general. If the masters succeeded in gaining access to their classrooms a penance was imposed and accepted quite cheerfully by the boys.

7   James Gillis (1802–1864), was Titular Bishop of Limyra and a coadjutor to Bishop Carruthers of Edinburgh whom he succeeded (1852) in the Eastern Vicariate of Scotland. He was born in Montreal of Scottish parents, returned to Scotland as a child and studied for the Priesthood in France.

    The Bishop Brown referred to is either Thomas Joseph Brown OSB (1798–1880), who was consecrated Titular Bishop of Apollonia and a Vicar-Apostolic (1840): He became first Bishop of Newport and Menevia (1850); or George Hilary Brown (1786–1856), Titular Bishop of Tloa, Vicar-Apostolic of the Lancashire District (1840). He became first Bishop of Liverpool (1850). John Briggs (1789–1861), Titular Bishop of Trachis (1833) coadjutor to Bishop Penswick Vicar-Apostolic of the Northern District, whom he succeeded (1836) becoming Vicar-Apostolic of the newly formed Yorkshire District (1840). He was the first Bishop of Beverley (1850).

Chapter Two

Schooldays in Scarborough 1815

I suppose I must have been between nine and ten years old when my father changed his residence and business to Scarborough. He there became popular by breaking down a system of union among the tradesmen to keep prices up at a point agreed upon, and cheapened the grocery, drapery and wine trades one after another.

Here I first saw the sea, the object of my aspirations from the time I read *Robinson Crusoe*, and I recollect all the circumstances of my first view of it from the top of the Northern Cliffs, and the expansion which that wonder of creation gave to my mind.

My second brother and I were placed as day scholars at Mr Hornsey's school, which had some reputation as both a boarding and day school. Hornsey was a genuine pedant as well as pedagogue and the fact of his having published an English grammar and some other elementary books did not diminish the importance of the man. We stood in awe of him, and his moral lessons given with pompous intonation when occasion served. But we took more kindly to his son and his usher who was preparing for the Anglican ministry. He taught his own grammar, but though I was quick and fond of knowledge, he never explained or taught us to apply the principles of grammar.

He once gave us a half holiday to see a man flogged in a state of nudity on the seashore, preparing the indulgence with a moral lecture on the example we should see, though fearing it could not benefit us, as some there were who even stole under the gallows.

He was a well-meaning man of the high and dry Protestant type, conspicuous from afar with his portly figure, white hat, clouded[1] cane and decided strut. I think, however, that I got my mind more enlarged through one of the boys, who had a

12

collection of voyages and travels, which he lent to his companions at a penny a volume.

Two of my brothers went to the school of a Protestant clergyman, a Mr. Irving, who was assisted by his two clerical sons. The school was held in the transept of the old church of St. Mary's, which was walled off for this purpose. It had formerly belonged to an Augustinian monastery. I remember how angry my father was when he found out that one of my brothers, following the custom of the school, had put out the eyes of Queen Mary with a pin, in Goldsmith's *History of England*.

While our education was going on in these Protestant schools we laboured under a great disadvantage in only having a priest at Scarborough one Sunday in six weeks. This was a great disappointment to my parents who knew there was a good chapel and presbytery in the place, but did not find out there was no resident priest until they had fixed their own residence. Mr. Haydock,[2] the editor of *Haydock's Bible*, came once in three months, and Mr. Woodcock, of Egton Bridge, also came once in three months. They were both Douay priests and as they generally dined at our house, I used to be much entertained with their college stories.

On the five Sundays intervening between the sacerdotal visits, it was arranged that the flock should attend chapel morning and afternoon as usual, and my father and Mr. Pexton, who had been a church student at Ushaw, but had given up the idea of the ministry, were appointed to act as readers on alternate Sundays. First the usual English prayers were said aloud, then all in silence read the prayers for Mass in the *Garden of the Soul*, making a sort of spiritual communion, and then the lector for the week read one of Archer's[3] sermons, which my father did from his usual seat, but Mr Paxton stood before the communion-rails facing the people. In the afternoon the usual psalms and prayers were said aloud and the children said their catechism to the lectors. None of us youths had made our first communion, and as to confirmation, we had none of us ever seen a Bishop, either at Pocklington or at Scarborough. There were only four in all England and Wales.

At twelve years old my father took me from school and put me to his business, with the idea that if I returned to school again after two years of trade, I should better appreciate the value of a school, and should be able to apply my mind with more practical intelligence to such mercantile education as I required. I trudged on for twelve months getting an insight into my father's three businesses, and his method of managing his books, but with no great taste for this kind of occupation. In the evenings I was indulged by being allowed to follow my passion for reading, which I did by running through all the books that tempted me by their titles in the two circulating libraries then in town. Voyages and travels were always my leading attraction, though I also ran through many rubbishy novels and romances. I followed my reading after everyone had gone to bed, and put my book under my pillow for a new start in the morning before business began.

This miscellaneous and undirected reading filled me with a strong desire to see the world, and as the only way of accomplishing this, I set my mind on going to sea. To this proposal my mother and father long and justly objected, but seeing that I was bent in that direction, they yielded at last, still hoping that I should sicken of it after trial.

A Scarborough ship was to be my destiny, and I was nearly put under the cruellest tyrant that ever sailed from that port, a man who had hung up his own son by the thumbs, and whose atrocities to his apprentices had become a proverb among seamen. But providentially my father found out his character in time to save me from him. Happily for me a fine brig was going to be launched, whose owners were my father's friends, and which was to be commanded by a captain superior to the ordinary run of mercantile captains, a man of gentlemanly manners and feelings, and whose wife, a superior woman, always sailed with him. I can never forget the kindness of Mr. and Mrs. Wrougham to me. Our officers and crew were also picked men, connected with decent persons in Scarborough. One of my father's assistants, a man of mature years, having taken a fancy to the sea, sailed in the same ship.

When, however, the Rev. Mr. Haydock came next Sunday to Scarborough, he looked very gravely on the notion of my going to sea. He saw its perils for a youth of my proud character, spoke seriously against it, and was evidently distressed. But finding it was all settled, he told me to go to him to prepare to receive the Sacraments before I left. But alas! in my boy's conceit, fostered by all this reading, by my fondness for isolating myself, and musing alone on the cliffs and sea beach, I fancied that the good priest was obtruding too much on what concerned me. I did not go to him at the time appointed, and even spoke of it to the Protestant shopmen and servants, who let me see that this did not edify them. Pained at my breaking his appointment, the good priest sent for me again, and when I reached the sacristy he made me stand at the door and gave me a grave rebuke, which did not advance matters. Had he been sympathetic perhaps he would have won me, but that is no excuse. I went to sea without the Sacraments.

Notes

1   Clouded = to darken in veins or spots; to variegate with colours; as, *clouded* marble. 'The nice conduct of a clouded can,' *Pope.*

2   George Leo Haydock (1774–1849), Priest and Biblical scholar. Entered the English College at Douay in 1785 but escaped from France at the beginning of the Revolution. He rejoined his Douay companions at Crook Hall, Durham, and was ordained in 1798. For eight years (1831–39) he was under a cloud resulting from a misunderstanding with his superiors and was forbidden to say Mass. Earlier, in 1812, he had published a new edition of the English translation of the Latin Vulgate. Bishop Challoner's 1750 text was the basis of the Old Testament and Dr. Troy's 1794 text of the New. Around the time Ullathorne speaks of he would have been in charge of the poor mission of Whitby.

3   James Archer (1751–1832), Priest. He was employed at a pub called *The Ship* in Turnstile Lane, Lincoln's Inn Fields where Catholics met secretly for Mass. Dr. Challoner was impressed with him and sent him to study at Douay when he was 28. After ordination, when 39, he returned to London to run the pub under both its guises. For many years he was Vicar-General of the London district. He received a Papal degree of Doctor of Divinity. He published a series of sermons which are referred to here. His portrait was engraved by Turner after a painting by James Ramsey in 1826.

Chapter Three

As Cabin Boy at Sea, 1819

We were proud of our brig, the *Leghorn*. She was handsome, quick and easily handled. We literally walked past most craft of our kind and trim. I was cabin boy, and my dear mother had stipulated with Captain Wrougham that I should not go aloft for the first three months. We took a cargo of merchandise from Newcastle to Leghorn; went thence to Barcelona and then to Tarragona, where we shipped a cargo of nuts for Hull. The nuts were brought by long strings of mules over the mountains, were then sorted on long tables by women in the storehouses and shot out of sacks into the hold like corn. The Captain treated me almost like his own son, kept me a good deal aloof from the sailors, except in the night watches, and never let me go ashore except with himself.

I soon attracted the attention of the sailors by beguiling the night watches with stories from my readings under the lee of the long boat, repeating from memory long portions, among other things, of Sir Walter Scott's earliest novels. This, with the knowledge they had of my friends, made me respected among them, although they did not fail to give me the rough side of their tongue now and then, especially for my want of smartness in action, the favourite quality of a sailor.

A specimen of this kind of regard for me was curiously exhibited at Gibraltar. As we entered the bay and looked upon the tremendous Rock with its projecting cannon, I was in a sort of romantic rapture, not at all diminished by a shot being sent between our masts from one of the batteries for neglecting to hoist our colours. Having care of them I made but one step off the companion ladder, and pitched on deck the horsehair bag that contained them, and the ensign was aloft in a moment.

My familiarity with Drinkwater's *Seige of Gibraltar* made the whole scene classic ground to my mind. But the Captain, in his good nature, allowed the men to purchase private stores of rum and, of course, they all got dead drunk, so that the ship at anchor was left to the care of the mate, myself and another boy, the only sober creatures aboard, for the Captain was ashore. The men lay sprawling, half on deck, half in the forecastle. One of them was so mad that he went to hit another for some fancied offence but when he found that he had struck the boy Bill (myself to wit) he was so vexed that he flung himself overboard and, had not the mate jumped into a boat alongside and caught hold of him, he would certainly have been drowned.

How many mad freaks have I witnessed amongst sailors always, however, arising from some imprudence in allowing them to have spirits under their own control. At other times sailors are generally as docile, however rough, and as kind-hearted as men can be.

At Tarragona the men bought buckets full of cheap, black Catalonian wine, and sitting round the bucket, bailed out the wine and drank it from the cans in which they cooked their tea and sugar on the cook-house fire until it was black and bitter. At one of these carouses, from which I always withdrew in disgust, they called on me, lying in my hammock, to have some, but getting nothing but silence in reply, they poured a can of it over me. It was simply a piece of their fun.

Lumpy as I then was, and was called, I got drowsy in the night watches and acquired the habit of walking the deck fast asleep. This was a serious habit, especially when having the lookout for ships approaching, and it was necessary to cure me of it. I walked the gangway steadily with folded arms and turned without touching any fixture as when awake, but if anyone stood in my way there was a collision. Sometimes a noose was put to catch my leg, and down I would come on my nose. Tar was put in my mouth and the burning substance so roused me that I seized a capstan bar to knock the offender down. Finally they pitched whole buckets of water on me from the rigging and shouted, 'A man overboard' and this kept me wakeful for some time to come.

The Spaniards who came aboard used to take to me as being a Catholic, which I was rather fond of letting them know. Whenever a group of monks or friars in their big hats and long costumes appeared on the shore, the men had a laugh and rough joke at my expense. At Barcelona, the two custom-house officers placed on board to prevent smuggling compassionated me in their hearts as a Catholic boy among heretics. They were overheard planning a scheme to get me ashore out of their hands. The Captain gave me sundry hints and threats which I could not understand. Many years afterwards, when a priest, I met him again and he told me of this plot, and how anxious it had made him, feeling his responsibility to my parents.

The walls and bastions of Tarragona were still in a ruinous condition from the two assaults they had undergone in the Peninsular War, the French first taking the city and the English retaking it. Our Captain, who had commanded a transport in that service, explained to me the English attack, of which he had been an eye-witness. The English approach was by a long viaduct spanning a broad valley.

The cathedral, with its cloisters and seminary, first revealed to my sight a great Catholic church with all its appointments, and enabled me to realise what York Minster once had been. Travelling, much later in life, with a venerable Spanish Bishop and comparing notes, I found that he had been a student in that seminary at the very time that I was cabin boy in the harbour. How often do these encounters in after life quicken the memories of the past!

Reaching[1] the Bay of Leghorn from Gibraltar, in this first voyage, the quarantine doctor came alongside and decreed that as it was reported that the Yellow Fever was at Gibraltar, we must have forty days quarantine, of which twenty at least must be passed at anchor in the open bay. This was a matter of unexpected consternation for there was no fever at Gibraltar and, besides the loss of time and consequent expenses, the bay was insecure and open to heavy gales. So the yellow flag was hoisted, our letters sliced, vinegared and fumigated, and all communication with the shore, except by long poles with the boats bringing provisions, cut off.

We rode out our twenty days at anchor in idleness, except setting up the rigging and doing odd jobs, and then came the doctor again. We had all to stand in a row and be inspected from his boat, and then to jump up and down to show our healthy condition. He then came on board and felt everyone under the armpits, after which he declared that we could enter the harbour. I shall never forget how desolate we were, wet to the skin and chilled to the spine. When we got into our berth at last, we were hemmed in by an Algerine on one side, and a Greek on the other. Our men, unaccustomed to the

Mediterranean, had strong superstitions about the Algerines, taking them for pirates, and the long robes of the captain, his white turban and long cherry stick pipe reaching to the deck, gave him a solemn appearance, whilst his men looked a truculent crew. On the other hand they were puzzled with the enormous baggy costume of the Greeks, who surprised them not less by their agility. The Algerines rushed over to the side. It was simply to suspend a defensive beam to prevent the ship's crushing, but so alarmed were our men that they determined to keep watch with handspikes over their shoulders. However, they soon got friendly with their neighbours.

For me, it was just that touch of romance that I enjoyed. The calm of the port, the change of those icy cold garments for dry ones gave me a sense of Elysian enjoyment such as I have never experienced before or since. I walked the deck with the new sights and sounds about me and a sense of revivification within me that approached to rapture. Our prime amusement during this tedious quarantine was the music-boats that played and sang around us, for the coppers that we flung them. Here I first got acquainted with Rossini's genius. An old grandpa, with his sons and grandchildren, male and female, the old man with his wall eyes, enthusiasm and bass viol, the rest with fiddles and voice used to give us the *Fra tanti Palpiti* which was then exciting a *furore* in Italy.

My ears had been attuned to music from childhood for not only did my father play the flute and flageolet, but my brothers and sisters cultivated various instruments as well as singing, and formed a choir in the chapel. My father also amused himself with engraving plates and etching, so that our artistic tastes got a certain encouragement. Yet in Leghorn I found nothing to gratify mine except the well-known statue of the Grand Duke Ferdinand, with the four bronze figures of Algerines chained at his feet, about which the sailors had many legends.

Our passage home was beset with storms and contrary winds that delayed us six weeks between Gibraltar and Portsmouth. In the Bay of Biscay our fresh water had turned putrid, and its stench was horrible. Our bread was filled with cobwebs and maggots and our beef (consisting of condemned stores from Gibraltar, which was all that was left) was, on the outside, like mahogany, though the inside was green and the men cut it into snuffboxes like any other timber, as curiosities. It had probably been ten or twelve years packed in salt brine, and buried in vaults of the Gibraltar Commissariat, should it be necessary for another seige.

Our first news from the English pilots was that old George III was dead, the Duke of Berri assassinated, and the English coast lined with wrecks from the terrible gales we had encountered. This last news made us grateful that we had not reached the English coast earlier, notwithstanding our short allowance of rations and their detestable quality. How eager we were to get some fresh water after we had rounded the Isle of Wight to the quarantine grounds, and with what glee the men hoisted the first quarter of beef on board.

Our long delay and the extraordinary number of wrecks had made our friends anxious about our safety. My father happened to be in the commercial room of a hotel in Hull when a person came in and announced that the *Leghorn* was lost with all hands. He called for his horse and rode forty miles to Scarborough, scarcely knowing what he did; but he had the discretion when he got home to say nothing of what he had heard. A day or two after the news reached him of our safe arrival off Portsmouth.

After discharging our cargo at Hull we took horses on board for St. Petersburg. In[2] our first voyage to the Baltic, when we anchored between Copenhagen and Drago, such a heavy gale came on that we had to cut cable, leave a buoy over the anchor and head for the open sea. There was a sort of ceremony on this occasion. When all was ready the Captain himself took the axe and cut the cable. But when we got off the isle of Bornholm the wind increased to still greater vehemence and a storm of sleet drove keenly in our faces. I and another lad were ordered aloft to furl the main-top gallant prior to reefing the topsail. But when we got on the yard the folds of the sail were so full of sleet, it so cut our faces, blinding our eyes, our hands were so benumbed, whilst one of my shoes blew off, that we could do nothing except hold on. It was a critical moment for we were on a lee shore without refuge. The curses sent up from deck did not stimulate us, so a man of light weight was sent up, and as we got down and jumped on deck, crack came a rope's end across our backs.

In the same voyage we had to run into one of the Swedish Sounds where, landlocked and in smooth water, we had to wait for the subsidence of the gale. Here it was my delight to ramble in the valleys gathering bilberries and strawberries and lying on a green bank to listen to the sounds that hummed in the air, the sounds of birds, insects, the silvery threads of waterfalls and the woodman's axe. Then the mate would take me with him in the jolly-boat with jib and leg of mutton sail and we would traverse the transparent water from shore to shore. So clear was the water that we saw everything distinctly at a great depth on the ground below. We saw oyster beds packed like tiles, and countless sea plants in great varieties of colour and form, crabs also, taking their lateral walks, polypi and anemones of brilliant hues, and fish pursuing their prey among the plants.

But we were not destined thus peacefully to conclude our stay. The men had been allowed to purchase a quantity of Holland gin, the Captain thinking it would be a comfort to them in bad weather. But sailors are children when their appetites are tempted and whilst lying in the Sound they had a regular drinking bout. They got full seas over, and this for days, so that the Captain, disgusted with the riot of the ship, landed his wife and there for hours they sat upon a high rock, looking down at the scene of revelry on board. The wind got fair and had slackened. It was necessary to make an effort to get the crew in order, and the cry was given, 'All hands, heave anchor!'

Then what a scene there was. Scarcely a man turned up with his proper garments in their proper places. The spectacle was ludicrous. They put their handspikes to the windlass, uttered a faint 'Yo he oo' but were as weak as cats and did not know what was doing. So after the first effort to restore discipline they were ordered to desist and, next morning, they were in a fair condition to get the vessel out to sea. There was no more grog allowed in the forecastle after that, except the rum served on deck whenever we had to reef topsails.

The summer skies of the Baltic enchanted me even more than those of the Mediterranean for I still had much of the poetic element in my composition. Elsinore, with its memories of Hamlet; Copenhagen with its islands and floating batteries recalling Nelson; the beautiful landlocked bays of Sweden, into which we ran when the storms began to rage; the short and almost nominal nights; the magnificent sunrises; the passing through the Russian Fleet; the tranquil sail up the Gulf of Finland; Cronstadt[3] with its, even then, prodigious batteries; then the Neva, up to the magnificent quays of St. Petersburgh glowing with its metal domes and spires; all these scenes worked on my youthful imagination like enchantment. The Russian people might not be very cleanly, the officials might require a good deal of bribing before the ships could get on smoothly, but the summer climate with its changing hues was fascinating. When, at a later period of life, I opened Comte de Maistre's *Soirées de St. Petersbourg*,[4] his description of his own fascination with the summer evenings on the banks of the Neva awoke a chord of memory unspeakably pleasant. Yet I was then but a cabin boy with my thoughts buried under a tarry cap.

Perhaps the most beautiful scene that I ever saw in creation was a sunrise in the Baltic, the summer nights in that climate were to me enchanting. The sun went down with a large glowing disc, and in a couple of hours was up again, so that one could read a good print at midnight. But on that wonderful morning the sun, as he rose, had fairly centered himself in a glowing sphere of amber, expanding beyond into a rich orange, which passed into crimson, and then into purple, covering half the hemisphere with these brilliant hues, whilst the opposite half-hemisphere was a pale reflection of the same, and the deck was chequered with those colours like a stained window. I once, and only once, saw a counterpart to this gorgeous spectacle, in a sunset in the tropics. It was on my first voyage to Australia. The whole western sky was banked up from the horizon with crimson clouds, presenting with their shades and salient lights the picture of a lofty mountain range, with a city piled in pyramidal form, like Algiers with its towers and battlemented walls, but all with glowing flame intense as a furnace. After a long gaze which seemed to subdue and entrance the passengers the vision slowly passed away.

One of the sights in the Baltic was an extraordinary shoal of mackerel. The sea was as smooth as a mirror, and there was not a breath of wind. As far as we could see, and as deep as we could look down, all was mackerel, and there was not a square inch where their bright blue and silver backs were not flashing and crossing one beneath another. In vain we tried a variety of schemes such as running lines from the jib-boom to the topsail. We could not catch even one. The mackerel pursues its prey, and when running with a rippling breeze of from four to five knots an hour, may be caught as fast as the lines with a bit of white and red flag can be let down.[5]

Before passing up the Neva we were, of course, boarded off Cronstadt from the guardship which gave us our pilot and examined our ship's papers. The Captain was well aware of the cupidity of the Russian officers of that day, and so his wife put everything out of sight in the cabin before they came aboard, that they could set their hearts upon. Of course he entertained them with that English cheese and porter for which they had a peculiar affection, and distributed his silver pretty freely. But one asked for the japanned waiter, on which I brought the bottles, and another, a young middy of the frigate, put his hands on a volume of *Pamela* which Mrs. Wrougham had left on the quarter-binns and, in broken English said, 'Oh, it was the book I am seeking, will you give it me?' Our pilot, a common sailor from the guardship, ran us on a sandbank off Cronstadt and there we thumped the sand until a long-boat came off to our aid, and got us warped off, when the poor fellow was taken off for punishment, and we got a pilot more capable who was no little proud of his success in taking us up to St. Petersburg.

The cooking-house of Cronstadt was an institution worth describing. In the ports of the Baltic no fire was allowed to be lit in the harbours. For cooking, a great house was provided on shore close to the port. In that dingy receptacle fireplaces with bars were ranged all round with wood fires, amid an atmosphere rich in reek and all kinds of culinary odours, blending the tastes of all navigating nations. At a certain hour each ship sent its boat, generally rowed by a couple of lads, to convey the cook with his provisions to the cook-house. It was often my lot to pull an oar, and once or twice I did the cooking. What a jabber of languages there was, and yet a kind-hearted, good fellowship, however incomplete the modes of expression between different nations. Now and then a little surliness, if one man trenched on another's bars, now and then an exchange of sly grogs, but in the main it was a merry, though weird, scene. Then, as twelve approached, all the boats reassembled to carry off the cooks with the steaming products of their labours. I saw, at the landing, a French sailor conversing with a Russian, when they found out that they had been opposed to each other at the Battle of Borodino, and then how affectionately they hugged each other, whilst tears came into the eyes of the soft-hearted Russian.

Then we moved near the famous statue of Peter the Great by the Winter Palace, and many a legend did I hear of his doings, and of the eccentricities of the Emperor Paul, whilst I witnessed the worshipful attitude of the people towards the Emperor Alexander.

The churches seemed to me Catholic and yet not Catholic, I could scarcely tell how, but I was greatly struck with the religious customs of the people. They made the Sign of the Cross on all occasions, commonly repeating it thrice. They seldom passed a church without entering, or at least uncovering and kneeling before they passed it. Nor was this custom limited to the poorer classes. The priests, in their beards and Oriental costume, were often striking and reverend figures. Even our sailors were impressed by the signs of religion which they saw, and spoke of them with respect. The blending of religion with habits of life showed externally even more visibly than in Italy or Spain.

I remember being in the serf's Sunday afternoon market with some companions when suddenly a bell rang out from one of the churches and the whole market, tradesmen included, knelt down in prayer. Whether it was something like our *Angelus* bell I cannot say but the Englishmen present felt they were amongst a religious people. After this silent prayer up rose the multitude and the babel of chatter was resumed.

Our object in the market was to buy pieces of Russian duck or canvas with which to make sea clothing with our sail cloth needles. We took in a cargo of hemp at Cronstadt, the stowing of which by means of jackscrews was the work of the Russian serfs, whose brawny limbs were fed on nothing better than black bread of a very sour flavour, and garlic. But they were kept in heart by glasses of fiery 'bottery'[6] which it was my office to give them at stated hours, and they lightened their heavy labour by improvised chants sung in untiring chorus under a leader who gave the improvisations.

There was a young man on board on my second voyage to Cronstadt, an officer from the custom-house, whose piety was altogether ascetic. He was singularly modest, courteous, and recollected. He was often praying and seldom without a pious book and it seemed a sort of Office Book. Though he had his meals in the cabin he never would touch meat. The Captain admired him much, and said that if he went not to heaven, there was no chance for any man. But this was my second Captain and I am anticipating.

Notes

1   The following four paragraphs do not appear in either the original or the revised manuscript but were presumably inserted by Mother Drane from the Ullathorne letters.

2   The following two paragraphs also appear to be from the letters.
3   Cronstadt, now more commonly Kronstadt or Kronshtadt, is a Russian naval base and port on Kotlin Island in the Gulf of Finland fourteen miles west of St. Petersburg. It is icebound for about five months of the year. The island was taken from Sweden by Peter the Great in 1703. At the time of which Ullathorne was writing Kronstadt functioned as a commercial port for St. Petersburg but the construction of a deep-sea canal in 1885 reduced its importance. Several naval mutinies took place in Kronstadt the last being in 1921 against the Soviet government.
4   Joseph de Maistre (1753–1821), French polemical author and diplomat. He lived in St Petersburg for fourteen years, as the envoy for the King of Sardinia, where he wrote the book quoted which is considered his best work. Baudelaire acknowledged that it was de Maistre who taught him to think.
5   The language is a little obscure here. He means that when they saw this prodigious shoal there was no wind so they could not catch any; however, in a decent wind, when the ship could do four or five knots, matching the speed of the mackerel, they could be caught. The line referred to is the lead line which has bunting attached to it at intervals to determine the depth of water beneath.
6   Mss.1. has vodka.

Chapter Four

Further Voyages

On returning to London I made acquaintance with my relatives who were very kind to me and on alternate Sundays, when I had leave on shore, I went to Mass with them at the Chapel of Somers Town.[1] They took me also, as a special treat, to St. Mary's, Moorfields, recently completed, and looked upon at that time as a wonderful advancement in Catholic architecture. It is a fact to be avowed that when abroad I had never tried to go to Mass, and probably I should not have been permitted to go alone. Yet I always stuck to the profession of my Catholicity and was proud of it.

The shipping trade was now slack and a charter could not be got on 'Change for a new voyage, so the Captain, who was part owner, resolved to put our beautiful brig for a time in the Newcastle and London coal trade. He would not, however, have anything to do with this dirty work but stopped in London with his kind-hearted wife and put in his place a coarse, rough, Newcastle skipper, and under this ignorant man my fortunes were changed.

We made a couple of voyages in the black trade and everyone cried out against the degradation of so fine a craft, but there was no remedy. What I vividly remember is, that when in harbour two of us boys had to land this Captain (no better than a common sailor) each evening that he might have his carouse with other coal-skippers of the same class, whilst we poor boys had to guard the boat — no trifling thing on the Thames where the wherry-men, jealous of all ship's boats, would not let us lie near the stairs, but compelled us to keep afloat in the tide, or to fasten on to some moored lighter for long hours. At last the skipper appeared with his fellow-skippers. Our boat had to carry them all to the smart ship, where they came for another glass, and then we had to row the visitors, half drunk, to their own ships, getting nothing but abuse from them and got back to bed, completely fagged, between twelve and one in the morning.

I had two narrow escapes of drowning in the Thames. Another lad, knowing I had a constitutional fear of dogs, set one upon me by way of a joke. I sprang from the bulwark of our own vessel to the loftier side of the next in the tier, calculating on catching on a moulding with my fingers, and so scrambling on board, but forgot at the moment that her sides had been newly tarred and varnished, so down I slipped between the two ships and sank beneath them. I could not swim, but being perfectly calm and self-possessed I paddled myself up with hands and feet. Alarm was given, the men sprang out of the hold where they were at work and one of them seized me by the head from the fore chains just as I emerged. It was considered a great escape, as few who sank in the tideway were ever saved.

The other case was in running down the Thames with wind and tide, having to get on board from a boat that hung by its painter. I seized the chain plates and the boat went from under me. I could not swing myself up and was too proud to call out, but a voice from another ship cried out, 'Captain Wrougham, that boy will be drowned there, under the main chains.' This brought a pair of hands down on my collar and a fair share of abuse on my person.

Being in the Thames after our second trip to Newcastle the skipper one day got very angry with me for eating a piece of pork for my dinner which he intended to reserve as a snack for the coal-metor, an officer employed by the City of London to measure the coal as it was unshipped, for the duty. He gave me a kick with his foot that wounded my pride to such a degree that I determined to abandon the ship. That night, accordingly, I packed up my bundle of linen, put on my best clothes and sat all night in the cabouse, or cook-house, on deck, lest I should not awake or be detected in getting on deck at a later period. I confided my secret to another youth, a respectable boy, who had been my schoolfellow, and he faithfully kept it. About eleven some of our men came from the shore half tipsy and the cook came into the cabouse for something he wanted, but as I sat low down on a bucket in the corner I escaped detection. About two o'clock in the morning I scrambled across the tier of ships in which we lay, got down into a lighter, and hailed a wherry at the landing. The man came but suspected me to be a runaway. We had a parley and half-a-crown induced him to land me. I wandered about the streets of London, gradually working my way towards the West End. I answered the policemen and patrols, who were suspicious of my bundle, in broad Yorkshire, as a simple country lad going to see my relations and received cautions in a kindly tone about not letting anyone carry my bundle. In due time I knocked at the door of one of my uncles who heard my tale, gave me breakfast, then took me to other relatives, three of whom agreed to drive me down again to the ship, and there have an interview with the Captain. My appearance thus accompanied produced a great sensation. It was thought on board that I must have been drowned. The skipper was nonplussed and had very little to say but referred my friends to the real Captain, who lived at some distance. We went to Captain Wrougham who, as usual, was very kind. He admitted the coarseness of the man in command, and proposed that I should go to my friends for the winter, and should rejoin the ship in the spring, when he hoped to resume command and enter once more on foreign trade. I enjoyed the spectacles of London for a time and then returned home. But our ship was at Scarborough before me. The other owners were dissatisfied with what the ship was doing and sent a special agent to bring her home. They agreed with my father to give up my indentures and I was free. Though always admired, the *Leghorn* was never prosperous. She was sold and, a few years afterwards, sank in the Bay of Genoa.

In vain did my parents try to persuade me to give up the sea. I had not much taste for shipwork, nor did I like the rude society in which I was thrown but I was fond of roaming to see the world, and was too proud to swallow the handspike. I had seen schoolfellows jeered at for deserting a pursuit supposed to have perils in it, and demanding a hardy disposition, and I believe that this opinion keeps many a youth at sea after he has had a sickening of it.

I spent the winter in studying the science of navigation under an old ship Captain called Houghton who had all Norrie's *Epitome of Navigation* off by memory, the table of logarithms included. He was clever, and had some half dozen pupils much older than myself. It was a strange sort of school; the old man kept no servant, cooked his own food, sometimes got tipsy and then he got teased, seized a two-foot measuring scale in his defence, some pupil seized another and then there was a fencing match. I learnt to keep a ship's way, to keep a log book, and to take observations of the sun, which we did with our sextants in fine weather on Castle Hill.[2]

In the spring I set sail once more. There was an excellent old couple of an old Catholic stock at Scarborough, a Mr. and Mrs. Craythorne. They had a vessel called the *Anne's Resolution*, a brig much inferior to the *Leghorn*. I was apprenticed for a short period to this ship, not altogether to my own liking, for I wanted to go on an Arctic discovery ship, or an Indian ship, or somewhere where I could have more adventure, and see a greater variety of the world. But my father wished to sicken me of the sea. A nephew of the Craythornes, educated for a time at Stoneyhurst and full of Catholic faith, was appointed mate. The Captain was a simple-hearted, good-natured man, with ordinary abilities, and very little acquirement. I stipulated that I should not again be cabin boy, but this threw me into the forecastle amongst a set of men whose conversation was the vilest imaginable. There were also one or two of the boys very corrupt. By the ears I learned to know everything about every form of vice, although my pride, self-respect and a certain refinement of feeling kept me personally from gross and exterior vice. Neither could I ever appreciate the necessity for the habit of interlarding speech with oaths, whether for mere embellishment, or as a means for expressing strong feeling. In harbour crews make acquaintance with each other, especially in foreign ports, and so my knowledge of this rude class became extensive. But with all their licentiousness, genuine seamen have in the main warm, child-like, kindly and generous hearts, and I have often compassionated these children of obedience. They were not without a sense of religion and of Providence in a vague way, and some few were even devout men.

We made a voyage to Cronstadt, and another to Memel[3] and thus I found myself again upon my favourite Baltic waters. After a time the Captain's health began to suffer and then he asked me to take care of the cabin as he wanted someone to look after his little necessary comforts. As he asked this in a gentle tone and as a favour my pride was disarmed, and being a soft-hearted boy when my proud spirit was not inter-fered with I could not refuse him, and so became cabin boy once more.

On my second return voyage from the Baltic we sighted Flamborough Head in a heavy gale that headed us. We lay to all night, in sight of the lighthouse, and our jib-boom snapped like a carrot. The wind increased and the Captain resolved to run as soon as daylight came into Scarborough. We were all very excited, for we should see our friends. We ran our twenty miles of ground, and as we neared Scarborough it blew such a gale that half the town mustered to see us make the harbour. A pilot-boat full of men got under our quarter with considerable difficulty, the men tumbled up on board, and so we felt ourselves well manned. Many of the newcomers were relations of the men on board, and I remember the father of one of our lads, a sailor of course, brought a little basket hanging on his neck. The mother could not resist sending the boy some fresh butter as her token of affection, though we should be in the harbour, and were then in a critical position, and the lad could not resist stealing below to eat some of his butter on his ship biscuit. I do not deny that fresh butter, even salt but especially fresh, is a very great luxury to a strong lad who has nothing but 'hard tack' (ship biscuit of the flint genus) sopped in his rough tea, morning and night for months past. But there was a touch of nature in this which was heightened to my mind when I afterwards heard that this same mother had gone to my own dear mother and had urged her to send me some also saying, 'Depend on it, ma'am, there's nothing like fresh butter when you come from sea!'

As we rounded into the harbour I was on the fore-topsail yard-arm, half a dozen of us being engaged in stowing the sail on the yard, when suddenly I heard the voice of one of my brothers − on the quay − crying out, 'There he is, up there,' and my father responding, 'Aye, there he is.' My heart jumped and my eyes searched the excited crowd, and I so got a jawing from my next mate for not handing up the crich of the sail smart and handy.

Two hours more saw the brig safe moored, and all taut on board, and my father had got leave through his friend, the owner, for me to go home till morning. I got home about eleven o'clock and there got my warm greeting and answered as many questions as I could, fired from all sides as they were in the rapid intervals between swallowing a hot supper that had been prepared more than once for my arrival. Scarcely had I ceased eating, and got all clear for fair talking, especially in reply to my dear mother who was then in delicate health, when up comes a messenger in hot haste, 'The brig's pitching and breaking all her fenders! On board directly!'

So off I bolted, running half a mile, and leaving the admiring circle in consternation at this sudden evocation. The day after that we sailed once more.

The great resource of a ship's forecastle, where the men live and sleep, is spinning yarns. In a vessel like ours there is no room to stand upright. Everybody moves to his place stooping and almost creeping under the hammocks. They sit on their sea-chests, the beef and biscuit is brought in wooden platters, like half buckets, each one takes a biscuit on his knee for a plate, pulls out his knife, commonly fastened to his pocket with a rope yarn, the knife which he uses for cutting rope with, and cuts off a chunk of beef with it. And so holding the biscuit in his hand, the beef on the biscuit and his tarry thumb on the beef, he saws away, knife and teeth, and when done with beef takes to the biscuit now unctuous with fat, and eats his plate as a final relish.

But the yarn-spinning thrives best of a long winter's night, riding at anchor, when most of the crew are below. A tin oil-lamp swings from a beam in the middle emitting a dubious light that plays on the ship's beam as the vessel rolls. The men lie in their hammocks smoking their pipes, and each in turn is called on for a yarn. The stories thus narrated are improvements on the incidents of their sea life, or shore adventures, or sea-fights or fairy-tales, or tales of monsters, many of them traditional and, like the letters of uneducated persons, they have all one form in which they begin and another in which they end. The beginning is in this wise:

'Once upon a time, when hogs were swine and monkeys chewed tobacco, there lived' etc.

The conclusion has a special allusion to sea-pies. And sea-pie is to a sailor the most perfect of all food, and only comes on great occasions. It is made after this fashion. First in the square iron fixed 'copper' is laid a well-seasoned stew, then a deck of paste over it, and finally to make a three-decker, another stew and another paste, which when well peppered and well cooked is a dish that a prince might envy. But the biscuit will not serve for this mess and wooden platters are brought into requisition.

The crime of all crimes on shipboard is to pass a mop through a ladder. This vicious act is sure to bring a storm, or even a wreck, sooner or later, or at all events a mast will go by the board, or contrary winds will prevail. Such a crime brings the whole justice of the crew upon the offender, and that with summary execution. There is but one remedy, and even that is at the best doubtful, and it consists in the same person passing the same mop between the identical steps of the ladder in the opposite direction, so as to 'unthread the rude eye of rebellion, and welcome back again discarded faith.' The worst feature of this crime is that it depends not on intention, and requires no proof of malice aforethought. A bungler ignorant of, or forgetful of, the law is as guilty as one who deliberately intended to invoke the ship's destruction.

A horseshoe nailed to the foremast is the preventative against witchcrafts and unlucky visitations. Yet if the seaman has his superstitions of a traditional sort, as well as his brethren on land, he is not without a vague and even strong religious sense, in so far as the action of God on the world is concerned, and upon the course of human life. He believes in the Divine Providence, and the efficacy of prayer and good conduct, whilst he holds cant and hypocrisy in singular abhorrence.

A Sunday at sea in fine weather has its especial observance. The colours are thrown over the capstan, and prayers are said by the Captain before an attentive crew in many ships. The men are quiet and subdued during the day, and in the afternoon after all is cleared up, you will see some of them reading their Bibles or other books, whilst the rest talk in a vein different from that of weekdays. And notwithstanding all the vile talk of the forecastle, they will sometimes strike into a religious vein in a vague, broad way, indicating the recent yearnings of their hearts, and ending by hoping that Almighty God won't be too hard upon a poor sailor.

I believe that no class of men would be more open to religious guidance than sailors if they could really have it brought to their souls on shipboard. Their peril lies in their excitement when they get on shore, where they are but helpless children in wit, whilst driven by all the passions of fallen human nature, and surrounded by every species of temptation, and that without any faith or force of grace to steady their minds and stay their hearts.

I cannot review the habits of a class of men in my grey hairs with whom I was so much associated in youth, without recalling the unspeakable gratitude I owe to Almighty God for having carried me through that perilous time without being utterly scathed, and for having rescued me from it by what was little less than a miracle of grace. It gave me a deep insight into the natural hearts of men, and especially of Man as he is isolated from the ordinary conditions of society. And when I had to deal with large classes of mankind in conditions still more exceptional, I found I had nothing to learn as to the working of such men's hearts which I did not already know – before I had studied a page of Moral Theology. The heart of the sailor is the most open and unreserved of all hearts amidst his shipmates, and his manifestation of himself is like a continuous public confession, with this difference, that it is void of all that disguise and dressing with which self-love contrives to clothe the formal self-manifestations of other men.

There was another youth on board, older than myself, who was not only steady but very anxious to improve himself. This led to a certain intimacy between us but we sometimes got into scrapes together. With my vivid imagination I was passionately fond of the theatre, but always kept away from low exhibitions. When in London Docks and we had leave on shore in the evening, I induced him more than once to accompany me to Covent Garden, and when the play was over we wandered through the streets until six in the morning when the dock gates were opened, and then we slipped on board before all hands were called. One morning, however, the mate appeared on deck before we returned which put an end to our theatrical enjoyments. In these nightly wanderings we made it a rule to keep to the main streets, to enter no place of refreshment, and to speak to no one.

Whilst in the docks I got a severe scald through upsetting some burning fat on my right instep and, being neglected, gangrene appeared. The doctor who was called in declared that it was a hospital case and serious; I was therefore conveyed up to my Uncle Longstaff's who then resided in the Polygon, Somers Town. Through the affectionate care of my aunt and the skill of the family doctor my foot was saved, and in due time I returned to the ship. I was one day engaged in tarring a cable when I suddenly heard my father's voice from the quay saying. 'I see his eyes, but nothing else of him.' I looked up and there I saw my father and uncle gazing at me. My father looked anything but contented, and coming on board said, 'Do you mean to say that you like this?' I suppose I was pretty well tarred myself as well as the cable.

However, I held on until we got to Memel, and there I found my deliverance.

One Sunday morning in that harbour Mr. Craythorne, the mate, said to me, 'William, let us go to Mass.' I fished up the *Garden of the Soul* from the bottom of my sea chest, and we set off through the flat town of Memel, with its numerous windmills for sawing timber, and its churches in the hands of the Lutherans, until beyond the town we reached a considerable wooden structure exteriorly not unlike a barn. There was a square yard of grass in front of it, surrounded by a low wall, and on one side of the walk to the door was a mound surmounted by a large wooden figure on a cross, round the front of which sat a number of aged and decrepit people singing and soliciting alms.

The Mass had begun when we entered the chapel. The sanctuary was profusely decorated with flowers and two banners were planted on the sanctuary rails one of which, I recollect, represented St. Michael the Archangel. I vividly remember the broad figure of the venerable priest and his large tonsure, which made me think him a Franciscan. The men knelt on the right side, the women on the left, all dressed very plainly and much alike. With their hands united and their eyes recollected they were singing the Litany of Loretto to two or three simple notes, accompanied by an instrument like the sound of small bells. The moment I entered I was struck by the simple fervour of the scene; it threw me into a cold shiver, my heart was turned inward upon myself, I saw the claims of God upon me, and felt a deep reproach within my soul. When we came out I was again struck by the affectionate way in which the people saluted each other, as if they were all one family. Whatever money was in my pocket went into the poor box, and when we got on board I asked Craythorne what religious books he had with him. He produced an English translation of Marsollier's *Life of St. Jane Chantal* and Gobinet's *Instruction of Youth*, which I read as leisure served.

The venerable figure of St. Francis de Sales and that of St. Jane Chantal introduced me to a new world, of which I had hitherto known nothing. A life filled with the sense of God, and devoted to God, was what I had never realised. Gobinet's *Instructions* again took me into my conscience. Still there was much fancy in me, and I lived in a sort of rapture of the imagination until we reached London. I then wrote home and informed my parents that I wished to leave the sea and return home. This was speedily arranged and I was again employed in my father's business. My dear mother, however, unacquainted with the change that had taken place in me, wrote to me before I left the ship expressing a hope that I should give no more trouble to them than the rest of the family.

I cannot remember how it was, but though there was then a young priest resident at Scarborough to whom I went and under whom, at his request, I resumed the catechism, I did not at that time make my First Communion.

I took evening lessons in French from Mr. Pexton, the Ushaw pupil of whom I formerly spoke, and in walks with him he interested me in college life and studies and I renewed my old habit of general reading. But in the midst of this course of life we happened to receive a visit from a linen manufacturer of Knaresborough who had a son studying for the church at the Benedictine Priory of Downside. He took a fancy to my brother James, who had a fine boy's voice, and was a principal singer at the chapel. He pressed him to go to Downside as a church student and spoke warmly about it to my parents. But my brother felt not the attraction, whereupon I made known how much I should like it, and made known the altered state of my mind. My father wrote at once to Dr. Barber, the Prior, and the matter was settled to my great delight. As Downside is near Bath I preferred going by London on board a packet sloop. But whilst anchored at the mouth of the Thames we were caught in a severe January gale and had to cut and run with about fifty sail more – of whom one, a Dutchman, went down – and got safe into Harwich, where, in consequence of floating ice in the Thames, I did not delay but went on by coach and arrived at Downside in the beginning of February, 1823, being nearly seventeen years old.

Notes

1   At the time when Ullathorne was in the habit of attending Mass at the chapel of Somers Town, Margaret Hallahan (see introductory letter p.1.) was an inmate of the Somers Town Orphanage. (Mother Drane's note.)
2   Castle Hill is in Scarborough.
3   Memel, now Klajpeda, in Lithuania.

Chapter Five

With the Benedictines at Downside

Arrived at St. Gregory's Priory, Downside, my life underwent a total and very earnest change. The new College with its chapel was in the process of completion, and everything was in a provisional state. I made the twentieth boy in the school. The first thing that struck me was the good feeling and piety that prevailed amongst the boys, and the kindly relations that existed between them and their masters. The whole tone of things was in such contrast to all I had ever known, and threw such a new light into my mind as to the real, practical bearings of my religion. The next thing that struck me with almost equal force was the absence of worldly knowledge and experience in the Superiors, who, nevertheless, by their quiet dignity, their piety and their kindness at once attracted my veneration.

In these days it will scarcely be believed that until I went to St. Gregory's I had never been present at Benediction of the Blessed Sacrament, or heard the Litany sung, except at Memel, but it now came with great sweetness to my ears and soul, and I had never before seen a cope. Such devotions in those days were chiefly limited to the few existing colleges and convents.

Mr Polding, afterwards the first Archbishop of Sydney, was our prefect and our director, and I found in him all that my soul needed.[1] To him I made my general confession, and he kept me long in training for it was not until Christmas night, 1823, ten months after my arrival, that I made my first Communion.[2] The letter which I wrote to my father on that occasion was found by my brother James many years afterwards amongst some specially private papers, and he sent it to Mother Margaret. I think it may probably exist among her papers. I remember it pleased her much.

I had now two things to look after, my studies and my soul, and in both had everything to make up; for I had never understood before either in what real study consisted, or how the soul could be advanced towards divine things. I began first with the Latin Grammar and elementary books, and the structure of language dawned upon me as a beautiful thing and one of deep interest, for old Hornsey's dry rules of English grammar had only served to perplex me in my eleventh year. I could repeat them, but the appreciation of syntax was a locked up mystery for the want of a teacher to draw them into exercise. I soon began other languages, for which I had a natural facility, and my private time was mainly given to history.

As to my soul, I worked first at Bishop Challoner's *Think Well On't,* getting a view of eternal truths. Then I took up Gobinet's *Instruction of Youth* again. In Butler's *Lives of the Saints* I found great delight; but my favourite book of this kind was Challoner's *Lives of the Fathers of the Desert.* They fed my still romantic imagination as well as my moral sense. After a while I took to the *Spiritual Combat*[3] using it as a sort of a rule of the inward life, and working at some of its principles. I had grave inward contests, on two points especially. But the year during which I stuck a good deal to the *Spiritual Combat* was what prepared me for the subsequent Novitiate. I still think it the best book ever penned for help in laying solidly the foundations of an interior life, especially when it is used, and worked at as a rule, bit by bit, and advancing in it by degrees.

Our first little retreat, made in Holy Week, each making his own meditation from the *Think Well On't,* and all saying the Jesus Psalter together, the nine parts in the course of the day, with the examination of conscience in the chapel, served as an oasis which brought my soul more deeply into the sense of God and of eternal things. And then came the awful functions of Holy Week to me for the first time, and above all the Sepulchre and the watching before the Blessed Sacrament whilst imbued with the almost living renewal of Our Lord's Passion in the functions. I was not like the innocent youths around me, but carried in my breast the memory of so much that contrasted with all that now I was for the first time entering into. The spiritual world with all its awfulness, its depth and its sweetness had come upon the experience and habituation of the profane world in which I had been prematurely steeped to the top of my head. My judgement as to human life was, I may almost say, matured; and though once more a schoolboy, working at the elements of learning, I had the gravity of a man. I thought much, felt much inwardly from time to time, but spoke little. My reserved ways, habit of observing, preference of books to games, and my quiet manner, got me the name of Plato, which adhered to me even for some time after I had entered the monastery. My readier habits of converse and lighter modes of speech belonged not to my boyhood, or youth. They came to me with middle age.

I was pushed up much too rapidly through the school, and did not get a fair share of scholarship, even as then understood in our colleges. I got no Greek, but picked up its rudiments later in teaching a class of beginners. I suppose this was because I was a late-comer. I was passed on from class to class at each two-monthly examination, so that in the course of twelve months I had gone through all the classes and found myself side by side with those who had been studying the languages for six or seven years. It is true I had a method of my own which gave me more of the book than they who had completed their year in it; but that was unknown to my masters. I got up the first lesson of the day as completely as I could, dodging the dictionary through all the roots and compounds of the words, and then went on in the book for the remainder of the time, so that I was soon ahead of the class by some hundreds of pages, yet had scarcely ever a mark against me. It was the practice after a lesson for the master to give a rough and hasty translation of the lesson for the ensuing day, each catching what he could of it. I thus compared his translation with one I had already made, revised the lesson at my desk, and then studied on in the book. Then I made a point of honour never to revise for examinations, having a detestation of secondary motives as something mean, but went on pursuing further studies. Yet the result was my transfer to a higher class. But I have always regretted this rapidity, which was beyond my own control; for though I have read most things privately, I have knowledge without due scholarship.

Of French I got but the rudiments, and that language was obtained later by dint of much reading of its writers. Of Italian I got the rudiments two years later in private hours from a fellow junior religious. Some Spanish I read for the first time aboard a Chilean brig on a voyage from Sydney to Chile in 1839 and some German from a fellow passenger between Sydney and England in 1836. The first time I visited my friends after my profession I took lessons in Hebrew from a Jewish Rabbi, but after a subsequent and laborious investigation into the merits of the systems of punctuation, I gave up the study, unable to satisfy my own judgement as to the best method to be pursued. Amongst the other studies of the course, the College attached considerable importance in those days to Finegle's system of fixing the chronology of history, using which system, we were taught Goldsmith's *English* and *Roman Histories*, and Reeve's *Church History*. I took to the Histories, but mentally discarded Finegle's method as cumbrous and overloaded with contrivances for a *memoria technica*. In recreation time I went through Rollin's *Ancient* and Hooke's *Roman History*.

On the feast of the Epiphany[4] I became a postulant together with four fellow-students. But the postulancy was managed in a peculiar way. We remained in the school and its dormitory as usual, never entering the monastery, but were called at five instead of six to attend Matins, Lauds and Meditation with the monks in choir. This was the only thing that distinguished us from other lay students.

We received the religious habit on March 12th, 1824, little more than a year after I had entered the school, bidding farewell to it and entering the Novitiate for a few days previous to our spiritual retreat and preparation. Dr. Polding gave up the prefectship at the same time to be our Novice-Master. I remember we were first assembled in the Sacristy where our master gave us an address which produced a deep impression in our hearts. All that I recollect of it now is that we were to be as wax in the hands of our master, to take whatever impression he gave us, and to respond to his influence in faith and simplicity. We were then set to scour the floor of the Novitiate as our first exercise.

Although the taking of the habit was made a great ceremony, and Dr. Barber, the Prior, read us one of his beautiful discourses, yet the rite itself was performed in a very primitive way. We were in the coloured clothes we had worn as schoolboys and without any soutane. The habit given us was a small scapular to be worn under our dress, and the one sample of the great choir-habit was put on the neck of each, until it reached the last, when it was put on him altogether. During the Novitiate we wore our old clothes, with a college gown, open in front, and a trencher-cap. Our Master was a man of warm and tender heart with true religious instincts, who formed our souls to detachment and the spirit of the Rule with unction and with genuine solicitude. We were devotedly attatched to him and affectionately united with each other. Before the novitiate terminated our numbers were doubled. After choir our mornings were devoted to the study of the Rule, commiting the ascetic chapters to memory. As breakfast was not a conventual meal, we daily asked for it on our knees, and before granting it and giving us permission to rise we had a chapter of external faults, each novice first declaring his own, then those he had noticed in his fellow-novices. Then came a brief exhortation, rebuke or penance from the lips of the Novice-Master, and so to breakfast, not with the community in the refectory but by ourselves in the novitiate, and that in silence.

Our public penances, those true searchers into nature, were generally between the choirs in the chapel or in the refectory; sometimes they were more or less eccentric in their character, judiciously taking hold of our pride or our human respect. Occasionally we were required to write down our morning meditation, distractions and wanderings of the mind included. This gave our Master occasions to offer us some kind advice individually that seldom failed to reach its mark.

Our chief text-book for the religious spirit was *The Practice of Religious Perfection* by Rodriguez to which our Master added instructions drawn from the Rule of St. Benedict. What took hold of me, as an idea at least, was the whole doctrine of Christian and Religious humility, and the example of the Fathers of the desert had a still greater charm, at least for my imagination. This, however, introduced a disturbing influence which set me a day-dreaming and so unsettled me. Abbot de Rancé's[5] book on the Monastic Life, his Life, and the four volumes recording the lives and deaths of the first members of his reformed monastery, took hold of me and linked themselves in my mind with St. Bernard, whom I had taken as my patron saint, and with his reform of the Benedictine Order. All this combined with the impression made on me by the Lives of the Fathers of the Desert, as drawn up by Bishop Challoner, had become to me what *Robinson Crusoe* had been to my earlier years – a grand, romantic, spiritual idea, to be somehow realised and acted upon. I earnestly entreated my Superiors to allow me to go to La Trappe, there to live a penitential life, buried from and forgotten by the world. A visit from Mr. Walmesley, an English gentleman, skilled in medicine, who was a lay-brother of that monastery, only increased my desire. My Superiors tried to divert me from it, yet in the kindest and most considerate way. Yet the notion acted upon me in a way that for a time overpowered my fondness for intellectual pursuits, for which I more than once got a smart rebuke. When it came to a question of profession, I opened my mind anew to my novice-master on the subject. He asked my leave to consult with the Prior. The result of their conference was to express to me their sincere apprehension of there being something of imagination in what I contemplated, and their fear that if I went to La Trappe I should most likely fail, in which case I should probably lose my vocation and return to the world. I was therefore advised to make my profession upon the understanding that, if after a period of two years I was still of the same mind, putting aside the thought in the interval, they would offer no further objections to my going to La Trappe. On this advice I acted; nor did I doubt, in later years, as I have known in similar instances, that all was a delusion. It left me, however, a valuable experience for the future guidance of souls.

Our Master was fond of exercising our memories. We committed to heart and repeated to him, not only the ascetic parts of the Rule, but also the Sunday Epistles and Gospels and, with the exception of those to the Romans and the Hebrews, the Epistles of St. Paul. This, however, was a task which extended into the Juniorate after profession. I never regretted the learning St. Paul's Epistles by heart in the Douay version. This exercise became invaluable to me as a preacher, though it gave me an involved style, which it took me years to shake off.

We also committed to memory the sixth book of the *Aeneid* of Virgil, Horace's *Ars Poetica* and Pope's *Essay on Man*. But our work was not all study, manual labour was sometimes added in the old Benedictine spirit and there can be no doubt that the man who can handle a spade, or do some mechanical work, will have more practical sense than he who can only handle books, not to speak of this veritable association with our poorer brethren.

Except for my romance with La Trappe, if it was a romance, our Novitiate was a happy one. Our numbers had been doubled during its course and, isolated as we were from the professed Community, on whom we looked with great respect, as well as from the school, we were closely united with each other. We observed the rule of silence strictly, and even if one of us glanced through the window in the way of curiosity at any carriage or group that passed before it, it became a subject of self-accusation at the next morning's Chapter. One of the most valuable influences exercised upon us was when from time to time at evening recreation our Master pointed some incident, religious event or pious history into valuable instruction. If a priest of our own or any Order, or one of the secular clergy, visited the monastery he had always something edifying to say about him, and inspired us on these occasions with the true spirit of the missionary life. That life, however, he used to tell us, was only for us if called on by the President-General to enter upon it; our real business there was to make ourselves good monks, and to leave our future disposal in the Hands of God, Who would manifest His Divine Will through the voice of superiors. This solid principle was also carefully enlarged upon, that the care of souls was an office so far beyond human powers that nothing could make it safe or effective but the grace attached to obedience; that it was essentially what the Divine Revelation declared it to be, a mission; and that mission consisted, not in selecting for ourselves, but in being *sent* by authority.

Four of us who had entered the novitiate together made our profession on Easter Tuesday, April 9th, 1825. It was a time of unusual fervour, as well in special preparation as in that greatest oblation to God of which man is capable. As I am in part recording the customs of those days in which the Catholic Church in England was first beginning to emerge into freedom, after its long state of obscurity, I may mention that our change of costume consisted in nothing more than a change from the old brown or blue clothes to what was then considered clerical costume, to wit, a black-tailed coat, shorts with gaiters, and a white limp cravat; and in the monastery a soutane, a college gown, and cap. In those days it was not considered safe to wear a religious habit even within the monastery. It was only done by the enclosed nuns.

Dr. Polding still continued in the office of Novice-Master and we, as junior professed, remained under his paternal care. He still directed our studies, and under him we studied Rhetoric, Logic and Mental Philosophy. During the year of

Rhetoric our text-books were Cicero and a manuscript by Eustace, the author of the *Classical Tour of Italy,* who was first a student and then a professor of the Priory when at Douay, though never a monk; Quintilian and parts of Longinus; whilst for private reading we had Blair's *Lectures*, Rollin on *Sacred Eloquence* and Cambell's *Philosophy of Rhetoric*. But for my part I read everything the library could produce. A little debating society was also got up later on, which some of the older monks joined; and thus one began to gain the habit of thinking on one's legs before an audience. Privately, I felt the need also of a certain physical training, for though no longer heavy and clumsy as in my sea-going days, because study had reduced my system, yet I was stronger on the left than on the right side, and had a lisp in my voice. I therefore worked myself through the postures and positions as figured in Austin's *Cheiromania* with dumb-bells and trained myself to freedom and ease of action until it became natural to me. I stood for hours at my studies, leaning at the sill of the window in my cell to get some power over the right leg, the nerves of my right side having always been weaker than those of the left. And to clear the lisp and get clear open utterance I repeated compositions walking uphill with pebbles in my mouth when I had the opportunity to do so unobserved. We also paid particular attention to pronunciation, making it a rule to correct each other, and keeping *Walker's Dictionary* on the table for an authorative appeal. And here let me express my surprise that so little has ever been done in the training of our clergy, to cultivate clear and effective reading for church use.

About this time I took up St. Augustine's *Confessions* as a spiritual manual, which, next to the sacred Scriptures is the book of greatest profundity, whether as regards the knowledge of God or of the divine operations in the human soul; no book ever opened my intelligence so much by setting before me the principles upon which human life should move. It is a book for the heart quite as much as for the mind, and reveals to us the divine operations of grace in its conflicts with nature with wonderful clearness. There is much truth in the remark that St. Augustine formed the religious intellect of Europe.

From Rhetoric, after an elementary course of Physics, we passed to Logic, using as text-books another manuscript by Eustace drawn up in Latin, *Watts*, and the *Port Royal Logic*. Here I found a study completely adapted to my taste, for few things have ever fascinated me more than the analysis of mental operations and the study of the mental and moral faculties. It has been more or less a pursuit through life. And I found myself at last in the open field of my predilection, when we entered upon the study of mental and moral philosophy. Dr. Polding himself was not a very deep or persistent thinker,[6] but with the use of his books he made the subject attractive. He first opened our mind with Reid[7] and other Scotch philosophers, and after thus interesting us in philosophic thought, especially in the beautiful style of Reid and Beattie, passed us on to the Catholic philosophy. All the chief systems were analysed excepting those of Germany which, at that time, were scarcely known in England. We were then set to analyse Hume, Berkeley, Locke and Hartley, and to write essays upon them. Then we were introduced to Natural Religion, which brought me into contact with the *Pensées de Pascal,* Paley, and the large works of Bergier and Bishop Butler. In private time I analysed and annotated most of these books on paper and, which I afterwards regretted, burned a great pile of these papers before going to Australia.

Nor was the study of Scripture neglected. These occupied the Sundays, festivals, and an hour each evening. Besides the *Prolegomena* we studied the Psalms, with the help of Menochius, Bossuet and South, and after studying one day wrote notes the next. I found South of great assistance in comprehending the style of the Old Testament, and the few lessons in Hebrew, which I had privately obtained at Scarborough from the Jewish Rabbi, gave me an insight into the structure of that language.

Our Professor of Theology had no taste for Philosophy beyond the Scholastic Logic. He caught me in the library one day reading Smith's *Theory of Moral Sentiments*, with Coglan on the Passions lying by my side. 'What are you reading?' he asked.

I told him.

'There is no theory of morals,' he said.

'No,' I replied,' but there *have been* many; and in its nature it is a system.' Comprehending the significance of my *have been* he let me read on. It became a habit with me to trace everything I could to its origin and principles. I endeavoured to think by principles, and the habit made me laconic in speech, for my style was a reflection of what was going on in my mind, and made me sometimes a puzzle to those to whom I spoke. This amused me, though it sometimes got me the credit of being inclined to be cynical as well as silent. One good *confrère* hit me with Horace's *brevis esse laboro, obscuro fio* – In trying to be brief you grow obscure. And I sometimes heard my former nickname, amplified into 'Old Plato'. I believe I was more or less a puzzle to Superiors as well as to brethren, and was left to do much after my own way. Thus I got into a habit of constant reading with very little relaxation; and excessive reading overlays solid mental, as well as moral, discipline. I read far into the night, beyond the time for extinguishing lights, and consequently was often found wanting in choir when Matins had begun. Nor was this noticed, as it ought to have been, until at last I went to the Prior, acknowledged my fault, and offered to submit to whatever correction he thought best. After which I received a public rebuke.

Notes

1   In the dedication to a volume of sermons, published in 1842, Dr. Ullathorne expresses his obligations to his director. 'You were my first, my constant, and my best instructor in the spirit of the religious life. It was you who early inspired me with that missionary spirit which counts itself as nothing in the pursuit of the salvation of immortal souls. And as I was brought up at your feet, so have I since been privileged to walk at your side in the Apostolic career, and to be guided by your light.' (Mother Drane's note.)

2   A letter is preserved, dated Downside, January 7th, 1824, in which the writer, addressing his parents, informs them of this event. 'I had the inexpressible happiness,' he says, 'of approaching Holy Communion for the first time on Christmas Day, and promised now to begin in earnest to serve God with all my heart, which, indeed, is a very poor return for all the mercies and blessings which he has vouchsafed to grant to such an unworthy being as myself. And now, my dear parents, I feel as if I were entering on a new being, so much happier am I than during my former course of life.' (Mother Drane's note.)

3   Most probably St Ignatius of Loyola's *Spiritual Exercises*.

4   1824.

5   Jean-Armand le Bouthhillier de Rancé (1626–1700), was the reformer of the Cistercian order at the Abbey of La Trappe, whence the name Trappists, though properly The Order of Cistercians of the Strict Observance.

6   The later manuscript has 'Father Polding himself was an extensive reader and large thinker on these topics' which would appear to be Mother Drane's misguided charity playing with words.

7   The original manuscript has Reed.

Chapter Six

The Great Conflict[1]

In the month of October, 1828, I received the Sacrament of Confirmation from Bishop, afterwards Cardinal, Weld. I had never before seen a bishop, except Bishop Baines, when he officiated at the opening of the old Chapel of St. Gregory, the year after I arrived at Downside. On the same day I received the Minor Orders, and on October 12th of the same year the Sub-diaconate, together with my companions, Messrs. Kendal, Davis, Dowding and Sinnot. On Ember Saturday, September, 1830, together with others of the brethren, I received the order of Deacon. On March 3rd, 1829, the aged bishop, Dr. Collingridge, of the Western District, departed this life, and Bishop Baines, who had been his coadjutor, succeeded him as Vicar-Apostolic.

Soon after this arose the great conflict between the English Benedictines and Bishop Baines, himself a member of the Order. Anxious to establish a great college with something of the character of a university, although this was contrary to the advice given him by his predecessor Bishop Collingridge, he bought Prior Park. But being without men or resources, he set his mind upon his old brethren, the Benedictines. He did his utmost at Rome to persuade the authorities that the English Benedictine vows were invalid, and their houses were without religious discipline. He opened a correspondence with the Fathers at Ampleforth, which had been his own monastery. He went there himself, remained a considerable period, and induced the Superiors, and several of the monks, to abandon their monastery, taking with them what students they could, and all the resources of the house that they could bring together, and to pass over to his own secular college of Prior Park.

Before this, however, there had been a prolonged Chapter of the Congregation held at Downside, and a severe contest between the two parties already dividing the body; the men of Downside remaining staunch to the Order, as well as other men of mark from the Northern Province. All that we young religious knew was that the Superior of Ampleforth and some others had given occasion to this contest. I have no wish to enter into this miserable history except in so far as it is necessary to explain my own. Miserable, I call it, although it redounded to the honour and credit of those who, by their constancy and perseverence in its defence, saved the Congregation, put it on its former footing, and restored its unity.

The day after the Chapter had dispersed, we young religious were invited into the stranger's parlour to meet the venerable Dr. Marsh, the late President-General, and Dr. Birdsall, the newly elected one. This, however, was something new to us. We were pleasantly excited, and still more so when our healths were drunk as the *spes altera gregis*, the other hope of the flock. Dr. Marsh arose and said: 'As I am an older member of the Order, and you are yet young, may I venture to suggest a word of advice, which you will take kindly. I have always made it a rule not to think about my own interest, but only for the good of the order, and I have found in that rule a source of content. And if you do so, I am sure you will find the same.' From the lips of this simple-hearted and truly venerable man fresh from his late contest in defence of the Order these words came with a singular grace.

He was a tall, gaunt man with a shrill voice, a small face, sharp features and bright grey eyes. And he walked with long strides and figure erect. The brown frock-coat he had on had been worn for fourteen years and was still clean and becoming. He had managed the escape from Douay amid the horrors of the French Revolution and had gone through some narrow escapes himself. He had founded Ampleforth, and afterwards refounded the old monastery at Douay. He had been in all the offices of the Order, and was still destined to be President once again, having buried, as I heard him say on the occasion of his next installation, several men who expected to bury him. He was a most frugal, self-denying man, given to prayer. He was looked up to as the man who had done incomparably more for the Order than any other man.

His successor in the office, Dr. Birdsall, was quite as tall, but the sternest man I ever knew, stern even to harshness, so that the younger monks trembled to approach him. His voice and his looks seemed to throw one off him by habit more than by effort, or by any indication of intention. He impressed one with the notion of his having had great and prolonged internal combats with his nature, but then he seemed to combat all natures, ours as well as his own. He was a labouring missionary and a first-rate catechist, but everyone was in awe of him. His self-denial was undoubted, he bore the brunt of the conflict with Bishop Baines, and suffered severely from it. Deficient in tact, I do not think he was aware to what an extent his manner and tone were trying to those who had relations of duty with him, yet I have been assured by ladies who had consulted him in days of trial and distress that on such occasions he showed how very tender and feeling was the heart within him, and how little he spared himself when he could do a real service. Spare himself he never did.

Ampleforth was broken up. Its Superiors and leading members deserted it for Prior Park. The conflict thickened, and the President-General sent Dr. Marsh and Dr. Brown, our Professor of Theology, to Rome to wage the conflict there. They were very coldly received, their own Order refused them lodgings in their monastery, spies were put upon them. They were supposed to represent a body of men devoid of all good religious discipline. Gradually, however, the truth came out. The first thing that opened the eyes of Propaganda was that these men read Rodriguez for their spiritual reading. The Prefect of Propaganda, afterwards Gregory XVI, began to esteem them and to see that the congregation had been grievously misrepresented. Meanwhile Dr. Baines had put an Interdict on Downside, and had suspended the President-General, who was a missioner at Cheltenham. The monastery was, of course, exempt, and the Interdict did not touch the internal faculties of the Superiors, and the boys of the College were considered as having the privilege of exemption. Still, Dr. Polding, their confessor, had qualms, and wrote to Cardinal Cappelari, who in reply told him not to disquiet himself. But for the servants and the people of the congregation a priest was sent over from time to time from Bath, one of those men who had deserted the Order in its needs, and he heard their confessions in the brewery, seated on a tub, as being outside the precincts of the monastery.

We young men were made partakers of the controversy, for as much as it was thought expedient that the whole community should sign certain petitions and documents sent to Rome. This necessitated the President-General and Prior's explaining the state of affairs to us, and the correspondence of our representatives to Rome was read to us. We were all staunch and loyal to the Order, and had no misgivings as to the merits of the case; but later on I could not fail to observe that the effect was somewhat to damage our simplicity. Hitherto we had known nothing of the affairs of the house or Order, and troubled our heads with nothing but our obedience. Henceforth, our judgements having been once evoked, we were inclined to exercise them a little in other matters concerning our own immediate government. This to my reflecting mind was a lesson stored up.

And this reminds me of another lesson which became valuable to me in the future guidance of religious houses. Soon after our profession we were called upon, as directed by the Constitutions, to deliver our judgement to the Council of the house respecting the question of professing another, who had for the most of his time been our fellow-novice. We all felt that he was unfit for profession, and each of us, as we were called in, declared as much. We were questioned as to the grounds of our conclusion, which was quite proper, but being ourselves but recently professed, and feeling shy in a somewhat odious line of duty, we could not analyse and express the grounds of our judgement with much clearness. So we were a little brow-beaten and made to understand that we were prejudiced. The Prior put off the profession for three months as the Constitutions directed, and then, without calling the community again, as was allowed by the Constitutions, professed him. The one who was thus professed became a great trouble, failed under every effort made to save him, and was at last expelled. This led me subsequently to reflect on the wisdom of St. Benedict, who says in the third chapter of his Rule: *saepe juniori Dominus revelat quod melius.* And in the seventh chapter: *aetas non discernetur in Ordine, nec praejudicet; quia Samuel et Daniel pueri presbyteros judicaverunt.* Let not age be a disadvantage for when Samuel and Daniel were young they judged the elders. There can be no doubt but that the young ones know most concerning those of their own standing, and position. They live with them, and they necessarily exhibit their real character to them with less disguise. But when the young ones are called to give their judgement on their companions on a question so momentous as their profession they will naturally be timid, speak with hesitating tones and find it difficult to assign the grounds of their judgement, when they are compelled by conscience to speak against them. Whereas the presumption is that they would wish these brethren to be even as they, if their conscience would allow them to say so. When, therefore, a real difficulty presents itself as to whether a novice is fit for profession or not, the wisest thing is to try to get at the sense of those who are on the most familiar terms with them. Although this mistake was committed once, as I have known it committed once in other houses, the Prior was a prudent man, a good spiritual guide, and one who by his general demeanour impressed the sense of authority on his subjects.

This is not the place for entering into further details of the great conflict. Bishop Baines was directed by the Holy See to take off the Interdict and to remove the suspension from the President-General. But he hesitated and delayed and the Holy See had to speak more than once before this was accomplished.

Notes

1   See the Preface for background to the Prior Park difficulties.

Chapter Seven

A Priest Forever

Soon after this my Superiors wished to advance me to the Priesthood before I had completed the course of theology, but thinking there might be difficulties with the Bishop about dispensations from time and interstices, a petition was sent to Rome through Cardinal Weld, who was a protector and kind friend of the Order, but he replied that it was below the dignity of a Cardinal to act as agent, and so to my individual satisfaction I escaped from what I thought a premature ordination.

However, I was not destined to continue my studies, but with the Rev. Mr Sinnot, a deacon as well as myself, I was sent to assist the new Prior in restoring the Monastery and College of Ampleforth after their great desolation.

Soon after arriving there I was appointed Professor of Theology to a small class, and had prepared the first lesson when the Prior changed his mind, put in an Irish Franciscan, and I was made Prefect of Discipline over the school. Although those who remained constant to the Order after the great desertion stood firm, yet there was still a flavour remaining of the spirit in which they had been trained. The new Prior was from the old house of Lambspring,[1] and an old Missioner, and was not accepted with perfect cordiality, still less the two members from Downside. This spirit communicated itself to the school, which had too intimate relations with one or two of the Religious, and no sooner had the new Prefect appeared than there was written all over the walls: 'No Hunt, No Reform'. Hunt was the leading Radical in the political world of that day. I let them enjoy their little triumph for the rest of the day, but next morning after prayers I told them I was surprised to find a set of College boys who showed the manners of a pothouse or a kennel. That if one or two had chalked the walls in a style insulting to one who was a

51

stranger to them as yet, the rest must have concurred in their conduct or they would have removed the disgrace fastened on the whole school. I will not, I said, be severe on you without necessity; I will give you the next vacation hour to get the walls cleaned of their disgrace. If it is not done then, I will stop all school work until I find out the offenders. If I fail to do so I shall conclude that the whole school is involved in the guilt and then I must punish by decimation. The walls were quite clean after the next recreation. Still, there was a rebellious spirit more or less fostered by those who had no right to interfere. I expelled one of the oldest students, flogged a younger one, and then we became good friends and understood each other.

One little incident more, and the rest of the house understood me also. There was a young man, son of a baronet, living amongst the Religious. He took liberties in the refectory so far as to come up and talk with boys at their dinner. I ordered him off. Stimulated by some unwise person, he came to me the next day before these youths and asked for an apology. I told him I generally did that kind of thing after the morning prayers and if he would then come into the school he should have an explanation in their presence. He came. I contrived to have most of the masters present and the Prior also. I then gave him an apology that made his ears tingle. He burst out into tears, and shortly afterwards, having a good heart, we became close friends, and I had no more trouble in any quarter.

The Prior was a clever but somewhat eccentric man. He had great and original powers of preaching, but was also passionately fond of controversy and of placarding brief replies to adversaries. This return of his old missionary habits very much interfered with the business of the College, got him entangled in hot water with the neighbouring Protestant clergy, and at last it came to lecturing in an adjoining village from one of the college wagons. All this caused a considerable excitement about the country and led to personal accusations in the way of recrimination, untrue but inconvenient to the College. I wrote an account of this state of things to my old Superiors, and finding that my letters were carefully read before being posted I wrote all the more plainly, perhaps too plainly. This led to some estrangement between us.

Meanwhile I had received the Order of Priesthood, together with Mr Sinnot, from Bishop Painswick at Ushaw.[2] This, to me, great event took place on the Ember Saturday of September, 1831. Reaching Durham, by accident we met with Mr. Walker, now Canon Walker of Scarborough, and one of the Gillows, both professors at the College. They arranged for our luggage to follow, and we walked to the College with them. I well recollect how Mr Walker gave me a specimen of his quality, questioning me in my philosophical and theological reading, and when he found I was not unacquainted with such writers as Hooker, Barrow, Jeremy Taylor and even Clarke on the Attributes he broke out on the impropriety of allowing young men to read such books, though he was both himself a young man and obviously knew something of these selfsame writers.

However, very different ideas than those furnished by Protestant divines were occupying me then; the Bishop and Dr. Youens, who was then Rector of the College, examined us and we got through pretty well. Several members of the College received the priesthood as well as ourselves, and the joyous burst of the *Te Deum* after the function, and the vigorous congratulations of their brethren shewed how much the whole College participated in the happiness of the newly made priests.

At the little entertainment given to the assembled College[3] on the day of my first Mass I poured out my feelings in picturesque language on the grandeur, dignity and power of the priesthood in a way that made a solemn impression on my youthful charges. As prefect I felt reluctant to employ my consecrated hands in punishing boys sent to me for that purpose by their masters. I mentioned it to the Prior, who rebuked me for my squeamishness. I put down some of my more earnest feelings in a sort of journal I then kept, and these papers were amongst a few that I preserved, and took to Australia, but leaving them with the Sisters of Charity for custody when I last left, they were entrusted to be conveyed to me in private hands and never reached me.

I need not dwell on the great change which the priesthood wrought in my spiritual habits. Only those who, after long preparation, have entered under obedience into that sublime state and office, can in any degree realise what the Sacrament of Priesthood does for the soul of the receiver. For weeks after my ordination I seemed to feel the sacred unction on my hands. The thought and feeling with which the Priesthood inspired me was one of *sacrifice*, making it appear to be the natural life of a priest whose soul has undergone a transformation into a new order of existence. The ideas of *monk* and *priest* appear to my mind's eye in singular correlation with each other: the monk, as the man spontaneously offered to God through the call of His election of grace; whilst the priesthood, imparting the distinctive character of Christ to the soul, absorbed the hidden life of Our Lord, and brought Him forth an open sacrifice for the souls of men. The tremendous mystery of the altar took visible form in my eyes, and was coloured to my inward sense as that Divine oblation of the Immaculate Lamb which on Heaven's golden altar was ever offered before the majesty of the Father, the earthly repetition of which made by mortal man seemed to make the material altar stream with grace.[4]

I believe the sense of sacrifice impressed on my soul at my ordination had a secret force and some conscious influence in rendering me prompt to respond to the call to the Australian Mission. Alas! That those deeper movements of the soul should slacken and suffer loss amid the strife and turmoil of subsequent life.

Soon after my ordination I was sent to the small mission of Craik and Easingwold on alternate Sundays. There I preached my first sermons and did the Sunday duty. It was at Craik that Bishop Baines first began, and I found there a copy of *Archer's Sermons*, covered with his marks for accentuation. It was there he first elaborated that style of delivery which made him afterwards such a perfect master of oratorical delivery. Cardinal Wiseman is inaccurate in one of his writings in stating that Dr. Baines spoke in a Lancashire dialect. He broadened and opened his vowels for effect, but he was the most polished man in speech and manners after a certain style that I ever knew, although one was always sensible that his manner was the result of elaboration.

Before I received the Priesthood I had lost my dear father. He received the last Sacraments surrounded by his family, and one of his assistants, who was likewise present, was so touched by the Catholic death-bed, the sacred rites which accompanied it, and the moving words of the priest, the Rev. Mr. Leyne, that he became a Catholic in consequence. It came out that he had hitherto been the secretary of an Orange Lodge, which he at once relinquished and, as he subsequently told me, the object of that Lodge was to do all the harm they could to the Catholic religion.

The contents of my letters, before referred to, had been reported to the President-General from Ampleforth, and I received a short and peremptory instruction to repair back to my own monastery *recto tramite*, by the shortest path. On the way back, as I had to pass through Cheltenham, I called on the General, in case, as I observed, he should wish for any explanations. He received me with more than his usual gravity, and simply remarked that I should have time to go on by the same coach. Yet, years after these events, I was told by my old Superior that these very letters of mine were produced in the General Chapter when I, in fact, was in Australia, and were used as authentic documents to enforce a change of authority at Ampleforth. This was discipline, and in so far it was good.

Notes

1   Lambspring, a monastery of the English Congregation in Germany, founded 1643, suspended by Prussia, 1802.
2   The College of St Cuthbert, then a combined College and Seminary, founded in 1804 to replace Douai which had been suppressed after the French Revolution. It is still one of the chief English seminaries.
3   We are now back at Ampleforth.
4   The greater part of this paragraph (from Only those who ... till the end) does not appear in either manuscript and was either added by the Archbishop at Mother Drane's request as edifying for her nuns or supplied by Mother Drane herself. The tone of flowery piety, far removed from Ullathorne's natural style, suggests the latter.

Chapter Eight

Preparing for a Voyage

I had scarcely settled in my own monastery to my great relief, when Dr. Polding received his Briefs of appointment as Vicar-Apostolic to test Mauritius where his uncle, Bishop Slater, was Bishop. But he feared lest the intense heat of the climate should relax his energies, and declined the appointment.

Through the intervention of Bishop Bramston, Vicar-Apostolic of the London District, Dr. Morris, a member of the Downside Community, who had for several years been the only member of any regular Order employed on the London Mission, was then appointed as Apostolic Visitor to the Mauritius, which appointment he accepted. The Vicariate of Mauritius at that time extended beyond the island over all South Africa, Australia, and the islands of the Pacific including New Zealand, and also over a considerable part of British India.

Dr. Morris naturally wished to obtain co-operators from the house of his profession. In reply to his application, he was told by the Superiors that if I was asked I should probably not be unwilling to go. The impression on the part of my Superiors was, I believe, derived from an incident that occurred several years before. I was suffering for more than two years from an acute inflammation of the liver, combined with sharp and continuous attacks of ague; the latter disease having been caught from an open reservoir in a field under our windows into which ran the entire drainage of the College and monastery. This mischief was not stopped for years until at last a medical man pumped it out as the cause of the sickness in the house. On its removal, I got better. But I was going with some other young Religious in Dr. Polding's company to Bath to consult the physician. As we drove on, Dr. Polding began to talk of the great want of missionaries in Australia amongst the convict population. He said there was no part of the world where there was such a field for missionary labour, or where it was so much needed. He spoke of the sufferings of the convicts as what was likely to open their hearts to the Divine Grace. He gave his own views as to the way in which such a mission should be managed. He mentioned his own attraction to that kind of work, and asked whether if he went any of us would join him. I said at once that I should be ready at his call, and so the subject ended.

This conversation had been laid up in Dr. Polding's mind, and had led to the mentioning of my name to Dr. Morris. When, therefore, Dr. Morris wrote to me, I replied that I had about a hundred reasons against going to the Mauritius, and almost as many for going to Australia. He at once responded that he equally wanted help for Australia, and asked me to go to New South Wales. I therefore submitted the question to my Superiors.

The Prior at that time was Father Turner, an old Douay monk, a very meek, holy and venerable man, who had for some time succeeded Prior Barber, whilst Drs. Polding and Brown filled the next offices. Dr. Polding in his kind and fatherly way showed me his correspondence about the appointment to the Mauritius which had been kept a secret, and was inclined to advise me to delay, thinking the time had not yet come for doing the work effectually, but left me at liberty. The others had advised me to write to the President-General for leave to offer myself for the Australian Mission. This I did. The General replied by a short and characteristic letter, that he gave me up entirely to Bishop Morris, adding a word in commendation of the work before me. Having received a small legacy from my father, I was allowed to devote it to my preparations, and to pay the expense of the voyage out.

I then proceeded to London where I received the greatest kindness from my relatives; nor can I forget the affectionate co-operation of my confrère and old Professor of Greek, Dr. Heptonstall, who was then in London as Protector of the Order, serving a small mission also at Acton.

Having now left monastical observance for a busy life in the world, let me pause and look back before proceeding on my solitary way. For truly my life was henceforth more solitary far than in the monastery. For the greater the crowd amongst which you move, the greater is your loneliness, if the key to which your soul is tuned is different from theirs, if your thoughts are not their thoughts, nor your ways their

ways. I loved the monastic life, had imbibed much light
from the Divine Office, especially during those years of my
training, and the spirit of the office was deepened in me by
the Gregorian Chant and by the recurrence of the Festivals
which celebrated the mysteries of Faith, and the great Saints
of the Order. I loved to read the ascetical writings of the saints,
and to muse upon the ways of the monastic saints who had
sought God with all their souls. But the English Benedictines
were not ascetic like the monks of La Trappe. They were destined to the work of education in the house, and were brought
into that work a year, or very few, after their profession, and
whilst still studying their Theology. And the prospect before
them was the English Mission, where they had not in those
days the discipline of their Order, but lived rather after the
manner of secular priests. In the monastery the Constitutions
were well observed, but on the mission the monastic life practically ceased.

The disturbing element in me was my fondness for reading
pursued to excess. No doubt I felt my own intellectual deficiencies, and strove to arm myself with whatever knowledge
I could compass, but I made all sorts of divarications from a
methodical method of study, and overlaid my brain with too
multifarious and too rapid a succession of ideas and forms,
besides diverting my soul from the steady pursuit of my own
spiritual advancement. I had so much light which I did not
wisely use. My Superiors should have guided me, for they must
have known of my ways, and this was, and often is, a defect in
monastical establishments, for which reason I mention it here.
I remember that once or twice our master of juniors, or our
Professor of Theology, visited our cells in study time, inquired
into our habits of using our time and methods of study, and it
did me a great deal of good. This ought to be done more frequently, as well in monasteries where studies are pursued as
in ecclesiastical seminaries.

Aware that Catholic books must be a rarity in those remote
colonies, and not knowing what I might need in an emergency,
I set to work in London to make up a select library of about
five hundred volumes. Although chiefly ecclesiastical, I added
some of the choicest classics in all the languages of which I
knew anything.[1]

I also paid a short visit to my family in Scarborough, who
generously helped me with more money, and I bade farewell
to my dear mother, brothers and sisters, expecting never to see

them again. Meanwhile a dispatch had come from the Governor of New South Wales to the Secretary of the Colonies which changed my position. There were conflicts between the three priests then in New South Wales, and conflicts between the senior priest and the Government respecting grants of land, which had reached a crisis, and Sir Richard Bourke[2] asked the Home Government to obtain that some Catholic ecclesiastic should be sent out invested with the authority to manage the affairs of that Church. Bishop Morris was in consequence invited to an interview at the Colonial Office, and he informed the Secretary of State that he had an ecclesiastic in view, whom he could appoint as his Vicar-General for Australia, with residence in Sydney, who would have all the authority required. This was agreed to and a stipend was assigned by the Government of £200 a year, an allowance of £1 a day while travelling on duty, and for voyage and outfit £150. The title assigned to me by Government, in documents, beyond that of Vicar-General, was that of His Majesty's Catholic Chaplain in New South Wales. I also received a letter from the Colonial Secretary, recommending me to the Governors of the Australian Colonies.

As I was a young priest but recently ordained, I felt that my youth, inexperience in ecclesiastical affairs, and ignorance of Canon Law would stand greatly in my way. I had no wish but to work as a simple missioner. However, I consulted my spiritual father Dr. Polding, and he said: 'You must accept it, but you had better write to the President-General and ask his leave.' My passage had already been paid for on the *Sir Thomas Munro* and I had deposited eighty guineas with the owners as my fare. I wrote to the General in all simplicity, but he gave me no reply. I wrote again, but he still kept silent. This put me in great perplexity and fretted my mind not a little. I could not see my way out of my difficulty, and it caused me much anguish of soul.

At last, a day or two before the ship sailed, I got a joint letter from Drs. Barber and Polding, written under the eyes of the General, and informing me in grave and formal language that my conduct in writing for leave to accept the Vicar-Generalship after he had given me entirely up to Bishop Morris was a sort of duplicity since he had consented to my going. When the ship reached the Downs, I got a second letter from Dr. Polding apologising for the tone of the previous one, adding that they had had considerable difficulty in inducing the General to let them write, and explaining its style on the ground that it had to be submitted to him. This pained me much. I wrote in reply that whatever I had done, I had done in simplicity, that it was purely by the advice of him, Dr. Polding, my old guide and Superior, I had written at all to ask leave to accept the responsibility put upon me by the Bishop, and that I thought this circumstance ought to have been explained to the General, which would have shown that I was really acting in obedience to one whom the Order had so long given me for a guide.

I added that now that I was in a position which required me to judge and to govern ecclesiastics, I could not avoid seeing that I had been treated with a great deal of unnecessary cruelty, and had been put into a most trying perplexity, all of which could have been avoided, had he said that I was simply acting in obedience to his advice. So bidding him an affectionate farewell, with gratitude for all he had ever done for me, I proceeded on my solitary way across the ocean.

Notes

1   This is from Mss.1. Mss.2. reads: I ... spent months in the old bookshops and among their catalogues, and gathered together about a thousand volumes of Theology, Fathers, Canon law, and sacred literature, in every language of which I knew something.

2   Sir Richard Bourke (1777–1855), sent as a liaison officer to the Spanish army in Galicia (1812) he impressed Wellesley. He rose to the level of Major-General and was sent as Lieut. Governor of the Eastern district of the Cape of Good Hope (1825–28). His appointment as Governor of New South Wales from 1831 to 1837 was characterised by strict impartiality and religious tolerance. He returned to Ireland (1837), served as High Sheriff of Limerick (1839), was made full General in 1851 and died at his seat Thornfield near Limerick.

Chapter Nine

Voyage to Cape Town

I sailed in the *Sir Thomas Munro* on September 16th, 1832. A large ship is a very different thing from the brigs in which I had sailed as a boy; and I was no longer a cabin boy, but a priest with a title expressive of responsible office. I had a good sized cabin which enabled me to enjoy retirement at any time. Although solitary as a Catholic, and unable to say Mass as a priest, and although I had but little in common with those around me, I never felt those long voyages tedious. I enjoyed the quiet and absence of solicitude, and the retirement of my cabin, that floating hermit's cell. From my boyhood I had a good deal of the hermit in my composition, preferring to be alone, and having no attraction for society beyond the sense of duty. My attraction was to books and my own solitary musings. And though for many years I had the credit of putting out a good deal of practical energy, that was when duty called and no longer. Archbishop Polding used to say, and with truth, that I required some exciting cause, or some difficulty to surmount, to draw out the sleeping energies within me. I never felt the disposition to take in hand the future before the present, and was thus saved from many useless solicitudes which torment the imagination. Experience has taught me that things do not occur as the imagination is apt to paint them by anticipation, and that by tormenting yourself with anticipations of events in which you are to be engaged you only jaundice your eyes and warp your judgement. Napoleon's remark that the eye of the general should be as colourless as his glass is applicable to all who have to deal with difficult human affairs. I did not therefore tease myself with the unknown future, but in some degree, on St. Augustine's principle, I 'joined myself to eternity and found rest'. And of that eternity I had all around me the image in the boundless sea joined to the boundless heavens, always the same, yet always living in a change that spoke of God's never ceasing action in the created universe. On how many tranquil evenings and starry nights did I drink in a deeper sense of God's grandeur as Creator and controller of the boundless air and ocean, and of the worlds that twinkled above me as from a point! There is nothing that inspires the sense of dependence on that sovereign will like the silent teaching of the trackless ocean through the process of the intelligence.

Early habits had made me indifferent to all but the necessities of life, and I discarded many of those useless encumbrances which people call comforts. In the cabin there was much more luxury than I needed, and I never troubled the twelve o'clock 'tiffin', or the eight o'clock assembly over the spirit bottles. For many years neither tea, coffee, ale, wine, or spirits suited my constitution; I had steam enough within me to keep up the movement of life. Most of my companions made themselves miserable with the heat in the tropics; and certainly the pitch would sometimes bubble up from between the seams of the deck, and your sticks of sealing wax would melt together; but these good people unnecessarily put fire into themselves, and heated themselves through the imagination by thinking about it. By keeping below when the ship was cool in the earlier part of the day, and coming on deck in the evening when the ship was hot, I was always cool when my companions were in misery. By little management I saved myself this torment, and tried to impart some of my philosophy to others, but without success; they seemed to think that our natures were not the same.

I had a sailor's heart for the poor fellows who manned the ship, and although I never spoke to them but a word or so on occasion, they seemed to know it by instinct, and always showed me particular respect. I fancy they liked to see the sturdy way in which I walked the deck in all weathers, and that independence of circumstances which came of the monk grafted on the sailor. Except the privation, therefore, of the Mass and Church services, I was always inclined to regret when the voyages came to an end, and the quiet and retirement that they afforded me. They were a sort of prolonged retreat, uniting a course of spiritual with a course of ecclesiastical study, by which I in some degree made up for my abridged course before ordination.

On board ship I adopted a rule of life, which I followed on all future occasions, and which never failed to give me influence on emergency. I followed a plan of studies in my cabin, from which I never deviated except on rare occasions, but after meals I mixed in the general conversation. A long voyage at sea, though it induces good fellowship, yet, as the passengers are of so mixed a description, and as all the individual infirmities that are commonly secrets within the family come out, as there is little to do, and as wine-spirits and malt-liquors are put on the table three times a day, a good deal of small jealousy, misunderstanding, and antipathy is apt to arise from time to time, especially where there are ladies as well as gentlemen, and some who are neither.

For instance there was a very quiet Methodist minister with his wife and family on board. They used the quarter-deck and had a large aft-cabin near mine, but had made a cheaper arrangement to have their meals second-class by themselves. They were very unobtrusive and respectable in their way, but they were teased and put upon by a number of young men, for no better reason than their own thoughtless amusement. But my reserved habits enabled me to act as their protector on various occasions and, as they suffered a good deal of discomfort, I privately sent them presents of wine and other things which had been sent on board for me as presents which I did not use.

Feeling my deficiency in Ecclesiastical law, I made it a point of special study, and directed special attention to what concerned the authority and jurisdiction of a Vicar-General. For, by my deed of appointment, this extended over the whole of Australia, Van Dieman's Land alone excepted, which was left to the only priest then in that colony. I knew that I should be some four thousand miles away from my Bishop, with whom the means of communication would be rare and casual. Even the consecrated oils for the Sacraments were received from London, much after date, and there was a whole breadth of the world between these colonies and the Holy See. I felt, then, that I should have to act almost as if the complete authority of the Church were concentrated in my office, and to rely on my own resources.

We put in at the Cape of Good Hope for fresh provisions. It was blowing a gale at the time from Table Mountain. The famous cloud called the Table Cloth was resting upon it and a rainbow in the cloud. We beat into the bay with such a stress of canvas, that we were at first supposed to be a man-of-war.

The Dutch have built Cape Town after the fashion of their streets at home, in broad, straight lines and at right angles, void of all protection from the fierce winds, sun, and dust, as if arranged for that special purpose. Even the gentlemen had to wear blue veils for the protection of their eyes.

I landed and put up with the priest, an English Benedictine belonging to Ampleforth, and an accomplished man. His congregation was a mixture from all the nations of Europe and the East, and what with his difficulties with them and his having no other priest to have recourse to he had got into a habit of grinding his teeth. And being very abstracted, he was afterwards brought back to England with the loss of his mind. This was the first opportunity of observing the impolicy of leaving a priest alone by himself in a remote colony. I was destined to see more of this evil later.

Enjoying the hospitality of the Rev. Father, I was much interested in the novel vegetation to be seen on all sides, and the diversity of races, and especially with the social customs of the Hottentots and the Malays.

I visited a chief supporter of the chapel, a loyal friend of the priest, who was quite a character. He was a West Indian Creole of mixed French and Negro blood, with a large family of children, who were eating oranges all day long. A large hamper of the golden fruit stood always in the hall for their use. He had begun life as a player on the violin, and had risen to wealth by supplying the exotic gardens of Europe with seed, and its menageries with wild animals. He had lions, tigers, ostriches, and other wild animals ready in iron cages for shipment. His establishment was a curiosity, and his house was hospitable.

Chapter Ten

Van Dieman's Land

Setting sail again, we ran with a fair wind and a stiff breeze all the way to the Australian coast. And sailing up Bass Straits, between Van Dieman's Land and New Holland, with both coasts in sight, we entered the harbour of Circular Head, so called from a huge rock, or rather mountain like a drum, rising sheer up and covered with trees, which advances into the sea and forms a horn of the little harbour.

This was the headquarters of the Van Dieman's Land Company which had received from Government half a million of acres on which to establish an improved system of agriculture. The manager was Mr. Curr, an English Catholic, and brother of a priest, from whom I had letters. The homestead was certainly in a flourishing condition, both as to vegetable and animal production but, with the exception of the manager, his family and a few superintendents, the whole settlement consisted of convict labourers assigned to the Company. Here I had no jurisdiction. The only priest in the island[1], about the size of Ireland, lived at Hobart Town, the capital, on the opposite side of the island. I received no more attention from the manager than the other passengers, to their great surprise and a little to mine, being invited to dinner once, as they all were, in successive parties, whilst part of our cargo was discharging, but not invited to take up my residence ashore. I baptised three of his children, two of whom were old enough to make their remarks and play with the end of my stole whilst I was administering the Sacrament, and their elder sister stood sponsor as the only Catholic available except the parents. Mrs. Curr had two convict men for her nurses because the convict women were so corrupt and difficult to manage. They found the men-nurses affectionate to the children and careful of them, though the children could not be kept so cleanly under their fostering.

Letters which I wrote from there, describing my first impression of the scenery, the singular trees, with their bark then dropping instead of the leaves for it was the Australian autumn, the sweet-odoured shrubs and scentless flowers, the rich-plumaged birds, and the sponges and shells that covered the shore, these letters with similar ones of later dates were long preserved by my brother Owen, but at his death they were unfortunately destroyed by his widow.

From Circular Head we sailed for Hobart Town. No one will ever forget his first welcome into Hobart Town Bay, its vast expanse and depth, its basaltic columns rising here and there out of the lofty cliffs like giant organs, its islands of basalt growing numerous as we approach the yet concealed mouth of the Derwent. And Mount Wellington towering in the distance to 3,000 feet, and marking the position of the captial. To enliven the scene a school of black whales were crossing the bay and shore boats were after them. We saw one that had been struck with the harpoon flying through the water with prodigious rapidity, the boat held by the cord of the harpoon stuck into its body flying after with its bows out of the water and the foam of the sea covering its fore timbers, while the men sat still as death. Another whale was spouting blood, lying exhausted on the surface. The harpooner was leaning on the end of his instrument from the bows of his boat and forcing it into the body with all his strength. We wound our way through the islands, having Bruny pointed out to us by the pilot as the best land for potatoes in the world, entered Derwent, and sailed up its broad stream between its beautiful sloping banks until, turning into Sullivan's Cove, we saw the town spread before us and Mount Wellington towering into the bright sky directly over the houses.

Father Connolly, the one priest and Vicar-General of this island, was absent on his annual visit to Launceston. I was hospitably lodged and entertained by Mr. Hackett, a native of Cork, and a distiller; a man of information, popular among the few Catholics, and influential in the town. Meeting the leading Catholics, all of Irish origin, I soon began to hear a sad account of the state of Catholic affairs, which my own subsequent knowledge but too much confirmed.

I must refer to my two pamphlets, *The Catholic Mission in Australasia* published in England in 1837, and the *Reply to Judge Burton* published in Sydney in 1839,[2] for the history of Catholic Affairs before my arrival.

The first priest who arrived with authority in New South Wales was the Very Rev. Jeremiah O'Flynn, who was invested by the Holy See with the title of Archpriest, with power to administer the Sacrament of Confirmation. He arrived in Sydney, by the ship *Duke of Wellington,* on August 3rd, 1817. All those Catholics who remembered him spoke with great reverence of his mild, religious character, his great charity, and his fluency in speaking the Irish language. He was of a Religious Order, and, if I remember rightly, a Capuchin.[3] There was no charitable institution at that time for receiving the helpless poor, and he took into his residence several aged and decrepit people, whom he lived with and maintained. But as he had come without any authority from the Home Government, the Colonial Government, influenced by a strong anti-Catholic party, illegally seized upon him, put him in prison, and sent him back to England by the first ship. This tyrannical act produced a great sensation at home: Mr Hutchison, of the Donoughmore family, member for Cork, brought the whole case before Parliament; and under the influence of Lord Bathurst two priests were sent out, Father Connolly and Father Therry, each with a stipend of £100 a year. They arrived in Sydney in 1820, but soon afterwards they disagreed, and Father Connolly went to Hobart Town, where he landed in March, 1821, and remained there until I landed in the beginning of 1833, without ever having the opportunity of seeing a brother priest or of approaching the Sacrament of Penance.

The people complained that they were treated with great severity and kept at a great distance; that the Sacraments were seldom approached and by few; that the priest spent his time chiefly among Protestant friends, and in a morning on the exchange listening to the remarks of the men of business; that he was the bosom friend of a suspended Anglican Clergyman, and that he claimed the large plot of ground, granted by Government for a church, as his own property; that this had led to a conflict between him and the Governor, and that the chapel was a wretched structure made of boards given by the Government when he first came, that had never been improved since, and that there was no Catholic school for the children. All this I found to be true.

I went up to the chapel to my Mass. It was situated on a plot of several acres in a beautiful position, but was in a most disgraceful state. There was a tidy little house enough, but the floor of the chapel consisted of loose boards of the gum tree, with their sharp edges curled up and the planks moving at every tread. The altar was a frame of wood with a most filthy old black antependium and altar cloths. The rough plaster at the back was covered with black-glazed cotton put up at the death of George IV and covered with filth. The other inner walls were but the first rough plaster, covered with dirt. The two sides and under the altar were refuse holes for the household, old discarded hats, lime-wash buckets, mops, brooms, all sorts of disgraceful rubbish heaped up and thrown about there. The altar linen, long unwashed, was thickly stained with port wine. There were no steps to the altar, but the same loose planks that formed the entire floor, and no seats for the people. The chalice and ciborium were tarnished as black as ink. Although assured it would give great offence, I cleaned the chalice and ciborium, laid short planks across in front of the altar to give a surer footing, got some of the worst of the rubbish away, and on Sunday I preached to the people, who were so unaccustomed to be spoken to warmly that they were moved to tears.

The Governor, Sir George Arthur, received me with great courtesy and invited me to dinner to meet also the Protestant Archdeacon Broughton, who was on a visit with his large family from Sydney, and who was afterwards the first Bishop of Australia. At the dinner-table the Governor said that Mr Connolly had treated him shamefully. The fact is that he consorted with the adversaries of the government and held out threats of writing a history of Sir George's government and, having a very sarcastic spirit, the Governor was afraid of him.

At a later interview the Governor opened up the subject of religion and we had a long private conversation on the subject. He was himself an earnest Evangelical. He, however, asked me some questions, which afterwards I thought scarcely fair without giving me warning that his friend the Archdeacon was then writing a controversial pamphlet upon those very points I had afterwards to reply to. Yet I recall with pleasure the courtesies I received from Governor Arthur.

Father Connolly returned home before I left Hobart Town. He expressed no discontent at what I had done in the chapel. He gave me his ideas of the state of things in Sydney, and we parted friends.

Notes

1   i.e. Tasmania.
2   *A reply to Judge British, of the Supreme Court of New South Wales, on the State of Religion in the Colony.* 1840
3   *The Catholic Encyclopedia* (1907–1914), speaks of this priest as Father Jeremiah Flynn, an Irish former Cistercian. Mss.1. mentions him as Flynn, without the 'O'.

Chapter Eleven

Sydney[1]

I made it a point of policy not to send any previous notice to Sydney of my coming, and when we arrived there in February, 1833, after a fortnight's sail, I walked straight to the priest's residence. There I found Father McEncroe[2], a grave, experienced man, formerly Vicar-General of Bishop England in South Carolina. He had come to Sydney from Ireland the year previous with Mr. Attorney-General Plunkett, his wife and sister. From him I heard a good deal of how things stood. Father Therry had gone to Parramatta. The housekeeper was the widow of the celebrated John Maguire who kept the British troops long at bay in the Wicklow mountains after the insurrection of '98 was over in the rest of Ireland. He surrendered at last on condition that he and his family should be sent safe to Australia. This was done. Father Therry had promised the gallant old man on his death-bed that he would protect his wife and family.

Two of the daughters lived in the house with their mother as well as another young person. There was also a young man residing in the house, a clerk to a bank, who had deluged the Vicar-Apostolic in London with letters in defence of Father Therry. All these were his staunch allies, and, although good people, I felt the awkwardness of their being in the house.

Father Therry arrived whilst I was having some dinner and was at once, as his housekeeper had been, very patronising, spoke to me, as she had done, of my very youthful appearance for a priest, and offered me, no doubt with kind intention, every assistance in his power to settle me in some part of the colony. I knew that his first impulses were generally sound, so after the cloth was removed and we three priests were left by ourselves, I produced the document constituting me Vicar-General and shewing me to be exclusively possessed

70

of jurisdiction in New South Wales. He read it and immediately went on his knees. This act of obedience and submission gave me great internal relief. That evening I went by invitation with Father Therry to the house of a gentleman, where I found myself in company with precisely the three persons with whom it was represented to me in England that I should find my difficulty. This internally amused me, and the more so when I found out afterwards that they had mistaken the newcomer for a raw College youth who, they said after I left them, might easily be disposed of to Bathurst, then the remotest part of the Colony. I confess that I had purposely humoured this notion until I saw my way to a decisive step.

The next morning as I came from Mass in the little chapel, Father Therry met me and said, 'Sir, there are two parties among us, and I wish to put you in possession of my ideas on the subject.'

I replied, 'No, Father Therry, if you will pardon me, there are not two parties.'

He warmed up, as his quick, sensitive nature prompted, and replied, with his face in a glow: 'What can you know about it? You have only just arrived, and have had no experience.'

'Father Therry,' I said, with gravity, 'listen to me. There *were* two parties yesterday; there are *none* today. They arose from the unfortunate want of some person endowed with ecclesiastical authority, which is now at an end. For the present, in New South Wales, I represent the Church, and those who gather not with me, scatter. So now there is an end of parties.'

That day I went by coach to Parramatta, to see the Governor at his country residence. Sir Richard Bourke had recently lost his wife, to whom he was much attached, and was ill in bed. But he was anxious to have the Catholic affairs settled, and gave me an audience in his bedroom. The fine old soldier was one of the most polished men I ever met. In his younger days he had been a good deal under the influence of the celebrated Edmund Burke, and was a man of extensive information as well as experience. The statue erected to his memory in Sydney bears recorded on its base the great measures by which he gave freedom and social progress to the Colony. Though not a Catholic, he had a great respect for the Catholic religion, and had many Catholic relatives and friends. He received me with great kindness, and we soon understood each other. I listened to his remarks, and then asked leave to see him again after I had enquired into the points of which he spoke. I returned to Sydney, and on the Sunday I announced my powers to the people from the altar, and stated that I suspended all affairs connected with the business of the Church for a fortnight, when, after making due enquiries, I would call a public meeting of the Catholics.

There were several difficulties on hand. First there was not a single church or chapel in the Colony fit for service except a small chapel attached to the priest's house for a weekday use. Father Therry was the most singular character I ever knew. He was a truly good man, had gone through all the first difficulties of providing religion for the convict population, yet was generally in conflict with the Government. He had been there, alone, for a space of ten years without ever seeing a brother priest, yet he always, every day, said Mass, whether under a roof or on a mountain top, carrying a vestment and altar-stone behind him on horseback or in a gig, or on the back of a man who travelled with him. He also said the Rosary publicly every evening with as many people as he could get together. But except Mass and the Rosary he never finished anything else. He never finished a church and, unless a person were dying, he never finished a Confession except with a few regular people. So that for twenty years after, if a poor convict turned up, and said he had been last with Father Therry, the priest knew at once that he must begin with the beginning, from the time he confessed in his native country. He was full of zeal, but wanting in tact, so that he repeatedly got into trouble with the Government, and sometimes with the successive ecclesiastical authorities. Hence the long difficulties which arose after he was superseded as Vicar-General in Tasmania by its first bishop. Having passed from trade to his studies, he·had sufficient knowledge of his duties, but was too actively employed to be a reader.

He had been building a great cathedral in Sydney for twenty years. It was roofed at last, just before I arrived, but not one of the sixty windows were in, nor the floor laid down, nor the plaster done. He never thought of getting more priests for this widespread Colony with its numerous townships, many of them far asunder, and its distant settlements. When one unexpectedly arrived, he seemed to think it was an intrusion on his province. As having been so long the only priest, and by certain popular ways of an odd kind, innocent but inimitable in their *bizarrerie*, he was wonderfully popular with the masses both of Catholics and Protestants. As an Irish settler from up the country said to me: 'They thought that Almighty God did not shine on any man as He shone on Father Therry.' Yet he was neither a preacher nor a man of business, though he dabbled in business in his own way a great deal. He could not put two ideas together on any subject, had quite a limited education, and yet continued to exercise his singular influence on public opinion. He had a hand or a hat for every poor and every well-dressed man in the street, always making the advance. He went into the taverns, so numerous in Sydney, where the rough men drank, calling everyone *Sir* and *Mister* and when they presented a glass for him to drink he just touched it to his lips, for he was a very temperate man, and so shaking everyone by the hand went out again.

When known to be in Sydney, he had a crowd at his door every morning, waiting for an hour or two, with papers to be signed for the Government offices, petitions, etc. After he had quietly breakfasted he would go out to them and say: 'My dear people, you see I am engaged, can't you come another day.' And they went away reporting that Father Therry had so much to do that he could not attend to them. Now and then he would slip around with some of those papers to Father McEncroe or myself, and get them certified or signed, as he was himself in hostility with the Government; and, of course, it was always Father Therry who did everything. After nightfall he would have lamps lighted to his gig and drive out to one or two sick calls and, of course, 'Father Therry was always working day and night.' And he was in bustle day and night, though it is wonderful how little came out of it.

Large tracts of land had been left him by will; for many of the emancipated convicts dying without relatives considered him as the representative of the Church. But he treated it all as his personal property, and yet he never properly looked after it. He did not seem to care for property, and yet he held to it with tenacious grasp, so that it could not be turned to use for supplying the necessities of religion. He begged everywhere after his own fashion, and had agents everywhere to raise money for the great Sydney church. And when he got an intimation that someone was coming out with authority from England, he went everywhere amongst the people, taverns included, with an agent, and got both Catholics and Protestants to sign promissory notes for one or five pounds, or ten or twenty, to be paid in instalments for a number of years to come, and thus get the future ecclesiastical revenues into his own hands. Later on, he attempted to sue in the courts both Protestants and Catholics for these notes, and I had to forbid a course which was both scandalous and illegal, for there was no equivalent to make these promises actionable. Now and again, his highly sensitive nature got so moved, and his head so heated with the notion that I was doing him some grievous wrong, that he would come to me and pour out in a way that was at once provoking and comical.

'Pardon me,' he would say, with reddened brow, and mincing manner, bowing all the time, 'I do not wish to offend you. But you are my greatest enemy. You are very learned, but you do not understand this Colony. You are very unjust to me. Oh, pray don't think I wish to say anything displeasing to you or inconsistent with your office.'

And after this sort of preface to which I calmly listened, would come out some vague expression of grievance, or perhaps very strong words, always balanced with apologies. Sometimes he would get upon some third person. 'I would on no account say anything disparaging of him, but he is a dishonest person, and a great scoundrel. I do not wish to say anything disrespectful of him.'

A few kind words often sent him away tranquil; but if he went too far, I used to say: 'Father Therry, you or I must leave the room. Which shall it be?'

'Oh, I will retire by all means.'

Then, next morning, I sent him a note by Father McEncroe, requiring him to withdraw his language on pain of my serious displeasure. Then he would make amends in a proper manner, and show any little kind note I wrote to him to his friends. Such was the man who kept everything from consolidating, and who had caused so much trouble that a well-disposed Governor had applied to someone with ecclesiastical authority to manage him.

In 1830 a priest of the name of Dowling had arrived in the Colony, a man of fervid popular eloquence, and heated imagination. He preached at Sydney. Father Therry and he soon disagreed. Dowling turned his eloquence upon the old missioner. Father Therry was in the habit of going down after

Mass in his vestments and standing at the door with the collecting box, giving loud eulogies to those who put in most, and making polite speeches to the people as they passed out. Dowling claimed some of this money, and both of them in their vestments or surplices, one Sunday, were dragging at the two ends of the box in presence of the people, and amongst their exclamations. When Father McEncroe arrived, Dowling went and settled at Windsor.

Notes

1   The following chapters, written forty years on, are general reminiscences and not necessarily in chronological order. The manuscripts themselves, particularly Mss.1., are piecemeal. A little effort has been made to shuffle them in something approximating a sequence but the author's own wording has been strictly adhered to.

2   John McEncroe (1795–1868), born in Ardsella, Co. Tipperary. He studied for the sacred priesthood at Maynooth where he was ordained priest in 1820. He taught briefly in the Meath seminary. Bishop England of Charleston invited him to join in the South Carolina Missions which he served for seven years. Ill-health forced his return to Ireland (1829). In 1832 he went to New South Wales as a chaplain to the penal colony. He served faithfully until his death in 1868. He was the founder of *The Freeman's Journal* in Sydney 1850, for many years the major Catholic newspaper.

Chapter Twelve

Establishing Authority in Sydney

Government policy was still strongly in favour of an exclusive Established Church under the Crown. A Royal Commissioner, Mr. Briggs, was sent out to report on the condition of the Colony.[1] Mr. Thomas Hobbs Scott, formerly a wine merchant, accompanied him as secretary. On their return Mr. Scott was made the first Protestant Archdeacon of the Colony, and on his arrival announced his intention to organise the Protestant Church, to establish parishes and schools, and to hand over to a corporation one seventh of the land of the Colony for that purpose. This was accomplished by a deed under the sign manual of George IV.[2] Moreover, in the orphanage established by Government at Parramatta, the children left without parents were all to be taught the Protestant religion.

This new state of affairs was very alarming to the Catholic population, and Father Therry addressed a letter to the *Sydney Herald* (which was at that time also the Government Gazette) on June 6th, 1825, in which he signified his intention of forming a Catholic School Society, and also of doing his best to establish Catholic cemeteries, which would prevent many inconveniences, besides avoiding collision with the Anglican clergy. But at the close of the letter he spoke of the Protestant clergy as entertaining for them, as it appeared in print, *'qualified respect'*. Father Therry explained that this was misprinted, and that he had written the word 'unqualified'. Nevertheless the letter was made an excuse for withdrawing his small salary, and of excluding him from officiating in any Government establishment, thus prohibiting him from visiting the prisons, hospitals and similar institutions.[3] This occurred under the Government of Sir Thomas Brisbane, and soon after the arrival of Archdeacon Scott with the purely Protestant scheme of an exclusive Establishment. It is said that Father Therry was offered a small sum of money, £300, to leave the Colony, but of that I never heard, and have no proof.

In the year 1829 Sir Roger Therry arrived as Solicitor-General and Commissioner of the Court of Requests. He was the first Catholic appointed by the Home Government after the Emancipation Act.[4] On taking office, the Protestant oath was tendered to him. He asked for the Catholic one. The official replied: 'Now that the point of honour is settled, it can make no difference.'

'It makes all the difference in life,' replied Sir Roger.

So the Catholic oath was produced. In 1832 Father McEncroe arrived, in company with Mr. Plunkett, his wife, and sister. Mr Plunkett came with the appointment of Attorney-General. These two Catholic gentlemen, both of high character, were the first men of position who were earnest in the practice and support of their religion, and their influence was of great value. Two other Catholic gentlemen had come out with office at an earlier time, but they concealed their religion until it was lost to themselves and their families. It was a saying in Sydney that Lady Therry's was the first bonnet that had appeared in the Catholic congregation. But when I arrived things had very much changed in that respect. In 1829 the Rev. J. V. Dowling also arrived and made his residence at Windsor. These were the only two clergymen besides Father Therry whom I found in the Colony in 1833, and both of them had stipends from the Government.

The chief difficulty on my arrival regarded the church in Sydney, which Father Therry had begun soon after his arrival, but which was not yet completed. It was on a very large scale, with transepts raised to a great height, with walls of massive solidity, and with large crypts beneath. The Government had granted the site for the church, and an ample space for whatever buildings might be required in addition; but it had never been conveyed to trustees, which the Government now required to be done. Moreover, Father Therry claimed an extent of land considerably larger than the Government admitted to have been granted, and there was no documentary evidence producible. The land in question formed part of Sydney Park, and the addition which he claimed would have made considerable inroad into the open space. The Government appointed its own surveyors to measure and mark out the grant, but Father Therry declared they were encroaching, took a stake, and threatened to knock the men down who put any marks of division within the territory that he claimed. No doubt he believed in his claim, and there was an impression on his mind that one of the earlier Governors intended to give more. But the Governor did not want the park spoilt by being built over, and there were really no proofs. Just before I arrived the Attorney-General, an excellent Catholic, was put in the awkward position of being directed to bring an action against Father Therry for his encroachments. This was suspended by my arrival.

On my second visit to the Governor I asked his Excellency to allow me to arrange that instead of six lay trustees, as demanded, I might be allowed to have three clerical trustees of my own appointment, and three lay trustees to be selected by the congregation. This, I said, would secure three very respectable laymen, in whom everyone would confide, but if six laymen were required we should have three emancipated convicts added to the list and it would lead to serious conflicts. Sir Richard at once understood it, and consented. 'Anything reasonable,' he said, 'for the sake of peace.' I then solicited his Excellency to join with me in completing the church for service; for we had not a single church completed. In Sydney we had only the use of a Government building, used for the Court of Requests, where we had the Sunday services and a school on week-days. If the Government would complete the woodwork, including the flooring. I would put in the sixty large windows. His Excellency agreed to this also.[5]

On the Sunday appointed for the meeting, I first said the Mass and then preached an earnest sermon on unity. Then I took the chair, on my own motion, and knowing that several people had come prepared to rake up stories of the past, and to load my ears with grievances, I put a stop to all this by saying that we were not met to talk, but to vote; that hitherto painful divisions had prevailed owing to the want of an authority, but as there was now a duly appointed authority, all good Catholics would adhere to it. And as to past troubles, the sooner they were forgotten the better. 'Let us put a ponderous tombstone of oblivion over them, and then leave them in God's hands. Let all the congregation, except the servants of the Crown (the convicts), put the three names they wish for trustees into the voting box.'

This was done. The three names turned up were those of Mr. Attorney-General Plunkett, the Commissioner Therry of the Court of Requests, and Mr. Murphy, the latter being a most respectable Emancipist, who had been unjustly transported, and was now a wealthy and much respected man.

I then appointed Fathers Therry and McEncroe, with myself, as the three clerical trustees. This ended all our troubles. And as I saw that all were in good humour, I said I should now be happy to hear any remarks that anyone felt inspired to offer. This brought out cordial expressions of thankfulness and unity from the principal leaders, and the meeting closed. I have been thus particular in detailing the steps I took to establish peace and unity, because after this stroke of policy it was never after interrupted.

Passing from the meeting to my residence, I was met at the door by a poor ragged Irishman, the only man in tatters I had yet seen in the Colony. He asked me if I would listen to what he had to say. 'Well,' I said, 'what is it?'

In reply he poured out a stream of hexameter verses, in perfect metre and harmony, describing the meeting, weaving in the names of the speakers and the incidents that had occurred since my arrival, winding up with a touching thanksgiving for the peace restored to the Catholic body. I asked my Irish troubadour with some astonishment what had reduced a man of his abilities and elevation of mind to such a condition. He replied: 'I am a child of nature, Your Reverence, and I cannot resist the drink which my countrymen give me in their generosity.'

Some years afterwards, when up in the interior country, I called at a wealthy settler's, a Catholic and a native of the country, when he pressed me very much to stay for dinner.

'I assure you,' he said, 'if you will stop, I will give you an intellectual treat.'

I stopped, and after dinner, in rolled my troubadour from the farm, in a good and fat condition, smiling all over his face. Standing by the door he resumed the history of my transactions in the Colony from where he had left off after the meeting, and rolled out a stream of sweet and harmonious verses, without halt or fault of composition for half an hour. I never saw or heard of my poet afterwards. He was a self-taught man, and a simple child of impulse, and spoke in tones whose sweetness, tenderness and pathos I recall completely whilst I write.

Notes

1   John Thomas Briggs (though his name is given as Bigge in the *Cath. Enc.*) was Special Commissioner in Australia from 1819 to 1822.

2   i.e. On 17th July, 1825 Royal Letters (George IV was still on the throne; he died in 1830) set apart one seventh of the whole territory of New South Wales – which, incidentally, then included the Moreton Bay District, now Queensland – to the ruling creed. This was revoked in 1834 but in the meantime 435,000 acres was in the hands of the Anglican Church.

3   'Whilst still under this ban Father Therry went to visit a dying man at one of the hospitals, but was stopped by the guard when about to enter. Father Therry said: "The salvation of this man depends upon my ministration; which is your first duty?" The guard lowered his arms and permitted him to pass. On another occasion, going to the infirmary to visit a sick person, the doorkeeper bade him wait till he should have ascertained from the attendant surgeon whether he could be admitted. Whilst he was away, Father Therry, who knew all the passages of the place, gave the sick person the consolations of religion, and on returning met the official, who told him he could not be admitted.' – Dean Kenny, *History of Catholicity in Australia*, p. 51. (Quoted by Mother Drane.)

4   March, 1829.

5   This is from Mss.2. Mss.1. reads: 'If the Government will put in the windows and doors, I will do the rest.'

Chapter Thirteen

Sydney Reminiscences

Writing home on the day of my arrival, with the window open before me, suddenly there came a darkness. I looked up and there was the head of the chief of the Sydney tribe thrust through the window to see what was going on. His black face painted red under the eyes, wild mass of hair, beetling brow, big jaws, crushed nose, white teeth, and naked shoulders, the grin on his face, the energetic nodding of his head, formed a picture so grotesque and unexpected that it required a little effort to return his greetings with politeness. Behind him was his *gin*, the poor princess of his tribe, peering out of the blanket with which she was enveloped. I gave them some coppers, and sketched them into the letter I was writing. We were the intruders into their dominions, not they upon ours, and their tribe had already dwindled down to half a dozen fighting men. Whenever the white man came, the tribe was ruined by the communication of his vices and by drink.

Father Therry was habitually kind to these poor creatures, who camped and held their corroborees and their funerals in a valley by the seashore, about half a mile below our residence. He often fed them when in want. But there was no making any religious impression upon them. Any allusion to a God reduced them to silence. But they had vivid notions of the transmigrations of their fathers' souls into new bodies of man, bird or beast. They also had great fears of a malignant spirit.

Father McEncroe and I once had a most interesting account from two young men, of the Botany Bay tribe, telling us their traditions of the arrival of Captain Cook in that bay.[1] When they saw the two ships they thought them to be great birds. They took the men upon them in their clothes, and the officers and marines in their cocked hats, for strange animals. When the wings (that is, the sails) were closed up, and the men were aloft, and they saw their tails hanging down (sailors wore pigtails in those days) they took them for long-tailed opossums. When the boat came to land, the women were much frightened; they cried and tried to keep the men back. The men had plenty of spears, and would go on. Cook broke a branch from a tree and held it up. They did the same. He came on and they came on, and they trembled and the women tried to stop them. Cook took out a bottle and drank and gave them rum. They drank, and spat out, calling it salt-water. Cook took some biscuit and ate it, and gave it. They spat it out and said: 'Something dry'. Cook took a tomahawk and chopped a tree. They liked the tomahawk, and he gave them it. Thus the first gift they saw the value of was the axe that was destined to clear their woods and to make way for the white man. Allowing for the broken English, that is an accurate narrative of the tradition of the Botany Bay tribe.

Dr. Bland, an old inhabitant, told me that in early days he had witnessed a fight between the Sydney and the Botany Bay tribes on the very ground before the house. After hurling their fourteen feet spears, they closed, and each struck his antagonist with his *waddy*, a club of hard wood, and then chivalrously presented his head to receive the return blow, striking alternately until one of them was laid prostrate.

I was walking on one occasion with Father McEncroe on the same ground, when a young native fled across our path naked and unarmed; a second, with his *waddy*, followed in chase, whilst a third appeared in the distance. The first plunged into the Government domain, an aboriginal forest with walks cut through it. We followed by the shortest cut in the same direction, but only arrived in time to find the first man killed with the *waddy* of the second, who had fled. The third came up in terrible excitement, his naked skin fretting and his eyes bursting. He was the brother of the man who was slain. Finding life extinct, he sent up one cry and then rushed after the slayer. The police brought the body into our stable and then an inquiry was made. But it was found to be a case of native feud between two tribes following their own laws. The body was given up to the tribe to whom it belonged, and I heard the funeral rites performed that night in the valley below. Nothing could be done for the souls of these poor creatures, corrupted as they were among the Europeans. Some youths, however were brought up in Catholic families, became regular communicants, and were steady up to the time of mandhood, when they flung off their clothes, ran off to the Bush and followed their native impulse for savage freedom.

Soon after my arrival in Sydney a venerable old man who lived by splitting timber in the woods came for his annual visit to go to his religious duties; for, like thousands of others, he lived in the Bush a long way from any priest. He remembered the early days when Sydney was nothing but a penal settlement. He was a tall man, with white hair and a bowed head, with much refinement of speech and manner, and an old Insurrectionist of 1798. He spoke much of Father Flynn, whom he had known, and said, with touching pathos: 'Oh, if Father Flynn had been let to remain, what would he not have done? He had the swiftest and sweetest tongue of Irish that ever my ear heard.'

Another tall, old man, with the same breadth of chest and shoulders, and with the bearing of a chief, used to be led from the convict barracks every Saturday, for he was stone blind, by a boy, to make his weekly confession. And always after concluding his confession, he made a brief but solemn Act of Thanksgiving aloud for the gift of blindness, as it shut out half the wickedness in the midst of which he was compelled to live.

Sir Richard Bourke remarked to me, at my first interview with him, that I should find the bulk of the Irish convicts very different in their moral feelings from the main body of the English ones. He said truly enough: 'It is commonly some impulse of deeply aroused passion which commits an Irishman, and not an habitually corrupted nature.' Unhappily, many of them who were horrified at the crimes they found prevailing amongst the vile classes amongst which they were thrown, contracted vices in the temptations into which they ought never to have been thrown. Bushranging with its venturesome hazards had naturally an attraction for them, and some of the most desperate bushrangers were Irishmen.

It was a rule amongst the bushrangers of all descriptions, English or Irish, never to touch a priest. They had a fixed idea that if they did they would never have luck again. So we always knew we were safe. Going in the late night on a sick call from Sydney to Liverpool, a man sprang out of the Bush with a blunderbuss over his shoulders, and seized the horse's head. I was sitting in the gig enveloped in a cloak, and at once disengaged my hands, and my man prepared for a spring upon him, throwing me the reins, when the man saw my face in the moonlight, and ran off among the trees.

Father Corcoran at Windsor got secret intelligence of a very notorious bushranger, on whose head there was a large price set, being in refuge in a cavern of the Blue Mountains, a few miles distant. He rode out to see him, and had repeated interviews, doing his best to induce the man to give himself up; for he had perpetrated several murders, and was sure to commit more if he remained at large, and had no long chance for his own life. His last interview was on a Good Friday, when, after conjuring the man by all the sacred memories of that day to surrender himself, and to die a Christian death, he succeeded in his entreaty, and was turning round to come out of the cave, and go to the magistrate to arrange for his surrender, when the police, who had suspected Father Corcoran's communication with him, and had followed the track, entered the mouth of the cave. The man instinctively sprang up with a pistol in each hand, and firing went on over Father Corcoran's head. He bent down to avoid the shots. The man was wounded and seized and carried off to gaol, and, of course, was executed. I might tell many anecdotes of this character, but these will serve as a sample. The men in the condemned cells have told both the Bishop and the priests of particular times and circumstances when they passed them by, lying in wait in their hiding places.

There were several soldiers who went to their weekly Communion, in the 17th Regiment, and at least twenty who went once a fortnight. One young man I particularly remember. He was quite a contemplative. He had received the Carmelite Scapular before he entered the Army from the Reverend Father Pope at Congleton, and had persevered in a habit of prayer and fasting. He spent the sentry watches in prayer. He had to stand sentry at the gaol by the gibbet one night after two men had been hung upon it, and such was his terror through the working of his imagination, in that ghastly spot, with the shade of night around him that, as he afterwards told me with a sense of gratitude, nothing but the earnestness with which he said his prayers, and so conquered his imagination, saved him from throwing down his musket and jumping over the parapet to run away. The incidents of the barrack room, and the rigours of military discipline, served him as subjects of self-mortification. And he certainly had both a tender conscience and an habitual sense of the presence of God. He kept several of his comrades steady to their religious duties, and from time to time brought others to the Sacraments. I have often wondered what ultimately became of that young soldier, who had then gone on well and holily for several years.

When that then admirably disciplined regiment went to India the Bishop got leave of the Lieutenant-Colonel for all the Catholics, about a third of the regiment, to have a day free to make their confessions, and to go to the Holy Communion. Every man of them came, for the Colonel gave them the leave on parade. One man, whom we had never seen before, was asked by the Bishop: 'What brought you here?'

He gave the military salute and replied: 'The orders of my commanding officer, Your Lordship.' This was just one of those cases that the Bishop delighted to get hold of.

There was a convict about thirty years old far up the country on the Bathurst Range beyond the Blue Mountains, who was quite a contemplative, a shepherd, always following his sheep over extensive pastures, and, except at lambing and shearing time, always in solitude, or nearly so. He spent his time in prayer and enjoyed his solitude. There was then no priest resident in all that country, and his master was so pleased with his steady, reliable conduct, and the care he took of his sheep, that once a year he let him come down to Sydney to receive the Sacraments, and gave him five shillings to buy food on the way. He walked upwards of a hundred miles for this purpose, praying by the way. He stopped a few days in Sydney. I gave him half a crown to help him back, and he returned to his solitude. He had the gentleness of manner which the habit of prayer and solitude gives.

Notes

1   Which, after all, had been little over sixty years before.

Chapter Fourteen

Sydney Reminiscences II

I was called to visit a dying person the day after my first arrival in Sydney, under circumstances which made a deep impression on my memory. The woman to whom I was called had been living with a man who in the course of the previous night had treated her with savage barbarity. He had beaten and bruised her all over her body and face, and thrown her down a ladder which led up to the loft, above the wretched, filthy wooden box of a room in which she lay near her death. Her face was much swollen, her eyes were both black and largely swelled. But, partially conscious, she constantly called out for water. She cried for mercy every now and then, but whether it was to God, or to the man, who then stood solidly by, thinking he was still in the humour to beat her, it was hard to ascertain. She expired a short time afterwards. The miserable scene and its history so impressed me, that I drew it, and one or two not very different cases to which I had been called, into pictures in sermons illustrating the consequences of these habits of crime which never failed to produce a deep impression, and to awaken a thrill of dismay in my auditors.

Sitting late one night reading, it might be between twelve and one o'clock, a man came to the door, a broad, thick-necked, surly-spoken fellow and said: 'My wife's dying.'

'I will come directly. Wait a moment.'

Providing myself with all things requisite, I set out with the man. I saw he had had some drink, though conscious enough of what he was doing. As we walked across the racecourse or park, as it was called, lying between our house and the city, I began to question him. When we had got about the middle of this open space, he suddenly stopped, turned to me and said: 'I beg your pardon, sir, but my wife is not ill at all.'

'You scamp,' I said. 'What do you mean by calling me out at this time of night?'

'The fact is, sir,' he replied, 'we've just had a desperate quarrel and neither of us will give in, and if Your Reverence will just come and put us together again.'

I walked on with him, found his wife in bed, gave both of them a good scolding. They cried, shook hands and I left them, telling them I should come the next morning and look into their goings on altogether.

The poor Irish girls, through being assigned to wicked masters, were not infrequently exposed to great perils, especially in lone country places. I recall one poor girl who had hard conflicts to protect herself, and like many others, she knew well that any appeal to a Court would only bring ridicule, perhaps punishment, upon herself. There was very little faith in a convict's statements. The theory was that they were always at some scheme or other; and too often this was true. The presumption, of course, stood for the master, especially when there was no witness except master and servant. But this was a really simple-hearted, modest girl, and in telling me her troubles she said with great *naiveté*: 'Whatever did they send a poor harmless girl all this way over the world to learn wickedness for? Lord Bless Your Reverence, it was only for receiving a stolen goose from a lad, and I didn't know it was stolen.'

Another poor girl was never safe from her master's importunities even in her kitchen, and she kept a carving-knife near at hand when he was about, to protect herself with. This knife she had to take in hand more than once.

Convict girls were sometimes foolish in marrying dissipated old men, for the sake of getting their freedom. A smart young girl came one day to my house with two witnesses and an old man to marry. The banns had been published, but I did my utmost to persuade both parties, and each separately and apart, not to marry, assuring them that they would only make each other wretched. But all in vain. Married they would be, and married they were. The next morning the old man took his young wife to the Police Court for having given him a cruel thrashing, of which he exhibited the signs. All the defence she put in was that she 'didn't know what the old fellow was driving at.'

Such were the miseries in which at times we were compelled to be unwilling co-operators. On the other hand, men who had got their freedom would go to the Parramatta Factory and ask for a wife from among the convicts there. This was made known to a certain class, who, with the prospect of freedom before them, volunteered to marry. A certain number came forth. The man cast his eyes over them, invited one whom he selected to a conference, and after a little conversation they were married. And the majority of these marriages, especially when they settled up the country, out of the way of the public-houses, turned out quite happy and thriving.

A man came to me at Norfolk Island from amongst the convicts, who was blind, and had had to grope his way for some years, and was consequently exempt from work. He came, however, to tell me that he never had been blind, and that he began to be suspected, and wanted to know what he ought to do. My advice to him was to manage to get his sight back, and as soon as he let the overseer know that he had got a glimmer of light the better.

Playing the old soldier was not an uncommon thing, to get rest and hospital diet, or to get out of the hands of some hard task-master. One way of doing this was to bring on a temporary fever by swallowing tobacco juice. Another way was to make a wound, as if received at work, or by accident, and to irritate it to inflammation by applying copper to it. One or two penny pieces were sufficient for the purpose. But contrivances of this sort were numerous, and traditional in the gangs, and often perplexed doctors to distinguish between them and reality.

Knowing there was a chain-gang employed in repairing a road a few miles from Parramatta, I rode off one Sunday afternoon with the object of seeing what Catholics were amongst them, and with the view of saying prayers for them. I found the gang, as usual, lodged in a number of wooden boxes, like bathing machines off their wheels, placed in the Bush off the road. They were, as usual, all locked up in these boxes, which was their usual condition when not at work or at their meals or washing their clothes. There was the usual military guard, and the overseers were loitering about. I asked what Catholics there were, and the overseers set to work to find out. As the first door was unlocked they said: 'Stand aside, sir,' and out came a yellow steam, the atmosphere caused by so many men packed together, with only some small square holes for ventilation. The men lay on shelves and on the floor, for there was scarcely room for them all to have stood on the floor together, however closely packed. Thus they remained all night and all Sunday except a certain time for meals.

I had the Catholics mustered in an open space, where the sentries could seem them all, and said prayers for them. I visited them thus on a Sunday as much to relieve them from confinement in that packed-up, sweltering condition, as to say prayers for them. Anything more demoralising than this system of treating men worse than dogs cannot be imagined. I have known the heat so intense that the sentry has dropped down dead under the weight of his accoutrements and the oppression of the atmosphere, and as he was carried off, another soldier, in carrying his body, also fell from exhaustion. A soldier had been brought to court-martial for being drunk on his post, and it was satisfactorily shewn to have been the effect of the heat.

The Reverend Bede Sumner was travelling along the Liverpool road, and leading his horse by the bridle down a hill. Two men rushed out of the Bush and, putting a pistol to his head, called for his money and his watch. Having light-coloured pantaloons on and a black stock, they did not recognise him as a priest. He gave up what he had, and then said: 'Do you know that you are robbing a priest?'

They replied: 'If you are a priest why don't you dress as a priest? Where is your breviary?'

He satisfied them that he was a priest, and they told him that they had taken to the Bush to escape the cruelty of a master who had a down on them, after they had suffered repeated floggings. They also said that they had been out several days and, not daring to go near the houses, had had nothing to eat but some cobs of Indian corn. Father Sumner gave them five shillings to get some food with and went on his way. The men, as it afterwards came out, then deliberated how they should contrive to get into a public-house without being apprehended as runaways.

They had robbed a policeman the day before, getting nothing, however, but a pair of handcuffs, and they hit upon the following scheme. One of them was to personate a policeman bringing down the other as convict to Sydney, and this one was to wear the handcuffs. In this plight they entered a wayside tavern kept by a man called Tim Ryan. After they began to get merry over their meal the landlord suspected they were too intimate in their merriment to be in the relation of policeman and prisoner, and went out and

watched them through a window. He then went in search
of a road patrol and, finding one, told him what he had
observed. 'I suspect,' said the policeman, 'that those are the
fellows who robbed me of my handcuffs,' and going to take
a peep at the same window, the sham policeman twigged him
and bolted. Whereupon the true policeman entered, took possession of the man, already shackled in his own handcuffs, and
conducted him to Sydney gaol.

I was often struck with the injustice that men habitually
commit in generalising the habits of criminals and leaving
them not one virtue or one human quality. I have sat at
the table of lawyers, solicitors and attendants at the criminal
courts and have heard them discuss the criminals they had
been engaged in trying or hearing tried, and have observed
how natural is the disposition even of shrewd men to apply
the principle: 'He who offends in one point is guilty of
all,' in a sense certainly never contemplated in the Sacred
Scripture. There the sense intended undoubtedly is that the
offender against one point of law is guilty against the principle upon which all law is based, and against the God whose
command is disobeyed as much in one point of law as in
another, and against that love of God which is the object and
end of all law.

But men of the world seem to have a common habit, fostered especially in law-courts, and amongst those who deal
with criminals, of concluding that once a criminal always
a criminal; and that to have been criminal in one point
implies a natural malignancy that is ready on occasion to
perpetrate every crime. Such monsters, however, are rare in
human nature, although there are many who are so weak
that whilst under prison discipline they are subordinate and
obedient, yet when released from the necessity of discipline,
and from a condition devoid of temptation, they are easily led
or driven into crime.

Thus many women there were in the Parramatta Factory
who, when there, were models of order and regularity as
well as of submissiveness, yet having no inward strength, the
moment they were free they became the wildest and most scandalous of reprobates. In a smaller proportion this may also be
said of men. But fewer men go into the opposite extremes
as far as women will go. There is also a class of criminals
who, had they been born and bred under advantageous circumstances, would have been heroes, but who, from a spirit

of pride and daring, are always prompt to lead in every fray, to let themselves be put forward by more malicious and cowardly men, and to keep that word with their comrades in cooler hours than they have uttered or sworn to in the hour of excitement. There are men who, as a rule, though they oftener incur punishment, and are looked upon as specially dangerous, not without reason, are yet often endowed with better qualities than their comrades, even with more real humanity, even with something of tenderness, when sincere kindness draws it forth; and such men, when convicted, will become very earnest and thorough penitents.

Often have I had the opportunity of comparing men as, from my secret knowledge, I knew them inwardly, with the judgement passed upon them by those who knew the same criminals, but by the outward evidence that is brought into courts of justice; and have seen the vast amount of practical truth embodied in the inspired sentence: 'Man sees in the face, but God beholds the heart.'

This singular experience has forced on me the proof of the necessity of a Divine Judgement to rectify the judgements of men more than all the high theories drawn up on the subject from the Treatise of the pagan Plutarch down to the reasonings of the Catholic De Maistre.

Men are sometimes executed for crimes which they never committed. And more often as a matter of course men and women also have been transported for the crimes of which they had no cognisance. This was no rare case during and after the Insurrection of 1798, and at other periods of bitter political strife blended with religious strife. And how many men were marked and transported for the most trivial causes after the famous Clare Election in O'Connell's days? I knew a number of these men, men doomed to a life of misery for the crime in fact, though not in form, of voting for O'Connell before the Act of Emancipation.

I knew a man condemned to death, I am confident without cause, whatever might be the appearance of the evidence. He got a reprieve after living some days in full expectation of death, and the agonies he suffered during that period were unusual in their keenness. He was sent to Norfolk Island for life, but conducted himself with so much propriety, and with such a sensitive self-respect, that he was soon made an overseer, and after some years obtained a full pardon.

I knew another man who had long been a bushranger, and had for so long a time staked his life on the hazard, and done deeds so desperate that when preparing for execution, though perfectly earnest to repent, and obedient to all injunctions, and praying much vocally, he could feel nothing. He felt his whole nature as hard as a stone, yet in will had but one desire, to die penitent. And he used to say: 'I feel very hard; pray for me.' His eye was hard, his face was hard, yet did he beat his breast and pray much for mercy.

Chapter Fifteen

Sydney Reminiscences III

Father McEncroe was subject from time to time to have his mind overcast with a terrible melancholy, accompanied by great internal heat and a peculiar twitching of the corners of the mouth; and then came on an intense longing for drink on this really otherwise very sober man. If then I took his shoes and his hat and locked his door to save him from sallying forth, he so far lost his senses as to get out of the window as he was and cross the park to some Catholic house, where he would implore the people for the love of God to put the light wine used in the country down his throat. And I used to have to go and seek him out and drive him home in my gig like a log.

When he came to himself nothing could exceed his distress and self-humiliation. And it was some time before these symptoms again returned. At such times he had no possession of his mind or moral faculties, and yet so admirable a man at other times. He was finally cured by giving up tea, coffee and all other stimulants. But this infirmity in my one counsellor and co-operator, with the uncertainty of its return, was the one great anxiety of my life. I never considered him a responsible man whilst the fit was on him, and when I could be with him he obeyed me like a child.

The affairs I had to manage led to no prolonged mental discussion, nor did they greatly distress me. I saw a crooked state of things requiring to be put straight, but was not inclined to hurry things before they were ripe for action. But when I struck, the blow was decisive as it was rapid, and it was soon found that I was not to be turned from my path. My decisions generally resulted from a combination of two forces, a sort of intuition of the right thing combined with an instinct of the characters to be managed in the process. I had faith in my office and faith in the people's faith in the authority of the church, and that I felt to be a match for all Father Therry's immense popularity. Him I treated with kindness and consideration consistent with what the exigencies of the Church required, and he could not but be sensible of this. His mistakes resulted from the limits of his mind, and his very brief ecclesiastical training, having, like myself, been in business, before he made his brief course at Carlow for the ecclesiastical state, as his old master Father Fitzgerald told me at a later period. And I could not but have a great deal of consideration for the arduous difficulties he had had so long to encounter, and that single-handed. It is true that that was one of his greatest crosses, for he ought to have got assistance, and might have got assistance, but who could think of that after all these years of solitary labour were past, and he suddenly found himself put down from that first place in the Australian church which he had so long occupied.

I was placed above jealousy, so was not teased with that devouring passion. I was not inclined to be suspicious and I gave credit to even difficult people for the good that was in them. Why do I say all this here but for the purpose of recalling those early lessons of providence and a certain temperament which I owed to my dear mother especially, and to the habitual influence of her calm, solid and practical good sense, shewn unceasingly in her example and at fitting seasons in her words of advice. The very sense of my responsibility kept me solid and reserved, and the necessity arising from my youthful appearance required me to bear myself with a gravity in those days, which the advance of age and grey hairs seemed no longer to demand in the same degree.

By Christmas night the great church was completed, and we began to have the services and devotions in a more becoming manner. I devoted myself a good deal to preaching and the Confessional, and communicants increased as the church began to be steadily served. With the aid of the Government I also began a school chapel on the Rocks, among the rudest part of the population.

Father Therry often made visits into the more populous parts of the interior. I visited various districts occasionally, and especially Maitland, on the river Hunter; St. Patrick's Plains, higher up the country; Newcastle, at the mouth of the Hunter; the beautiful district of Illawara; Bathurst, beyond the Blue Mountains; and sometimes Parramatta. Our usual way of travelling was on horseback, with a servant on another horse carrying the vestments and altar-stone. We always carried the Blessed Sacrament in a pyx in the breast pocket, not knowing where or when we might come upon the sick and dying. The Holy See has since prohibited this practice; and recollecting that we often had to stay the night in taverns, and in more miserable places, I think there was a wisdom in the prohibition. My oil stocks, through wearing a hole in the pocket, were lost in the desolate Blue Mountains. But, strange to say, a Frenchwoman passed that way, found them, and concluded that they must belong to a priest, and so they were finally recovered. A silver snuff-box lost in the same region was never recovered, although my name was upon it and I offered a reward for it. I valued it as a gift from my mother.

Generally, as I have said, we used the police courts for our chapels, but at Bathurst I used a ballroom built over the inn stables. At Apin I said Mass at a room of the tavern and preached a sermon against drunkenness. The men rallied the innkeeper upon it, but he said: 'Oh, we'll take anything from his Reverence.' Wherever we went, the Catholic innkeepers entertained us and our horses, and anyone in our company, always refusing payment. When we reached a township our custom was to ride round the country visiting the farms, calling also at Protestant houses to ask leave for the Catholic convict servants to come to Mass and the Sacraments, and looking after any sick who might require attention. Then the day came for Mass, and the missionary work began. The whole day would be occupied with people coming and going, and perhaps a second day was required for Communions. The heat was often intense, and in riding the rounds both horse and man got quite exhausted, while the heat vapour overhung in grey masses beneath the trees, and we had to drink some little, both horse and man, at almost every farm. Approaching a farm required a little management. As soon as you approach a whole chorus of dogs runs to meet you. Then you must stand perfectly still with the pack around you until someone advances from the house, calls them off and takes you under their protection. After this the dogs admit your claim to be let alone, or simply greet you with their wagging tails. But woe to you if, calculating on a night's lodging, you are met with the salutation: 'What a pity. We are just going to kill,' for that means that there is no meat in the house, and that your diet will be damper and tea with an egg or two after your hard ride, damper being a very bad cake baked in the ashes, and no doubt so called from the damp it puts on your digestion. Hospitality, however, with a hearty welcome to all that is in the house, never fails in the Australian Bush.

But you sometimes get into queer places and meet with odd incidents. Archbishop Polding was sleeping in a log hut and saw up through the rafters a couple of lights like stars. He puzzled as he lay to make out whether it was the bright moonlight sky peering through two holes in the roof or two actual stars, when pounce came a cat from the spot on his face and clawed his nose!

Having a sick call from Sydney to Illawara, a ride of eighty miles, a very heavy rain came on, and I stopped at a wooden hut for shelter. As the downpour continued the good people offered to lend me a beautiful blue cloth cloak, which hung up in the room and which someone had left there for a time. When it was taken off at the house where I stopped the whole inside of it was covered with bugs, as if it had been sewn with pearls, and it had to be hung upon a tree and swept with a broom.

The sick woman whom I went to visit, and whom the messenger, who had ridden all the way to Sydney, reported to be near death, came and opened the door. She was quite well and had only had a fit of ague.

I stopped the night at a log hut in the neighbourhood, and was awakened the next morning by a very loud and extraordinary noise. Shrieks and wailing were predominant, whilst a certain harmonious discord in two parts ran through the shrill notes. I got up and inquired, and was told that it was *the settler's clock;* a species of kingfisher that lives on snakes, against which it is protected by a ruff of feathers round its neck. Owing to its destroying so many poisonous snakes the bird is held sacred. From the extraordinary dialogue of sounds with which the male and female salute the rising sun, Governor King gave it the name *the laughing jackass*, by which it is commonly called.[1]

Returning from that most beautiful district at the ascent of Mount Keera, the forest was on fire on both sides; a not unusual occurrence after a high wind on a very hot day. I stopped to examine if it was safe to proceed and, looking at the horse's feet, found a kangaroo rat,[2] which is an exact copy of the larger kangaroo in miniature, cowering under the horse's hind legs for protection from the fire. Halfway up the pass was

a huge hollow gum capable of holding inside of it both ourselves and two horses; we entered and put it to the test and
found room to spare.

Sleeping that night at the inn at Apin, I was told next
morning when at breakfast that a settler wanted to see me.
'Tell him to come in.'

He stood at the door squeezing his hat. 'Good morning,
your Reverence, I am glad to see you.'

'When were you last at your duties?'

'Oh, it's not that, your Reverence.'

'Well, what is it then?'

'Saving your Reverence's presence, I got beastly drunk, and
I promised my wife on my knees that I wouldn't take a drop
for a year, saving and except through the hands of a priest,
and if your Reverence will only let me take a bottle of rum
through your holy hands to keep Christmas with ...'

'Well, I'll make a bargain with you. Father Therry will be
here about Christmas and if you promise to go to him to your
duties, and will drink the rum at home with your wife, and
not take more than two glasses a day, you shall have a bottle
of rum.'

I rang the bell. 'Mr. Carey,' I said to the landlord, 'give
that man a bottle of rum.'

It came, the landlord looking perplexed. 'There, give it him,
and let him pay for it.'

'It must come through your Reverence's hands, if you
please.'

'Well, come here. There now, go and keep your promise.'

He lingered at the door, held the bottle to the window,
and said, 'It looks very nice. Won't your Reverence have a
little drop?'

'Now come, go along.'

'Ah, if your Reverence would only let me have a little
drop now.'

'Come, go along. Give the bottle to your wife and don't
touch it again till Christmas Day. And I shall ask Father
Therry if you kept your promise.'

These incidents in one sick call to the Illawara give a fair
specimen of a priest's journeying in the Bush.

I had no sooner written the above paragraph than the letter
given below was handed to me. The son of the very landlord
of the Appin inn comes to my door in a state of distress,
though I had heard nothing of Appin, or of its landlord, or

of his family for thirty years until this moment. And I find
in his letter that Apin, as I had spelt it, after a little reflection
should be *Appin*, and I find it so on reference; and the landlord's name is not Carey, as I wrote it, but *Carbray*, as his son
writes it, and as I at once distinctly remembered it, on seeing it
written, although he was generally called Carey. I remember it
through a stupid joke I made at Appin. I asked a scholar as
a piece of nonsense if my landlord was the English translator
of Dante's *Divina Commedia*, and he said not quite, as his
name is not spelt Carey, but Carbray.

The letter which led to this correction is as follows:

*Reverend Father in God and respected sir, very humbly I beg
pardon for this liberty, but the poor wretch who writes this
letter is a stranger in this great country but without friend
or home. I am a native of Appin, New South Wales, and
seeing your name on Wednesday, I believe you, Father, are
the gentleman that my beloved mother always spoke in Holy
terms of and at that mother's house you have stopt when you
blest that country with your presence nearly forty years past. If
I am wrong, forgive me, but I am, sir, very poor. Still wishful
to be your dutiful child and servant*

Charles Carbray.

'Bring the man up,' I said.
'He is in a most wretched condition,' was the reply.
'Never mind, bring him up.'
The man appeared. 'How do you spell your father's name?'
I asked.
'Sir, the people always called him *Carey*, but his real name
was Carbray.'
'You are right.' I then asked a number of questions about
his father, mother, and the localities about his father's house,
which he answered accurately. 'Why,' I said, 'your father was
a worthy man, and your mother an excellent woman; they
were in good circumstances and well respected. When you
were a boy I must often have put my hand on your head,
and often talked to you; whatever has brought you to this
condition?'
'Drink, sir. I have just come off a South Sea Whaling
voyage, where I was a mate of the ship. I went where
I should not have gone, and had £40 stolen from me,
besides my best things, and a crucifix my mother gave
me, which I always carried about me, and which you gave

to her. And now I have nothing decent about me to get another place.'

'Well, I should like to give you a decent suit of clothes. But how can I be sure you won't pawn them?'

The strong man burst into a hearty fit of crying. When he had recovered himself he said: 'I did not expect this, sir. I thought you might give me a shilling or two, in memory of old times. But if you will send your young man with me to a clothes shop, I promise on my knees before God, they shall be sacred, and I will never part with them.'

What a singular correction! Such are the ups and downs; such the contacts of human life.

Breakfasting at Bathurst in a hotel after saying Mass, a young lady came to me in great distress of mind. She had but recently arrived alone in the Colony, and had brought me a letter of introduction. 'Whatever are you doing,' I asked in some surprise, 'in this remote place?' Through her tears she told me that she had come with the view of buying land; but that she was lodging with a Catholic farmer in the neighbourhood, who would not let her have her horse, and was trying to force her to marry his son.

'Do you really mean to say that you have ridden all the way from Sydney, and have crossed those lonely Blue Mountains without any guide or protector?' So it was, however. 'Go back to your lodgings,' I said, 'and tell the people that I shall be there in two hours' time.' On my reaching the door the whole family came out. They were so sorry, but the lady's horse was loose in the Bush, and could not be caught.

I said to my man: 'Put the lady's saddle on your horse, then go back to the hotel, get another horse, and follow us as soon as you can over the O'Connell Plains. As to you (turning to the settler), see you send that lady's horse and things to the Bathurst Hotel by tomorrow morning, or you will hear through the magistrate.' No sooner was she mounted than I gave her a canter of some eight or ten miles, when I deposited her with a worthy surgeon and his wife, who kindly undertook to see her off to Sydney by the next public conveyance, and to send a trusty man with her horse. I thus lost a day in rescuing a distressed damsel from toils woven by her own folly.

Going to the convict hospital at Bathurst to visit the sick on a Monday, I found the men busy erecting the black triangle in the middle of the square round which the hospital was built, and from which the sick in their beds, both men and women could see through the large windows.

I asked what they were going to do.

'To flog some men,' they replied.

'What!' I asked. 'You are not going to flog the invalids?'

'Oh no, your Reverence, but there are always men from the police court to be flogged on a Monday morning.'

'But why before the eyes of the sick?'

'It's more convenient for the surgeon to dress their backs afterwards.'

I said no more. But when I reached Parramatta I waited on the Governor and told him what I had witnessed, and he immediately sent an order to every hospital in the Colony to prevent the recurrence of such scenes in the midst of the sick men and, I may add, the sick women.

Whenever we got the loan of a court house up the country as a chapel I invariably found a Bible on the bench for administering oaths, on the back of which a paper was pasted the full length in the form of a cross; most commonly consisting of two crossed pieces of coarse brown paper. When anyone had to be sworn, the clerk asked: 'Are you Protestant or Catholic?' If Protestant, the book was opened and its pages kissed; if Catholic, the brown paper cross was presented to be kissed. I wrote a letter to the Governor, pointing out both the indecency and the illegality of this practice, as well as the prejudice which it caused. By a circular to the magistrates the abuse was put an end to.

But enough has been said to give an idea of the manifold claims upon a missioner's attention when travelling the Bush and visiting the settlements.

In Sydney we did all our outdoor work in gigs, both on account of the heat and to save time. Besides the usual flock, forming a fourth of the population, we had to look after the prisoners' barracks, a huge gaol in which the convicts were put on landing and to which they were sent from all parts of the Colony for punishment. We had to attend the felons' gaol where about forty executions took place in the year. We had to look after a large chain-gang upon an island in Sydney Cove. Also to be visited was the great convict hospital in Sydney, another at Parramatta, fifteen miles off, and another at Liverpool, twenty miles off. Again there was the Benevolent Asylum, a refuge for decayed people, who had come to poverty and were without friends to help them. This was no uncommon state of things amongst a convict and emigrant population. There were the funerals also, outside the town, at least every other day. Parramatta had to be served regularly from Sydney, and Liverpool from time to time. Father McEncroe and I had the brunt of this work. But he was subject to his infirmity, which deprived me of his services from time to time and gave me great uneasiness as well.

Another field of occupation was the examining and signing of papers of the large convict population. No one of that class could obtain their ticket of leave, enabling them to work for themselves on certain conditions, or their free pardon, or leave to marry, or the privilege of having their wives and children sent out at Government cost, or petitions of any other description attended to, unless the documents had been examined and signed by their clergy. Thus we had a good many civil matters to look after.

In my office of ecclesiastical Superior or head of a department, to use the official term. I had also a fair amount of occupation of another kind. I had relations and correspondence with the Colonial Secretary's Office, the Survey Office, the Architect's Office, the Audit Office, the Treasury, the Military Department and the Convict Department.

There were grants of land to be obtained for church, schools and presbytery in every new township; payments to be arranged and certified for priests and schoolmasters; aid to be sought for raising new buildings, and plans to be settled upon; arrangements to be arranged about duties amongst the military, and providing for the exercise of their religion; matters to be settled about attending convict establishments; favours to be gained for this or that person in the way of mercy through personal influence; arrangements to be made for special journeys in the Government service by land or by sea.

I always found the heads of department friendly and considerate, and the official dinners at Government House strengthened our good understanding. On those occasions His Excellency was always considerate enough to invite the Protestant Archdeacon and myself on different days, so that each of us in our turn had the place of honour assigned and said Grace. I remember on one occasion we were amused at finding that though there are only two soldiers amongst us, the whole of the fourteen guests were Generals. These were the Auditor-General, for instance, the Surveyor-General, the

Commissary-General, the Vicar-General, Solicitor-General, and so on. These entertainments were very pleasant. Sir Richard Bourke was a man of refinement, and good feeling was promoted at his board. Now and again I was invited to pass a day or two at his private residence at Parramatta, and there his guests were on the homely footing of private friendship.

Notes

1   The kookaburra, the *jackass* of the title of this volume. See Introduction for explanation.
2   i.e. A wallaby.

Chapter Sixteen

Sydney Reminiscences IV

What I was most solicitous for was to obtain more priests for New South Wales, and to get things put on a better footing in Van Dieman's Land. I wrote to Bishop Morris by one of the rare ships that sailed from Sydney to the Mauritius, and described the state of things both in that island and in New South Wales, and after a long time got an answer that His Lordship was about to send off a priest to Van Dieman's Land which would remedy the state of things there. But he never came. I had also written at the same time for two marriage cases which were beyond my delegated faculties. Instead of the dispensations, I was told in reply that they would be attended to in a subsequent letter, but I never heard again from the Mauritius.

The Bishop lived there, but he never visited or looked after the other portions of his extensive jurisdiction. I held my office without any support or co-operation from my Bishop. This led me into grave reflections. I saw that we wanted something more than clergy. We wanted a Bishop of our own. I observed that wherever these remote missions were left in the hands of a Vicar-General, Apostolic Prefect or Archpriest, he was but the first among equals. This not only made his administration unnecessarily difficult, but he did not possess the creative power which Our Lord left to the Church. He could not make priests, nor could he attract priests to his help as a Bishop had the power of doing. Being young myself, and looking youthful, I had to demean myself with a gravity and reserve to hold my position firm, and to put forth all the watchfulness and tact that the exigencies of that position demanded.

There were other Colonies founding at remote distances from the mainland of New Holland, where there was no priest. New Zealand was but a thousand miles distant, and though

Protestant missions had been established there for a considerable time, no priest had ever reached it. Norfolk Island was a penal settlement, quite as far off, but no priest had ever visited it. Moreton Bay (now Queensland) was another penal settlement far to the north of Sydney, which had only been once visited by Father Therry. A new Colony was also beginning to be formed in the extensive region which finally took the name of Victoria.

Loaded with this heavy responsibility, I wrote to Dr. Polding at Downside and described the state of things, pointing out the necessity of a Bishop. This set the English Benedictines on the stir, and they opened a communication with Rome for Dr. Polding's appointment.

Meanwhile, with the assistance of the Government, I began to build a chapel school in the most populous part of Sydney, a church and school at Parramatta, a church at Maitland, and another church was rising at Campbell Town. To each of these buildings the Government gave handsome contributions, besides giving good-sized pieces of land. But there were no clergy to live at those churches. They could only be visited from time to time.

A priest arrived unexpectedly from England. He had been burnt out of a ship in which he had sailed on the coast of South America, and left the vessel in a boat with a few others, quitting the ship when a great number of passengers and sailors left behind were being burnt to death in the flaming ship. They saw them dropping from the bowsprit and rigging into the water as they rowed away. After rowing two hundred miles on very small quantities of provisions and water, they reached the Brazilian coast, and he came in on a ship that touched at Rio de Janeiro. I did not find his papers very satisfactory, and he had come out under a fictitious name, and was not in good health besides. However, I got him a salary from the Government, and gave him some employment.

Unhappily, not long after this help arrived, after a painful investigation, I had to suspend one of the priests, not, however, the one just alluded to. This left me both maimed of help and distressed for, to add to the trial, in a colony everything is known everywhere, and I was compelled to communicate with Government, because I could no longer certify his being in duty for receipt of salary.

After that, for six months I had to officiate at Windsor, a distance of thirty-five miles, every Saturday evening, and there put up at a Protestant tavern. Next morning at six I said Mass and preached in a chapel that had been a barn, and attended the convict hospital. I then drove to Parramatta, a distance of twenty miles, there to put up at the Woolpack Inn, and say Mass in the military guard house, a long, dark room with a couple of wooden shutters for windows, built over the prison of a chain-gang. The soldiers turned out on the burning lawn, not a green lawn generally, but drab-coloured, as the grass was burnt up by the sun, and I and my flock turned in. The altar was erected, and the wooden shutter opened at the back of it, through which, whilst saying Mass, I could see all that passed in a busy tavern opposite. When I turned round to preach I got a Rembrandt view of the first row, whilst the rest of the congregation were buried in darkness. The convicts locked up beneath were often cursing and swearing. When two Catholic ladies were staying at the Governor's house at Parramatta, on a Sunday, and would go to Mass, Sir Richard Bourke told them they could not possibly go to such a place. But they persisted, so he sent his aide-de-camp to select two steady Catholic sergeants from the regiment to kneel behind them.

After this work was over, and the baptisms, marriages, etc, I breakfasted at the hotel, then visited the convicts' hospital, and the military hospital, a good distance from each other, and then drove the fifteen miles to Sydney to preach at the evening service. Next day, about eleven o'clock, a sort of prostration came upon me, a reaction from the Sunday's labour. I then lay on a sofa for a few hours with a light book, and that brought me round again.

On one of those occasions at Windsor, I had a sick call after night came on, which was a couple of miles beyond Hawesbury. When I and my man reached the river, there was no getting the ferry-boat across for a very long time. The convict ferry-men were sleeping in their hut on the other side of the river, and were unwilling to hear with all our shouting. It was a cold, sharp night in the open air, and we got back to the inn at a quarter to twelve. I was hungry, with fasting till one o'clock before me. Everyone else was in bed, so I searched all about the house till I found a piece of bread and a jar of pickled walnuts, of which I made a hasty supper before midnight, which I had to regret the next day.[1]

Father McEncroe generally attended the executions and prepared the condemned for death. They occurred quarterly, and two-thirds of the Protestant criminals sought the aid of the

Catholic priest. This, at last, made such an impression on the population that the Protestant Archdeacon printed and circulated a thousand copies of a pamphlet, intended to remove the feeling awakened. He said, amongst other things, that these poor creatures had very little religion and had expended their moral sense; and that the soothing ways of the catholic priests, and their less guarded system of Confession, acted as a fascination to these poor criminals in their last hours.

Soon after my first arrival I had replied to a pamphlet of the Archdeacon's, and to another written by one of his clergy, but I thought it best to leave this curious publication to answer itself and it certainly did no harm. I once went to see a fine-looking young man, a Protestant, lying under condemnation, and I said to him on entering his cell: 'Why have you sent for a priest? You are not a Catholic.'

To which he replied: 'I want to tell what's on my mind, and if I tell it to a parson he will tell it again.'

Two men, after their condemnation, were sent by sea to Newcastle, to be executed on the scene of their crimes. It was for beating an overseer to death in the midst of a chain-gang employed in making a breakwater. One of them, though not a Catholic, applied for a priest, and I went with them a distance of about seventy miles from Sydney. On arrival at the gaol in Newcastle I was told by the Governor of the gaol that the Protestant chaplain particularly desired to see me. I thought it singular because, though a stranger to me, he had recently written an attack on me in a Wesleyan magazine. On his entrance he was embarrassed. He said that he was quite unaccustomed to executions, and as he had to attend one of the two men, he would be much obliged to me if I would give him a few hints as to what he ought to do. With a view to the poor man's benefit I told him what I should do myself, and he left me with thanks.

The execution was to take place on a promontory, on a lofty scaffold, surrounded by a thousand convicts in chains and their military guard, and that as early as five o'clock, as the deputing sheriff and hangman had to go further up the river afterwards to hang some black natives. Before we started with our men to walk across half a mile of sand-hills to the place of execution, this clergyman wished to see me privately again. He was very nervous, and asked me what he should do as we walked along? What after the men were cast off? Would I walk first? I told him that as we went along

I should repeat a Litany, which the poor man, who was well instructed, would answer, and I should occasionally address words to him suited to his state.

'Very good, Sir, and what will you do on the scaffold?'

'The man,' I replied, 'is well taught to offer his life to God for his sins, which he will do with me in the words I have taught him. And when the executioner is quite ready for the drop, he will give me a sign, and I shall descend the ladder and pray for his soul.'

'Very good, Sir. Will you please to walk first with your man?'

'Certainly.'

As we approached the peninsula the wind from the sea was furious, and the sun arose upon an awful spectacle. A thousand faces marked with crime and dull from bondage were turned upon the lofty scaffold, their frieze[2] garments made up of alternate pieces of brown and yellow. In their rear stood the rigid troops, loaded with bayonets fixed. I knelt at the foot of one tall ladder, the Anglican at the foot of the other. The wind hurled my ladder from the scaffold, and had I not, with a sudden impulse, pulled my Anglican friend back it would have gone right across his neck. The ladders were tied up after that, and I mounted with my man. I always arranged with the hangman beforehand to give me a sign when he was ready to let down the drop. The man wanted to harangue the convicts. I would not let him, for I knew how much of vanity was displayed in these dying speeches and how they thus died with their comrades' applause in their minds instead of God. He obeyed, and attended to his prayers. But so fierce was the wind that I had to plant my foot back on the framework of the scaffold, and hold him by the back and shoulder, lest we should both be blown off whilst the hangman was preparing the rope. At last I got the sign, pressed his hand, and he was cast off. I had not a single sense at leisure to see what the other clergyman did. But as we walked away he turned to me with a melancholy face, and said: 'Sir, this is a very painful and humiliating duty, and had I known I would be subject to such, I would never have taken Orders.'

This nervous man, with his sense of ignominy attached to duty, was actually the cause on a previous occasion of three men dying without any clergyman to assist them. The men had been lodged in Newcastle gaol, and though Protestants, called for a priest. There was none there, but there was a Pole, a carpenter, the very man who set fire to the mine at Leipsic, which cut Napoleon's army in two, and lost him a division of his troops in the retreat.[3] This good man went to see them and lent them Catholic books, telling them to ask for a priest when they got to Sydney. But the Protestant clergyman, hearing this, went to them, took away the books, and wrote to his brethren in Sydney to take care that the priests did not get hold of them. They were sent to Patrick's Plains to be executed. When they got to Newcastle they expected the clergyman there to accompany them. He was not to be found, had in fact ridden off fifty miles to visit a friend. The men sailed up the river, were carted up the country for thirty miles in a burning sun, crying out for a clergyman, but there was none then in that part of the country. And they were executed, still crying out for a clergyman to the horror of the spectators. The Attorney-General, who was still resting awhile in the country, witnessed the whole scene and heard the whole account from the window of a hotel, and repeated it to me afterwards.

Riding on my first visit to the Hunter[4] with Mr. Walker, the chief supporter of the Catholic religion at Maitland, and making our way through the rich forest on the alluvial flats near the river, I heard a whistle, and the crack of a whip, and then its reverberation. 'What is that road near us?' I asked.

'There is no road hereabout,' he replied, 'it is all Bush.'

'There again,' I said, 'I hear the drayman's whistle and his whip. There must be a road.'

'No,' he said, 'that is the Coachman. It is not a man but a bird.'

I took it on faith, and saw these birds afterwards, but I was completely deceived for a time. Had I heard the Bellbird which frequents the banks of that river at the same time, I might have mistaken it for the bells round the oxen's neck that drew the waggon.

Notes

1   Until the revisions made by Pius XII permitting evening Masses Catholics were required to fast from midnight before receiving Holy Communion.
2   A kind of coarse, woollen cloth, originally from Friesland.
3   1813.
4   i.e. The Hunter River.

Chapter Seventeen

Sydney Reminiscences V

After his arrival in the colony, Sir Roger Therry opened a correspondence with Mr. Blount, then member for Steyning, on the religious wants of that distant penal settlement. Mr. Blount, in consequence, made an energetic appeal to Parliament upon the injustice and cruelty of sending away the criminals of the country to the other extremity of the world without providing them with adequate provision for their religious instruction or requirements. He dwelt with strong emphasis on the religious destitution of the Catholics.

Meanwhile, Sir Richard Bourke was devising a systematic plan for meeting those wants, which ultimately took shape in his celebrated dispatch to Lord Stanley, at that time Secretary of State for the Colonies, now Lord Derby, of date, September 30th, 1833. About the same time I addressed a letter through the Governor to His Lordship, asking for four additional Catholic chaplains. His Excellency begins his despatch by stating that he has received the order of the King in Council for dissolving the Protestant Church and School Corporation; but without any information of the views of His Majesty's Government as to the future maintenance and regulation of churches and schools within the Colony.

His Excellency then points out that there are large bodies of Roman Catholics and Scotch Presbyterians, and that probably one-fifth of the whole population of the Colony were Catholics. 'The charge on the public treasury next year would be: for the Church of England, £11,542; for the Scotch Presbyterians, £600; and for the Catholic chaplains and chapels, £1,500. The Catholics possess one large and handsome church at Sydney, not yet completed, and to aid its completion the Government had given donations at different times amounting in all to £1,200. The sum of £400, included in the £1,500, had been appropriated in aid of private subscriptions for erecting

Catholic chapels at Campbell Town and Maitland. A chapel was begun in Campbell Town and in Parramatta some years ago; but neither have been completed for want of funds. Such an unequal support cannot be acceptable to the colonists, who provide the funds from which the distribution is made.'

Sir Richard then proposed the following arrangements, to be applied equally to the Church of England, the Catholics, and the Scotch Presbyterians. That whenever a congregation applies for the erection of a church and clergyman's residence, on their subscribing not less than £300 and up to £1,000, the Government shall give an equal subscription, the building to be invested in trustees. That where a hundred adults, including convict servants living within a reasonable distance, shall subscribe a declaration of their wish to attend that church or chapel, £100 a year shall be paid out of the Treasury to the clergyman of that church. That when two hundred adults so subscribe, £150 a year shall be paid; and that when 500 adults so subscribe, £200 a year shall be paid; beyond which no higher stipend shall be paid by the Government. Thus the three great denominations of England, Ireland, and Scotland were to be treated alike and on the same footing. Before the warrant was issued for payment by the Treasury, a certificate was required from the religious authority at the head of each denomination that the clergymen were in performance of their duty. In the same despatch his Excellency was pleased to say a kind word of the Catholic Vicar-General, preliminary to stating that 'he thought £200 a year too low for the office, and that it might be advantageously be raised to £400, to enable him to visit frequently the chapels in the interior.'

Before this despatch was sent the Governor kindly gave me an opportunity, through Sir Roger Therry, of seeing it. I could only express my gratitude for a scheme so well calculated to meet all requirements, whilst it left ecclesiastical authority in such perfect freedom. Sir Richard had privately expressed his opinion that the result of this scheme would be to provide the Colony with all the clergy required, after which the Government, supported by popular opinion, would cease to give its support to any religious denomination, and thus the several communions would support their own churches. To use his own phrase, 'they would roll off State support like saturated leeches.' And so it has come about.

The scheme received the complete approval of the English Government, and was passed as an Act of Legislative Council on July 29th, 1836. About the same time a scheme of denominational education was arranged, in which the schools were supported by the Government, partly by a fixed annual sum, partly regulated by the numbers in attendance.

In May, 1834, my old Novice-master, Father Polding, was appointed first Bishop of Sydney by Gregory XVI. He undertook to provide the other three priests applied for, and the four received the usual passage and outfit provided by Government. Meanwhile Lord Stanley had replied to my letter of application for additional priests (Lord Stanley had sent a copy of Sir Richard Bourke's despatch to Mr. Blount, and stated that he should consult Bishop Bramston as to the priests to be sent out), not only approving my application, but adding that, should our wants increase, he would be happy to attend to any further recommendation supported by the Governor of the Colony. Not long after, Sir Richard Bourke received a letter from Lord Stanley, announcing the appointment of the four priests, one of whom, Dr. Polding, was invested with the dignity of Bishop.

He then expressed his regret at my being superseded, and proposed that I should go to Hobart Town with the same stipend. When Sir Richard read the letter to me, I laughed, and said: 'Your Excellency will understand our ways better than Lord Stanley. I should be of material use to the Bishop in the beginning. Let him take the stipend of £400 a year which you recommend for the Vicar-general, and let me take the ordinary stipend of a priest.'

'Well,' he said, 'there is no other man in the Colony who would have made such an offer.'

So I remained in my old position, and the Bishop received £400 a year. My next point was to secure a proper residence for the Bishop before his arrival, a residence that would suitably represent his dignity as the head of the Catholics of Australia. I succeeded in renting a large and stately house, built for the first Protestant Archdeacon, and which at that time alone occupied the Vale of Woolloomooloo, with an extensive domain attached to it. It joined the Sydney Park, in which stood his Cathedral.

Meanwhile, however, the work went on. I received a letter from Father Connolly asking for a priest to visit him in Hobart Town. After weighing the matter I thought I had better go myself. The voyage was eight hundred miles. I took, as was my wont, the first vessel that offered, and it proved to be a small schooner, very heavily laden. I found three women and seven children cooped in the small cabin, and no one to talk to except a young artist. We encountered a very heavy gale with adverse winds off Bass's Strait and laboured heavily, laid to under a storm. The bulwarks were stove in, the anchor was lifted off the bows, and several casks of brandy carried off the deck, whilst we were driven off from our bearings at the rate of some hundred of miles in the twenty-four hours. The poor women and children were in a sad state, with scarcely room in which to move. At last, after some days in this critical state, the wind moderated and veered round, and we ran into port.

I found things much as I had left them, and after a fortnight returned to Sydney.

My return voyage was in a large Scotch ship from India manned by Lascars. We reached Sydney Heads in the night, and could get no pilot off, though we fired gun after gun. The captain had never been there before. However, I was able to point out where the danger lay, and we ran through the Heads and came to anchor.

Chapter Eighteen

Description of Norfolk Island[1]

Norfolk Island is about a thousand miles from Sydney. It is small, only about twenty-one miles in circumference; of volcanic origin, and one of the most beautiful spots in the universe. Rising abruptly on all sides but one from the sea, clustering columns of basalt spring out of the water, securing at intervals its endurance with the strong architecture of God.

That one side presents a low, sandy level on which is placed that penal settlement which is the horror of men. It is approachable only by boats through a narrow bar in the reef of coral, which, visible here, invisibly circles the island. Except the military guard, and the various officers and servants of Government, none but the prisoners are permitted to reside on the island; nor, unless in case of great emergency, can any ships but those of Government showing the secret signals, be permitted to approach. The land consists of a series of hills and valleys, curiously interfolded, the green ridges arising above one another, until they reach the shaggy sides and crowning summit of Mount Pitt, at the height of 3,000 feet above the level of the sea.

The establishment consists of a spacious quadrangle of buildings for the prisoners, the military barracks, and a series of offices in two ranges. A little further beyond, on a green mound of Nature's beautiful making, arises the mansion of the Commandant, with its barred windows, defensive cannon, and pacing sentry. Straying some distance along a footpath, we come upon the cemetery closed in on three sides by close, thick, melancholy groves of the tear-dropping manchineel,[2] whilst the fourth is open to the restless sea. The graves are numerous and recent − most of the tenants having reached by an untimely end the abode to which they now contribute their hapless remains and hapless story. I have myself witnessed fifteen descents into those houses of mortality, and in every one lies a hand of blood. Their lives were brief, and as agitated and restless as the waves which now break at their feet, and whose dying sound is their only requiem.

Passing on by a ledge cut in the cliff which hangs over the resounding shore, we suddenly turn into an amphitheatre of hills, which rise all round until they close in a circle of the blue heavens above – their sides being thickly clothed with curious wild shrubs, wild flowers and wild grapery. Passing the hasty brook and long and slowly ascending, we again reach the open varied ground. Here a tree-crested mound, there a plantation of pines; and yonder below a ravine descending into the very bowels of the earth, and covered with an intricacy of dark foliage interluminated with chequers of sunlight, until it opens a receding vista to the blue sea.

And now the path closes, so that the sun is almost shut out; whilst giant creepers shoot, twist and contort themselves upon your path, beautiful pigeons, lories, parrots, parroquets, and other birds, rich and varied in plumage, spring up at your approach.

We now reach a valley of exquisite beauty in the middle of which, where the winding, gurgling stream is jagged in its course, spring up – the type of loveliness – a cluster of some eight fern trees, the finest of their kind, which with different inclinations rise up to the height of fifteen or twenty feet, a clear, black, mossy stem from the crown of which is shot out on every side one long, arching fern leaf, the whole suggesting the idea of a clump of Chinese umbrellas.

Ascending again through the dark forest, we find rising on every side, amongst other strange forest trees, the gigantic pine of Norfolk Island, which ascending a clean stem of vast circumference to some twelve feet shoots out a coronal of dark boughs each in shape like the feathers of an ostrich, indefinably prolonged until rising, with clear intervals, horizontal stage above stage, the great pyramid cuts with its point the clear ether at the height of two hundred feet. Through these we at length reach the crown of Mount Pitt, whence the *tout ensemble* in so small a space is indescribable, of rock, forest, valley, cornfield, islets, seabirds, land birds, sunshine and sea. Descending we take a new path to find new varieties.

Emerging after a while from the deep gloom of the forest, glades and openings lie on each side, where, among many plants and trees, the guava and lemon prevail. The fern tree springs gracefully out, and is outstripped by the beautiful palmetto raising 'its light shaft of oriental mould' from above the verdant level, and at the height of twenty-five feet spreading abroad in the clear air a cluster of bright green fans. In other places the parasite creepers and climbers rise up in columns, shoot over arch after arch, and again descend in every variety of Gothic fantasy. Now they form a long, high wall, which is dense and impenetrable, and next comes tumbling down a cascade of green leaves, frothed over with the white convolvulus.

Our way at last becomes an interminable closed-in vista of lemon trees, forming overhead a varied arcade of green, gold and sunlight. The orange trees once crowded the island as thickly, but were cut down by the wanton tyranny of a former Commandant, as being too ready and too great a luxury for the convict. Stray over the farms, the yellow hulm[3] bends with the fat of corn. Enter the gardens, especially the delicious retreat, 'Orange Vale', there by the broad-breasted English oak grows the delicate cinnamon tree – the tea, the coffee, the sugar plant, the nutritious arrowroot, the banana with its long, weeping streamers and creamy fruit, the fig, all tropical fruits in perfection, and English vegetables in gigantic growth. The air is most pure, the sky most brilliant. In the morning the whole is drenched with dew. As the sun comes out of its bed of amber, and shoots over a bar of crimson rays, it is one embroidery of the pearl, the ruby and the emerald. As the same sun at eventide slants his yellow rays between the pines and the mountain, they show like the bronzed spires of some vast cathedral flooded in golden light.

Notes

1   In both manuscripts Bishop Ullathorne refers to his description of Norfolk Island given in his pamphlet *The Catholic Mission in Australasia* London 1838. Mss.2. quotes it in full, and it is inserted here as a separate chapter.

2   A lofty tree of the West Indies, *Hippomane Mancinella*, (Horse apple) so called from its effect on horses which eat of it. The wood is valuable for cabinet work, being beautifully veined in brown and white, and capable of receiving a high polish.

3   I can find no reference to this word in any dictionary at my disposal. Perhaps it was a misprint in the original for holm as in Holm-Oak or Holly.

Chapter Nineteen

Visit to Norfolk Island

In the year 1834 a conspiracy was formed among the convicts in the penal settlement of Norfolk Island, to overmaster the troops and take possession of the island. A larger number than usual pretended sickness, and were placed in hospital for examination. Those employed at the farm armed themselves with instruments of husbandry, and the gang proceeding to their work were to turn upon the guard.

The guard was assailed by the working gang, those who had feigned sickness broke their chains and rushed to join their comrades, but the men from the farm arrived too late. In the skirmish which ensued one or two men were shot and a dozen were dangerously wounded, of whom six or seven died. A great number of men were implicated in the conspiracy. A Commission was sent from Sydney to try them, and thirty-one men were condemned to death.

After the return of the Commission the Governor sent for me, told me that a new Commission was about to proceed to Norfolk Island, that there were several men to be executed from the last Commission for the bringing of them to Sydney for trial was a cause for their murdering each other for the chance of being brought out of the penal settlement, that he had engaged an Anglican clergyman to go for the occasion, that I should oblige him if I also should consent to go, and that we should receive hospitality at the mansion of the Commandant.

As the Government brig which conveyed us was limited in its accommodation, the captain, a Catholic, kindly gave me his cabin.[1] Our voyage lasted a fortnight, during which time I had several conversations with my Anglican companion. He was of Cambridge University, was an amiable man, with a limited experience of human nature, and he held some peculiar doctrines. For example, he maintained that the efficacy of Baptism depended on the prayer of the parents and sponsors. In a special case, he told me he had sent away the applicants without giving Baptism, because he did not think them in a becoming state to pray for the child. I asked him if he had taken care to have that child baptised afterwards; he replied that he did not think it necessary.

I cannot but think that one of our conversations had a material influence on his conduct on the island. My remarks in substance were to this effect: 'I cannot understand how you gentlemen profess to be healers of souls, when you know nothing about your patients. You seem to me like a medical man who goes into the wards of a hospital, takes a look round, directs that all shall be clean and well-aired, and then prescribes one and the same medicine to all the patients. Now, we examine the condition of our patients one by one, and give the remedy required by each.' My remarks on the Confessional and on its influence as a source of moral discipline seemed to have struck him and I think the result of this conversation will be seen later on.

All who have seen Norfolk Island agree in saying that it is the most beautiful place in creation, but it is very difficult of access. There is no harbour, and the only approach to the settlement is by boats over a bar in the coral reef that girdles the island, and which can only be crossed in calm weather. If the weather is unfavourable for landing at the settlement the vessel must proceed to the opposite side of the island, and there put off a boat, which lands the passengers on a ridge of rock that is slippery with wet seaweed. We had to adopt this last course on the present occasion.

Reflecting in my own mind that this was the first time a clergyman had ever visited the island, I resolved to be the first to land, for which I had grave reasons, which will appear directly. We were told to be ready to jump one by one, as the boat approached the rocks, as the oars would be at once reversed to prevent the boat being staved by the rock. I got into the stern sheets and sprang the first, when back went the boat. Major Anderson, the Governor, was there with his tall figure, at the head of a company of soldiers, drawn up in honour of the Commission. Before anyone else landed, I walked straight up to the Commandant and, after paying my respects, asked leave to go at once to the prison where the condemned men were confined. I requested to be furnished with a

list of those who were to be reprieved and of those who were to
be executed. These were kindly furnished me, as they had just
reached his hand from the vessel. I then asked how many days
would be allowed for preparation of the poor men who were
to die; and after kindly asking me my thoughts on the subject,
five days were allowed.[2] A soldier was then appointed to guide
me to the prison. We had to cross the island, which was about
seven miles long by four in breadth. The rest of the passengers,
when landed, proceeded to Government House.

And now I have to record the most heartrending scene that
I ever witnessed. The prison was in the form of a square, on
one side of which stood a row of low cells, covered with a
roof of shingles. The turnkey unlocked the first door and said:
'Stand aside, Sir.' Then came fourth a yellow exhalation, the
produce of the bodies of the men confined therein. The exhalation cleared off, and I entered and found five men chained
to a traversing-bar, and, as the hot sun had been beating on
the shingle roofs all day, most of them had thrown off their
clothes for the sake of being cooler. I spoke to them from my
heart, and after preparing them and obtaining their names I
announced to them who were reprieved from death, and which
of them were to die after five days had passed. I thus went
from cell to cell until I had seen them all.

It is a literal fact that each man who heard his reprieve
wept bitterly, and that each man who heard of his condemnation to death went down on his knees, with dry eyes, and
thanked God.

Among the thirteen who were condemned to execution three
only were Catholics, but four of the others put themselves
under my care, thus leaving four for my friend the Reverend Mr. Short.[3] I arranged to begin my duties with them at
six o'clock the next morning, and got an intelligent Catholic
overseer appointed to read at certain times under my direction
for those who could not read, whilst I was engaged with the
others.

Night had now fallen and I proceeded to Government
House, a handsome structure built on an elevation overlooking
the settlement and flanked at some distance by the military
barracks. Cannon were planted before it, the windows were
thoroughly barred, and the interior so arranged that in the
case of insurrection, the inmates might fight their way from
room to room without the danger of being taken in flank or
in rear by inopportune doors.

At Government House I found a brilliant assembly, in strange contrast to the human miseries in which my soul had just been steeped. It may seem strange to the inexperienced that so many men should prefer death to life in that dreadful penal settlement. Let me, then, say that all the criminals who were executed in New South Wales were imbued with a like feeling. I have heard it from several in their last moments, and Father McEncroe, in a letter to me, which I quoted to Sir William Molesworth's Committee on Transportation, affirmed that he had attended seventy-four executions in the course of four years, and that the greater number of criminals had, on their way to the scaffold, thanked God that they were not going to Norfolk Island.

There were two thousand convicts on the island, all of them men, all retransported for new crimes, after having been first transported to New South Wales. Many of them had, at one time or another, received sentence of death. They were a desperate body of men, made more desperate by their isolation from the outer world, by being deprived of access to all stimulants, by the absence of hope, by the habitual prospect of the encircling sea that isolated them from other lands by the distance of a thousand miles, and by the absence of all religious or other instruction or consolation.

Besides the criminals, only the military force and officials with their wives were permitted on the island. No ships, except those despatched by Government, and exhibiting the secret signals, were allowed to come near the land. Everything was on the alert, as in a state of siege. I had an opportunity of witnessing this. I was walking with the Commandant in a wood, he was conversing with secret spies he had among the convicts, when suddenly a shot was heard from a distance. Off went the shots of the sentries in all directions. The Commandant ran off to his post, and I after him. The troops were moving in quick time to their stations, and then came the inquiry. To our relief, it turned out that a young officer, just arrived by our vessel and ignorant of the rules, had been amusing himself by firing at a bird. But what an ear-wigging the young officer got! The rule was that no shot be fired on the island except to give alarm. A ludicrous scene occurred in the Court when the shot was fired. The Commissioner was sitting with a military jury, but the moment the gun was heard, the officers and soldiers rushed out to their posts, leaving the judge and the two lawyers alone with the prisoners on trial.

So sharply were all on the alert, for there had been three attempts by the convicts at different times to take the island, that I never ventured to move after nightfall without having a soldier with me to answer the challenges. A little incident that I witnessed made the sentries all the sharper. I was walking in the evening with the Commandant, when a sentry at some distance from us presented arms instead of giving the challenge. The old soldier, who had been a warrior from his seventeenth year, and had been in fifty battles[4], from Alexandria to Waterloo, was a martinet, and was up to the sentry in a moment.

'Why did you not challenge?'

'I knew you to be the Commandant and presented arms.' (He was much the tallest man in the island and his figure could not be mistaken.)

'You deserve a court-martial. Anyone might have put on my clothes. You ought to have challenged, and if I did not come up at the second call and give the password, it was your duty to fire at me.'

I spent the first week in preparing the men for death, and inquiring into the condition of the convicts generally. This took me daily from six in the morning till six at night. Then came the executions. The Commandant had received orders that all the convicts, to the number of two thousand, should witness them. As he had only three companies of infantry, some contrivance was required to prevent a rush of the convicts on the troops, as well as to conceal their number. Several small, but strong, stockades were erected and lined with soldiers, between the scaffold and the standing ground of the convicts, whilst the rest of the force was kept in reserve close by, but out of sight. The executions took place half one day and half the next. One thousand convicts divided into two bodies were brought on the ground the first day, and the other thousand on the second day. Thus all passed off in tranquillity. I had six of my men put together in one cell and five in another, one of which parties was executed each day, and executed in one group, whilst the Protestants were executed in another. My men asked as a special favour, the night before, to be allowed some tobacco, as with that they could watch and pray all night. This indulgence was granted.

When the irons were struck off and the death warrant read, they knelt down to receive it as the Will of God, and next, by a spontaneous act, they humbly kissed the feet of him who brought them peace. After the executioner had pinioned their arms they thanked the gaolers for all their kindness, and ascended the ladders with light steps, being almost excitedly cheerful. I had a method of preparing men for their last moments, by associating all that I wished them to think and feel with the prayer, 'Into Thy hands I commend my spirit; Lord Jesus, receive my soul.' I advised them when on the scaffold to think of nothing else and to say nothing else. The Catholics had a practice of sewing large black crosses on their white caps and shirts. These men had done so. As soon as they were on the scaffold, to my surprise, they all repeated the prayer I had taught them, aloud in a kind of chorus together, until the ropes stopped their voices forever. This made a great impression on all present, and was much talked of afterwards.

As I returned from this awful scene, wending my way between the masses of convicts and the military, all in dead silence, I barely caught a glance of their suspended bodies. I could not bring myself to look at them. Poor fellows! They had given me their whole hearts, and were fervently penitent. They had known little of good or of their souls before that time. Yet all of them had either fathers or mothers, sisters or brothers, to whom they had last words and affections to send, which had been dictated to me the day before.

The second day was but a repetition of the first. The Protestant convicts were executed after the Catholics. The Anglican clergyman had three to attend to each day. Then came the funerals, the Catholics at a separate time from the Protestants. A selected number of convicts followed each coffin to the most beautiful cemetery that the eye of man could possibly contemplate. Churchyard Gully is at some distance from the settlement, in a ravine that opens upon the sea, being circled on the land side with dark thickets of machineel, backed by the bright-leaved forest trees, among which lemon and guava trees were intermingled. Beyond there the ravine ascended and was clasped in by the swelling hills covered with wild vines and grapes. Above all this was a crown of beautiful trees, beyond which arose Mount Pitt to a height of 3,000 feet, covered with majestic pines of a kind peculiar to Norfolk Island.[5]

Arrived at the graves I mounted a little eminence, with the coffins before me and the convicts around me; and being extraordinarily moved, I poured out the most awful, mixed with the most tender, conjurations to these unfortunate men, to think of their immortal souls, and the God above them, Who waited their repentance. Then followed the funeral rites. So healthful was the climate, that all who lay in the cemetery had been executed, except one child, the son of a Highland officer, over whose tomb was the touching inscription: 'Far from the land of his fathers.'

After the return of the procession it was found that the men who composed it were sore and annoyed. The executioner had followed the coffins as though chief mourner, at which they were indignant. Yet the man did it in simplicity, and actually had a friend among the dead, yet to them his presence was a contamination. He was a man whom Sir Walter Scott would have given anything to have made a sketch of. A broad-chested, sturdy-limbed figure, broad-faced and bull-necked, who had won his freedom by taking two bush-rangers single handed at Port Maquarrie. But in the struggle he had received a cut from a hanger,[6] across the mouth, that opened it to the ears, and left a scar over his face that was alternately red and blue. Yet he had good-natured eyes. Whilst pinioning the arms of one of the men, he suddenly recognised him and exclaimed: 'Why, Jack, is that you?'

'Why, Bill,' was the answer, 'is that you?'

Then he shook his old friend by the hand and said: 'Well, my dear fellow, it can't be helped.'

Notes

1   This is from the later manuscript. The earlier reads: '... as the Government brig which took the party was pinched for room, the Protestant clergyman and myself had to back into one two-bed cabin.'

2   The earlier version gives a week.

3   This is not good arithmetic and there is confusion in both texts but as the Reverend Mr. Short is said to have had the pastoral care of four of the condemned men on each occasion he is refered to, it can probably be assumed that Father Ullathorne ministered to the other nine. Moreover, there were probably more men condemned to death by the Commission which travelled on the brig with Father Ullathorne.

4   The earlier manuscript has 'thirty pitched battles' though one assumes that after certain number of battles a soldier loses count.

5   The Norfolk Island pine, *Araucaria beterophylla* is a smaller member of the Chile Pine, *Araucaria imbricata*, family which is more commonly known as the Monkey Puzzle, so called because its branches are said to be so tangled that they baffle monkeys wanting to climb them.

6   A short, broad sword, incurved towards the point.

Chapter Twenty

Visit to Norfolk Island Continued

After the executions I devoted the rest of the time to the convicts, instructing all who came together for the purpose, and
got a man to read to them, whilst I heard about a hundred
confessions. Many of them had not seen a priest for some
twenty years, others since they had left their native country. I
had also duties at the military barracks, where I said a second
Mass on the Sundays. As Major Anderson was much engaged
with the dispatches for the returning ship, Mrs. Anderson, a
most kind and accomplished lady, on my return from my long
labours, seeing me worn and exhausted, used to have horses
and a groom in readiness, and rode with me herself through
the beautiful island before dinner. She saw that my burden
was heavy, and wished to give me a diversion. I shall never
forget the extreme kindness of these excellent people. They
saw their other guests in the course of the days, but I could
only see them in the evening.

During these evening rides we had a good deal of pleasant
conversation, but one day the lady suddenly drew bridle and
said: 'Do you think there is much affectation about me?'

'That is a strange question?' I said. 'Why do you ask it?'

'Do you think, at all events, that I am more affected than
the Protestant clergyman?'

'You perplex me yet more. I have not seen affectation in
either of you.'

'Well, I will explain myself,' said my companion. 'Mr.
Short said at the service that he could not admit anyone to
the Sacrament at Christmas unless they first had a private conversation with him. The officers smiled when they heard it, but
as I have to give a good example here I paid him a private
visit, when he charged me with affectation, and I found it
was because I paid proper attentions to my husband's guests

which my place required. But I turned to him and said: "Mr Short, there is some mistake. I am not Mrs. Short."'

I am afraid I was the innocent cause of this misadventure. My reverend friend had taken such a fancy to my ideas about the Confessional that he had got the men he attended at the gallows to tell their histories to him, and he repeated the poor men's stories of their criminal lives at the Commandant's tables; witness my own ears. This surprised people very much and made my friend, the Attorney-General, who was so good a Catholic, very indignant. When, therefore he told these very people, when present at the barrack service, that he could not give the Sacrament without some previous conversation the rest shrugged their shoulders, but our hostess found to her cost what that conversation meant.

The hospitable dinners and social converse every night, however pleasant in itself, completed my exhaustion, and on Christmas night I awoke in bed very sick and with my spine like an icicle. I rallied next day, but only when I got on board ship did I find all the effect of what I had gone through. For a week I was reduced to a sort of coma, and almost complete suspension of my intellectual powers. I passed into a sort of dull but very peaceful existence with but faint gleams of mind and feeling. I could not read. I saw the letters of a book without imbibing their sense. I was like a person dead yet conscious of a suspended life. I lay a good deal on my bed, but when I went on deck or to meals I seemed like one in a dream. It was *the gentle life*. It felt so calm, even though the privation of inward power inspired the sense of want. Gradually I recovered from this stupor, and by the time we reached Sydney I began to be as usual.

Before the executions the Commandant asked me privately if I had any reason to believe that there was a conspiracy to escape from the prison. I replied: 'My dear Major, of what I know of those men, I know less than of that of which I know nothing.' He apologised with the remark that he had for the moment forgotten the rigid secrecy of the Confessional. But after all was over I told him I had been authorized by the departed criminals to say that there had been a conspiracy to escape. That their chains were filed and ready for breaking, and that the plan was to mount on each other's backs to get at the shingle roof, and so to help each other out, take to the dense bush and contrive to make some kind of boat in which to put to sea. More than one party had, on former occasions, gone off to sea in this way and had never been heard of. But as soon as they heard there was a priest arrived they told me they gave up the scheme and thought it better to die like Christians. 'And now,' I said, 'if you will go and examine the fetters you will find them sawn and filled with rust and bread crumbs.' On going to examine the turnkeys were confident that the fetters were sound, and tinkled them with their keys. But the Commandant said, 'I am sure of my information,' and on closer examination it was found that they were all cut.

My last act before leaving the island is worth recording, as an example that the most desperate men ought not to be despaired of. The Major at breakfast told me of a case that gave him a great deal of solicitude. Among the convicts was one who was always in a round of crime or punishment. He was one of those who had been reprieved, and yet was already again under punishment. I asked if he were a Catholic. He thought so.

'But how can I see him; we are just about to sail?'

'If you will see that man,' he said, 'I will send a message on board that they are not to sail until I have been on board and I will send you a notice at the last moment.'

I found the man chained in a cell with three others, and I asked him to come out a while, as I wanted to speak with him. He was a tall, strong-built man, and I saw he was one of those proud spirits that would not seem to cave in before his comrades. I told him the turnkey would take off his fetters if he would only come out.

He replied, 'Sir, you are a kind gentleman, and have been good to them that suffered, but I'd rather not.'

I turned to the others and said, 'Now, men isn't he a big fool? You would give anything to get out of this hot place but because I am a priest, he thinks you will take him for a softy, and chaff him, if he talks to me. I have got something to tell him, and then he can do as he likes. He knows I can't eat him. What do you say?'

'Why, sir, you are such a kind gentleman, he ought to go out when you ask him.'

'And you won't jeer him as a softy because he talks with me?'

'Oh, no, Sir.'

'Well, take off his irons.'

I wanted to get him into a private room, but he would not go out of eyeshot of the other men, and nothing could induce him. I did not like to shut the door on them, lest it might be taken for a trick.

I said, 'Let's go to the turnkey's room.' No, he would not. So we walked up and down the yard, with a sentry on each side a short distance off. I found he was a Catholic, made an earnest appeal to his soul; but he held himself still, and I seemed to make no way.

A sailor came up. 'Anchor short hove, Sir. Topsails sheeted home. Governor and his lady waiting by the boat.'

I felt bitter. It was the first time I had found a soul inaccessible. I threw up my arms, looked him full in the face and poured out the most terrible denunciations upon him for neglecting the one opportunity of saving his soul, for I never expected that he would have a chance of seeing a priest there again.

I then left him. Bidding a warm farewell to our kind hosts, and loaded by them with every luxury for the voyage that the island produced, we set sail under a salute of guns. But though I did not know it till fifteen months afterwards, his heart was changed. As soon as I left he asked to be put in a cell by himself, got a turnkey, who was a Catholic, to lend him books, and became a new man. In going on board I said to the Commandant: 'You must not mistake that man. There is nothing mean about him. He would not tell a lie. But if he says he will thrash an overseer, he will do it. And if the man resists, he will kill him.'

The hint was taken. After a time one chain was taken off him, then the other. And on my return, after fifteen months, I met him smiling as he worked among the flowers in the Government garden. He proved most useful among his fellow convicts, and was my reader to the convicts as I heard their confessions. He was precisely one of those characters who, with a different training, would have been a hero. Proud and high-spirited, he would do any bold and daring thing and stick to it when once he had said it, egged on more by his cunning and cowardly companions.

He ultimately got his liberty and became a respectable man.[1]

Soon after my return to Sydney I placed the state of the convicts at Norfolk Island before Sir Richard Bourke, and strongly represented the great evil of their being locked up at night in the dark, without any division between the men and any watchman to control their conduct. I earnestly pointed out the necessity of partitions, lights, and watchmen under proper superintendence. But that was not effected until long afterwards, when the representations of Bishop Willson prevailed. But I put my attempt on record in my evidence before Sir William Molesworth's Committee in 1838.

Notes

1   Ullathorne also notes, in the first manuscript, that: 'the continuance of this man's history will be found in *The Catholic Mission to Australasia.*'

Mother Drane, in her rather edifying style, also adds a note here: 'A singular circumstance in connection with this story deserves recording. As Bishop Ullathorne was in the act of penning the above lines a letter reached him written by the very person referred to therein, and relating his subsequent history. After alluding to the last occasion on which they had met, the writer went on to say that after recovering his liberty he had settled in another colony, where he had gradually risen to a position of some eminence, and was bringing up his family in various professions. He had remained faithful in the practice of religion, and acknowledged all the happiness of his changed life as due to the impressions he had received from Dr. Ullathorne.

Chapter Twenty One

Arrival of the Bishop

Soon after returning to Sydney an effort was made to upset the denominational system of education for the people and to establish in its place a general system with the Bible as a prominent class-book. A public meeting was called to be presided over by a philanthropic Quaker, who was on a visit to the colonies, partly for benevolent, partly for botanical purposes. The Governor did not approve of the scheme and hinted in a note to Mr. Therry, commissioner of the Court of Requests, that he would be glad if he and I went and opposed it, which we were already prepared to do.

The meeting was in the great room of the Pultney Hotel. Some ladies went with us to see what they called 'the fun'. We found the Chief Justice, Sir Francis Forbes, also waiting to set his countenance against the scheme. As soon as we appeared and took up a front position there was a considerable stir and whispering on the platform, chiefly occupied by Evangelicals and dissenting ministers, and the chairman stated that no one was to speak more than quarter of an hour. Up I rose on that point. Up rose Mr Therry after me. We fatigued their patience upon their violation of the common law of public meetings, and then Mr. Therry proposed a resolution to the effect that their plan was not adapted to the wants and wishes of the people. Their own secretary, a dissenting minister, arose and seconded it, and it passed. We then rose and retired to a private room, where the whole platform fell upon the poor minister as an enemy of the Bible, he, poor man, pleading that it was the only way to get the enemy away. This stroke of policy put an end to the agitation in its infancy. I published an elaborate pamphlet in consequence entitled, *The Use and Abuse of the Sacred Scriptures*, which was republished in England by Keating.

On September 13th, 1835, the Right Rev. Fr. Bede Polding, Bishop of Hieroccæsarea,[1] Vicar-Apostolic of New Holland and Van Dieman's Land, arrived in Sydney, accompanied by three priests and four ecclesiastical students. He had stayed for a time in Hobart Town where he was received by Governor Sir George Arthur with marked courtesy and hospitality. He found things in the same state in which I had found them, but left there a Benedictine priest, the Rev. Father Cottram to serve Launceston, and one of his ecclesiastical students, afterwards Dean Kenny, to begin the first Catholic school of that Colony.

The Bishop's house was ready for his reception. The Catholic population received him with great joy, and presented him with a handsome carriage and pair as expressive of their wish to maintain him in his dignity. He was well received by the Governor and the chief officials, to most of whom he was the bearer of letters.

The Bishop wrote to me requesting that all the clergy in the Colony might be in Sydney to receive him on arrival. We were present except Father Therry, who started far up the country and remained there for some six weeks, having his agents in Sydney to tell him what was passing.

Knowing that the Bishop had brought with him one person who had been a perpetual failure, the first thing I did when I met him in the harbour was to strive to impress upon him very solemnly the duty of sending that person back on the very first opportunity. After which we had our cordial and affectionate greeting. That person was unfortunately retained for two or three years on one ground or another until he got the Bishop into a good deal of trouble, and was then shipped off. He was the very man against whose profession we young religious had protested in vain. His coming damped my joy in the Bishop's arrival considerably as, in a Colony, every folly and weakness gets to be known everywhere.

Everything in the church now assumed larger proportions. The Bishop took a position which gradually raised the tone and spirit of the whole Catholic body. We had pontifical functions with as much solemnity as our resources could command, which very much impressed the people to whom they were new. Then the vast body of the Catholics who had never been confirmed received this Sacrament. As the Bishop's house was large he turned half of it into a boarding school, over which I presided for a time. Thus was begun a solicitude for raising the sons of the settlers who were acquiring property, that they might take their suitable position.

At last Father Therry arrived and the Bishop sent for me to devise how we were to get possession of the papers by which he held the promissory notes obtained from the people before my arrival, and which his salaried agent was constantly hawking about for payment to himself. I devised the following plan. I advised the Bishop to keep the good priest in talk whilst I went and sent his agent down with the papers. I sent for the man, told him Father Therry was with the Bishop, and that he must take down to them all the papers he had connected with the Church. He took them, and was sent into the room where they were conversing. As soon as he entered the Bishop laid his hands on the papers and asked if they were all there. The man said yes! As soon as he had retired the Bishop said: 'Father Therry, you must not leave my presence until you sign over these papers to me. I will relieve you from all responsibility respecting them.' A document was drawn up and signed, and thus a great difficulty was at an end. Of course, I had all the outpouring afterwards, but that was of no importance. Father Therry still continued to hold the extensive landed possessions. He died but recently,[2] leaving a curious will, but leaving all he had for religious purposes. He also assisted the Bishop in enlarging the Cathedral. He was sent to Hobart Town as Vicar-General after I left the Colony, which put things into a long confusion and very much embarrassed Dr. Willson after he became the first Bishop of that See. Still, he was always a good and pious man.

As the Bishop was inexperienced in public business, the Government correspondence, which began to increase with the expansion of the Church, was still left in my hands. After a while I was placed at Parramatta to complete the church, form the mission, and attend the factory, which was the central prison for female convicts, where they were first placed on arrival and whither they were sent from all parts of the Colony for punishment. There were generally some fifteen hundred women in this place. I attended the Confessional there some hours in the day, and sometimes went home quite sick, even physically, with what I had gone through, or rather with what had to pass through my mind. I also attended the convict hospital at Liverpool, about ten miles distant, and occasionally had Mass there. I rode over to Sydney once a week to attend to the Government correspondence and to talk over general affairs with the Bishop.

I had also to look after the completion of the church begun at Maitland, and to start another at Parramatta. I had the assistance of the Government architect in devising the plans. But what was my surprise, on arriving one day at Maitland, to find that without my knowledge Father Therry had been there, and had doubled the number of windows in the walls. This was one of his singularities, to put as many windows in a building as the walls would allow, without any consideration for the intense glare of heated light. Thus in the old Cathedral of Sydney he put seventy large windows, two rows in one wall. At Campbell Town his church was like a cage. At Maitland he spoiled what would have been a well-proportioned nave in the old lancet style. His taste in architecture was for what he called *opes*; if a plan was brought to him, his first question was: 'How many more *opes* would it admit of?'[3] He could not understand the idea of adapting the light of a construction to climate.

And the Bishop began at once that wonderful course of missionary labour amongst the convicts, which attracted so much attention, produced so great an influence, and more than any other part of his ministry, drew so great a veneration towards him. He had not merely the heart of a father, but the heart of a mother towards them. When they came into his presence he wept over them, and they could never resist the influence of his words. The first step he took was to obtain leave from the Government for all the Catholic prisoners, as they arrived by ship, to be retained in the convict barracks in Sydney for ten days before they were sent up the country. When a ship arrived from Ireland there would be as many as three hundred to look after. They were brought to the church at six in the morning and remained until eleven; again marched to the church at three, and remained until six. It was a kind of retreat adapted to their circumstances. The Bishop was there the whole time, assisted by the Sydney clergy. After an address by the Bishop they were classified by the clergy into those who had not performed their religious duties for one, for three, for five or for ten years. After the clergy had examined into the amount of instruction which each possessed, they were reclassified for instruction. The ecclesiastical students acted as catechists, and some of the men were picked out as monitors. Then began the confessions, in which the Bishop took his large share. He gave most of the instructions and after the religious duties were completed by Holy Communion, a special course of instruction and advice was given to them regarding their position as convicts, what power their masters had over them, how the law affected them, to what dangers they were exposed, and how they would most effectually succeed in obtaining mitigations, good treatment and their ticket of leave. After this they proceeded to their assignment.

I need scarcely say that this system produced a most beneficial result, that was widely recognised. In my evidence before the Parliamentary Committee on Transportation in the year 1838, I was able to quote a letter from the Bishop stating that of 1,000 prisoners who had already gone through this system, only two had found their way into the Sydney gaol and that, whereas hitherto our clergy had attended not less than twenty executions yearly, during the six months since this system was adopted, only one Catholic had been executed, and he for a crime of three years standing. In short, it was a common remark among the clergy, that those whom they had in hand on their arrival very rarely found their way into gaol.

This was but a part of the Bishop's labour among the convicts. At regular intervals he visited the felon's gaol, instructed the Catholics, heard their confessions, and said Mass for them in the press room. Shortly after he had said his first Mass there, the head gaoler, a good Catholic, and a man of mild manners though of resolute will, said to me: 'I will tell you something, Sir, and I will tell it to no one else. You know how this place is infested with small vermin, so that even our rough men can hardly stand it. Well, when we are crowded, we are obliged to put a lot of men in the press room of a night to sleep. But ever since the Bishop said Mass, there is a rush of the men to get to that end of the room, because there has been no vermin there since that time.'

If there were men to be executed he always prepared them, although a priest attended them on the scaffold.

Every Sunday morning the convicts were marched from their barracks to the last Mass in the Cathedral where they crowded to the Bishop's confessional, and when he had to officiate the congregation had consequently to be detained a long time before the service began. Occasionally it became my duty to represent the great inconvenience to the congregation.

He would then weep and say: 'Anyone else I could put off, and I cannot resist these poor creatures.'

After the Sunday Vespers he would mount his horse, and proceed to a large chain-gang on Goat Island, or perhaps to some other chain-gang working on the roads, but boxed up in wooden huts on a Sunday. There he would have the Catholics drawn out and, after an earnest address to them, would use some retired place for a confessional. After the hard labours of the day were over, he delighted to have all the Sydney clergy at his house to a late dinner, and took that opportunity to invite any lay gentleman to whom he wished to show respect.

When he went up the country the convicts were always his first care, and he got as many of them to Mass as he could, and spent much of his time with them. When they knew he was coming, the Catholic settlers met him on the confines of the district on horseback and conducted him to the church, if there was one, or to the temporary place where he was to officiate. He made it a point, before leaving, to ride through the district in company with the priest, calling at the house of every Catholic or Emancipist who respected himself or was of good conduct. But if a man was not living properly, or neglected his duty to his family, he rode past his house without taking any notice of him. He thus inspired the Emancipists to respect themselves, and with the same view he established respectable schools for their sons, and founded a Catholic newspaper, which taught them their public rights and duties.

Having such an influence over the convicts they ran to him, as to a father, in their hours of distress. Let me give an example. He was walking in his large garden on a certain day, saying his office, when a man in wretched plight came from his hiding among the trees, and knelt before him. He then told his story. He had absconded from service 150 miles up the country, because the overseer had a down upon him and had unjustly reported him so often to his master, that he had had him flogged several times. He then showed his back covered with wounds and scars, and declared he was so miserable that he could bare it no longer. He had come all that way, avoiding the roads, and had had nothing to eat for three days but a green cob of maize, for he was obliged to keep in hiding. After questioning him closely the Bishop sent him to the kitchen for food and went straight to the Principal Superintendent of Convicts, an office of great authority. To him he told the whole tale, expressed his conviction of its truth, and pleaded for mercy. The Superintendent replied: 'The man must be sent to the barracks, and must be punished. But I promise you he shall be sent to another master, and to one who will do him justice.'

The Bishop's servants were mostly convicts and, of course, he was kind to them. There was an old man among them who worked in the garden who was very simple and in the main honest but, seeing the Bishop's jewelled mitre on a table, he could not resist a sudden temptation. He took up the mitre, wrapped it in a cloth, carried it to the principal hatter's in the city, said it was a curious Indian cap, and asked the master of the shop what he would give him for it. The master suspected at once that it was something belonging to the Catholic Bishop. He detained the old man and sent a messenger to the Bishop's house. A priest went to the shop, took possession of the mitre and the old man, and on his arrival at home he was saluted with general laughter. No more notice was taken of it. The old man worked on, but he never heard the last of the mitre from his fellow servants.

Our wants of all kinds increased so much that the Bishop thought it desirable that I should go to England, and on to Ireland, and do the best I could to provide for them. As, however, things were in a very unsatisfactory state in Hobart Town, His Lordship wished me first to accompany him thither, and so start on the long voyage from that port. Our visit was attended with very painful circumstances. We found the chapel and its altar still in a most disgraceful state. The people were still much neglected, and very dissatisfied. Father Connolly claimed the Church property for his own, though given by the Government for public purposes. The Bishop suspended him, and put the chapel under interdict. This caused a great excitement, especially as I had to put men with posted bills through the town on the Sunday morning to inform the people of the Interdict and to let them know where to go to hear Mass.

Father Connolly brought an action against the Bishop, and retained the Attorney and Solicitor-General in his cause.[4] We called a shrewd and clever Catholic who then held a public office to our council, and decided to appeal to the Governor for protection. The Home Office had sent a despatch by Bishop Polding and, in announcing his appointment, had directed the Governor to give him every countenance and support in his office. As the Bishop was leaving the Governor's house after this interview, he was served with a writ at the very gate, to prevent his departure from the Colony, or his return to Sydney.

The Catholics got word of these matters and quickly collected a public meeting, sending delegates with an address to the Colonial-Secretary, and invoking protection for the Bishop.

Upon this I took a letter from the Bishop to the Governor and lodged a complaint against the Attorney-General for having taken a retainer against an official recognised by the Government, whereas he might have to defend him in his official capacity. This visit enabled me to go into the whole merits of the case. His Excellency then sent for the Attorney-General. On his arrival we had a short, but somewhat sharp, altercation in the Governor's presence. It ended by His Excellency turning to him, directing him to return the fee, and requiring him to take up the Bishop's defence as a Government official. However, he asked him in my presence if there was anything actionable in the Bishop's official conduct. He smiled and said: 'No. But I understand there have been some remarks made outside of his official acts.' The Attorney-General was then requested to call on the Bishop, which he did, to say that the case was given up, and that he was free to depart, and the Governor sent his aide-de-camp to the Bishop in the most formal way to express his regret at the annoyances to which he had been subjected.

The Bishop, leaving Mr. Cottram, the only priest in the island, in Hobart Town, returned to Sydney, and I embarked for England.

Mr. Connolly died suspended.

Notes

1   A titular bishopric. Titular bishops are those who have been appointed by the Holy See to a diocese which had been canonically established in former times but at present has neither clergy nor people. It is essential that the titular diocese did once exist, and ceased to exist through death or defection of clergy or faithful, or pagan settlement and government. Hierocæsarea Thyessus was a See near the present town of Manisa in Turkey, a little to the north of Izmir. In 1888 When Bishop Ullathorne obtained leave from the Holy See to resign his diocese he was given the

title of Archbishop of Cabasa. Cabasa is the present town on Al-Qasabi in the Nile Delta.

2   Mss.1.

3   Perhaps this is a mild linguistic joke, deliberately using the Latin ops, opis = strength might, with the English idea of an opening.

4   i.e. Paid a retainer.

Chapter Twenty-Two

Voyage to England

After completing affairs in Hobart town, I took the first ship that offered for England. It proved to be a heavy tub with not only an uncultured but an incompetent captain, and we were a full six months on the voyage. I found the cabin passengers to be a naval surgeon returning home after taking out a cargo of convicted women to Hobart Town, a pleasant companion; a young Englishman educated in Germany, equally agreeable; an uncultured Scotch Presbyterian minister, who had originally been a carpenter, a kind-hearted man, but going home in trouble. A young Scotch settler who, though a Presbyterian, looked to me for guidance and a Jewess, who was a widow with two young daughters.

[1]It was a singular mixture and I had unpleasantnesses to encounter on account of this German Jewess. When I was not visibly present, but in my cabin, her conversation was anything but edifying. I could not but observe that she was laying traps for the young men, but in this she failed, and the silly captain was caught in her toils. I therefore refused to sit with her at table. I then ordered the steward to bring my meals to my private cabin. So soon as this was done the Scotch minister thought he ought to do the same. The woman at once declared that on no account would she be unpleasant to me, but she set upon the poor minister and gave him the most violent rating that I have ever heard from the lips of a woman. After this state of things had continued a couple of days, as I sat at my solitary meal in my own cabin, I heard the gentlemen passengers talking amongst themselves, and saying: 'This ought not to go on. We are deprived of the one who makes our society agreeable.'

Hearing this I went out to them and said: 'Gentlemen, will you have the kindness to accompany me on the quarter-deck, and be witnesses of what I shall say to the captain. I do not ask you to say anything, but simply to witness what I shall say.'

They followed me and it looked as though I were spokesman for all. I told him I had retired because my feelings and character required it, and I could neither appear in the cabin or on deck where that person was. He asked me what I complained of. I replied: 'You had better not ask. By your own account you have a wife in England as well as your owners, and there we are going. I have respectable witnesses besides your own conscience. I am willing to fix certain hours when I shall neither be in the public cabin nor on deck, but I cannot meet that person'. She heard it all from the cabin window, and came and begged that it might be as I proposed, and so it was arranged, and she took her meals in her cabin. But the evil went on, and when we got to London she still remained with him, until his wife got intelligence of it, and interfered.

So unskilled a navigator was the captain that he run us into sixty-six degrees South latitude far beyond Cape Horn, where we were entangled among icebergs for nearly a fortnight. The men lost all confidence, got low spirits, and proposed to the chief mate that he should take command of the ship. He very properly told the captain, and so the conspiracy was stopped. I counted more than seventy icebergs in sight at once, and we must have passed through some 2,000 of them. Some of the largest, as measured by the quadrant, were 150 feet in height above the sea and a quarter of a mile long. But most of them were much smaller. The weather was squally as well as foggy and a look-out had to be kept day and night from the fore-yard. It was intensely cold but we passengers agreed to have no cabin fires, but to wrap warm and take plenty of exercise. All our livestock, sheep, pigs, goats and poultry died of the cold and the shrewd old surgeon watched the dying moments of the creatures to see they were thrown overboard, and not brought to the table. He was a good-natured, facetious man, who had seen the world, and was a pleasant companion.

According to my custom in long voyages, I had my course of reading and made a sort of retreat. I also wrote some essays on the Convict System which, though never published, were of use to me in other publications. When I reached England and observed how little was known there on the subject I saw I had made a mistake in not having gathered copious materials for a complete book on the subject. I was, indeed, urged by a friend in Hobart Town to go back to Sydney for the purpose before coming home but, in fact, Church affairs were pressing, and

I left at a very short notice, having only a day in which to arrange my affairs, and set my house in order.

After clearing the icebergs we run[2] to Cape Horn and, strange to say, were becalmed off Staten island for a whole day. Four little cape pigeons accompanied us the whole way from the coast of New Zealand to the Horn; they never rested on the ship, but sometimes on the water, and flew about us the whole run, picking up anything the cook threw overboard. At the Horn they left us, and another came about us with a string tied to its leg. In a fortnight we ran from Cape Horn to the Brazils where, in the rapid change from cold to heat, we most of us caught cold. After a long spell at sea the sense of smell becomes acute on approaching land. We were in a fog and could see nothing, but the odour of land was rich with perfumes. Suddenly the mist cleared and the land revealed itself, covered with orange trees in flower and fruit. Our next object was to make for Rio de Janeiro to obtain fresh provisions. But the captain again blundered. He had clear observations the day before, sighting the bold land about Rio de Janeiro, but mistook it, and sailed back some sixty miles, when he fairly confessed that he knew not where he was. We got a man off on a boat from the shore and I was able to understand him. We were near, he said, to the Bay of Angra dos Rios. He undertook to pilot us into the bay, and there we came to anchor off the town. I landed with the captain to assist him in finding a ship agent. We found a respectable young Englishman acting as American Consul, and he undertook to provision the ship.

Two hills rose above the town on one of which stood a large Benedictine monastery, and on the other a Carmelite Convent of men. The next day I took my young Scotch friend as a companion and went up to the Benedictine monastery. The Prior received us with true religious courtesy and hospitality, and we stayed the night that I might say Mass in the morning. There were but very few religious to take care of the property, for the religious orders had been suspended through the influence of the freemasons. My Scotch companion was awestruck with all he saw, and he was quite nervous as we passed through the long cloisters, lighted by a single lamp to our rooms. The negro slaves of the property, about forty in number, were chanting the *Salve Regina* after returning from their work. The next morning, however, my Presbyterian companion was quite fascinated with the kindness of the monks.

There was an Irish medical man who had married a native Portugese, who possessed considerable wealth, and had built for himself a beautiful mansion outside the town. In this mansion he invited me and my companion to take up our quarters, and assembled a party to meet us.

I found religion at a low ebb generally, and most of the clergy in a low condition. One old priest, famed for his jokes and convivial tastes, attacked the Popes and clericial celibacy, in the presence of the Scotsman and the English Consul, among others. I gave him a sharp rebuke in Latin. He coolly repeated what I said in Portuguese, and said that he admired me for doing so. This was, in part, a consequence of the revolution, but I have reason to believe that there has been considerable improvement of late. But at that time scarcely anyone went to Confession, unless in danger of death. Fathers would not allow their wives and daughters to do so. I found one Parish Priest, however, who was truly pious and earnest, and paid him all the attention I could.

The public school was in beautiful order, but this priest assured me that they were not allowed to teach religion in it, not even the Doctrine of the Holy Trinity.

Angra dos Rios is the great coffee growing district. I was impressed with the modest demeanour of the slaves; the women and the men on the roads, even with loads on their heads, stood still as we passed and asked a blessing in the name of Christ. We entered a large barn-like place on a coffee plantation where an old negro woman had care of the infant negros, and a strange sight it was to see such a number of little blackies crawling all over the long floor with very slight clothing in the great heat. The mothers came from their work at certain intervals to suckle them.

Our host invited us to a good long ride into the country to visit a collegiate establishment. The soil was wonderfully rich, abounding in plantations of coffee, sugar, tapioca. Palms, orange and cocoa trees were profuse on the roadsides, and the pineapple grew everywhere like a common weed. The head of the College was an excellent Portuguese Oratorian, a man of considerable attainments as well as piety. He read a little English and shewed me his English books. There was a specimen of our scientific writing, of our literature and of our theology, he told me. The first was an odd volume of an old *Repertory of the Arts and Sciences,* the second was Hervey's *Meditations on the Tombs,* the third was Miss Bodenham's

Mrs. Herbert and the Villagers. He was surprised when I told him that they were not fair samples of our English thought and letters. Just as we were sailing I received by a messenger a letter from this good Father written in beautiful Latinity. He sent me some money, asking me to purchase with it, and send him, some good books in English. I was obliged to return it as I could not reach him without some address at Rio Janeiro. He also sent me a present of a large bird, which he said was a stranger in that country. It proved to be a very fine specimen of the Great Horned Screamer, so called from having two large horns in front of each of its wings. I had hoped to take it home as a present to the Zoological Society but knowing nothing of its habits we could find nothing it would eat, and so it died. I gave it to the surgeon to stuff for the Army and Navy Surgeons' Museum.

Nothing particular occurred during the rest of the voyage, except that the young man who was teaching me German had a quarrel with the big carpenter, a Shetlander, whom he throttled and nearly strangled, when I had to interfere and restore peace.

I landed in my native country towards the close of 1836.

Notes

1   The following paragraph has been crossed out of the later manuscript, presumably by Mother Drane. Perhaps she thought it unedifying for her nuns. Given the times, it is a measure of Ullathorne's moral stature that he can relate the incident as objectively as he relates anything else.

2   Whether the word *run* was used as an alternative past participle in those days, or whether peculiar to Ullathorne's Yorkshire dialect, I cannot say but here, as elsewhere, there is no mistaking *run* for *ran*.

Chapter Twenty-Three

The Eternal City

I then passed the two most eventful years of my life in obtaining aid for the Australian Church; mostly in England, but a good deal in Ireland, being always on the move. At the invitation of Cardinal Weld[1] I also went to Rome to give a report on the state of the Mission to the Holy See. So little was then known respecting Australia in England, and especially respecting its singular productions, the condition of its convict population, and the state of religion, that my narratives were everywhere listened to with great attention, and as something new and surprising. Kindness met me wherever I went, but becoming a sort of celebrity for the time, I found it very fatiguing.

My memory will not serve me so far as chronologically to arrange my proceedings during these two years. Although it was some time after my arrival in England before I proceeded to Rome, it will be better to dispose of that visit first.

The occasion was a letter received from Cardinal Weld, requesting me to go to Rome and make a report to the Holy See on the Mission of Australia. At Paris I met some of the devout Catholics of that city, and among others the future president of the Society of St. Vincent de Paul, then a young man, who kindly drove me to the principal churches and charitable institutions. I also made the acquaintance of the Venerable Abbé Dubois,[2] who had long been in India, but had published a discouraging book about its missions as they were at that time. Father O'Meara, then tutor to the present Mr. Hornyold,[3] also introduced me to several of the leaders of Catholic affairs, whom it was interesting to know.

At Chalon-sur-Saône I fell in with the celebrated Abbot Guéranger[4] on the steamer in company with Father Brandes,[5] afterwards Novice-Master at the great monastery of Einsiedeln,[6] and author of several Benedictine

142

books. They were on their way to Rome to gain approval for the new foundation of French Benedictines which Guéranger was establishing. I was the first professed Benedictine they had ever seen, and they asked me if I belonged to the Monastery near Bath which had had such a conflict with Bishop Baines. They were going to the monastery of St. Calisto in Rome, expecting that the Procurator of the English Benedictines, who lived there, would be of use to them. I also was going to the same house, and we joined company. I found the Abbot well versed in the Fathers and Church History and we had much interesting conversation. He maintained the authenticity of the works ascribed to St. Dionysius, and spoke of writing on the subject. He had completed the first volume of his *Origines de l'Eglise Romaine*[7] of which he had copies for Rome, but his great contest for restoring the Roman Breviary to its integrity in France and his magnificent work, *Institutions Liturgiques*,[8] prevented its ever being completed. He was an enthusiastic lover of art, and a valuable companion in visiting Genoa, Pisa and Florence, and the cities between there and Rome.

Genoa, the first real Italian city that I saw, amazed me by its splendour and by the radiant magnificence of its churches. Stepping into the church of the Annunciation, that glorious rainbow of art, and examining its details, and then the cathedral group of Pisa, I got possession of the principles of a style and a harmony of many arts of which those who have never crossed the Alps can have no real conception. At Florence I received an ineffaceable impression from the frescoes of Fra Angelico at St. Marks. They seemed more like visions of the divine purity of the spiritual world than paintings invented by a mortal man. And especially I was captivated by the mystical spirit and soul painting in the fresco of the Crowning of the Blessed Virgin. In Siena we found our own Gothic refined and worked out with a wealth of material and a minuteness of artistic finish, which united the genius of the two sides of the Alps in one single structure.

At Lyons I was introduced to the managers of the Society for the Propagation of the Faith, then in its early years. I do not forget the kind attention I received from them. At their request I drew up a full account of the Australian Mission and of the Convict System, to which I added a description of the country and of its most curious productions. It filled nearly a number of their *Annuals*, and being so completely new, was said to have advanced the interests of the Society. The Society voted a handsome allocation of money to Australia, and it was continued for many years.

We arrived at San Calisto in Rome on the morning of the Holy Saturday, 1837. As there was no Benedictine Cardinal at that time the suite of rooms for the use of that dignitary were vacant and the Fathers put them at my disposal. So soon as I was refreshed I went out with Father, afterwards Bishop, Collier, to see St. Peter's, and attend the Pontifical functions in the Sistine Chapel. When he brought me in front of the Colonnade I said: 'This is not St. Peter's. You have deceived me. It is some miniature of it.' It was so dwarfed by distance that I really believed it to be nothing else. But as we approached it grew upon the eye into the enormous temple it is.

We entered the Sistine, but I had no sooner got a glimpse of the Pope than I was turned out by the Swiss Guard. 'Is this the Roman welcome?' I said to Father Collier. 'Coming from the far end of the world to report a new continent for the work of the Church, I am at once turned out of the Pontifical Chapel.' He then, however, recollected that the frock coat was the sin I bore upon me. I ought to have been in the habit of my Order. But that I had never worn, and it had yet to be made. The Pontifical Chapel is part of the Pontifical Court, and requires some kind of Court costume.

When I was presented to the Cardinal Prefect of Propaganda, the mild and gentle Cardinal Franzoni, as Vicar-General of Australia, His Eminence, after a quiet inspection, exclaimed: '*Qual giovane!*' and after answering a few questions I retired. On my presentation to Pope Gregory XVI by the same title, His Holiness uttered the same exclamation: '*Qual giovane!*' What a youth! But he was truly paternal and expressed a hope to see my report. On fire as I was, and that habitually, with the interests of the Australian Mission, and anxious to awaken like interest in Rome, these receptions considerably cooled me. I felt I was looked on as a mere boy, and I therefore kept out of sight, and set to work with my report.

I drew up my report at considerable length in four parts. It was put into Italian by Dr. Collier and was revised by Abbot Peschiatelli. I presented it one part at a time until I knew that the whole had been printed at the Propaganda Press. I then called upon the Cardinal Prefect who expressed warm interest in the report, and became very cordial. He also informed me, to my great satisfaction, that a Canon of the Cathedral of Vienna, moved with what he had heard of that country, had given a foundation for the maintenance of a priest at Norfolk Island. I think that his informant must have been the late Baron von Hügel who, in his early days, had made a tour of the Australian Colonies, and whom I had the pleasure of meeting with his family in England in his latter days. As he had heard it was so rude a place he had seriously thought of sending two Capuchins, as probably only men of rigid self denial would be able to endure such a position. I then explained to His Eminence that the position of things in that island was very peculiar, that probably the Government, which allowed no one on the settlement not appointed under its own approval, would probably not accept of foreigners, and especially of men in religious habits, that the priest appointed there must be not only a zealous man, but also a man well acquainted with English manners and character, that he would require to have a certain polish too, and a knowledge of the world, as he would have to consort with the officials and keep up an influence with the Governor, in order effectually to serve the poor criminals. After this explanation the Cardinal concluded that the priests appointed there had better be British subjects, and left the matter in my hands.

I took the opportunity to observe to the Cardinal Prefect that as both His Holiness and himself had remarked, with apparent surprise, upon my youthfulness, I begged to observe that I had not sought the office, that it was imposed upon me, and that I was most ready to resign it. His Eminence replied that the report I had given was fully approved, that I had worked the Australian soil a good deal, and that I was not to suppose there was any dissatisfaction. His Holiness also directed that I should receive the diploma of Doctor of Divinity. I then began to understand Rome in a way that long experience has confirmed. When persons go there with great ecclesiastical or religious interests to be settled, they are commonly treated with a certain reserve, if they are strangers, until their spirit and character are seen through when, if satisfactory, they are treated with every kindness and consideration.

I saw that when Cardinal Franzoni interrupted my earnest remarks, in which I was pressing on his attention the work and the wants of New South Wales, with some bizarre question, such as: '*E sono tutti neri eh*?'[9] he was taking the measure of my character.

As Cardinal Weld had invited me to Rome, he gave me a cordial welcome. At his table I met his son-in-law, Lord Clifford; the Miss Clifford who was afterwards first Prioress of St. Scholastica's, Atherstone; and the present Cardinal di Luca, then secretary to Cardinal Weld. The next day the Cardinal was taken ill. He was repeatedly bled according to the medical system of Rome at that time, against which all the English exclaimed, and in the course of a week he died. His departure caused a universal regret. His great piety, his charity, and his edifying and recollected demeanour, so marked on all occasions, had drawn towards him a very high degree of respect. Besides the solemn requiem at his funeral, at which the Pope himself assisted, Lord Clifford had a requiem celebrated at San Carlo in Corso to which all the English in Rome were invited, and at which Dr. Wiseman[10] read a long oration recounting the history of the Cardinal's life. This gave rise to a singular scene for so solemn an occasion, and that in a Roman church. The music was the celebrated *Requiem* of Mozart, performed by the best singers with instrumentation. But Mozart is rarely heard in Roman churches, and it attracted the artists and musicians. But when the thrilling tones of Mozart had become interrupted for a long time by the monotonous reading of Dr., afterwards Cardinal, Wiseman in the harsh sounding English language, however interesting to the English, the Italians could stand it no longer, but set up a hissing all through the church. After a few moments Dr. Wiseman got a hearing, and by a few words of grave and dignified rebuke restored silence until the lecture was completed.

This was the only time at which I ever knew Italians to misbehave in a church. As to the misconduct of the English, it was at that time proverbial. On the very next day after my arrival, which was Easter Sunday, I saw an Englishman striving against the Swiss Guards to force his way into the dress circle at the Pontifical Mass. The Captain of the Guard came up to remonstrate, the Englishman squared his fists at him. The Captain clapped his hand on his sword, but three halberdiers quietly put their shoulders against the Englishman and as quietly moved him back out of the way.

Just before my arrival a most disgraceful thing occurred. Three young Englishmen of good family were staying in Rome with their sister. The Pope was walking in the suburbs in his white silk costume in advance of his carriage and guards. The three young men met him on the way. The three young men linked their arms together and obstructed the firm path so as to force the Pope to turn aside into a mud-hole. The Pope stood a moment, and said in Italian: 'Look gentlemen,' pointing to his white garments downwards and then to the road. They gave a stifled laugh and moved onwards together in the dry path. The Pope stepped into the mud almost, as he afterwards described it, to the knees. His carriage came up. He got into it, rode to the Vatican and sent for Cardinal Weld. The affair, of course, produced a great sensation. The Marquis of Anglesea, who was then at the head of the British circle in Rome, when spoken to about it, could not at first believe that English gentlemen could have been the authors of such an outrage. But after a little inquiry, he said he feared it was too true. Mr. Bodenham was sent by Cardinal Weld to the young men's residence. They kept out of the way and the sister received him. On his stating why he had come, the sister expressed indignation at such a charge being laid to her brothers, but Mr. Bodenham said: 'I come as the brother-in-law of Cardinal Weld, who has just come from the Pope and I have to inform you that unless your brothers apply at once for their passports, and quit Rome without delay, your residence will be immediately entered by the police.' They took the hint and at once departed.

Notes

1   Thomas Weld (1773–1837), was the eldest of fifteen children of one of the great English recusant families. On the death of his wife and the marriage of his only daughter he became a priest in 1821. He was consecrated as Bishop for Upper Canada in 1826 but ill-health prevented him from taking the See. While visiting Rome in 1830 he was raised to the Cardinalate. He died very shortly after this meeting with Ullathorne.

2   Mss.2. has *Ducot* but presumably Ullathorne had confused the name after all the years. Jean-Antoine Dubois (1765–1848), was a priest who went to India at the outbreak of the French Revolution. He was there for thirty-two years, and much loved and respected but made no converts among the Hindu population and returned somewhat disillusioned. His *Manners, Institutions and Ceremonies of the People of India* is still an important work.

3   Hornyold was an ancient Catholic, Worcestershire family. Late in the eighteenth century Teresa, the daughter of Thomas Hornyold, married a Gandolphi, of ancient Genoese nobility. The Hornyold to whom Ullathorne refers here was John Vincent Gandolphi Hornyold (1818–1902) who assumed the name of Hornyold by Royal Licence in 1859. He was a knight of the first

class of the Noble Order of Christ (1840). Two of his daughters entered Religious orders one son became a Jesuit priest. His uncle, Thomas Charles whom he succeeded. is mentioned below as a benefactor of the English Church. A forebear John Hornyold (1706–1778), Titular Bishop of Philomelia, was a Vicar-Apostolic of the Midland District.

4   An abbot at the time of writing, but not when met here, in 1836. Prosper Louis Pascal Gueranger (1805–1875), wished to re-establish religious life in France, under the Rule of St. Benedict, which had been suppressed at the French Revolution. When Ullathorne met him he had bought the once famous monastery of Solesmes back from private hands and was on his way to Rome to obtain official sanction for the enterprise. Today Solesmes has achieved a worldwide reputation for its devotion to the liturgy. One of its many daughter houses is Quarr Abbey on the Isle of Wight.

5   Mss.1. spells this *Brandes*, Mss.2. *Brandis*. For uniformity we shall stay with *Brandes*.

6   In the Canton of Schwyz, Switzerland. Founded originally as a hermitage in the middle of the ninth century, it was said to have been miraculously consecrated by Christ himself assisted by the Four Evangelists and St. Peter in 948. This legend has been investigated and confirmed by a number of Popes, the most recent being Pius VI in 1793. It still flourishes and has a number of daughter houses in the United States.

7   Paris 1836. Mss.1. calls this *Origines Ecclesiae Romanae*.

8   Paris Vol. i 1840. Vol. ii 1841. Vol. iii 1851. 2nd ed. 4 vols. 1878–1885.

9   And they are all black eh?

10   Nicholas Patrick Stephen Wiseman (1802–1865), was later to become the first Archbishop of Westminster and a Cardinal. He was one of the first to study at the new English College in Rome, which had been closed for twenty years after French occupation. He became a Doctor of Divinity in 1824, was ordained a year later and after three years more, while still only twenty-six, became the Rector of the English College. When he met Ullathorne in Rome he had just returned from a year in England, his first as an adult and a priest, and was full of fervent hopes for the future of Catholicism there after the Catholic Emancipation Act of 1829.

Chapter Twenty-Four

The Eternal City, Continued

Dr. Wiseman was then head of the English. Dr. Cullen[1] of the Irish, and Dr. Grant[2] of the Scotch College, from all of whom I received a great kindness. Bishops Walsh[3] and Griffiths[4] were also on their visit to Rome, and were lodged at the English College. The Pope treated them with particular attention. I was invited to accompany them, under the guidance of Dr. Wiseman, over the roof of St. Peter's and on ascending the dome we four just filled one quarter of the metal ball beneath the cross.

Dr. Wiseman gave a characteristic anecdote of these two devout prelates. They were riding across the Campagna towards Monte Porcio, to see the country house of the College, and had expressed a curiosity to see a herd of buffaloes. When in the midst of their office a herd swept by and the doctor whispered: 'These are the buffaloes, My Lords,' the good Bishops kept steadily on, with their eyes upon their breviaries. By the time they had finished and closed their books Dr. Wiseman said: 'The buffaloes are gone. You can just see something dark in the distance and that is all.' Whereupon Bishop Walsh turned his eyes in that direction in his very quiet way for an instant, and then said: 'I am glad I saw the buffaloes.'

Their piety and recollection was so complete when in the Sistine at the functions, notwithstanding the novelty of everything around them, that everyone used to ask who these two prelates were. And the English felt pleasure at hearing the reply: '*Sono vescovi Ingles*'.

There was one Cardinal whose kindness to me, a young stranger without introduction to him, I ought on no account to forget. Cardinal Castracane not only took a great interest in my mission but he called upon me, shewed a great interest in all my proceedings and presented me with a valuable painting

149

that had been bequeathed to him by another Cardinal, an *Assumption of the Blessed Virgin*, supposed to be by Guido Reni.[5] I took the picture to Australia and finally presented it to the Sisters of Charity for their covent at Parramatta. What became of it when that convent was broken up after my departure I do not know.

Amongst my occupations at Rome I collected a quantity of old pictures at a cheap cost and, of course, of no great artistic merit, to cover the walls of our Australian churches. Amongst them I was glad to get a picture of a black saint, having an eye to the aborigines. In a country where there were then no paintings I knew that they would be valuable. I kept in view the increasing of my library both abroad and in London, and also received a gift of books from the Propaganda Press. I had further to look to a provision of church plate and of vestments, missals, etc. for nothing of this kind was obtainable in the colonies. And this reminds me that Mr Hardman,[6] then recently married, offered me a present of the first monstrance ever used in the Australian colonies.

I had a brief interview with the celebrated linguist, Cardinal, then Monsignor, Mezzofanti[7] in company with Abbot Guéranger. He was waiting to accompany the Pope in a walk through the Vatican Library. I was struck by the great meekness and modesty of his demeanour, the wedge-like form of his brow, and the facile pliability of his mouth which so readily gave itself to every form of language and dialect. It was one of those faces we can never forget, presenting, as it did, such a perfect individuality of soul, a character unique and thoroughly simple.

Another instructive reminiscence of this visit to Rome was a private visit to Overbeck,[8], to whom I was introduced by Abbot Peschiatelli who was on intimate terms with the reviver of Christian painting. The advantage of this introduction was that I was allowed to see his painting then in progress, which he did not generally let be seen, but only his cartoons and completed paintings. He was then at work on his chief picture, representing the influence of Religion in the Arts, now in the Frankfort Gallery.[9] He spoke with warmth on the missionary life, considered himself a sort of missioner to souls, and quite warmed me with his gentle enthusiasm. Whilst he explained his great picture I could not fail in observing how much he had drawn the oval faces and calm, harmonious features of his Christs unconsciously from his own.

The tranquillity of the monastery and the religious influence of Rome were very grateful after the rough work of Australia, and the toils and solicitudes that followed my return to England. The paternal charity of the Benedictine Fathers increased the sense of tranquillity and the home-feeling, and there was this additional transformation that, although I had been a professed Religious for now some twelve years, it was the first time that I had ever worn the religious habit, and the religious habit controlled my habitual rapidity of motion, and consequently, of my thinking. The gentle-hearted Father Glower of the Gesu was my Confessor, and after kneeling by his side we generally sat down and had some useful conversation. He put into my hands the books published in America revealing the secret mysteries of Freemasonry up to the highest grade, as practiced on the Continent, and which were published by members, after the murder of Morgan[10] for betraying its secrets had created such a sensation; and this enabled me to comprehend, in a practical way, the mischiefs and machinations of that secret society, which is so little understood in England.

Searching everywhere for devoted priests for Australia, I was told of a priest who had founded a new Institute of missioners in, or near, Turin of self-denying and laborious men. Now one thing that fretted me in Italy was to see such a vast number of priests, many of them apparently with little to do, whilst in Australia souls were perishing without pastors or sacraments. I could not help talking of this. But I soon ascertained that the really competent men in Rome were engaged in one important occupation or another, and that a certain class of priests, then numerous, were men on their little patrimonies, or chaplaincies, mere Mass-saying priests, who would have been more in our way than a help to work like ours.

I asked Father Glover's opinion about the new Institute of missioners near Turin. He said the name of the founder was Rosmini,[11] but that his writings were suspected of having a taint of novelty and unsoundness. I then asked if there had been any reply to them and he mentioned the works of Gioberti,[12] which could be got at Genoa. But when I inquired of the booksellers at Genoa they told me that his books were prohibited by the State, and he himself sent into exile. In the year 1848 I sailed in the same vessel with Gioberti from Genoa to Civita Vecchia, and was surprised to observe his extremely

nervous state of body. His head and his limbs shook continually, and I was told by those who knew him that he was always
more or less in a fever, which appeared to be confirmed by the
red and inflamed condition of his eyes. I never could understand his fundamental position on ontology, of which the
American, Brownson, made so much, that in every affirmative
proposition we affirm *ens creat existentias*; for creation is a
free act of the Divine Will and is not therefore an object of our
mental intuition. And St. Paul teaches that 'by faith we know
that the world was created by the Word of God'. Then exist-
ences are contingent, and of contingencies we have no mental
intuition.

I stayed at Rome until after the great festival of Corpus
Christi, witnessed the great procession at St. Peter's, which
impressed me more with the religious grandeur and resources
of Rome than anything I had yet seen, and then I made
my preparations for departure, although Cardinal Franzoni
pressed me to stay for that of SS. Peter and Paul. The
Pope at my farewell audience gave me some kind words of
encouragement and told me to learn Italian for my next visit
to Rome. I had an affectionate farewell to the good monks
whose paternal charity towards me has never diminished on
my subsequent visits to the Eternal City, and started with
a party by *vetturnio*[13] to return by the Alps. Provided with
letters from the Benedictine Abbot, I visited the monasteries
of Perugia, Florence and Bologna on my way, and was cordially received by the brethren. In Bologna I visited the tomb of
St. Dominic, little then thinking that I was destined in after life
to have such intimate relations with his Order; but the Fathers
were very courteous in shewing me everything in that great
church, introduced as I was by one of the Benedictines.

Hearing from the Benedictine novice, Charles Brandes, that
there was an excellent young priest, son of a magistrate, in
the district of Bellinzona, who was anxious to go on the
foreign mission, I took a letter of introduction from him to
that family. But before I proceed, let me recall my second
acquaintance with Charles Brandes. Ten years after my episcopal consecration,[14] I was sent by medical advice to spend
some months of summer in the Alps. I then visited Einsiedeln.
When I presented myself at the door of the great monastery,
I sent in my card, and asked for someone who could speak
French or Italian. A Father came, and fraternally greeting me
in French, said: 'Your Lordship is no stranger here. I hold

in my hand the German translation of your book on La Salette,[15] which has done much to make that shrine known in Germany. We will send for your luggage to the hotel. Our best apartments are at your disposal.' Conducting me towards the Abbot's apartments, the Father suddenly stopped and said: 'There is a father here, the Novice-Master, who speaks French fluently.' Knocking at the door it was opened and revealed the master surrounded by his novices. He looked, and I looked, peeringly, into one another's faces for a moment. Then he threw his arms around me. It was my old friend and companion Father Brandes. I found him a truly spiritual man, full of zeal for Benedictine piety and discipline. We had three delightful days together beneath the hospitable roof of the Abbot's quarters, and on parting he gave me his translations of the *Rule and Life of St. Benedict* and his *Manual of Benedictine Piety*.

I visited the family of Leoni residing in a beautiful country near the Lake of Lugano, and there presented the letter of Father Brandes, who was then but a novice. The family received me with warm hospitality. The old magistrate was a man of patriarchial simplicity, living among his children and grandchildren, all under one roof after the old medieval manner of Italy. I was much edified during my three days' stay with the simplicity and unity of this large family. There was a purity of thought and piety of heart, a gentle yet free courtesy in this happy society which was very endearing. The head of it was a mild, firm and benevolent character, evidently much respected all the country round. On Sunday was the monthly procession of the parish round the church where the old magistrate was distinguished from the rest by carrying a larger and more ornamented candle, and walking last. The young priest, however, was not at home, but with his brother, the principal architect of Turin. I therefore drove to the Largo Maggiore, crossed to Savona, and took the diligence for Turin. During this journey I was much taken with the gentle simplicity of a young Franciscan friar, also going to Turin. He had got his passage for the love of God, and intended to ask for a fare in the diligence for the love of God, and he got it.

At Turin I stayed some days with the Leoni's, who took me everywhere. I called to see Rosmini, not yet losing sight of his missionary institute, but he had gone to visit his mother, who was ill. I found the young priest more heavy and less spirited than the rest of his family, but as he was eager to go I took him, his brother paying the expenses. But at London he lost courage, and returned home.

Notes

1   Paul Cullen (1803–1878), later Archbishop of Dublin and a Cardinal. He was a brilliant student and a noted linguist. At seventeen he was sent to the College of Propaganda in Rome and at the age of twenty-five lead a disputation before Leo XII and an audience of Cardinals and Prelates which included the youthful Abbate Pecci, the future Leo XIII. It was Leo XIII who declared in later life that the brilliant talent and singular modesty of the Irish student had made an indellible impression on him. Cullen was Rector of the Irish College from 1832 to 1850.

2   Alexander Grant (1810–78), Rector of the Scots College. John Henry Newman refers to Dr. Grant as one suspicious of the future Cardinal's orthodoxy. See *Newman the Oratorian* p. 434 Dom Placid Murray OSB, Fowler Wright 1980.

3   Thomas Walsh (1777–1849), was consecrated Bishop of a titular see in 1825 and became Vicar-Apostolic of the Midland District in 1826, which post he held during his visit to Rome. Propaganda had resolved that Bishop Walsh should be the first Metropolitan of the new Hierarchy but he died before that could be realised. Ullathorne was reportedly the next choice but in the event it went to Wiseman.

4   Thomas Griffiths (1791–1847), was educated at St. Edmund's, Old Hall, where he was ordained in 1814. Four years later he was chosen as President, which post he held for fifteen years. He was consecrated Bishop of a titular see in 1833 and three years later became Vicar-Apostolic of the London District, the first, and only, cleric wholly educated in England to hold that post. When he died unexpectedly in 1847 Ullathorne himself preached the funeral sermon.

5   Guido Reni (1575–1642), an Italian painter of the generation immediately following Carracci and Caravaggio.

7   John Hardman was a rich Birmingham manufacturer who, in the tradition of his staunchly Catholic family, was noted for his generosity to the Church. One of his sisters, Mary Juliana, was instrumental in introducing the Sisters of Mercy into England and was the first Prioress of the community at Harmsworth, Birmingham.

7   Giuseppe Mezzofanti (1774–1849), was said to speak thirty-eight languages perfectly and have a working knowledge of a further thirty along with some fifty dialects of these languages. He came from Bologna and was the son of a poor Carpenter. He had finished his theological studies before he was old enough to be ordained and so devoted his time to the study of Oriental languages. At ordination he held the chair of Hebrew at the University of Bologna. When Ullathorne met him he was Custodian-in-Chief of the Vatican Library. He was created Cardinal in 1838.

8   Friedrick Overbeck (1789–1869), German Painter from Lubeck, a Catholic convert, who regarded traditional, pre-reformation religious art as an expression of genuinely religious minds satisfying the spiritual needs of the community. He lived chiefly in Rome where his influence was vast and where he became known as the 'Father of the Nazarines'.

9   It was, in fact, bought by the Prince Consort.

10   An anti-masonic movement was ignited in 1826 by the mysterious disappearance of William Morgan, a bricklayer in Western New York, who supposedly had broken his vow of secrecy as a Freemason by preparing

a book revealing the organization's secrets. When no trace of Morgan could be discovered, rumours of his murder at the hands of Masons swept through New York and then into New England and the Mid-Atlantic states. *Ency. Brit.*

11 Antonio Rosmini-Serbati (1797–1855), founded his Institute of Charity, better known as the Rosminians, and was encouraged by Leo XII and later by Pius VIII. His missioners spread throughout Italy and England, notably to Prior Park. His writing were always controversial and in 1854 the Pope ordered an examination of all his works while not disparaging the author, his Institute, or his exceptional service to the Church. He died the following year, before the investigation had been completed.

12 I can find no reference to Gioberti among Rosmini's critics but there were so many of them, mostly Jesuits.

13 Stagecoach.

14 The trip referred to actually took place in 1857 which was more like seven years after his episcopal consecration.

15 *La Salette* (1854) concerns an apparition of the Blessed Virgin to two shepherds, Melanie Calvat, a girl of fifteen, and Maximin Giraud, who was then eleven, in the parish of La Salette in the diocese of Grenoble on September 19th 1846. There are interesting similarities between this apparition and those of Lourdes (1858) and Fatima (1917).

Chapter Twenty Five

Dublin

One of the first things I did in England was to publish, in pamphlet form, *The Catholic Mission in Australasia*. This at once awakened a warm interest in the missionary work of that remote country. Several English priests offered themselves for the work, but their Bishops could not spare them. One effect which it produced, and which I did not anticipate, was to send several ladies into English convents. Active Orders had not yet begun in England, so this result surprised me all the more.

Besides publishing five editions of that pamphlet, I took to lecturing on the Mission and its wants in the churches of Lancashire, and in the course of seven weeks obtained offerings to the amount of a thousand pounds. The Jesuit Fathers were particularly cordial in their co-operation. Ladies occasionally put their jewels on the plate. A convert lady gave me another thousand. Contributions came in from other quarters.

I then went to Ireland, and met its Bishops assembled at Maynooth, who took such an interest in the wants of Australia that several of them promised that, if any of their young priests were willing to offer themselves, they would account every year served in Australia as two towards obtaining a parish, in the event of their ultimate return. Several Bishops invited me to visit them at their homes. But from none of them did I obtain more earnest co-operation than from Archbishop Murray of Dublin, and Bishop Kinshela of Ossory.[1] With him I had many pleasant days. Travelling with him I had the opportunity of seeing the whole system of working an Irish diocese. He gave me the run of his Seminary, with leave to take as many young men as offerd themselves for Australia. I selected one priest and five students, who afterwards turned out valuable priests. Thus, while working in the interests of Australia, I was gathering useful experience for myself.

I also received very great assistance from Dr. Montague, the President of Maynooth, a remarkably shrewd man, who possessed a surprising knowledge of the character of every priest in Ireland, and could point out where the most devoted men were to be found. Nor must I forget the extreme kindness that I met with from all the professors of that great College. Dr. Gaffney, the Dean of Discipline, was of special service in recommending students to me, and at his request I gave a spiritual retreat to students in preparation for ordination.

At that time the Irish Prelates were seriously thinking of founding a College for educating priests for the British Colonies and Foreign settlements, and the Primate, Archbishop Crolly, asked me to draw up an estimate of the probable numbers that would be required. This I did, and gave it into his hands. I also made the intimate acquaintance of the Franciscan Fathers of Dublin, who had recently completed their large church, still called *Adam and Eve*, owing to a tavern which formerly occupied the site, and bore that sign. The peculiarity of their establishment was that their convent, for want of space, was built on and over the top of their large and lofty church. Two of the fathers volunteered for the Australian Mission. One was Father Geoghegan who went out with me and who founded the Mission in Melbourne and became the second Bishop of Adelaide. The other was Father Coffey[2] who followed later on and succeeded me at Parramatta. When Bishop Polding was laying the foundation of a little church on the banks of the River Hawkesbury and the ceremony was proceeding, a herd of wild cattle came rushing down from the hills and, attracted probably by the sight of the Bishop in his cope and mitre, and the clergy in their white surplices, came rushing on to attack the whole function like so many demons. Imagine the consternation! But Father Coffey, with his stout, rotund figure, ran up to the Bishop and cried out: 'My Lord, give me your crozier!' Armed with which he faced the furious herd as they came wildly on in loose order, and so effectively brandished the crozier in their glowering eyes that they all turned tail and retreated into the bush.

It was in this Religious house that I contracted a close friendship with Father Maguire, the celebrated controversialist, who used to come from the bogs of Leitrim to give his Lenten lectures. Few people in these days will recollect the famous platform controversies of Pope and Maguire, and Gleig and Maguire, but at that time he was giving a great course of controversial lectures at the new Franciscan church, which was most densely crowded four night in the week by an audience, Protestants as well as Catholics, who listened with close attention for two hours' duration.

What struck me most in these lectures was the wonderful amount of freshness and vigour which Father Tom, as he was familiarly called, gave to old and familiar texts. They came out under his handling with a force and cogency which quite surprised even those who would before have said that their pith and marrow had been drawn out over and over again by our controversial writings, even to exhaustion. He took his time in preparing your mind, but when the point came at last it came irresistibly. His eloquence had a flavour of the Leitrim bogs, but its fervid flow and skilful reasoning seemed only to acquire more force from this rustic simplicity. He generally spent the first twenty minutes in short and pithy replies to the letters he received from Protestant auditors in reply to his previous lecture, and then he took up his subject. When he descended from the pulpit, his garments were saturated through with perspiration. He had immediately to change them, after which he descended into the common room of the Fathers, where he was met by a number of his friends. A red hot poker was in the fire, a tumbler of whisky and water on the table. He seized the poker, plunged it hissing into the beverage, and drank it off. Thus guarded against cold, he sat down to a table surrounded by a circle of his friends, clergy, lawyers and wits, some of them leaders in O'Connell's agitations, and then began a flow of wit and learning such as I never witnessed before or since. When we broke up Father Maguire dropped me from his car at my lodgings before going to his own.

Father Thomas Maguire was a tall man with a high, tapering forehead, broad jaws, florid features and a small mouth with tall teeth and, for his proportions, narrow shoulders. He had great abilities, but required the stimulus of another mind to bring them out. The person who did this office for him was Coyne, the publisher, who had an extensive and minute knowledge of old controversial books. He never would ascend the pulpit for these lectures without Richard Coyne, whom he called his father, at his back.

The origin of Maguire's intimacy with Coyne is curious and worth telling. I had it from Coyne at his own table in Maguire's presence. When Maguire was holding his public controversy with Pope, that first made him renowned, Coyne went to see what was going on. He soon observed that Pope was not using his own materials, but was borrowing all his matter from *Lesley's Case Stated*, of which Maguire knew nothing. After the day's discussion was over Coyne went up and introduced himself to Maguire, and asked him to come and dine with him on Sunday. Maguire excused himself, as he must go that day to Maynooth to extract from the Fathers.

'I will give you the Fathers in a nutshell,' replied Coyne. 'Come and you will not repent of it.'

Accordingly Maguire went, and when he entered the house Coyne put a book into his hands, open at a particular page, and asked him to read on from there. As soon as Maguire had read a few pages he fell on his knees and thanked God for the gift. The book was Manning's *Lesley's Case Stated*.[3] In this book the Catholic Controversialist incorporates Lesley's whole text, replying to it not only with great accuracy and ability, but also with a pleasant humour and the *argumentum ad hominem,* in a way that was admirably adapted for the controversial platform. The history of the controversy after this was as follows. Pope retired exhausted to bed, having a friend to read to him from time to time the portion of Lesley required for the morrow, whilst Maguire was working at Manning's reply and prepared himself by a discussion during a walk with Coyne in the Phoenix Park. The result of the controversy was that Pope, who for some time had been a celebrated itinerant controversialist, retired into privacy. He took up residence at Bangor in Wales, and corresponded on friendly terms with Maguire on various points of religion until Maguire's death. Coyne then published a new edition of *Lesley's Case Stated* which he dedicated to Father Maguire as the 'Bossuet[4] of the British churches'.

One anecdote more to exhibit a little of the humour of Maquire's circle and I leave the subject. Always looking after opportunities to add something choice to that library which I left in Australia, I picked up a great rarity in a shop in Dame Street, Dublin. It consisted of most of Martin Luther's publications, the original editions, tracts, pamphlets and sermons without any of those expurgations of his abusive language and obscenities which were effected in the collected editions of his works. They were bound up in a dozen quarto volumes dating from 1519 to 1545, with the curious woodcuts on the title pages, beginning with the tiara, St. Peter's pontifical keys, etc., all such pious emblems as the printer had in stock, but growing more and more anti-Papal as time advanced, until the Pope was at last figured in the most grotesque and diabolical forms. Coyne set his heart on obtaining these books from me for Maquire, and the scheme he adopted was this.

He asked Maguire, myself and a number of our friends to dine, and after dinner he pushed his good claret (wine, however, I never drank, in fact it did not agree with me and I always suffered more or less, even from a single glass). When all were well cheered and in warm fellowship, Coyne suddenly tapped the table and called out to Maquire at the opposite end of it: 'Tom, my son.'

'What, Dickey, my father?'

All were silence and attention.

'Here,' said Coyne, 'is Dr. Ullathorne, who has got possession of a rare collection of the original, unexpunged tracts of Martin Luther, and I am sure he agrees with me that they can in no way be better placed than in the hands of the great controversialist of Ireland. That's you, my son Tom.'

All looked at me, I rose and said: 'My dear Father Maquire, I know how much value you would set on such a collection and how useful it would be in your controversies. The mere exhibition of the woodcuts would be sufficient to reveal the base character of the foul heresiarch who has cast so much confusion into the world. I also know how much my friend, Mr. Coyne, with his great knowledge of controversial books, appreciates the possession of such a book as this. I only know of one copy more of it, and as we are all three agreed upon its value, I think we shall further agree that it is desirable that there should be a copy at each end of the world. My copy shall be packed shortly for Australia.'

I heard a good deal of able and fervid preaching in Dublin such as is not often heard in England, preaching that really went from soul to soul, and was much struck with its many charities, and the spirit with which they were supported. Catholic Dublin is a city of churches, and every Sunday in the year there was a charity sermon for one institution or another. These sermons were always preached at two o'clock to enable persons from all the parishes to attend them. They were preceded and followed by music and singing. Called upon to preach in the Jesuit church for the Institute of the Good Shepherd, which then bore another name, I found it rather a nervous task, especially as many of the city clergy did me the honour to attend, and were seated round the pulpit. That sermon was printed in my volume of *Sermons With Prefaces*. Lucas justly criticised that particular discourse as being too elaborate and as not leaving the story to tell itself in its own simplicity.

With Mrs. Aitkenhead, the foundress of the Dublin Sisters of Charity,[5] I had several long interviews. Being a great sufferer she sat in bed, with a little low table over the bed on which she wrote and had her working materials. She was of a full habit, and much flushed in the face when speaking, which she did with great earnestness and rapidity. She was a shrewd, clever woman, and though bedridden knew everything that passed in the religious world of Dublin, as well as in her own houses. After one of these interviews, I was told, she was so much exhausted that she had generally to go into a warm bath. Her Rule is based upon that of the Jesuits, and a Jesuit Father was her chief assistant in drawing it up. I arranged with her for a filiation of five sisters to accompany me to Sydney, for which the approval of Archbishop Murray was readily obtained.

I also visited Miss McAuley,[6] foundress of the Sisters of Mercy, and saw her surrounded by her first community. But as I then observed them it struck me that there was something much too formal, a defect of freedom, in their tone and bearing. This did not strike me as being the case with the foundress herself, but only in her community. The habit of all sitting formally on the two sides of a long table with writing desks before them gave them the air of so many clerks interrupting their work in the office to have a conversation.

Another acquaintance in Dublin whom I recall with great respect was Father Kenny, the Jesuit, then advanced in years. He was a man who said but little, but was endowed with an eminent wisdom and prudence, as well as sanctity. He was consulted by Bishops as well as by many priests, and was a singularly wise and solid director. I have known several persons placed in distracting, secular positions in life who always ascribed their fidelity to their religion to the early guidance of Father Kenny. He came somewhat late to religion having originally, I was told, been a coachmaker.

The Earl of Mulgrave was at that time the popular Viceroy of Ireland, Lord Morpeth was Secretary, and Mr. Drummond, who took so great an interest in the welfare of the Irish people, was Under-Secretary. There never was an Irish Government so thoroughly adapted to the exigencies and feelings of the country. The Under-Secretary sent for me, and ask me if I would write something calculated to remove from the minds of the people the erroneous impression that Transportation led ultimately to the improving of the convict's condition, and put him in a better state than fell to the lot of honest labourers at home. I promised to do so, and wrote a little pamphlet entitled *The Horrors of Transportation*. I got it put up in type at Coyne's, sent a copy of it to the Secretary, and said that it was entirely at the service of Government. When Lord Morpeth had read it, he directed a large quantity, some twenty thousand copies, to be printed and had it sent in quantities to all the parish clergy and the gaols throughout the country. I have no copy of this production, and I have not seen it for many years, but it was supposed by the clergy to have exercised a useful influence. But it is time to conclude these reminiscences of Dublin, where I passed so many profitable and pleasant days, and where I found so much co-operation in the object of my mission.

Notes

1   Mss.1. gives Bishop Kinsella of Kilkenny.
2   Mss.1. has Father Coffin.
3   Charles Leslie or Lesley (1650–1722), a non-juror (and a forebear of Shane Leslie, editor of *From Cabin boy to Archbishop*), the presumed author of *The case stated between the Church of Rome and the Church of England*. The repost referred to as *The Reply* was by Robert Manning, whose date of birth is not known. He was educated at Douay where he was later Professor of Humanity and Philosophy. On his return to England he appears to have been Chaplain to Lord Petre. He died in 1731.
4   Jacques Bénigne Bossuet (1627–1704), French preacher and Bishop of Meaux who, both in content and delivery, is still considered one of the greatest of pulpit orators.
5   Mary Aitkenhead (1787–1858), Sister Mary Augustine in Religion. She was chosen by Archbishop Murray of Dublin to carry out his plan of founding the Congregation in Dublin. The first members took their vows in 1815. In 1831, over-exertion and disease shattered her health, leaving her an invalid.
6   Catherine Elizabeth McAuley (1788–1841), founded the Congregation in Dublin in 1827. The Sisters were introduced into Australia in 1846 and into New Zealand in 1849. They still have many houses in those countries.

Chapter Twenty-Six

England

In the early part of 1838 I was summoned to give evidence before Sir William Molesworth's Committe on Transportation. The pamphlet I had written on the Australian Mission had awakened attention, and without my knowing it Dr. Lingard, the historian of England, had written a letter to a Member of Parliament recommending that I should be examined before that Committee. On my arrival in London Sir William Molesworth invited me by note to a private interview. I went to his house and was amused to find him in a dandy silk dressing gown, covered with flowers like a garden, and tied tight with a silk cord with flowing tassels. He had my pamphlet before him, and tried to coach me up as to the best way of giving evidence. When we came to a very embarrassing[1] point, I told him it was doubtful whether I ought to speak on it. He pulled up his head, gave me a menacing look, and said: 'Do you know how grave would be the consequence of your refusing?'

I looked into his eyes whilst replying: 'You have read that book and ought to know that I am not a man to be talked to in that way.'

He tried to laugh it off, and I said to him gravely: 'At present I have conscientious doubts whether I ought to speak on that subject. I will consult some of our best theologians and act on their advice.' The printed evidence itself will show in what manner both the Chairman and myself approached that subject, and how I contrived to throw the weight of the testimony on other shoulders. Before the Committee, being in a new position, full of matter, and like a young soldier for the first time under fire, somewhat excited, I spoke with such rapidity that I had to be repeatedly stopped by the members, that the reporter might be able to record the words. The report of that Committee forms a large volume, and in the appendix will be found a good deal of my correspondence with the Secretary for the Colonies concerning the clergy whom I sent out from time to time.

Knowing the importance of interesting Members of Parliament in my transactions with the Government, I made it a point to sit in the Strangers' Gallery on most nights of that winter during the debates. Sometimes Mr. Philip Howard would come up and sit with me, sometime Mr. O'Connell,[2] sometimes others; but the man I found most difficult to converse with was Mr. Shiel, who then held office, but who was too quick and restless to listen to details, and wanted to jump to conclusions at once. Avoiding obtrusiveness, I took every opportunity of studying men and things, but I learnt more of the ways of Parliament in its routine business, than during great debates; although Parliament was very different then to what it is now. Then, during great debates, everyone was absorbed and there was no speaking to anyone. I witnessed remarkable scenes and exhibitions of character in the old house of St. Stephen's,[3] but this is not the place in which to record them.

I must not forget to notice the invaluable services of Mr. Howard of Carlisle during the whole of my mission to England, he was always at my service with his kindness and industry, and I took the first opportunity on my return to inform the Catholics of Australia of what he had done for them.

At this time Sir Richard Bourke was attacked in certain letters to the *Times*, to which I wrote a reply that was well received in New South Wales.

I obtained, sent out, or took out with me fifteen priests, four of whom became Bishops at a later period, five Church students prepared to begin their philosophy, five Sisters of Charity from Mrs. Aitkenhead's convents in Dublin, and two or three school-masters, one of whom became the able editor of the first Catholic newspaper in Sydney. It cost nearly £2,000 in passage money to convey all these people to Sydney. A fair amount of this, however, was paid by the Government. Lord Glenelg was then Secretary for the Colonies, and Sir George Grey[4] was Under-Secretary. But the man who really pulled the wires in that office was Mr. Stephens, well known in the Colonies under the name of King Stephens, as he was supposed to have been long supreme in that department.

I had one rather curious correspondence with Lord Glenelg. I was very anxious to get a priest allowed by Government for the penal settlement of Norfolk Island, with a proper salary and passage and outfit paid by the Colonial Office. We intended to send two, but could only expect to have one supported by Government. The usual allowance for passage and outfit for a clergyman in a colony was £150, but that was paid from the Colonial revenues. When I had got the priest, I was informed that he would be only allowed £100 for his expenses. This nettled me a good deal. He had to travel a thousand miles further after he reached Sydney, and it was on record that such was the impression about that dreadful class of cannibals in that solitary place that no Anglican clergyman could be induced to go to it at that time, and they were obliged to be content with the services of a dissenting minsters (*vid.* correspondence of Sir Richard Bourke in Appendix to Transportation Committee of 1836). I therefore paid the priest for Norfolk Island his £150 and sent him on his way. I then wrote to Lord Gelenelg, told him what I had done, represented the much greater sacrifices that awaited him, besides his having to undertake a second voyage, and added that unless the additional £50 were paid I should have to beg it of friends, and that I was sure it was not the intention of Government that I should fit out the servant of Government with the beggings of charity. The result was that the other £50 were paid.

Having occasion to call on Sir George Grey, who was then new in the office of Under-Secretary, I was received with an amusing check. Instead of waiting to hear my business, by the time I had reached his official table he had pulled himself up into what some people would call great dignity, and said: 'We never interfere between a priest and his Bishop.'

'Pardon me,' I said. 'I am well aware of that. But I call as the representative of the Bishop of Sydney, and am known to Lord Glenelg, with whom I have had several transactions.' He then entered into business.

I must mention here that I had obtained the services of the Rev. Francis Murphy, then senior priest of St. Patrick's, Liverpool who, having been educated at Maynooth, went over to that College and there induced several young priests to join him.

I had a curious interview with Bishop Baines. Dr. Brindle had called on me in London and asked if on my next visit to Downside I would call at Prior Park as Dr. Baines particularly wished to see me. I did so accordingly. I found his Lordship residing in the little cottage called the Priory, with Miss Crewe. It was very handsomely furnished. The Bishop said he had two priests to offer me who would be useful in Australia. I asked their names, and on hearing them I said: 'One I do not know, but as to the other, I knew him formerly as a layman when he was fond of ardent spirits, and I am surprised he was ever ordained. Let me say that I feel a great weight of responsibility upon me, and if I take out one priest to disgrace himself I shall do more harm than I can do good for the rest of my life.'

He said there had been some weakness in these men, but nothing so very grave. That in a country where most of the Catholics were Irishmen, if anything happened the people covered it over and would not see it. This speech moved me inwardly, and more so when, seeking for a letter of the priest unknown to me, he put the wrong one into my hands by mistake.

I said: 'Your Lordship need look no further. He says in this letter that he is without money, friends, or character. I do not forget Bishop Griffith's advice to me when I first reached London. He said: "Put not your trust either in Bishops or Archbishops."'

At this his Lordship reddened, so I concluded: 'I think that was sound advice. A Bishop is apt to think that a man who has failed with him may succeed elsewhere.' We lunched and then parted.

The English Vicars-Apostolic I met assembled at York. They were very kind but, though several English priests and divines offered themselves to me, and that with earnestness, owing to the wants in England I only succeeded in obtaining two. My invariable plan was to put all the difficulties and labours of the Mission before those who offered themselves, and none of the advantages. By this means I secured volunteers who were animated with the spirit of self-sacrifice.

I also assisted at the opening of the chapel of New Oscott[5] at which all the Bishops were present, as well as a hundred priests. On that occasion the more ample form of vestments was first introduced in place of the old form derived from France. Pugin,[6] with his dark, flashing eyes and tears on his cheeks, superintended the procession of the clergy; he was in raptures and declared that it was the greatest day for the Church of England since the Reformation. Dr. Rock, who had been Pugin's assistant in the restoration of Gothic

Art, was conspicuous by the novelty, to English eyes, of a black *zuchetto*, or skull cap, and when somebody asked Mr. McDonald which was Dr. Rock, he replied: 'The man with the pickled walnut on his head.' It was an enthusiastic gathering from all parts of England, and Dr. Weedall[7] preached an elaborate discourse on Catholic education.

Notes

1 The word delicate is deleted here in Ms.2., and embarrassing substituted. (The incident isn't reported in Mss.1). The problem which Ullathorne refers to is homosexual practices among the convicts, a problem which greatly concerned him at this time [see Hughes, *The Fatal Shore* pp. 264ff (London 1987)].

2 Daniel O'Connell (1775–1847), 'The Uncrowned King of Ireland'. He had been elected to Westminster in 1828.

3 The Palace of Westminster had been virtually destroyed by fire in 1834. Only Westminster Hall and fragments of the cloister and the former chapel of St. Stephen, the House of Commons, remained.

4 Sir George Gray (1812–1898), later made Governor of South Australia (1840) and twice Governor of New Zealand, and was also its Prime Minister (1877–79). He received his knighthood in 1848 so was still Minister at the time Ullathorne met him.

5 St. Mary's College, on the outskirts of Birmingham. It was founded in 1793 as an establishment for the education of the sons of the Catholic nobility and the clergy in an English atmosphere. Hitherto most students were sent abroad but the French Revolution had changed that. It was very successful and this New Oscott was a grander building two miles from the old college.

6 Augustus Welby Northmore Pugin (1812–1852), one of the great British architects of the 19th century. He converted to Catholicism in 1834 and taught for a while at Oscott.

7 Dr. Weedle was the principal of the College at the time.

Chapter Twenty-Seven

Return Voyage to Australia

I now began to prepare for my departure. All the priests whom I had enlisted had already started in two groups, at different intervals, except two. These and the five Sisters of Charity, and the Church students, joined me in London, and we embarked on the *Sir Francis Spaight* at Gravesend towards the end of July.

When we got afloat I scanned out fellow passengers with some solicitude, and took measure of the Captain. He was a big, soft sort of man without much inward strength of character. The first mate was a lump. He proved incompetent to manage the crew or the ship, and was put out of office, living secluded in his cabin for most of the voyage, whilst the second mate, a brother of the Captain, a very nice, quite a gentlemanly man, took his place.

As to the passengers, who were sufficiently numerous to crowd the cabin table, they were a very mixed assortment, and much inferior as a whole to those I met on my former voyage. Most of my companions of my former voyage were educated persons, including three university men. Here there was not much of that sort. Some were young men, evidently sent out to amend themselves. One was an American with his wife, son and daughter, who came on board with one name on his luggage and the title of American Consul which he changed, effacing the Consul also, as soon as we were out of the Channel. The rest were quiet and harmless persons enough, but placed in a situation of first-class passengers to which they were not accustomed.

To my surprise I also found that one young priest, nephew of a Bishop, had brought his sister with him, which I only discovered after we had got to sea. She was a respectable, fine looking, well educated girl but awkwardly placed, especially as both she and her brother were country brought up,

168

and ignorant of the ways of the world. The other priest was Father, afterwards Bishop, Geoghegan, an experienced man on whom I could rely.

I saw very soon that I should have an anxious voyage, and that I must make some stringent regulations at once. The nuns had two large stern cabins. They would necessarily hear all that passed in the main cabin, but that could not be avoided. I arranged for them to retire from table immediately after the cloth was drawn. Three of the number were happily of mature age. I had myself a large private cabin, where I could muster my little flock and say Mass, which I did every morning when the sea was tolerably calm. The chalice was on the altar only when wanted, and held on the foot by another priest, firmly secured in a corner. As for myself, I could always rely on my sea legs, and on my feeling by the soles of the feet what a ship was going to do next in the way of motion. Hence I had no fear of accidents. For the nuns' confessions, it would not do to bring them down to my cabin when no one else was there, so I determined on a bold course, but one which from its regular recurrence would explain that I had some duty to perform. Every Saturday, immediately after breakfast, I walked into one of these two private cabins with a book under my arm. They all then went into the adjoining cabin, coming to me one after the other. Twice a day at a fixed time, they came on deck for an hour or so, and I always arranged to be with or near them. It was soon comprehended that they did not converse on deck with the other passengers but only at table, except now and then a little with the female passengers and by a tacit understanding that part of the deck was then left to them and to me.

As to the Church students, I began with them their course of logic, giving them exemption from school whenever the topsails got a reefing, and they soon learned to understand when that process was going on. I also gave them spiritual instructions and we all made a retreat. Thus we sped for five months and a half, in the old fashion before the circular system of sailing was introduced, touching at no port on the way. But as I had anticipated, from time to time we had our troubles. Attempts were made to play on the simplicity of my young men for the purpose of extracting amusement. By a little extra gravity, however, with the offenders and one or two private admonitions to their butts[1] I got that stopped.

The American, a thorough bully and a vain creature to boot, was fond of inventing little schemes of annoyance, first against some defenceless person and then another, enjoying them privately afterwards with some of the young and thoughtless men. For example, carving one of the chief dishes, he would send to a female, and even to a man, a lump of fat and little else. There were a couple of very simple men, shy from the newness of their style of life, to whom he would do the same. I had to watch and get this put right by sending back the plate. One very quiet man was so provoked by incessant insults in this and other ways to his equally quiet and patient wife that he could stand it no longer and, as they came on deck, in his boiling indignation he struck the insulter a blow with all his strength on the neck. The daughter of the American rushed down screaming to my cabin and implored me to come up as her father had drawn a big knife. With quiet steps and grave face I mounted to the quarter-deck. The poor man who had struck the avenging blow was cowering at the stern by the man at the wheel. The broad-built Yankee sat on his companion seat with swelled-out lips and distorted eyes, giving diabolical looks at the poor fellow in the intervals of whetting a long blade on his boot thrown up on his knee. The passengers about were in consternation. The Captain was out of sight. I walked slowly up and down for a time, keeping a fixed eye on the American as I approached him, until I saw him begin to tame, and then said to the other man: 'Go down to your cabin.' Taking the widest berth of his opponent, he went. Gradually the American cooled, shut up his long knife, and I left him. We heard no more of it.

One poor man got nervous with the idea of pirates, and the Captain was foolish enough to enter into the humour of these men, got up a sort of a sham fight after dark, firing off his two cannon and his muskets, bringing the seamen into the poor joke, and stunning the poor man with pistols fired close to his head, thus exposing him to the ridicule of the whole ship.

The next mischief was a story cooked up by the American that the priest's sister had stolen some of his wife's silk stockings. It got all about the cabins. Her brother was a spirited young man but too unused to the world to manage a matter like this. Although this innocent and well-behaved girl had come without my knowledge and I found it inconvenient enough, yet her protection now required that I should henceforth take charge of her. I arranged this with her brother, and then faced the American. I took the accuser under the lee of the long-boat, where I asked him for his proofs. He stammered and could give nothing but conjecture. I told him plainly that unless the matter was put right within four and twenty hours I should hold him responsible. The next morning at breakfast there was an apology. His wife said she was 'very sorry but they had found the stockings under the bed.' After that I put this young person in the care of the nuns, and she joined their Order on reaching Sydney, and became a valuable Religious.

We were quiet for some weeks after this, and then the Devil turned up in a new shape. By a little scheming the soft-hearted, soft-headed Captain was got to pay special attentions to one of the younger nuns. She was more clever and witty than she was altogether wise, though a woman of good education. At first these things were too slight to take hold of, but they grew, and everyone that had eyes must observe it. The other Religious were very anxious, but my hints and then plain words seemed not to go to this consecrated nun under solemn vows as much as they ought to have done. I saw the Captain one evening take her shawl and put it on her as she came out of the cabin to join her sisters. I went down to my cabin, turned the subject over in my mind, had a good cry which I had not had since I was a little boy, and then screwed myself up, and through the steward sent a message to the Captain that I wished to see him in my private cabin. He came, and I had it out with him very plainly, and to clinch the matter I told him that I knew there had been a sort of conspiracy to force him to run into the Cape of Good Hope for provisions, that it was merely a scheme to see the Cape, that I had been asked to join it, that I had replied that I knew the ship was well provisioned, and disapproved of the proposal; that, moreover, I knew my name had been used with him as if I had been the chief promoter of the scheme to turn him aside in his voyage. He was completely moved, and declared that Mr. --- was the most deceitful man he had ever come across.

'Then, Captain,' I said, 'as your eyes are opened, know your true friends, and let us have no more annoyance. You ought to know how much your return-cabins will depend for their being filled on my report of you at Sydney.' We had no more trouble with the Captain, but one more vile act on the part of the other man. He induced two young giddy fellows to pitch overboard certain conveniences belonging to the ladies, which the steward put on the forecastle daily for purification. For this vile act, attended with so much inconvenience for the rest of the voyage, I was determined to put him and all his belongings into Coventry. I arranged it with my own people, and the other decent persons on board were too glad to follow suit. At dinner we spoke not to them, nor on deck, and if he tried to start a conversation with anyone I turned my back towards him, led off the conversation with someone else in another direction, and reduced him to a nonentity. This continued until we reached Sydney.

I have been thus long in this narrative to show how hard the Devil tried to annoy the first nuns that ever entered upon the New World. I must say that for once I was glad to get to the end of a long voyage.

Yet despite these disagreeables it must not be supposed that all was disagreeable. We had our pleasant days, and even weeks, and the majority of the passengers were good, inoffensive people, only the most of them were too simple or too little-spirited to put down these offences by the force of a common action. We had also our diversifications. For example, in a dead calm, surrounded by a number of albatrosses, that most magnificent of sea-birds, some floating on the water, some flying in the air, some hauled on the deck with a fishing-line, others, poor wretches, being shot with rifle balls, I read to the Sisters Coleridge's *Ancient Mariner* as they sat on the deck. And so touching proved the wondrous tale under the circumstances that their eyes dropped tears of compassion. And long after they were wont to murmur the closing lines:

> He prayeth best who loveth best
> All thing both great and small:
> For the dear God who loveth us
> He made and loveth all.

Another day, when there was half a breeze and the sea was moderately up, a white or sperm whale was gambolling about the ship; what he took us for I never ascertained, but in one of his plunges he came up right under the ship and struck us underneath, tossing up the ship and heaving her over on the side as if we ourselves had struck a rock. The man at the helm thoughtlessly ran from his post to look over the counter, which made the position yet more nervous, until a thundering volley of oaths sent him back again, and another man to help him. The Captain was terribly excited, the crew in consternation. I got the Sisters and priests by the bulwarks amidships to see the monster, who disentangled himself after a few instants and lifted his huge head close up the side of the ship, so that they could almost touch it, as it rose, covered with what looked like weed and barnacles. He then got himself clear to windwards of the ship; and how he did sport and blow and spout after his accident. Everyone was relieved and drew an easier breath, and a smart young fellow said: 'I should not like to sleep in the same cabin as him!'

'Why not?'

'If that's his breathing, what must be his snoring?'

The laugh at this joke broke down the suspense and set all minds free again. The Captain, though alarmed, was prompt in trimming off the ship. Though a long piece of softness, he was a good sailor.

The only thing like this that I remember was when a lad in the Mediterranean. It was fine weather, and we were most of us below at tea, when the brig was suddenly struck as against a rock. We rushed up and there was a big grampus that had struck the vessel amidships; he raised his giant body into the air, fell splash upon the water, and went on blowing with redoubled energy. He had left his mark, however, on the copper.

Many years ago a whaler was actually sunk by a sperm whale. She was a cranky old craft, commanded by Captain Rankin. When a calf-whale is caught the cow-whale will follow the ship. It was so in this case. The mother-whale, furious at having lost her young one, attacked the ship, came again and again at her hull, until with her ivory horn she stove in her timbers, and as the vessel was sinking the crew took to their boats, and had to pull some three hundred miles before reaching the Australian coast; after which Captain Rankin gave up the sea and established a cheese factory near Bathurst, the only one of any importance in the Colony. In my days Rankin's cheese was to Australians what Stilton is to Englishmen.

One episode more and I have finished with this voyage. The Captain got very angry with the man at the wheel one day and struck him a blow. The man said calmly: 'Captain, if you do it again I shall be obliged to defend myself.' He did, and the man returned the blow. Of course, the mates were summoned and he was put in irons and lodged on the quarter-deck. I forget how, but there had been some ill blood and two other men had been put into irons. The men were very determined to hold out peaceably and bring an action against the Captain on arriving in Sydney, and their comrades, who could speak to them when at the wheel, encouraged them to stand out and remain in their irons. The Captain got very anxious about the consequences. He had already had his chief mate deposed, and it was awkward that his brother was the only man to take his place. The two senior Sisters of Charity felt much for the poor men and at last mustered courage to ask the Captain to allow them to try their influence on the men. The Captain was too glad of the offer but had the imprudence, in his anxiety, to peep through the cabin window to see how they succeeded, and the men perceived him there, which spoiled the whole thing.

When the sisters came to them the men rose up, uncovered, and said: 'Ladies, we have no words to say how much all the men reverence you. We know that you have given up every-thing for the sake of poor people and that you are our true friends.'

Their gentle persuasions failed nevertheless, the men declaring that they were acting on the advice of their comrades and, though they would act quietly, and disturb no one, they felt it their duty to hold out and get righted in Sydney. Next morning I asked the Captain if he would put the affair in my hands for half an hour and act on my advice. He was glad to do so, so I then went to the men, sat among them and said something like this. 'Now, mates, I have been a sailor like you, and have furled many a topsail. My heart always warms to a sailor. The Captain was wrong to strike the man at the wheel, but I don't think you know how to go about these things. I know Sydney better than you. If you land as pris-oners you will have the ship agents, the consignees, against you. They will get learned lawyers and you'll have nothing but land-sharks. And you'll get all the worse for holding out against your duty. If your irons are taken off, and you return to your duty, you will still have your case if you choose to follow; and won't be in a worse, but in a better position.' I then went to the Captain and said: 'Now, Captain, if you will send your mates to take off those men's chains, and you say quietly to them: "Now men, will you go to your duty?" I think they will obey you.' This was done, and being good-hearted fellows they soon forgot all about their grievance.

On December 31st, 1838, we reached Sydney, having been five months and a half on the voyage.

When we landed, and the nuns were lowered in the swing-chair over the sides into the boat, all the crew stood alongside the bulwarks with their caps off, saying in subdued tones: 'God bless you, ladies! God bless you, ladies!'

The Captain was invited by the Bishop to dine once more with the Sisters before entering their convent, along with my other companions, at his residence, and a sumptuous dinner was prepared, but so shy and ashamed was he, I suppose by reason of certain reminiscences, that, although the real object of this dinner was to part with him kindly, there was no getting him to feel his natural freedom, or putting him into any shape of ease.

Notes

1   i.e. the Church students; the butt of their jokes.

Chapter Twenty-Eight

Work Again in Australia

Scarcely had I landed a day, when I found that I was, and for some time had been, the object of universal indignation in the Colony, and indeed throughout the other penal settlements.[1] Several chief officials and other leading men had given evidence, and that in language both plain and strong, on the evils and vices of the convict system, before Parliament as well as myself; but I had been selected as scapegoat for all. Others they ironed, me they resolved to skin. Besides my very plain evidence, there was my little book, *The Catholic Mission in Australasia,* which had been got hold of, extracted from, and in the usual newspaper fashion distorted in garbled extracts with sinister comments. It must be remembered that the Australian Press was to that of England in those days, what Australian society was to English. Nor did it slacken the fire of that burning anger, which was by no means put on, as far as the colonists were concerned, that I had associated my statements and my judgements of the way in which some forty or fifty thousand criminals were managed, with the interests of the Catholic Religion, and had succeeded, as their organs said, by that very means, in procuring the ecclesiastical aid of which we stood in need.

I had deeply wounded both freemen and emancipists in two ways, had touched them in two most sensitive points, in their pride and in their pockets. I had made the degrading state of things widely known at home, and indeed throughout Europe, and I had exposed the evils and vicious results of the assignment system. But on the continuance of that system depended the principal wealth both of emigrants and emancipated criminals. The land derived its value from the number of convicts that its owners could get assigned to them. Thus they got work without paying wages and the more criminals, the more wealth. Moreover, trade and manufacture depended on the same resource, and even the domestic servants of both sexes were assigned criminals. But the system had already, after the evidence given against it, been vigorously attacked in Parliament and in the British Press, and its reformation was already looming in the prospect.

In the Colonial Legislature the subject of the evidence had also been discussed before my return. Even then I became a special object of warm animadversion, and my old friend, Attorney-General Plunkett, a man of the highest character and the only Catholic there, defended me in such a hesitating half-and-half style, that it made things look all the worse. When my pamphlet was so mangled and misrepresented by the Press, the Bishop had an edition printed in Sydney, with a view of correcting these false statements by its issue, but as the assault grew more furious, he did not venture to put it out, and I found the copies all carefully packed up in a store-room.

My landing was a signal for the storm to rage anew, and the newspapers daily gave me a vast deal of notoriety. I had often half a dozen columns in the daily Press collectively to my personal share, and they insisted that I had exposed the Colony for my own purposes. No one defended me, no one stood by me. The Bishop and the clergy were dismayed. All held their tongues; and so did I. Judge Therry, however, who was more thoroughly versed in the criminal history of the country than any other man, told me that every word I had written was true, and that if I retracted a syllable of it, he would never forgive me. I had no intention of doing so. One step, however, we were compelled to take, and it resulted in great advantages to the Catholic body. Hitherto the Catholics had supported the *Australian*, a newspaper written by a very clever barrister, the son of Judge Stephens. But this paper attacked more furiously than the rest, even than the one edited by the notorious Dr. Lang, the chief Presbyterian Minister, and a violent politician. Stephens went so far as to attack the Bishop as well as myself, and held him up to ridicule. In consequence of this I and another priest went to the office and asked whether they intended to continue that policy, in which case the Catholics must establish a newspaper for themselves. I added: 'I am fair game, but you have no right to attack the Bishop.'

They did not believe we would or could establish a paper, and though they apologised to the Bishop, they took the words from my mouth that I was fair game, adopted it as a test, and went on more merrily than before. Then a few Catholics met, put down funds, and started a newspaper, giving the editorship to a Mr. Duncan, a shrewd, clever Scotch convert from Presbyterianism, whom I had brought out as a schoolmaster, and he gave blow for blow. The chief value of this move was that the Catholics now had an organ, and one which soon exercised a considerable political influence.

Various public matters with which I had to deal later on increased my popular unpopularity, and I grew before the public eye into a species of monster to be pointed at as I passed, and shunned. But going up the river one day to Parramatta, on a somewhat crowded steamboat, after a group of settlers had, by their glances, let me know that I was the object of discussion, one of them stepped up to me and said: 'We can't forgive you, sir, because what you said was all true, and that makes it the worse for us. We could have dealt with a pack of lies like the "Major's".' The person here alluded to had given his evidence in a most exaggerated style, and had published a book in England which had brought him into court for libel. The settler thus gave an unexpected but honest statement of the case.

But, besides the external difficulty of my position, I soon found that I had also internal difficulties to meet where I least expected them, and these fairly brought upon me at last a consciousness of internal anxiety, a sense of which I had never had much awakened in me before. The time has come for me to go into these matters, cost what they may, for they are the only solution that can be presented of my subsequent history, and can alone explain my return to England at a subsequent period.

Some years ago, the official Chronologist of the English Benedictines wrote and asked me to give him a sketch of my Bishop, and especially of my reasons for leaving Australia, adding the reason which he had heard alleged for that step. I replied, declining the request, and adding that the motive he had heard had a shadow of truth in it, but was inaccurately apprehended, and only entered, besides, among the minor and subordinate motives. The real facts will come out in some degree in the course of the narrative.

I had forgotten to state in its due place that I had visited Norfolk Island a second time, a little prior to my going to England, in company with a Special Commission, consisting of judge, lawyers, and a military jury. I was received with

joy by my former penitents, most of whom had persevered
in their resolutions, and had stood to their religious practices
despite the ridicule of their companions. Nearly sixty of them
had learned to read their prayers. The Commandant whose
hospitality I again enjoyed, assured me that crime had considerably diminished, and to my delight I found that for the
fifteen months that had passed since my first visit, there was
not a single Catholic brought before the judge.

A short account of that visit will be found in *The Catholic
Mission in Australasia*, a copy of which is attached to this
manuscript and should be kept with it.

On reaching Sydney I found that Father McEncroe and
Mr. Gregory, afterwards Abbot Gregory, had been placed
at Norfolk Island to take charge of the mission amongst the
criminals in that settlement. Mr. Gregory, although ordained,
had still to study his theology. Had they been in Sydney I
think the state of things might have been different. But I had
scarcely been half a dozen days on shore when I found that
two priests whom I had sent out, both of mature age, and
residing with the Bishop, exercised great influence over him.
One of them had chief charge of the cathedral mission, the
other managed a school in the Bishop's residence. I found
that, although Vicar-General, and although the weight of all
grave business in the diocesan administration was still vested
in me, I was not to have the position which the responsibility
laid on me required.

The first sign of a change of relations exhibited itself in a
request that I would give an account of all I had received and
expended in my absence. This was so completely alien from the
confidence that had existed between the Bishop and myself,
that I knew it had been prompted by these two clergymen,
and indeed it was admitted. I could only say that whatever I
had received I had paid to Dr. Heptonstall, the Bishop's per-
manent agent in London, that I had left Sydney with nothing,
had almost entirely met my personal expenses from my Government salary. I had sent out fifteen priests, five Sisters of
Charity, five Church students and some school teachers, had
arranged for all except the students being supported on Government funds, and had brought nothing back of my own
except a few books, part of which had been presented to me
by Propaganda, and that whatever remained over and above
what had been expended, would have been accounted for in
Dr. Heptonstall's accounts.

I had deposited all I had collected with him in the first instance, and had drawn on him as money was required to pay the passage of those I sent out, who were not paid for by Government, or to purchase church furniture etc., for the missions. This explanation over, the Bishop wanted me to go to Parramatta, where I should be able to take care of the nuns I had brought out.

They were required to visit and instruct the great central female prison at Parramatta, called the Factory, and they were also to teach the school there. I was to visit the Bishop in Sydney once a week for the purpose of talking over administrative business and writing the Government correspondence. To this arrangement I consented without hesitation. I had brought the nuns out expressly with a view to that work, and I had already built a church in Parramatta, and a good schoolhouse had been raised close beside. It was understood before I left for England that a Mr. William Davis, a wealthy emancipist, would provide the convent for the nuns, and he paid the value of a good house and garden for them, very near the church. I had to rent a very inferior cottage, the only place I could get at all near. I also took a young Irish priest with me chiefly to teach him his theology. Of course, I maintained him. He also went back to do duty at the Liverpool Hospital occasionally. One day he came back, having gone the night previously, entering the house wringing wet, and looking very pale and haggard. I saw something had happened, and waited for him to say what it was, but he kept silent. He could not, however, resist telling the nuns. It was his first ride in the Bush and he got his imagination stirred with fear of the blacks. Night drew on before he reached Liverpool, and rain began to fall, and so vividly was his imagination stirred that he backed his horse under a tree, fancying every moment that the natives were coming to spear him. So there he stood all night, hearing the great clock of the hospital strike each hour and not venturing to proceed until daylight came, when he rode on, did the duty he went upon, and then returned half dead with the effect of his nocturnal fears, and the rain which had poured all night upon him. He had a habit of studying with a music-box always going to soothe him, so I got the old tunes stealing through his door on my own ears for half the day.

The influence of Sisters upon the women in prison soon told upon the entire colony, from which, and to which, they were constantly coming and going. And the magistrates repeatedly bore testimony to their services from the bench. There were commonly as many as 1,500 women in this prison, five or six hundred of whom were Catholic. The prisoners were distributed among its three well-known wards or classes.

All the Sisters went to this establishment at six o'clock in the morning for an hour, and again at six o'clock at night. They sat on chairs in the middle of the yard, and the women sat round them on the gravel, taking one group one day, another another, until all were gone through. I, of course, at my hours, took the Confessional. One of the nuns' great difficulties was to prevent these poor creatures telling their confessions to them, which some were very anxious to do.

As I did not like the nuns always walking home at night in the dusk over the same unprotected ground, without some security, especially as convict men or ticket-of-leave men used to hang about the walls outside to establish communications with the women within, I generally walked on and accompanied them back, or continued to have my own work there so as to walk in silence near them on their return. They began, however, to think that this looked awkward, gave me a hint of their feeling, and I desisted. But before a week was over, as they were walking along, they met a man dressed in woman's clothes, who passed them in a way that startled them. Then they sent me a note, that they saw the prudence of their being protected, and begged of me to accompany them home as before. I consented on condition that they all expressed that wish to me in writing, that I might hold a testimony of the need to which they were put.

The work at the Factory was very laborious and often distressing, but it was amply repaid. The third-class prisoners were the worst, their heads were shaved, and this was never done without a great struggle, showing how women, under all circumstances, will cherish their hair. Then their work was coarse, some of them were set to break stones for the public roads. Then, again, the second-class consisted of unfortunates nursing their children, and their attachment to these poor children often led to severe quarrels and fights between the mothers about their food, or bits of clothing, or their own little quarrels amongst each other, and of course their language was what they were.

I was preaching to the third-class women in my familiar way on one occasion when from the other side of the wall sprang up a great howling, shrieking and swearing amongst

the nursing women. The mass of poor creatures before me
began in various subdued ways to express their horror at this
conduct. I improved the occasion, told them it was very much
what they did themselves many a time when my eyes were
not upon them, and that I wished they would just see themselves in it. Then some began to cry, and most of the rest
joined in sympathy, and I left them. But somehow they got
the notion that this ordinary quarrel in the other ward was
got up to annoy the priest, and that night they got into the
other ward, and there was such a fight and pulling off caps
that half a dozen had to be taken to the hospital, and several
others were severely injured. All this reached the ears of the
nuns, and the matron told it to me. On another occasion the
third-class women jammed up the matron in a corner and cut
all the hair off her head.

Years before they had broken out to see the races and it took
several days to get them back again. Old Mr. Marsden, senior
Protestant Chaplain of the Colony, and chairman of the committee of management, told me that they were at a certain time
in such a state of rebellion that he had to send for the troops.
They were in the stone-breaking yard, the troops drawn up
within the gates, with fixed bayonets, and the women took
the stones and pelted the soldiers as they stood in their ranks.
The captain in command said: 'We can't fire on, or bayonet
the women. What are we to do?'

The clergyman, an old magistrate, replied: 'Drive them in
with their own weapons.' So, as he told me, the soldiers
actually pelted the women into their ward-room, where they
were then locked up. But the influence of the Sisters, most
of them mature in age, and well-named, besides belonging to
respectable families, effected a change of spirit amongst the
Catholics which did not fail to communicate an improved tone
to the entire establishment.

Sir George and Lady Gipps[2] showed their appreciation
of the sisters by repeatedly calling upon them, when at
their country house at Parramatta; sent them presents from
their garden, and would have invited them in a quiet way
to their mansion, only they received hints that it would
be against their rule. And here I may mention that, on
their arrival the Governor expressed to me his readiness to
allow them pensions, but as they refused to accept their
passage and outfit from the Colonial office, to the great
surprise of Lord Glenelg, so they declined the offer of

the Governor, thinking it best to keep themselves independent.

Notes

1   All manifestations of public feeling were not, however, so hostile. The Bishop has forgotten to allude to a great meeting of Catholics held on January 6th, 1839, in the course of which many fervent expressions of gratitude were offered in acknowledgement of his great services to the Church in Australia. Alluding to his recent visit to England, Mr. Justice Therry reminded them that it had been undertaken solely for the spiritual benefit of the Catholic community, and not for the advancement of any commercial interest. 'I never once inquired how wool was sold at Garraway's'.

    In his reply Dr. Ullathorne took up this remark. 'Mr. Therry has observed,' he said, 'that whilst in Europe I never mentioned the price of wool, though doubtless I was often questioned about it. This is quite true. "How is land selling in New South Wales?" some person's would ask me; and I would reply that I had been so much occupied with the cultivation of sheep that I had not paid much attention to land. "Well, then, how is wool selling?" "Why, you will think it strange," I would reply, "but though my flocks are numerous, they don't bear wool, and if they did we should not fleece them."' – Kenny, *History of Catholicity in Australia*. (Note by Mother Drane.)

2   Sir George Gipps succeeded Sir Richard Bourke as Governor of the Colony.

Chapter Twenty-Nine

To Adelaide

I went to Sydney frequently, for the Bishop often needed me for one thing or another, and occasionally, when there, the Governor would send for me. For example, my old acquaintance Archdeacon Broughton had become the first Anglican Bishop of Australia, and the equal position awarded by Government to the Catholic Bishop was not palatable to him. And when our Bishop appeared at the Levee for the Queen's birthday in his rochet and purple soutane, the Protestant Bishop sent in a formal protest against it. The Governor sent for me to talk over the matter. He had evidently no personal objections, for he said the only thing that struck him was that it was a very pretty dress. For he was aware that the Bishop was backed in his protest by a party of zealous Anglican officials, and as his protest had received but little attention he requested that it should be referred to the Home Government. Consequently, we sent a document to the Governor in which it was stated that, properly, the robes in question were the domestic wear of a Catholic Bishop, and so far from being *appropriate* to a Bishop, they were worn by certain other ecclesiastics of lower rank, and even by canons. The two documents were sent home together, and in course of time the reply came from the Colonial Office, that as the Catholic Bishop had stated that the robes worn at the Levee were not appropriate to a Bishop, there was no question to go before the legal adviser of the Crown. But, to prevent all further nonsense on the subject, the Bishop went henceforth to the Levee in coat and feriola.

At the Bishop's request I gave a retreat to the clergy of the diocese, assembled at his residence. The priest, however, to whom I have alluded before, after the first instructions, absented himself, though actually living in the Bishop's house.

The assaults of the Press still went on, and every new piece of intelligence that reached from England respecting the reforms recommended, or in course of parliamentary discussion, awakened the animosity anew, of which I was the object.

Two newspapers wrote some gross libels on Father Brady, afterwards Bishop of Perth, an excellent and hard-working priest, who was doing much to advance religion in the Hawkesbury District. I took up his defence. We also brought actions against both papers. One of them was ruined in consequence. The editor went and established a new paper in Melbourne, and was always afterwards a friend when Catholic questions arose in that Colony.

Father Geoghegan was sent to found the Church in the new Colony of Melbourne, now the most flourishing of all the Australian Colonies and, though the gold mines had not yet been discovered, he succeeded in building a very large church, which became the cathedral, when a Bishop was appointed.

The Bishop asked me to pay a visit to Adelaide, the capital of the new province of South Australia, distant eight hundred miles from Sydney. Mr. Lynch, one of the young priests I had brought out, took my place at Parramatta for the time and, according to my custom, I took the first vessel that sailed.

She was a small schooner and when I got on board I saw only some uneducated women, their children and one or two men of the emancipist class for cabin passengers. I thought I should have no one conversable for the fortnight's voyage but, leaning over the bulwarks, I saw a young man near me of gentlemanly bearing who suddenly turned towards me and said: 'The last time we met was under the leaning towers of Bologna. It is owing to my conversation with you then, that I am now settled in South Australia.' I then remembered him and our having dined in company, and his asking me a good many questions about the country in which we had once more met.

When I landed in Adelaide, the city, a few miles from the port, was but four years old. Laid out in a square, most of its streets were yet but marked out by chipping on the standing trees. And the houses were scattered about here and there upon an extensive site. Some six miles beyond Adelaide rose a high range of mountains, and the flat prairie between was covered with a carpet of the most beautiful flowers. They were of the Australian flora, peculiar to the South, and many of them scented like the hyacinth. In a cottage where resided a Catholic man of business, looking upon this beautiful prairie, I was hospitably received. The lady of the house was a converted daughter of a clergyman with her young family around her. I baptised her youngest daughter, but recently born, and a few years ago she wrote from Sydney to remind me that I had said she must be a nun, and that, in fact, she had been recently professed with the Benedictines at Parramatta.

The Government of this Colony was then but partially in its Governor's hands, being mainly in the hands of a commission of merchants and others, who had been its chief founders. I called more than once on the Governor, but somehow could not get to see him. He and his whole family were devout Evangelicals, and a good deal of this spirit, together with Presbyterianism, prevailed in that Colony. I could see that the arrival of a Catholic priest was not a welcome event with the men of power. I called on the Chief Commissioner, a Scotch Presbyterian, to ask leave for the use of a large public building, which had been lent to every sect until they got places of their own. I had a civil reception but was told I should receive a reply in writing. The reply was a refusal without any reason assigned. This was so contrary to the courtesies and services we were accustomed to receive in the other Colonies, that it took me by surprise.

I opened a correspondence with the Governor's secretary, stated that I was not only a Catholic priest, but a Queen's chaplain and Vicar-General, not only recognised, but paid as such by the Colonial Government of New South Wales at the instance of the Home Government, and I expressed my surprise that His Excellency the Governor had given me no opportunity to pay my respects to him. This brought a tart reply as to style, a half-apology as to substance and an interview was appointed. But I got no more notice from Government House than a quarter of an hour's general conversation with the Governor. This treatment was soon noised about by the few Catholics; and a Protestant, who dealt in chinaware, was so indignant that he offered me the use of his shop for a chapel, putting his crockery down in a cellar twice a week to give me clear use of his shop on the Sunday and Thursday night.

There then I said the first Masses and preached the first sermons ever heard in South Australia. It soon became obvious that the Catholics were few in number, the Government unfavourable, and as there was no convict settlement there was no ground for obtaining Government assistance towards supporting a priest. Then the Bishop had wisely decided never to put one priest alone anywhere unless he could visit another priest and return on the same day. In the vast and thinly populated districts of the interior of the Colonies two priests were always put together, one of whom remained at home whilst the other passed through half the tract of territory, holding one station after another for a month or six weeks, and soon after his return the other started on his course through the other half of the district.

I remember one priest reporting from Muneroo Plains that he had traversed a district of 10,000 square miles in the course of a year or eighteen months. Nothing then could be done for South Australia, for the present but to visit it from time to time. So things continued till the Australian Hierarchy was established. I was then at Coventry. But at the very time that Bishop Murphy was being consecrated at Sydney as Bishop of Adelaide, to commence the mission there aided by one priest only, and when they did not see the way to obtain support for them without making subscriptions for the purpose in the other Colonies, a most precarious resource; Mr Leigh of Woodchester, then residing at Leamington after his conversion, called on me and stated that he wished to establish a Catholic Bishop in South Australia. He explained that he had a property there, that out of that property he had destined four acres in the township of Adelaide for the site of a Protestant cathedral, one hundred acres in the country, and two thousand pounds in money towards building a church and maintaining a Bishop; that he had actually paid the money into Protestant hands, but since his conversion had got it back again, and that he wished all this now to go to a Catholic Bishopric. Thus the Mission was founded, and Mr. Leigh got plans for a church from Mr. Hansom[1] which was subsequently built. The money having been invested early by the Bishop in the Burro Burro copper mines, brought a good income, and the Australian Church was established, and is now under its third Bishop, the two deceased having both been of the party who went out with me in 1836.

Next door to my host lived Captain Sturt,[2] one of the celebrated explorers of Australia, who had then nearly lost his sight from what he had gone through. From him I learnt many

interesting details of his expeditions. I was particularly struck
by his account of the time when, after a long course of thirst,
they had to drink the blood of their horses. Their men lay
prostrate and groaning, not excited, they were past that, but
half dead and despairing. He wondered how ever he was able
to keep himself up.[3]

I puzzled my friends in Sydney by telling them that the
streets of Adelaide were fitter for the study of astronomy than
for commerce. The fact was that miles of marked-out streets
had scarcely a house in them, the forest was still standing
around, and the ways, after a heavy Australian rain, were
full of little lakes, through which my good hostess waded to
the china-shop chapel for the evening service in her husband's
boots. And the brilliant stars of the southern hemisphere were
reflected up from beneath your feet in the clear pools.

It must have been soon after my return from this mission
that I wrote my *Reply to Judge Burton*, the most important of
my colonial publications, for it has become the textbook for
the early Catholic history of New South Wales. On a visit to
England, Judge Burton, who had been a sailor in early life as
well as myself, published a large book in which, whilst advocating the interests of Protestant ascendancy in Australia, he
had not spared us. He had also given certain judgements from
the bench, reversed afterwards indeed by his brother judges,
but which, had they stood, would have invalidated all the
Catholic marriages in the Colony up to a quite recent period,
would have illegitimised the children of those marriages and
have upset the tenure of their property. And this he had done
on the mere plea of the applicability of English laws that were
not at all applicable to the Colony.

On these two themes I wrote, and the pamphlet made a great
sensation. I not only handled his delinquencies plainly, but
with considerable severity, for he had shown a strong animus,
and it was necessary to produce an impression. He was still
in England, and one of his brother judges sent him the sheets
as they were printed. We took care also to send copies of the
pamphlet to the Colonial Office in England and to the library
of the House of Commons. It was thought even by some of
his friends that he would not be able again to appear on the
bench in Sydney. He returned, indeed, just before I left the
Colony, had a great dinner given to him by his friends, when
in a speech he endeavoured to explain and smooth down what
he had written. But soon after he was removed to India, where

he remained eighteen years, after which he returned as Chief Justice to Sydney for a time. But this stern policy did not improve the feelings of the High Church people towards me. Nor did the lawyers as a body like to have one of their ornaments attacked. A leading barrister, who ventured to say at a public meeting that this pamphlet was unanswerable because no one thought it worth answering, was hissed into silence by the general sense of the assembly.

Another conflict in which I was concerned was with the Tract Society. This was something new in colonial life. But the influx of clergy of all sorts through Sir Richard Bourke's Bill led to the introduction of a good deal of the old English anti-Catholic prejudice, to which we had hitherto been strangers, and we had to contend for that position of perfect equality which the law and policy of Government had assigned to us. From this Tract Society anti-Catholic tracts began to be distributed at the doors of the Catholic families, and we noticed that men who held leading official situations attended the meetings of the Society, not only subscribing but making speeches in its support. To meet this and sundry other machinations, we established a Catholic Association which met monthly. Generally the Bishop presided and opened the subject, the exposition and enforcement of it being left to me, who also had a previous understanding with the other chief speakers as to how the whole discussion was to be guided to its conclusion. Thus we had a perfect unity of plan and treatment, a rare thing at public meetings.

When these tracts began to fly about into the doors of Catholics I told them from the cathedral pulpit to accept the next that came and to bring them to me. 'Don't,' I said, 'put them on the sacred altar whatever you do, but bring them to me.' A quantity came. We selected samples of those which were the most calculated to raise ill-feelings between the two classes of Her Majesty's subjects, made extracts from them, and then prepared a list of Government officials who were supporting this Society. We then called together a great meeting of Catholics, and after the Bishop had addressed the meeting in vigorous yet dignified terms, I rose and brought forward specimens of the kind of publications with which the Catholics were insulted at their very doors, and then showed how sundry officials, receiving larger salaries that they might devote their energies to the well-being of society, were lending their names, and that influence which office gave them, to a Society the result of whose operations was to create ill-feeling, dissension and strife amongst the Queen's subjects. I ended by proposing that a statement of the facts should be drawn up, a list of those officials appended to it, and the whole be sent with an address to Her Majesty's Secretary for the Colonies. This was done, and the Society's rooms were henceforth cleared of all officials.

Although a fair interval of necessary and administrative labour came between these public acts, there were other public matters which arose and demanded attention from time to time. Nor may my memory serve to narrate them in the order in which they occurred, although each of these transactions remains distinctly impressed in my mind in all its leading details. The whole period, however, after my return to Australia to my final departure could not have been more, with all its crowded incidents, than a year and a half.

Notes

1   Joseph Aloysius Hansom (1803–1882), Architect and inventor of the Hansom Cab (1834). He and his younger brother, Charles Francis Hansom, a supporter of Ullathorne's Coventry Mission, were partners from 1859 to 1861.

2   Charles Sturt (1795–1869), explorer of Australia whose expedition down the Murrumbidgee and Murray rivers is considered one of the greatest explorations in Australian history. He was born in the Bengal Presidency of India where his father, Thomas Lenox Napier Sturt, was a puisne judge. He joined the army in 1814 and saw action in France and served in Canada. In 1827 he became Military secretary to the then Governor of N.S.W., Sir Ralph Darling, after which he set out on his expeditions. Exhausted and nearly blinded because of poor diet and overexertion he recuperated in England between 1832 and 1834 leaving the army in July 1833 and returned to Australia with a 5,000 acre grant of land near Adelaide. He married Charlotte Christiana, daughter of Colonel William Sheppey Green, Auditor-General of Calcutta. He made another expedition after Ullathorne met him, the first to penetrate the centre of the continent. He returned to England with his family in 1853, and lived at Cheltenham until his death on 16th March 1869.

3   Mss.1. here reads: ... the men were sunk down in complete prostration and despair, whilst he, having his sense of responsibility still kept up, was able to think for the whole party.

Chapter Thirty

The Very Reverend Agitator-General of New South Wales

My position between Parramatta, my actual mission, where Mr. Lynch continued to assist me, and the Bishop's house, whither I had so frequently to go, began to be very inconvenient. The Bishop was a wonderful missioner. His work amongst the convict population had produced almost incredible results. He had every set of Catholics who arrived, and whole ships came from Ireland, given up to him for a week after their arrival. Assisted by a few clergy, he gave them retreats, instructed them in the elements of religion, heard their confessions, gave them the Sacraments, wept over them until they became as children in his hands, and most wonderfully changed the character of many of them. The whole Colony felt the change and confessed it. He was also very popular. He also did much for the children, prepared the general Communions when they made them for the first time and, again, he was much in the gaols and in the other penal establishments. He was more frequently and longer in the Confessional than many of his priests.

On State occasions the Bishop kept up all the state he could, but at all other times he was the hard missionary workman. He could drive, for example, to Government House on the Queen's birthday with his four horses and two servants, one being a black native. He even prepared the criminals for execution in the condemned cells though, of course, he did not go with them to the scaffold. On one of these occasions he was anxious to bring out of a man if he really was guilty of the murder which he resolutely denied. For sometimes these men held out even with the priest until the last hope of reprieve expired, clinging to the last hope that even the Bishop might be inclined to strive to get their lives if he thought them innocent. Generally in saying aloud the psalm *Miserere*, the culprit would thrill with horror on coming to the words: 'Deliver me from blood, Oh God; God of my salvation.' On this occasion the Bishop repeated the words when he came to them with great feeling and solemnity, but the man looked hard at him, as much as to say, do you think to catch me that way? This, however, was a rare occasion for the Bishop had that unction and tenderness towards these poor creatures that gave him possession of their hearts from the first.

This example in the Bishop worked a vigorous missionary spirit in the clergy, and raised the Catholics into a religious people. But my difficulty was this, that the episcopal work dropped behind so much to give place to the missionary, so that I was obliged to be constantly urging its claims, and to think a great deal about it, and look a good deal into it whilst, as my own mission was distant fifteen miles, I found my difficulties by no means trifling. News came to me of this or that going on, and that the Bishop, always extremely sensitive about his popularity, no doubt chiefly on account of its influence for good, was in low spirits and depressed. Then I would go over, rouse him up, and get him to look the matter in the face. He always inculcated that it was my business to receive the brunt of attacks, to do the odious things, and to keep the Episcopal Office in the odour of sanctity; and this I was ready to do. But most times the real prudence and safety lay in promptitude, when he was very reluctant to act. It was also very awkward to have the Bishop resting on me in difficulties, when the two clergymen to whom I have repeatedly alluded were at his elbow, and I at a distance, or when there, as the other clergy said, going about the house like a poor relation.

For this state of things was not palatable to the body of the clergy. The priest who never took to me, though I sent him out, now and again let out sneers at me even at the Bishop's clergy dinners, which were practically inconvenient and were not checked by the Bishop. For instance, the young priest with me, going on a mission of his own, had been complimented at the Bishop's table by the Bishop and clergy present. He rose, and with generous emotion, spoke out his gratitude for what I had done for him. He said that when he went to Parramatta, he thought in his youthful conceit that he knew a great deal, that he soon learnt from my teaching and methods how little he did know, and then began really to know. But whilst the young priest thus spoke his open-hearted feelings, this priest threw sneering exclamations between each fervid sentence that was uttered. Yet of this no notice was taken. On another occasion, all the clergy being there, and the servants present, he made some allusion to my having looked after my own interests when in England, and that in an offensive way that called the general attention. When the servants had retired, I called on him for an explanation. I am almost certain there was also a lay gentleman present. A few words of mumbled explanation were all that were elicited. These things would be trifles, were it not for the continued influence which this priest and his colleague, who was over the school, exercised, in secret, in a way that embarrassed my position. One day when a new attack had come out on me in the Press, on the old score of my evidence, I happened to meet him as I was walking across the park from the house. He pulled up his horse and said, alluding to this attack: 'The fact is, that we shall have no peace, so long as you are in the Colony.'

I thought it time to speak plainly to the Bishop. I explained to him how difficult my position was becoming. I represented that, as Vicar-General, and as one called in to decide or to act in emergency, I felt I was anomalously placed. I proposed to resign my Vicar-Generalship and keep to my mission, or even to leave the Colony. Of neither proposition would the Bishop hear. He said we made a complete man between us, and that I was needful to supply in those points in which he was deficient. In the midst of this conversation, Father Brady happened to come in. He was an humble as well as a zealous man, and the Bishop's confessor, and I took the opportunity of his being present to go completely into matters, and that with considerable plainness. I had become so harrassed with a combination of difficulties of various kinds, all centering in the duties I had to perform for the Bishop, and in the difficulties put in my way by his nervous apprehensions of public opinion, or his reluctance to move, that it was wearing me down, and my health began to break. I had even brought matters to a point in another way, by sending in my resignation to the Governor, resolved to bring our matters to a crisis, one way or another. Thus I startled the Bishop and he saw that things could not go on as they were. He also said that he could not possibly see me in the suffering state I was in without feeling himself very anxious. At his earnest requests I withdrew my resignation. The Governor, on receiving it, had himself sent for me, expressed his sincere regret that I should think of giving up, and asked me to give him my views on the subject of popular education, as he was anxious to revise the system then in operation.

Let me give one or two specimens of the kind of difficulty I had to endure, although the narrative will necessarily be somewhat long. A young person came to the Colony from Ireland. She apostatised and became a sort of Maria Monk[1], professing to be the neice of a priest, and to know the secret abominations of the Catholic religion. She was taken up by an anti-Catholic set of people who were not without social influence. From time to time letters appeared in the papers signed with her name, Agnes Bryne, evidently drawn up by more skillful persons, and professing to expose the abuses of the Catholic Church. The Confessional, the paying for the forgiveness of sins, the acts of money-making and various other slanderous things were the subject of the letters. The Bishop wished me to reply. I did so, submitted all the letters I published to his revision, and sometimes putting a stronger passage in, at his suggestion. My letters were, of course, roughly handled by the adverse Press, and my conduct in the matter of the evidence before Parliament, in driving the officials from the Tract Society, and similar delinquencies were not forgotten. I was still, as they loved to call me: *The Very Reverend Agitator-General of New South Wales.* Whilst the Bishop was represented as the head of a reformed Catholicity, that was universally charitable and tolerant, I was upheld as the representative of all the old, mediaeval bigotry and intolerance. Still no sign was given in any way that in these matters we were of accord, and acting together, or rather, that I was acting under episcopal direction.

This Agnes Bryne came to reside at Parramatta in the house of a retired colonel, and she was there put forth as a set-off against the nuns, whose visit of charity was not at all relished by those who were the leaders of Protestant zealotry in that town, which might be called the Bath of New South Wales. But as she was put offensively forward, and as her letters still continued, with the Bishop's approval I resolved to give a lecture in the church, which I advertised, for the purpose of refuting her calumnies. This, of course, was fresh food for the newspapers. Soon after this, Agnes Bryne quarrelled with her protector, and left his house, and as she was going on a lonely road, she was beset and assulted by convicts, who happened to be Irishmen. Of course, it would have been the same with any woman they had met. They knew not who she was. They were looking out for an opportunity. Happily she was rescued but up rose the Press, ascribing the whole affair to my influence, and the *Australian* headed an article with:

'DR. ULLATHORNE AND BLOOD'

in large capitals. The object of that article was to maintain that I had been the instigator of the men. Such was the feeling excited that the Chief Justice, when the trial of the men came on in the Sydney Courts, found it necessary to address the jury before proceeding, and to instruct them that I had nothing whatever to do with the matter. This had become necessary in consequence of the popular excitement raised by the newspapers. I remember that soon after this assault occurred, I was going from Parramatta to Sydney in the steamer, and Captain Westmacott, aide-de-camp to the Governor, was also on board. I knew he had been at the lecture which occasioned all the hubbub, and I told him I felt in a somewhat awkward position, as I had sent in my resignation, might have to return to England, and did not see how I could go, unless these matters had first subsided. It would look like cowardice and would be misconstrued. He said with some earnestness that there was nothing in that lecture that could be fairly complained of, especially as it was but a repelling of attack, and advised me not to let the state of unjust opinions influence any of my movements. Yet I had to stand through all this as I might without any support from anyone.

I was invited to a great public dinner given on St. George's Day by the leading Englishmen in the Colony to the Scotch and Irish. I was invited as the guest of the chairman, the Bishop preferring that I should appear as representative of the clergy rather than himself. In returning thanks for the clergy, my words were much applauded, until I happened to make some allusion to the Catholics as having a long ancestry. This moved an Indian judge, who was also a guest, to interrupt me with some very sour remarks. Opposite him sat the Chevalier Dillon, a warm-hearted Irish Catholic who had been titled by France for having discovered the remains of their famous navigator, La Perouse, on the Fiji Islands. Dillon seized an apple and threatened to drive it down the judge's throat if he did not stop. This effectually quieted him. On sitting down I turned to Captain, now General, England, who sat next to me, and asked him to tell me frankly if I had said anything inappropriate. He said: 'Upon my word, no. If I thought so I would tell you without hesitation.' But the papers, ever on the lookout for the old offender against the convict system, brought it home to me as a new crime. I had caused what was a near approach to a fracas amongst gentlemen on St. George's Day. Perhaps it would have been as well for me to have avoided the allusion, however innocent, especially as I was living under so much public suspicion, but certainly it would have attracted no especial notice but for this touchy evangelical judge, whose name was nearly like my own, being Doneythorne. Who knows but this accidental resemblance might have, unconsciously, deepened his jealousy, especially as it was then in such bad odour. This reminds me that years afterwards I met with Catholic officers from India who told me in jest: 'We know all about you in India; as to your Bishop, he is an angel, but you are the Very Reverend Agitator of New South Wales.'

Notes

1   In 1835 a book entitled *The Awful Disclosures of Maria Monk* was published. The lady herself professed to have been a nun in the convent of the Hotel-Dieu in Montreal and tells of murders and immoralities supposed to have been committed there by priests and nuns. The narrative was refuted on its initial appearance by even Protestant authorities. Furthermore it was proved that during the time the authoress alleged to have been a nun in the convent she was, in fact, plying her trade as a prostitute in Montreal. She died in prison in 1849, whence she had been consigned for pickpocketing. Her book was still being sold and distributed well into the present century.

Chapter Thirty-One

Further Sydney Reminiscences

In the year 1838 Bishop Pompallier[1] arrived in Sydney from France, on his way to begin his Mission in the Islands of Oceania, and was accompanied by several Fathers of the Marist Institution. From Sydney they proceeded to New Zealand, where they first began their labours. And this recalls to mind the conversion of a New Zealand chief, which took place some years before in Sydney. A worthy Irishman wished to marry the daughter of this chief, but being a truly religious man desired first to make her a Christian. He brought her and her father over to Sydney, and then came and told the Bishop that he wished to present them to him, in the hope of their conversion. The Bishop fixed the time, and received them in rochet and mozzetta, attended by two priests. The Irishman acted as interpreter. The man was told that the chief of the Christians received with respect the chief of the Maori, which was duly acknowledged. After some more conversation in the way of politeness, the Bishop took a large crucifix and held it before this eyes. The chief gazed at it for some time, after which the Bishop said: 'You are accustomed to avenge the wrongs of your tribe?'

The chief nodded his head.

'Well this is a case of revenge, and a case of torture. Did you ever see torture like this?'

Still gazing the chief shook his head.

Then the Bishop slowly said, and the Irishman interpreted: 'The Great God of heaven, Who made all men, was angry with man, and would not destroy him. But the Great God had a Son like Himself, and He made a man of Him and he revenged the wickedness of men on His Son. And this was what His Son suffered; He is ready to pardon every man who begs pardon of Him and obeys His laws.'

The chief was deeply moved and tears flowed from his eyes. The essential point of the mystery of redemption had entered his mind. He and his daughter received a course of instruction, were baptised, and the daughter married to the Irishman.

I was thinking over this incident, before writing it, in the year 1888, when I received a visit from my friend, Dr. Redwood,[2] Archbishop of Wellington. To him I repeated what I have just written. The Archbishop asked: 'Do you remember the name of that Irishman?'

I confessed that I could not recall it.

'Was it Paynton?'

'Now you mention it, I am confident that that was his name.'

'Then,' said the Archbishop, 'he and his family have always been good, practical Catholics, and the chief as well. It was in his house that Bishop Pompallier was first received on his landing. It was in that house that he said the first Mass ever said in New Zealand. And that house was always looked on with respect by all the Catholics, until it was burnt down not so very long ago.'

Later on came another group of Marist Fathers, on their way to the South Sea Missions. Among them I particularly remember Father Bataillon,[3] who converted the Wallis Islands, became the first Bishop of Central Oceania, and whose life has been recently published in France. I also remember making the acquaintance of the Blessed Father Chanel,[4] who was martyred for the faith in the island of Futuna, and who has been recently beatified; but wherever met, I do not remember, unless it were in New Zealand. I also remember calling upon the Bishop and his companions, destined for New Guinea, and whispering to Dr. Heptonstall: 'Look well at the heads of those men.'

When we had left Dr. Heptonstall asked: 'Why did you tell me to look at those men's heads?'

'Because,' I replied, 'I know something of the savage race of New Guinea, and am confident that some of their heads will be knocked off before twelve months are out.' And it did occur, that landing in a boat, from the vessel that took them from Sydney, the savages met them in the water with their clubs, battered the Bishop's head to pieces and his body was taken back to Sydney.

In the year 1841 we were preparing to lay the foundation stone for a second church in Sydney, St Patrick's. The history of the site given for this Church was almost an abridgement

of the history of the Catholics in the Colony. It was the
cottage and garden of that William Davis who had paid
for the convent for the Sisters of Charity at Parramatta.
The old man had been transported on the charge of having
made pikes for the Irish Insurrection of 1798, for he was
a blacksmith by trade. When there were no priests in the
Colony, in the rough early times, he had been repeatedly
flogged for refusing to go to the Protestant Worship. He
had been put in the black hole for the same offence. When
he got his freedom he built this cottage on about the highest
point in Sydney, by what then was the market, just opposite
the one and only Protestant church. Father Flynn, the Archpriest, during his short stay in the Colony, used to say Mass
in that house but he was unwarrantably seized, cast into goal
and sent out of the Colony so suddenly that he was unable to
consume the Blessed Sacrament, and there it remained with no
priest nearer than the Isle of Mauritius, for two years, when a
French expedition of discovery arrived there, and the chaplain
of it said Mass in Davis' home and consumed the Hosts. For
that two years the Catholics assembled there to pray, and
Davis, with the Ark of the Covenant under his roof, was
blessed and prospered like Obededom[5]. By his industry and
integrity he began to gather wealth for good mechanics were
few. 'I love the Church,' the old grey-haired man of many
sufferings used to say, with a voice, hoarse, from the depth
of his feelings. 'I love the Church.' And now he had offered
to give his house and garden, the ground of which had become
so valuable, for a site for the new church, and to put £1000 on
the foundation-stone. The Government gave another £1000.
The rest had to be collected. For years there had been weekly
collections made through the city for it. For years there had
been weekly meetings of the Catholics in a large room, where
speeches were made, and the collections paid in. It was at
those meetings that I first adopted that free colloquial style
of speaking in blended anecdote, narration and instruction
which proved attractive then, and which I afterwards found
so valuable in advancing the Coventry mission.

It happened that at this time a scheme was being agitated
for establishing a general system of elementary education.
The Governor wished to introduce a common, instead of the
denominational, system of which Bible-reading would have
formed a part, conditions which no Catholic could have
accepted, in consequence of which the Bishop and myself

had an interview with the Governor, Sir George Gipps, on the subject. After considerable discussion the Governor brought the interview abruptly to a conclusion by saying: 'In short, I must adhere to the strongest party, and I don't think that you are the strongest.' After that we determined to make a public demonstration for we knew that, if not the strongest by numbers, we were by our union.

The time approached for laying the foundation-stone. There was to be a grand procession from the Cathedral through the chief streets of the city, which came on the line of route, up to the elevated ground of the new church. The people were bent on having green banners and scarves, and the women green trimmings, and great cost had been gone into already in these preparations. Hitherto national distinctions had been instinctively avoided in the Colony; all prided themselves on being Australians. The rumours afloat about this national exhibition began to alarm the Government. They were afraid that it might lead to Orange reprisals. The Governor sent for the chief police magistrate. He called upon me and expressed his fears for the peace of the city, and lest the demonstration should lead to the formation of party organisations. It must be remembered that the Colony was still a penal settlement. The Attorney and the Solicitor-General and the Crown Solicitor, all at that time Catholics, also thought that things, however innocently intended, were going too far. But meetings to complete preparations continued to be held. Warm speeches were made and they were resolved to go on. The Bishop, though he saw the difficulty, shrunk from stemming the popular tide. The clergy of Sydney, all Irishmen, were reluctant to do anything but let the matter go on. The Chief of Police called and urged that what might be construed as party insignia should be omitted. 'Suppose,' he said, 'some man in the crowd were to hoist an Orange flag, in what state would we have the peace of the city?'

I was compelled to take the matter in hand with the Bishop. After I had made all representations I could, without inducing him to interfere, I retired to another room and wrote him a letter, which I sent into him, stating that I had now done all I could in the way of representation, and felt free from further responsibility, but that as the whole object of the procession was to conduct his Lordship to the foundation-stone, I still felt that the representations of the authorities ought to be attended to. He then sent for me and asked what I would recommend as he did not see his way. I then said that if he would leave it to me I would get him through it, and I was left to act on my own judgement.

I got Mr. Therry, the Solicitor-General, and one or two others, to accompany me and went to the Catholic meeting then going on, on the very eve of the appointed day. The great room was densely crowded and speeches were going on. In a speech of an hour's length I gradually worked the assembly round until I came to the point, when the chief leader of the popular voice arose and called upon the multitude to comply with my request and put away the insignia which had cost them so much and to which they had attached so much importance. Thus the point was gained. Mr. Therry, who had been a leader in the great Emancipation meetings under O'Connell, was much struck with the whole affair, the excitement I had to meet at the outset and the gradual working round of the audience, and said it was like one of those great and agitated assemblies he had so often shared in.

When I got back and told the Bishop the result he flung himself with tears on my shoulders and said I was always saving him. But this was my very difficulty. I had so great a reverence for him, my old Master and Superior, and now my Bishop. I owed so much to him, from my days of turning to religion, and yet I had so often to set my judgement against his reluctance to act, or to act in an effective way. This wore me beyond anything, for it harrassed all my best feelings.

The procession started from the Cathedral and the Catholic population was in a state of exalted enthusiasm. Bands of music were provided. The cross preceding, magnificent banners following along the line. Three hundred girls clothed in white followed the cross, the rest of the children forming a long line. Then came the Catholic people, who were 14,000 out of a population of 40,000. After them the acolytes and the clergy in their sacerdotal vestments, whilst the procession was closed by the Bishop in an open carriage with mitre and cope with his attendants. Such a procession had never been seen in Australia. The shops were closed, business ceased, the whole population was in the streets or at the windows, and as we reached the place of the new church, on one of the highest points in Sydney, by every descent you might have walked on the heads of the people as far as the eye could reach. All Sydney was there, and many from the country as well.

The foundation-stone was suspended in the air, visible to the multitude. At the Bishop's request I was mounted upon it, and thence I gave the touching history of the house which had now disappeared, which had been the centre of Catholic devotion in our days of trial and persecution, and which had now made way for the church which was there to rise on the most elevated point in Sydney. It was on the very catacombs of the Catholics that this church was to repose.

As the procession returned, people were heard saying: 'Only the Catholics could do this. We must come second.' The children re-entered the Cathedral and with the Bishop and clergy in the sanctuary the children ranged themselves in concentric circles round the altar steps, and raised Handel's triumphant song *Sound the Loud Timbrel*, and that with an enthusiasm which deeply moved the people. This was a revelation to the Colony of our strength, and our reply to the Governor's remark. And we heard no more of the new scheme of education. It must be remembered that, in those days, we had to meet the long cherished traditions of Protestant supremacy, and to *assert* that equality before the law, which the law itself had given us.

To return again after this long explanation to the point where I had sent in my resignation, and had the interview in the presence of Father Brady, the Bishop, of his own accord, resolved to make a radical change in his surroundings. He sent off the two clergymen of whom I have repeatedly spoken, one into the interior, the other into the city, and asked me to come and reside with him. This sudden change gave great satisfaction to the body of the clergy, who expressed their feelings in various pithy sentences, such as: 'Hurrah, the Tories are out.' I undertook to direct the school, as well as the cathedral work and my official duty. The school, however, proved too much with other occupations, and after a while it passed into other hands.

Notes

1   Jean Baptiste François Pompallier (1801–1871), Titular Bishop of Maronea and Vicar-Apostolic of Western Oceania (1836), Bishop of Auckland (1860), Titular Archbishop of Amasia (1869).
2   Born 1839 in Birmingham he was taken to New Zealand at the age of three. Educated in France, he joined the Society of Mary. He was consecrated Bishop of Wellington in 1874 by Cardinal Manning and in 1887 was created Archbishop and Metropolitan of New Zealand.

3   Spelt *Battalion* and *Batalion* by Ullathorne, this is Pierre Marie Bataillon
     (1810–1877), a French Marist, first Vicar-Apostolic of Central Oceania in
     1843. He died on Wallis Island.

4   Pierre-Louis-Marie Chanel (1803–1841), Protomatyr of Oceania. He was
     ordained in 1827 and joined the newly-founded Society of Mary (Marists).
     In 1835 he was sent to the island of Futuna where he was brutally matyred
     six years later. It is interesting that Ullathorne refers to him as 'Blessed' as
     he wasn't formally beatified till 16th November 1889. Ullathorne himself
     died eight months before, on 21st March, St Benedicts Day.

5   2 Kings VI, 10. Douay or 2 Samuel R.S.V.

Chapter Thirty-Two

Final Days in Australia

My time, however, was far from being all engaged in these troublesome and weary conflicts. Occasionally I visited some of the remoter missionary districts. For instance, the River Hunter district had always been one of my favourite missions. I had begun the church in Maitland, as well as a parish in Newcastle.

On my last visit there I was riding with two zealous priests, one of whom had been with me at Parramatta, and we met a farmer who rode rapidly past and turned his head from us. 'There,' said one of our priests, 'goes one of our miseries. We have had so many of these men to deal with, who are living wrongfully and will not get married. We denounced two, and both soon after came to a wretched end, and we dare not mark that man for fear of something terrible coming on him. You saw that he durst not look at us.' This was said with a good deal of feeling. Alas! The man had not ridden half a mile further when his horse threw him and killed him. Our greatest difficulty in the early days of the Mission was to get the people married, and their children baptised, especially in the interior. They had adopted the law of nature when there was scarcely a priest in the Colony, or a clergyman of any sort, and by habit they continued in it. Then there were so many who, having been transported, had left a wife, or a husband, at home of whom often we could gain no intelligence. For many years this continued to be the most difficult part of the priest's work, to settle the marriages of so many of the people. Still, religion progressed, and progressed wonderfully. The first year of my arrival there were but a hundred Easter Communions in Sydney and but few elsewhere. A year or two after I left there were a thousand at the Cathedral alone.

The agitating period of my last residence in Australia was not all spent in action. I had my quiet hours in retirement surrounded with my books. And I also gave Retreats to the nuns as well as to the clergy, and always found in them a resource for the restoration of my own spirit. I had a good deal of preaching, and while for the mysteries and festivals Bossuet was my favourite guide, for moral preaching I found my chief resources in St. John Chrysostom. The sermon which I published against drunkenness was to a great extent drawn from the writings of that saint. Yet it was so adapted to the exigencies of that period, that it was widely circulated, even by Protestants. An old soldier to whom it was thus given, at Bathurst, and who was a veteran toper, gave his idea of it to the donor in this sentence: 'The gentleman who wrote this, sir, must have drunk very hard in his time.' Nor were his ideas made much clearer when he was told that I had been a water-drinker all my life. The Colonial Secretary, a Protestant, a man of much religious zeal as well as distinguished in science, told me that he read it every fortnight to his convict servants. He pressed me with particular earnestness to publish one on profane swearing, the second great vice of the Colony. And in compliance with his request I did so, but that discourse owed much also of its pith to St Chrysostom. My other discourses will be found in my volume of *Sermons With Prefaces*. I also inserted in the same volume the discourse delivered on the occasion of the profession of a Sister of Charity, the first nun ever professed in the New World. This sister was Miss Williams, an orphan whose father, an officer of Cavalry, was killed at the battle of Talavera. She received a pension in consequence. She was a cousin to Mrs. Fruin who founded the two houses of Sisters of the Institute of Mary in this Diocese,[1] and who died in the convent at Leek. it was this early association between her cousin and myself which attracted Mrs. Fruin to make her last foundations in this Diocese.

Amongst my books I had some valuable ascetic writings, especially the best Spanish edition of *St. Teresa* by Palafox, and Father Baker's *Sancta Sophia*, and I was still a monk at heart. I also received the *Université Catholique* as it came out in Paris, and that valuable series of papers, written by the ablest pens in France with the view of supplying the absence of a Catholic university, had a freshness, vigour and depth, to which I owed a good deal of mental expansion. Digby's volumes on *Christian Chivalry* and on the *Ages of Faith* helped much to refresh and elevate the heart amidst the din and conflict and the sordid surroundings of a penal settlement. But when I wanted rest and nothing but rest of mind, I not unfrequently betook myself for a few evening hours to the pure humanities of Sir Walter Scott. Of one kind or another, after weariness and anxiety, I always found a book the pleasantest pillow on which to rest my mind, and the quickest restorative to healthy spirits.

One thing I had long striven to impress on the Bishop's mind, and that was the importance of obtaining a second Bishop for Van Dieman's Land, now called Tasmania. During my absence in England he had sent Father Therry to Hobart Town, and that with authority as Vicar-General, there being only two other priests in the island. This removed a difficulty from New South Wales, but created a serious state of things in that island for Father Therry proceeded just in the same style as formerly when alone in Sydney, beginning but never finishing anything, and driving about upon his restless impulses, without organising anything. I repeated on every fitting occasion that Van Dieman's Land was 'the sore point on the episcopal conscience.' At last the Bishop took it seriously to heart and resolved to go to Europe for that and other affairs of the Australian Church. I was to manage the Diocese until his return.

But when he showed me a list of names to be presented at Rome with my own at the top of it for the proposed Bishopric of Hobart Town, I at once took alarm, I had seen enough of Bishops thoroughly to compassionate but not to envy them. I saw that if I should be appointed, being at so vast a distance from Rome, I should scarcely be free to exercise a judgement as to accepting or declining, that I should be driven to a kind of necessity to accept or to let the country go on for years more without having a Bishop. I therefore told Dr. Polding that unless he consented to take my name off, and to promise he would not bring it before the Holy See, I should be compelled also to go to Europe until that affair was settled, because I could not otherwise be left a free agent in case my name were accepted. He pleaded the difficulty of leaving the Colony without leaving one behind who had been in the centre of affairs. It was then proposed that I should go, and though this seemed not much to mend matters as far as the Bishopric was concerned, as I should necessarily have to negotiate the appointment, yet I did not refuse, and actually went to engage a cabin in a ship about to sail. It will shew the feeling in the Colony respecting my character as drawn by the newspapers when I state that a wealthy and worthy merchant went to engage places for himself and family, and hearing I was likely to go in the vessel, he declined going in it. The captain, who had commanded the *Thomas Munro* on my first voyage out, in vain tried to remove the impression formed, from his personal knowledge. However, the matter was delayed and the family went in that ship.

The Bishop began to think that he ought to go and pressed me to remain. Having a sort of half-understanding about the Bishopric, I consented, though reluctantly. I knew I should have great difficulties, and my health was a good deal changed through my continued anxieties, for I had many solicitudes and many things to combat which it is unnecessary here to record. I was quite sallow, indeed as dark as a mulatto then, and for years afterwards, until I began to recover tone. I remember my dear mother writing that a lady had called on her at Scarborough who had seen me on a Parramatta steamer six months before, and was astonished to see how careworn I had become.

At the last moment almost, my deliverance came in a way I had not anticipated. The clergyman to whom I have so often alluded made some representation that I ought not to be left without some check upon me, and the Bishop proposed that that clergyman and Father Brady, who lived thirty miles off, should form a council with me for the administration of the Diocese. I saw at once that this could not work. Father Brady I should have no difficulty with, but the other priest was precisely the person who would give me trouble and hamper my action, and make his own statements to the Bishop at a distance. It was not that we were not always on good terms externally, not a word of unpleasantness had ever passed between us except on the one passing occasion which I previously mentioned; but our characters were so different that we could not have understood each other. At that distance also from all authority of a higher character, and with the critical emergencies apt to arise in so anomalous a state of society, unity of government was essential. Admitting this proposition then with the other question about the Bishopric, I told the Bishop I must be either removed from the Vicar-Generalship or go with him, and so it was settled with very few words. Dr. Gregory was to accompany us, and passages were engaged in a Chilean brig bound to Talcahuano, the Port to the City of Conception, but to call at New Zealand on the way where the Bishop, Dr. Polding, wished to visit Bishop Pompallier at Korarika in the Bay of Islands; the French Bishop having long wished for such a visit, for the sake of the influence upon the natives. Our intention on reaching Chili[3] was to ride through the Pampas across South America to Buenos Ayres *sic*, and there to take shipping for England, and for that purpose we took our English saddles as part of our equipment.

The Catholics prepared a splendid demonstration to shew their respect for their Bishop on his departure, and collected a considerable sum of money as an offering for his expenses. I was asked what I should like, but I told the declaration that I would not interfere with a testimonial to the Bishop by accepting anything myself unless it were a trifle, such as a snuff-box. So they presented me with an address and a silver snuff-box filled with fifty sovereigns.

On the last morning I said Mass for the nuns whom I had landed in the Colony, now increased by an addition of members. They came down to Sydney for the occasion. Poor souls, they wept all the Mass, feeling that the one person who thoroughly understood them, who had looked to their interests, and had guided them, was leaving them most probably for ever. They had never been thoroughly sympathised with except by myself. They feared their Rule and Institute would be tamperd with, and that proved in aftertimes but too true. They withstood the change, and those I took out took refuge in Van Dieman's Land except one, who after many years managing a hospital in Sydney returned to the parent house in Dublin. Some of the younger ones who joined them in Australia remained, were cast in a new form, and still continue. What they feared, and I confess that I feared also, was their encountering the spirit of improving away the old, already approved by the Holy See and in full operation in the parent houses, and replacing it by 'improvements of Australian manufacture.' They could not and did not conceal their distress up to the moment of our departure, and I confess that the well-being of those Religious whom I had taken from their homes and placed among strangers was the chief thing which made me reluctant under the circumstances to quit the new Colony. As we turned from them, still kneeling and weeping, the Bishop said to me: 'They are good religious but very much distressed.'

It is only a fortnight from writing this that I celebrated with them, the breadth of the world between us, a singular jubilee of thanksgiving. They wrote to remind me that on December 31st, 1888, it would be fifty years since I first landed them in Sydney, and asked me to join them in their thanksgiving for all the benefits they had received and, I may add, for all the good God had enabled them to do during those past fifty years. But the most interesting part of their letters recorded the present state of their Congregation in Australia.

There are now 110 members. They have a large hospital in Sydney, with 150 beds, which is well supported; another in Parramatta in the house in which I placed them; an orphanage in Hobart; a young ladies' college in a well-constructed building; and they teach 3,000 children besides. They are also about to erect a hospital at Melbourne, towards which they have received a sumptuous offering. Of the five members who landed with me, one alone survives, who is still Superior of the orphanage, at the advanced age of eighty-nine years. Here is a theme for gratitude.

From the Cathedral seven thousand people walked with the Bishop to the boat. It was a universal holiday. The strand was covered with the population, the habour with boats, and all the ships hoisted their colours. A large steam vessel covered with the Bishop's friends accompanied the vessel down the magnificent harbour and out to sea. Guns were firing on all sides, cheering was incessant. At last we found ourselves away and all alone on a tranquil sea. The captain, a warm-hearted little Englishman, who had married a Chilian and had become a Catholic, did his best to provide for us. When a lad he had been in Lord Dundonald's ship, when he commanded the Chilian fleet, during the war of Independence, and he was full of anecdotes of those stirring times. He told me how much surprised he was when he met me, as from all he heard on shore he concluded I was some big, rawboned man fitter to handle a shillalah than anything else.

One thing I did before I left Sydney, which ought to be recorded. It was something very obvious, to me at least, but no one else seemed to see it. A great deal of speculation was going on, and land in Sydney and other townships rose enormously in favourable positions. It was said that land had been sold in one principal street at a higher price per foot than it had ever been sold at that time in Cheapside, London. Many millions of paper money had floated from the banks, but at that time the *Government Gazette* published the amount of specie in the Colony, which did not amount to more than £600,000.

Anyone with a little knowledge of finance ought to have seen the consequence, but no notice was taken of it. I then wrote three letters in the *Australian Chronicle*, the Catholic paper, addressed respectively to His Excellency the Governor, to the City of Sydney, and to the Colony at large, in which I predicted that great troubles were on the wing, and that a great deal of property must soon change hands. I regret I have not a copy of those letters. I lent them to the British Consul at Talcuhana and never recovered them. They were received with incredulity, but after a time came the crash, and many failures. Land ran down rapidly in price, and sheep, the staple of the Colony, came from twenty-five, to five shillings a head, and even half-a-crown until coppers were sent from England to boil them down to tallow for exportation. Nor did the Colony recover itself until the discovery of gold. Meeting my old friend Sir Roger Therry long years after, on his return to England, he said: 'We did not believe your letters. We were rather amused at them. But we were awfully punished.'

If I were asked how I was affected by those long and persistent attacks of the Press, and from the opinion this generated, though it never touched the Catholic circle, I should say that, being then a young man, I was not without an annoying consciousness of it, yet it was less the object of thought than of a certain dull pressure as from the enduring of hostile elements. But it was a valuable training, as it made me indifferent to public opinion for the rest of my life where duty was concerned. In my book *On the Management of Criminals*, I have spoken of the way in which the Colony ultimately did me justice, how the time came when all the inhabitants of New South Wales, as well as of the other Australian Colonies, came to my way of thinking.

I was probably sitting in my room in Birmingham, or pursuing some tranquil occupation, quite unconscious of what was passing in Sydney, when a hundred thousand people under their leaders met from all parts of the Colony in that park I had so often traversed, in front of that Cathedral where I ministered, and of that house where I lived; in sight also of that court-house where a Chief Justice had to arraign a jury, guarding them against supposing I had anything to do with a most infamous assault committed by convicts, guarding them against any supposition that there was any truth in the newspaper articles, such as that headed: 'DR ULLATHORNE AND BLOOD'.

And the object of that huge assembly, speaking in the voice of the whole Colony, was to proclaim the convict system an abomination and a pollution of the land to be got rid of at any cost, and to utter the solemn resolve that never again would they allow a convict ship to touch their shores.

Amongst the speakers who addressed that monster assembly arose my old friend Archdeacon McEncroe and reminded them how they had pursued me for broaching similar sentiments in milder terms. Then there arose three cheers for the old advocate of their new views. Such is opinion, that Queen of the World, who has so often to revise her judgements.

Notes

1   Birmingham.
2   Now an hotel.
3   Ullathorne's spelling throughout his writings.

Chapter Thirty-Three

New Zealand

We left Sydney on the brig *Orion* on the 16th, November 1840 and after about a fortnight's voyage we cast anchor before Korarika in the Bay of Islands. The town consisted of a native pale, a British settlement and a French mission. We were met on board by Mr. Waterton, brother of the celebrated naturalist, who was then residing at the mission, and spent his time in botanical excursions. When we reached the mission-house we found that Bishop Pompallier was absent, making a tour amongst the islands of the Pacific in his little schooner. The missionary Fathers of the Marist Congregation, who had all received our Bishop's hospitality on their way out, and most of whom afterwards became Bishops, received us with joy.

Their residence was built of wood, and a little wooden church stood adjoining, bright all over with green paint. Small as it was, it had its confessional, font, and every appointment complete. Soon after our arrival the evening service began for the native tribe. Of course, we entered the church and joined the service. One chief object of our visit was to remove an impression created by the Anglican and Wesleyan missionaries, that the Catholic religion was not the religion of Englishmen, but of a people with whom they had nothing to do. And this statement had been embellished with fantastic stories of the old anti-Catholic type, but seasoned for the New Zealand palate with an accumulation of horrible accompaniments of the Foxe's *Book of Martyrs* school. One Father read prayers and another intoned the hymn *O Filii et Filiae*, adapted in the New Zealand language to the native comprehension. Their scale of notes was as limited as their alphabet. The Alleluia which ends the stanza became *Arr-a-oo-yah* in their mouths, and they dropped the concluding tones into the lowest notes that their voice could reach, giving the concluding drop, as if the voice had suddenly lost all capacity of sustainment.

After this earnest act of devotion, the senior missioner began to address them in their own language. Sometimes he pointed to us, and all eyes bent upon us, then again he pointed to himself. But whether he pointed to himself or to us we always heard the word *Picopo*. After the service was over, we asked the Father the meaning of the word *Picopo*. He then explained. When Bishop Pompallier commenced his mission he was obliged to coin new words for the expression of ideas new to his neophytes. Their language being formed chiefly of vowels and liquids could only employ thirteen letters from our alphabet, and there was this additional peculiarity, that two consonants could not be sounded together, nor could a word end otherwise but with a vowel. The words Bishop or *Eveque* were unpronounceable, so to designate himself he took the Latin term *Episcopus* and changed it into *Picopo*, and his religion became also designated by the same word. So *Picopo* both designated the Bishop and the Bishop's religion. It meant a Catholic as well as the head of Catholics. When he then addressed the natives he pointed out to them that we were English and yet Catholics, exactly as he and they were Catholics, and that they saw an English Bishop seated on the same chair of authority on which the French Bishop sat. There was the *Picopo Poryaxono* as well as the *Picopo Wee Wee*. *Poryaxono* meant an Englishman, for as his own proper designation was unpronounceable, the natives gave the Englishman a name derived from Port Jackson, the harbour of Sydney, which many of them had visited in the whaling ships. Whilst the Frenchman was called *Wee Wee,* from their having constantly heard him pronounce the affirmation *oui, oui.* We then were pointed at as the *Picopo Poryaxono* in unity with them, the *Picopo Wee Wee.*

We went to visit them in their lovely huts, into which they crept, and in which they sat but could not stand. They are the most magnificent race of men in point of height, bone and muscle that I ever saw, and are singularly quiet and intelligent. They were fond of reading and writing and could all do these feats. The men had remarkably expressive and even dignified physiognomies, especially the chiefs, and the tattoos upon their features gave depth to their expression. The women were coarser in feature for their sex, but inspired with an incessant cheerfulness, often expressed in laughter. We

found a chief at our first visit under *taboo*. He had had his
hair cut that day, and so could not use his hands until the
day following. He sat with his hands crossed on his breast,
and his wife and daughter were feeding him. This operation
was done in the following manner. A skillet with about half
a peck of boiled potatoes stood before him, and nowhere are
potatoes finer or larger than in New Zealand, though dark in
colour.[1] The wife put a potato into his mouth ready peeled,
on *one* side, and when that disappeared, the daughter had
one ready peeled and prepared for the same journey on the
other. He was a grand specimen of his race, received us very
politely, apologising to us, as we stood at his door, through
our interpreter, for being unable to rise or give us his hand
in consequence of being *tabooed*, and added that if he were
not fed by others he would be obliged to go without food.

The missioners told us that in consequence of their recent
cannibalism, the necessity they themselves felt of removing
every spark left of that inveterate habit, and the difficulty
of handling the cognate doctrine of eating Christ's flesh and
blood, without confounding things in their minds, obliged
them to revive the ancient discipline of the secret with their
first catecumens. They taught them only that the Mass was
the highest degree of worship, and whilst one priest said the
Mass, another kept them occupied with prayers and hymns
whilst it was going on. When nearly prepared for baptism,
they were then taught the mystery of the Real Presence.

We rowed up the Bay for some miles to pay a visit to
the Governor, for the Bay of Islands was at that time the
chief settlement. Captain Hobson, R.N. received us cour-
teously and talked freely about the British position amongst
the native population. He was particularly anxious to avoid
a collision with them, which they then seemed somewhat
inclined to provoke. He had a native in prison for murdering
another. They had let him escape once, but the natives themselves brought him back. Bishop Pompallier was on very good
terms with the Governor, and had given his wife lessons in
the native language, and yet the old sea Captain had a sore
grievance against him, a grievance which Dr. Polding could
not comprehend but which to an old sailor like myself was
obvious enough. The Bishop by his account had brought an
American vessel for his missionary purposes, sailed her with
a French commander and crew, had no regular papers and no
national flag, but only some fancy device of his own, an image

of the Virgin represented on white bunting. 'If I met her at sea, concluded the Captain, 'I should certainly seize her for a pirate and take her into port.' And no doubt the Law of Nations would have justified him. It was proof of my friend the good Bishop's simplicity in the world's ways. But the Captain, who was crusty on the point astonished Dr. Polding with his final remark that the Bishop who could do such a thing 'must be either a very good man, or a very bad one.' Dr. Polding defended his brother Bishop's goodness, whilst I was simply amused at the whole scene, comprehending the way in which the Captain was paying covert homage to the good Bishop's innocence of a certain point in the law of the seas. At a later period the Bishop adopted a British flag, and registered his ship as belonging to New Zealand.

About a mile from the residence, the British troops were encamped under tents, and we went to pay them a visit. Right in front of them was a *Pah*[2] situated on a lofty eminence scarped and strongly fortified. The water approach from the bay was strongly palisaded, and the steep passage of ascent as well. The officers said that, in the event of a collision, there would be no getting at the enemy except by throwing rockets. It certainly looked formidable except to artillery, of which they had none, either there or in Sydney. After hospitable treatment in an officer's tent, we returned to the mission.

On another occasion, through Mr. Waterton's urgent recommendation, we made an excursion to see, amongst other things, a remarkable geological formation. Accompanied by Mr. Waterton and two of the missioners, we pulled up at the bay, then entered a river for some distance, landed, and walked some miles along the back of those winding ridges and across valleys that characterise that island. At last we came to a broad valley with a stream rushing through it, on one side of which rose a mountain of marble prolonged for a considerable extent, obviously cleared on all sides at some period or another by the action of water. It presented the most fantastic shapes as of gothic ruins, covered with trailing plants, and indented with caverns. The marble itself was white with salmon-coloured veins. By the stream stood a native village as silent as the grave. We entered it and found not a soul, nothing but a dog and a few calabashes. The population had gone to their potato ground at a distance. A yawning cavern just opposite shewed by the feathers suspended that it was *tabooed* as their cemetery. It is death by native law to violate *tabooed* ground, but they soon found it expedient to consider Europeans as not under the law. We ventured to enter, but only found a strong odour of human remains and an old musket, and quickly retired.

Their provision of corn was, as usual, deposited in little circular thatched cots, elevated on top of long poles, to keep it from the rats, and *tabooed*, to make it sacred from human intrusion. Even an enemy in time of war will not touch anything made sacred by the *taboo*. As we crossed a wood on our return we came upon a withered old woman who, when she saw the missioners in their soutanes and triangular hats, set up her wailing cry of joy. They had made a Christian of her, and she had not seen them for some considerable time. After a mutual greeting and some exchange of kind words, she continued wailing her joy until we were out of hearing. The New Zealanders invariably expressed deep feelings of joy by loud crying, prolonged according to the depth of feeling awakened. A mother who came from a distance to see her son, a youth of fourteen, who was studying under the missioners at their house, in the hope of becoming a priest, cried for half an hour, sitting looking at him and hugging him alternately.

We passed near a Protestant school in which about forty women and children were busy reading. Curious to see what was going on, I approached the window when, at sight of the obtruding *Picopo*, up rose the *odium theologicum* in the hearts of the women, and with sudden exclamations they clapt-to the door, and the wooden shutter which closed the window. We crossed one of those magnificent pine forest valleys filled with lofty stems and the darkest of foliage just as night was falling, and so to our boat and home.

Mr. Williams, the head of the Protestant mission, crossed over the broad bay from his handsome house in his beautiful boat, manned by natives, to pay us a visit, and on the following day we returned his call. He had been some twenty years in New Zealand and had accumulated a large property. The extent of land and stock which he and other missioners had acquired had often been the theme of attack both in the Sydney Press and Legislative Council, and I was curious to see with my own eyes what those large properties really were. They had preceded the settlers as well as the Catholic missioners some twenty years, and had fairly taken possession for trifling considerations, it was said, of the best land. The Protestant Bishop had stated in the Council in their defence that 'it was their duty to provide for their children, and that by the gift of God no persons had been blessed with a more numerous progeny than the New Zealand missionaries.' On the other hand, the French Bishop and his clergy obtained no more, and that by regular purchase, than sufficed for their residence and garden. It was also said that these missioners had carried on an extensive traffic, amongst other things in spirits, and in New Zealanders' heads, as curiosities, and for museums and surgical collections, until the Sydney Government at last made the latter article contraband. In war, the New Zealanders cut off the heads of their fallen enemies as trophies, baked them, then exposed them to a current of cold air which hardened them, and so ranged them on a shelf in their huts as trophies of their valour. I had one, given me by a surgeon in Sydney, for a considerable time in a bandbox over my bed's head, intending to get it to England for the Downside museum, but the maggots got at it and I was obliged to bury it.

The natives soon found out that the French missioners neither entered into traffic or cared for land, and remarked that whilst the one class sought for their land and their produce, the other sought for their souls, and about forty thousand of them, those who had not already given in adhesion to the Anglican or Wesleyan missioners, put themselves under the Catholic mission.

Bishop Pompallier told me at a later period that when they first landed they soon found the most extraordinary notions rife amongst the natives respecting those horrible *Picopos*. Amongst other wild stories, they understood that they were a sort of cannibal from religious motives, eating human flesh. On his first visit to a tribe at a distance they looked at him with a notion in their heads that he was a sort of magician, and had the power of fascinating and devouring them. He seated his tall and handsome figure, smiled through his mild and beautiful features upon them, and then said: 'I have come to eat you, but before I do so let me give each one of you a blanket.' After they had got their blankets he explained to them that he had not come to eat their bodies, but to bring their spirits to the Great Spirit. And as they grew free and familiar with him, they told him: '*The mikoneri* always sold their blankets very dear.'

Mr. Scott, an Irish gentleman and a convert, told me after a voyage to New Zealand from Sydney for England that he found his best introduction to the Catholic tribes was to tell them he was *Picopo* and to make the Sign of the Cross. He had once introduced himself thus to a chief, when he soon found his mistake. The man shook his head and said: 'God very good, Maria very bad.'

'Who is Maria?' asked my friend.

He pointed upwards and said: 'The woman, very bad.'

Coming on another occasion to a group of natives, he found them surrounding one of their number, who was preaching to them. He had a burning stick in his hand and was making gestures illustrative of his theme. He asked his Catholic native guide what the man was saying, and it appeared he was explaining a place called Roma, where the *Picopos* came from. He told them that the people of Roma burnt those who would not be *Picopos* under the arms and in other parts of the body to which he pointed with his fire stick, and that they tied them to wild horses and tore them to pieces. He had been obviously led to confound the cruelties of Pagan to Christian Rome, and had got the *Book of Martyrs* in his head in its newest edition.

Curious then to see with my own eyes one of those great missionary farms of which so much had been said, and wishing to be able to speak of them from my own knowledge, should I ever be called upon to do so, in company with Father Bataillon and Dr. Gregory we started in a boat for a long pull over the breadth of the vast bay and up the principal river for a distance of some six or seven miles. We had for our crew the tailor of the mission, a boy, and a native who was to leave us on the opposite shore. We calculated on sailing back with the evening breeze. After a long pull we got on a small island for a rest, and finding quantities of small oysters cleaving to the rocks, taking stones, we hammered them off, sucking the juicy 'sea-fruit', as the Italians call them, until we had cut our hands pretty freely through the clumsy operation of detaching them.

We then sailed on to a native Catholic village where, seeing the triangular hat approaching, we were met by the chief and all his subjects of both sexes, young and old, crying their joy. The salutes were warm without interrupting the crying, and the tall and burly chief rubbed his cold blue nose against mine with energy befitting the occasion.[3] Then we all went on our knees in the long grass, and Father Bataillon began to say prayers in which they all joined. After some merry gossip with the good Father that was Sanskrit to us, the wind began to blow stiffly and the water to get agitated, and it was decided that it was not safe for us to venture further, but that we should have hard work to get home again, the wind heading us, or nearly so. After holding a little council we decided on taking a reach to an island at some distance, hoping after that to be able with sails and oars to gain the harbour of Korarika. The natives gave us a hearty shove off, and then came the heavy tug. We just caught the island, and found a young Scotch couple its only inhabitants. They cultivated a garden for the Korarika market. They gave us some food, and pleased us by their kindly welcome. After I reached England I read in a newspaper that this good, simple-hearted couple were found murdered and their place plundered. We launched once more, the wind stiffened into a gale and the boat laboured a good deal, running her lee gunwhale almost into the water. I took the helm, and held the sheet of the sail in my hands, ready to let slip in the event of a sudden squall, and put the boat before it. The others pulled the oars, and now and then baled out the water thrown over our bows. The ships in the harbour watched us with their telescopes, anxious for our safety. We set up the *Salve Regina*, and then the Litany, and they were seldom sung with more earnest devotion. Long was the tugging, close and watchful the sailing. Night came upon us. We failed to reach the harbour, but caught a point beyond it, hauled our boat on the beach and walked home, after making our thanksgiving, quite ready for a supper.

One excursion more, which for its amusing incidents is worth recording. Bishop Polding, Dr. Gregory, a son of Mr. Justice Therry, a boy of twelve years whom we were taking to College, and two of the missionary Fathers started again in the boat to visit a first class *pah* and to see the country. The *pah* was a formidable structure, square in form, enclosing a considerable population, and formed in its defences of upright stems of trees driven into the ground, the corners being huge thick boles, with grotesque and grinning figures carved at the top of them. Stockades protected the entrance, but even when these were passed the difficulty of effecting an entry was by no means surmounted for the entrance from the exterior was only into a long and narrow passage formed by other stems of trees, which only gave an exit into the interior after it had run for a considerable distance on to the centre; and it left the invaders to the mercy of the warriors, firing or using their spears through chinks and loopholes. A hostile tribe or, more likely, a confederation of tribes, might lie in ambush for months, watching some opportunity to scale over, make a breach into or slip through these defences or undermine them.

On our return we came to a bend of a river, having to cross over where a native village stood. A woman pushed a bark canoe across, too frail for more than one passenger at a time, and leaky as Charon's ferry craft, witness the water that covered the precarious footing which it offered. A priest crossed, standing upright, and the Bishop followed the example. He was in his purple stockings and large shovel hat. The frail bark, that was mere bark, cockled from side to side. The Bishop squatted for safety down into the water, and the olive-coloured ferry woman raised a merry laugh in which we all joined in chorus. Arrived at the other side, we inspected the cooking of a dog that was going on. Their style of cooking, if simple, is perfect whether applied to hog, dog, or human subject. The following is the recipe:

Just make a hole in the ground of convenient size. Then pave it with good round stones. On the stones make a wood fire. When the stones are thoroughly heated cover them with leaves. Then put in the dog, properly prepared and rolled up. Next put leaves over him, then stones that have been heated over that. Throw some earth lightly over all, and after a time the pile will begin to smoke. Let experience regulate the time required for cooking, and then when you take out the baked animal you will find it not only the tenderest of food, but also filled with gravy, of which a drop has not been lost.

We had now to make for our boat, and I set my mind on proceeding in its direction along a range of hills covered with forest, which promised a fine prospect of country. The natives shook their heads and declared we could not go that way. The Fathers declared we could not safely neglect their opinion; but in a headstrong mood and self-confident I resolved to try it, and persuaded Dr. Polding to join me, who took young Therry with him. The missioners and Dr. Gregory wisely took another course. From the hills we had to descend into a green plain to gain the stream; but alas for my presumption! We found ourselves plunging into a black and sloppy bog, covered over with the treacherous grass. We got up to our knees. Young Therry every now and then left a boot sticking in the slush, and it was difficult recovering it. At last we carried him on our backs, in turns. Amidst our difficulties there appeared a deliverer in the shape of a long, half-naked New Zealander. He came up to near where we were, holding a brace of wild ducks in his hand, quavering which he exclaimed: 'One *talara* two *talara*.' Yes, yes, we were ready to give him two dollars to help us out. He came up, stooped, and I mounted first on his broad shoulders. He laid me on a green mound, from which I could see the boat at a distance with the Fathers in it. But when I turned again to look for the Bishop, I saw him mounted on the copper-coloured New Zealander, his purple legs sticking forward, and on his shoulders, rising above his broad hat, rode young Therry, from whose hands hung the wild ducks. This human pyramid advanced with solemn pace upon the two long copper legs, and after a hearty laugh at the whole adventure we handed our dollars, giving something extra for the ducks as a memorial, and joined the boat.

After a very interesting fortnight at Korarika we again set sail, our Captain having failed to dispose of much of his remaining cargo of *jarke (chaire cuite)* or sun-dried Chilean beef. The pork of New Zealand, fed in the woods, was so abundant and so superior to anything that goes by that name in England, being something with the united qualities of veal, wild boar and ordinary pork, that the colonists lived chiefly upon it, as well as the missioners, and never tired of it. This great supply of hogs had sprung from the few left by Captain Cook. The dog had been previously left by the Spaniards and still retained the Spanish name of *perro*. Having had no quadruped but the rat before that may explain the practice of eating the dog, as it may also explain the practice of eating men, dating from earlier periods. There is no doubt that they also had a sort of diabolical sacramental notion that in eating a warrior they partook of his warlike qualities.

One missionary anecdote from the lips of Bishop Pompallier, and then we will leave this interesting people. A daughter of one of the principal chiefs had been a follower of certain dissenting missioners, and her name was Hoke. But coming under the influence of the Bishop, she became a zealous Catholic. She was intelligent and well instructed. The missioners, concerned at losing such an influential proselyte, came and remonstrated with her. They said: 'Well, Hoke, we are surprised at your going to those *Picopos*, who will not give you the Holy Book.' And on that theme they enlarged. Meanwhile Hoke sat and listened, with her arms across, for they are very polite. When they had finished, Hoke arose to speak, and they had to sit and listen. She began: 'You mick'oners, you say you come from God. But if you come from God, you don't tell lies.' She then said to a girl attending her: 'Fetch my books.' She took up one little book and said: 'Look! That teaches all I have to believe. It explains the Apostle's Creed. Look!' She laid it down and took up another: 'Look! That explains all I have to do. It explains the Ten Commandments. Look!' She took up a third and said: 'Look! That explains all I have to ask of God. It explains the Lord's Prayer. Look! If I was blind, of what use would be the Holy Book. But the *Picopo* came, and he spoke to my ear living words, and the words went to my heart, and the light of God came with them, and I saw and believed. And now you have told lies. – Go, go, go!'

Notes

1   Not only the potatoes, but the pork also of New Zealand, was often praised by the Bishop as superior to anything of the kind grown in Europe. He used to relate how both these comestibles figured on the occasions when peace was established between two tribes after a period of war. The ceremony in use at such times was peculiar. A wall was built, composed of roast pork and potatoes, mixed together; the rival tribes established themselves at either end of the wall and steadily ate their way through it till they met in the middle, and when this happened the peace was considered as concluded.

2   *Pah* or *Pa*. A fortified Maori village.

3   In Ullathorne's last illness when someone spoke of his feeling cold he replied, 'Not so cold as the nose of a New Zealand chief, that is the coldest object in nature that I know of.'

Chapter Thirty-Four

South America

But though various other remembrances of this fine race of men crowd into my mind, it is time we were on the broad Pacific, where a strong wind is almost always blowing in the direction of Cape Horn.

In the Bay of Aranca[1] I read over again the celebrated epic of Ercilla's[2] on the scene itself. The unconquerable Arancanians have not yet been conquered and the Chilians subsidised some of their leading chiefs to keep them tranquil, giving them nominal commands in their army. Passing Juan Fernandez on a bright day with a fine breeze it was impossible not to recall Alexander Selkirk, Rogers and Robinson Crusoe, although the scene of that enchanting story is laid in the Carribean Islands. The lofty island still abounds with goats but Chili has made it a penal settlement, a sort of second Norfolk Island, which destroyed its poetry. The Andes towered up at a great distance on our right and volcanic ashes fell in fine dust upon our deck, though we saw nothing of volcanoes. At last we turned into the Bay of Talcuhana where the friends of our Captain, Captain Saunders, whose brother-in-law was Governor of the town, came crowding on our deck.

We soon learnt that there was a furious civil war raging in Columbia, and that it would be not be safe for us to take our proposed route across the Pampas owing to the confusion on the other side of the Continent.[3] The City of Conception was seven miles inland from the port. A new Bishop had just been appointed and he was on his way to receive consecration at St. Jago, the capital, attended by fifty horsemen, on a ride of some six hundred miles. As there was no suitable inn at Talcuhana we remained on board, going ashore to say Mass and to look about the country. For both the City of Conception and the town of Talcuhana had been utterly destroyed by an earthquake seven years previously to our arrival, and

223

this was the third destruction by similar causes. On the last occasion a great wave came upon Talcuhana and washed it into the sea and the first town of that name lay at the bottom of the Bay.

Being English the people could not get rid of the notion that we must be Protestants, and that young Therry was the Bishop's son. Even though they saw us say Mass in their churches, they only concluded that the Protestant service was very like their own. We had also to encounter a prejudice on the part of the Governor of the Province, which came of a very innocent cause. Colonel Frere, a member of a wealthy family near Talcuhana had been exiled with some of his companions for their share in one of the numerous insurrections which, from time to time, agitated that country. They were sent to one of the South Sea Islands in a gun brig. Calling at Sydney on their way our Bishop heard of them and with his usual kindness called upon them, offered them hospitality, and sent them presents of provisions which might conduce to their comfort. The governing authorities of Chili heard of this and mistook the courtesy of a Catholic Bishop to Catholic gentlemen under a cloud for sympathy with their cause. The Bishop therefore on arrival received no attention except from the family of the Freres who did all they could to show their gratitude, and put their finest horses at our disposal. But Captain Saunders and his friends bustled about, explained the spirit and intent of the Bishop, and went to the Governor at Conception to lodge an explanation with him, and told him what a disgrace it would be if the Bishop were neglected because of a pure act of humanity. We were consequently invited by General Bulnoz[4] to his mansion in the City of Conception. This Bulnoz was the brother of the hero who had conquered the Peruvians on their own soil, and who at that time was the President of the Republic.

We started on the beautiful horses lent by the Freres accompanied by our Captain and the British Consul, and after a ride of seven miles reached the splendid residence of the Governor, which had been rebuilt since the earthquake, and covered a large space of ground, as the whole was on the ground storey, a precaution against new earthquakes. On surveying the city we found that it had been utterly destroyed. All that remained of the once most magnificent cathedral in South America were the broken steps of the high altar. All the churches as well as the convents had been completely destroyed. The population for several years had lived under tents. The town was being gradually reconstructed, but all on ground floors. The bells of the provisional churches were suspended in low, wooden cages. It was curious to notice the sparkles of gold in the broken bricks of the ruins, but they were not worth extracting.

The heads of the clergy, of the Religious Orders of men, and the chief notables were invited to meet us, and such a dinner was laid on the table as only Chilians or Peruvians could understand. The courses were endless and eating went on for seven mortal hours and a half, from four o'clock to half past eleven. None of the party spoke any language except their native Spanish, for though we understood their speech pretty well, we did not venture to smatter in it. So Don José, one of the canons, a man quick of speech, acted as interpreter, through the medium of Latin, not a prompt instrument for modern conversation.

Towards the end of the dinner, at which the sweets were introduced in the middle, and then meats followed anew, a negro servant undertook to produce an English dish in our honour. The dish was produced amidst general expectation and consisted of five boiled ducks floating in hot water, with skins as tight as the skins of unripe gooseberries. Although it was the etiquette to take of each dish everybody rebelled against the English dish, and it was taken away.

After the prodigious labour of this dinner we rose from the table near midnight. We left the Bishop in a suite of handsome rooms and Dr. Gregory and I took our way to the British Resident's where we found accommodation. On our way thither we met first one, then another of the city police, mounted on horseback, trotting along and blowing a whistle all the way, except when it was interrupted by chanting *Ave Maria purissima*, or calling the hour with a cry of *Viva Chili*. It struck us as an effective way of warning the thieves and evil doers to get away.

The next morning the Bishop said Mass in the principal provisional church, but the people still had the impression that they were present at a Protestant Bishop's Mass. We visited all the churches and convents accompanied by a curious crowd, the bells of each, suspended in their wooden cages, ringing as well as they could at our approach. The furnishing of the churches was excessively tawdry. Behind every high altar there was a blind of white silk which, at the moment of Elevation, touched at a spring, flew up and revealed behind and above the Blessed Sacrament, a dressed-up image of the Blessed Virgin, ascending from amidst a mass of artificial flowers into a painted heaven. This was very distracting at so solemn a moment, nor was I edified when the British Consul leaned towards me and whispered, 'Look, she is a pretty lass.' But the feature most strange to our eyes in the church was the glass cases arranged along the walls in which, as in a museum, were arranged a number of wooden figures with staring eyes, clothed in habits and standing close upon each other, as representations of the Saints. They looked exactly like the blocks that carry clothes in a shop window, and suggested nothing but clothes. Religion was confessedly at a low ebb in the country, and the Sacraments but little frequented. We did not visit the convents without getting a penance for, receiving us with all honour and kindness, at each one that we came to the nuns, or the friars, insisted on our taking thick chocolate with sugar biscuits, which no refusal could save us from, and with which we were almost choked.

The Trinitarian nuns, a large and flourishing community with a respectable boarding school, threw open the folding doors of their enclosure and received us in a body, standing on one side of the enclosure while we stood on the other. Benedictines though we were, they insisted on our receiving the Trinitarian scapular, and sent for their chaplain to confer it in their presence. As the Bishop tamely submitted to the function we, of course, followed, however uncanonical the proceedings.

After lunching with the Governor, His Excellency proposed to drive the Bishop back to Talcuhana. A great company, consisting of the chief clergy, Superiors of Religious houses, military officers and gentlemen assembled on horseback with a guard of honour. A singular vehicle consisting of a sort of tub with the sides and a seat mounted on four wheels was produced and the Governor, an enormously stout man, mounted together with the Bishop and we were ranged in order and proceeded. It was a strange and variegated scene and the English Consul and I soon dropped behind that we might talk freely and enjoy the spectacle. It reminded us of Flaxman's procession of the Canterbury pilgrims. Military men were mixed with civilians in their broad sombreros, and the cloaks and scapulars of the religious men flew out in the wind, whilst their heads were covered with large-brimmed straw hats. After going about a mile, the seat of the carriage broke down between the big wheels, evidently owing to the immense weight of the Governor. The two riders disentangled themselves. After examination the vehicle was pronounced incurable and to the great relief of the Bishop, who was a celebrated horseman, led horses were brought forward for them to mount. On approaching Talcuhana we were met by another escort, headed by the chief men of the town, where, bidding farewell to our entertainers, we returned to our ship.

Notes

1   Ullathorne's spelling differs from the currently accepted Araunca.
2   Alonso de Ercilla y Zuniga (1553 – 94), Spanish soldier and poet, author of *La Araucana*, the most celebrated Spanish Renaissance epic poem and the first epic poem about America. He fought in the wars against the Araucanian Indians and his poem, which consists of thirty-nine cantos, is based on his experiences in those battles and shows great sympathy for the brave resistance of the Araucanians.
3   There was indeed a civil war in Columbia at the time Ullathorne was in Chile but Columbia seems a long way off from their proposed destination of Buenos Aires to have much direct effect on travellers.
4   Mss.1. has Bulnez.

Chapter Thirty-Five

On Board a French Whaler

In the harbour was a French whaler which, after two years in the Pacific, was returning to Havre de Grace. We arranged for a passage in her, the mates and harpooners giving up their cabins for a small share of the fare, and were soon once more at sea. They still kept the crow's nest at the masthead, as they were not full, and still hoped to fall in with a whale or two, but were disappointed. The Captain was an able man, well mannered and agreeable. The numerous crew were light-hearted, easily amused and always gay. They had no allowance of rum as on an English ship, but drank spruce beer, made on board from twigs of the spruce tree. They had neither the economy nor industry of English sailors, where not an inch of rope is wasted. As we neared France coil after coil of rope was thrown overboard, which English sailors would have been employed in turning into spinyarn, knittles[1] etc. The reason alleged was that they would have everything new for the next voyage. Yet with all their leisure these men never quarrelled.

One night we were awakened in our cabins by an awful scream from aloft. It had begun to blow and a light youth was furling the main topgallant sail when he slipped from the yard and hung suspended by his hands to the foot rope. The Captain, a little, wiry man was on deck, and shouted out, 'Hold on a minute!'. He threw off his pea jacket, ran up aloft like a cat, got astride the yard like lightning, seized the man by the collar, flung him over his shoulder like a child, and brought him down. The moment he was on deck the excitement of this daring and gallant act turned him sick. This was the third life he had saved in the course of his maritime career.

A little incident that occurred during the voyage will throw some light on the later part of my Australian narration. A

228

copy of Fenelon's *Telemachus* was in the cabin. The Bishop read it through remarking, when he had done so, how very different the beautiful composition struck his mind when thus read, than when merely used as a school book. This remark led Dr. Gregory to read it. When he had finished the thirteenth book he said to the Bishop in his frank, laughing way: 'Why, Idomeneus is yourself and Dr. Ullathorne is Philocles, and Mr--- and Mr--- are Protesilaus and the other man.'

'Yes,' replied the Bishop, 'But I sent them about their business and recalled Philocles.'

I did not, of course, hear these remarks, but they were repeated to me by Dr. Gregory. Now the pith of that character is contained in the following sentences, addressed by Idomeneus to Mentor. He says:

'The frankness and integrity of Philocles disgusted me: he saw himself decline under the ascendency of Protesilaus without a struggle and contented himself with always telling me the truth, whenever I would hear it, for he had my advantage, and not his own interest in view.'

This incident offers an opportunity for making some analysis of the difficulties which so much embarrassed my later position in New South Wales. The passage I have just quoted from the conversation of Idomeneus with Mentor, if not strictly applicable to the letter, was not without a certain truth of application to my own case. At critical moments I did speak plainly, sometimes more plainly than was palatable, yet always with an element in our relations that needs to be taken into account. For the greater part of his life, beginning with his youth, and ending with the appointment to the Bishopric, the Bishop had been prefect of a School, or Master of Novices, and the peculiar habits imbibed from these offices clove as a matter of course. And I had been a boy under him as well as a novice, and moreover he had been my spiritual father, and had even first prepared me for the sacraments. His heart was, moreover, of that character which claims for those under its influence an affection and a loyalty of that kind which sons give to their mothers. Then from his life in a monastery he had not that practical skill in the world's ways, being also himself unworldly, which my less fortunate history had given me.

A second position is always more difficult than a first, but these conditions, on both sides, made mine particularly difficult. Then there was this additional circumstance, and such things tell more than they are habitually realised, as it were, in the undercurrent. I had held the ecclesiastical authority in the Colony before the Bishop appeared on the scene and had, as matter of necessity, become mixed up with all its affairs. The Bishop, again, was more attracted to missionary labour than to the conduct of affairs, which threw the thinking them out a good deal upon me, who alone, besides himself, had the key to them. The Bishop himself expressed this state of things more strongly than even the reality warranted, or than I could admit, when one day, as we were riding together, he observed in the course of conversation that we made up a Bishop between us, and that in drawing the burden of our affairs, he was in the shafts and I, too, therefore. Yet, though I took all odious things upon me before the public and really did my best to keep him in good odour, although I never acted unless by his direction, I was left to bear the exclusive responsibility before the world, left as unsupported in an emergency as though I had acted from myself. All these things in combination were both trying in themselves and quickening to one's native sensibility, and wearing to one's spirit.

But there was another difficulty springing less from intention than character. Seldom was a case put to me, or a circle of facts communicated, but something or other that was important to decision, and had to be kept in view in action, was reserved and never came out. The Bishop had not that valuable faculty of saying out in a few words of all that was essential for putting one at the very centre of a subject under consideration. One got fragments, never being certain of having got the most essential ones. It is this which has embarrassed so many of his affairs with the Holy See, and caused him to be so often misapprehended. He never detailed a case well, so as to secure its being seen both from the centre and all round. Thus something might come out to confuse a line of action after it had been adopted and set in operation. One was sometimes tempted to imagine that there was a feeling that to part with one's knowledge of a subject was like parting with all one's prerogatives, yet this was not so much the case as it was the not realising the importance of steadily looking a difficulty all through, before taking it in hand to deal with it thoroughly. Again, there was the uncertainty of holding firmly to a course after it had been settled in council, and one had got committed to it in action.

During the earlier part of the voyage I had thought much of the religious wants of Australia. There were then five Colonies, remote from each other, as well as the distant settlement of Port Macquarie and the penal settlement of Norfolk Island. And yet the one Bishop was entirely occupied with New South Wales alone, and could know little of what passed in the other Colonies. Besides, until they each had a Bishop, they were not likely to be properly provided with priests. It was also a great temptation to send difficult priests to those remote Colonies, as Father Therry had been sent to Hobart Town, there to make things more impracticable for the future than if there had been no priest sent there.

At the same time I felt that at so great a distance from the Holy See, there ought to be a point of unity, and a centre of control over the whole of the Colonies. It appeared to me that what was really wanted was a Hierarchy. I also thought that the Bishop would enter into the schemes of multiplying Bishops more readily if a Hierarchy could be gained instead of Vicars-Apostolic. I therefore drew up a scheme for a Hierarchy, alleging the reasons for it that I thought expedient, and specifying the Sees to be gradually filled up. This document I gave to the Bishop, and urged the subject upon his attention in various conversations, until he became quite disposed to see the importance of the proposition, and to enter into it.

This document, as Bishop Polding afterwards informed me, was made the basis of the plan when recommended to the Holy See. And Archbishop Nicholson, then Father Nicholson, the Carmelite, let me know that it was chiefly through his instrumentality and influence at Propaganda that the plan became successful. But of this later on. Let us proceed on our voyage.

The Bishop never lost an opportunity of drawing souls to God. I remember his saying that the sublimest act of his ministry that he remembered was on a dark night, travelling through the bush with a boy for his guide, the son of an Irish emancipist settler. Talking to the boy, as he led the way through the dark forest, he found he had not been to his duties for a long time and, though the rain was pouring heavily, the Bishop got off his horse, led him to a tree and sitting on the stem of another that had fallen, he heard the boy's confession, kneeling in the wet grass by his side. Some time after, in travelling the same way, he turned aside to enquire after him and found that he had been killed while felling a tree.

On board the French whaler the Bishop got a word first with one man, then with another, and gradually formed a little class that came down into the cabin for instruction. The class grew until it embraced the whole crew, officers included, who came down in their watches below. To one or other of us, as their fancy suggested, they came to confession. At twelve o'clock on Easter Eve, lying in my cabin, I heard the men creeping into the cabin in their stockings, and when assembled those simple-hearted men went on their knees and sang the cantique, *Réjouissez-vous, O Chrétiens*, as a greeting to the Bishop at the dawn of Easter Day. Next morning, the weather being fine and the sea smooth, an awning was stretched over the main deck, an altar erected, and the Bishop with Dr. Gregory and myself as assistants, sang High Mass for the crew, all of whom went to Holy Communion. Having most of them been choir boys when young in their village churches, they sang the Mass in Plain Chant and acquitted themselves well. At the offertory the cook unexpectedly presented himself on his knees with a loaf on a cloth, especially prepared for the *pain bénit*, to be eaten after Communion after the French custom. Often after that day did we hear the men singing pious *cantiques*, especially during the night watches.

Crossing the line we made it a festive occasion and requested the Captain to give up to them some of the fresh provisions intended for us, a couple of sheep or so, perhaps three, included. The Chilian sheep, by the way, of which a large stock were brought on board, were so thin that, when hung up, if a candle had been put inside of them, they would have made beautiful red railway signals in the night, revealing at the same time the anatomy of the animal. We also added sundry dozens of light wine. How grateful they were, and how gay, and how they danced all day, making music of an old speaking trumpet and a few jingling bars of metal and yet, with the help of their mouths, the musicians contrived to accentuate their favourite tunes.

And how they sung and danced at once, singing favourite village songs that were perfectly innocent. One of their favourites was to lilt hand in hand around the mainmasts singing out:

Je m'en irai, où je boirai bon soir à la compagnie;

Je me'n irai, où je boirai bon soir à la compagnie ...

and that in such a merry tune. They were so childlike, and they were so courteous to one another, yet in no mockery, and they were so gratified at having us looking on, and entering into their enjoyment. At first one, then another, came up to us feeling the privilege of the day to do so, and saying how all their life this would be a great remembrance, and how they would have to tell their fathers, mothers, wives or sisters, how the Bishop had mingled in their happy fête. I could not resist throwing in this little event, it struck us as such an illustration of what Christianity can do to make the hearts of men of a rude occupation, simple, and as presenting such a contrast to the stiff, self-conscious, more than half-ashamed exhibition we might have had from a set of English rustics. But sailors, even English sailors, are incomparably more simple and genuine men than their brethren ashore. If only, as in this case, they could have religion brought to them on the seas, and could be guided as children need guiding, when out of their element on shore.

The Captain was a steady, religious man who always made his Easter duties. The only one who hung back was the young surgeon. One saw that it was nothing but a little of the pride of the *esprit fort*, and that more in show than in reality, for he was really a good-hearted young man. One smooth day Dr. Gregory asked him to go up with him into the maintop, there to lie down and have a talk in the cool air. After a time Dr. Gregory, who was a strong, muscular man, seized him by the collar, as if going to pitch him into the sea. The little doctor, startled, called out: 'Ah, Monsieur Gregory! *Tenez, tenez!*'

'What is the matter?' said Dr. Gregory. 'There must be something not right in your conscience that makes you feel afraid. The fact is, the Bishop has sent me for you. He wants to speak to you in his cabin.'

'Oh, Monsieur Gregory, will you make my apology?'

'Certainly not. Is that your French politeness? Go and make it yourself.'

They came down. The little doctor reluctantly descended to the Bishop's cabin. Dr. Gregory pushed him in and closed the door. After an interval he came out with a happy face and went to Communion soon after, to the delight of the crew. He then told Dr. Gregory that he had been piously brought up, and that his First Communion Day had been the happiest of his life, but that he had been diverted from the exercise of his religion through the influence of certain college companions, though never in his heart had he abandoned the Faith.

About three hundred miles off the river La Plata we encountered a gale such as I never elsewhere experienced. It had been blowing already and the sea was rough, when there came a tremendous gale that laid the sea flat, the foam running over the surface like cream. We put before the wind under bare poles and as it grew more moderate the sea rose furiously. On sounding the pumps there were twelve feet of water. We took our spell with the men at the pump handles, but after twelve hours pumping it was found there was no leak, it was the result of the strain upon the hull for the time.

As our vessel entered the Channel we got an English newspaper from a pilot boat, and the first thing upon which my eyes fell was the failure of the Wright's Bank. This was sad news for the Catholics of England, and for Catholic institutions, and we were apprehensive for our own small resources. But our agent, Dr. Heptonstall, had divined the state of things, and had drawn everything out just in time.

On reaching Havre de Grace the ship's company presented the Bishop and his companions with a grateful and touching address drawn up, and read, by the doctor, and they had it inserted in the Havre newspapers.

Notes

1   Small lines used for various purposes at sea, such as to reef sails from below, etc.

Chapter Thirty-Six

Further Travels in Ireland

We landed in England from Havre towards the close of May or beginning of June, 1841, and reached London in time to assist at the aggregate meeting of the Catholic Association, at which O'Connell made one of his great speeches. The Bishop was particularly solicitous to appear at the great assembly, as an opportunity for bringing the Catholic affairs of Australia before the Catholics of England. He said to me: 'I will skirmish, if you will explain our great wants systematically.' The Bishop spoke, but Lord Camoys, who was in the chair, overruled my speaking in the committee room, on the plea of want of time, and though repeatedly called upon I thought it prudent to sit still. However, the meeting brought us into contact with the leaders of the English Catholics.

As the vacation was approaching at Maynooth it was thought desirable that I should proceed there without delay to endeavour to obtain some ecclesiastics, or rather, prepare the ground for the Bishop's obtaining some, whilst he himself proceeded to Birmingham to assist at the opening of the Cathedral of St. Chad. When I arrived there I was received with great warmth and kindness by the President and professors, and Dean Gaffney asked me to give the Retreat to the students prior to ordination, and the break-up of the College. Aided by a copy of the works of St. Alphonsus Ligouri, that had been put in my hands, I did so, and took an opportunity, with the sanction of the Rector to give a discourse on the Australian Mission. This led sundry of the students to offer themselves to the work of the Australian Church. I wrote to Bishop Polding telling him how important it was that he should be on the spot without delay, as the vacation was so near; that otherwise my work would be frustrated. He replied that he would leave Birmingham immediately after the opening and that, as I suggested, he would not even wait for the assemblage of the leading Catholics from every part of England in the Town Hall afterwards. Yet, though His Lordship faithfully complied with my request thus far, I was destined for disappointments. I waited three days in Dublin for him and he did not appear. At last I went off to England in search of him. Meanwhile, from being inexperienced in railway travelling, he had reached Liverpool too late for the boat. He was advised to go to Holyhead, reached there too late again for the boat, returned to Liverpool, and at last reached Dublin after the vacation had commenced. This misfortune was serious, as the freshness of the call to Australia wore off before another opportunity came round.

We made a journey together to the South of Ireland, where the Bishop had many friends and I not a few. We received a genuine welcome at Carlow, where the College was having its exhibition, and there met the celebrated Bishop England, of South Carolina, as also Bishop Clancey, of Demerara.

Thence we paid a visit to the Cistercian Monastery of Mount Melleray,[1] where for the first time I found myself in a centre of that ascetic life to which I had once aspired. The monastery was large, the Community numerous, the church capacious; but everything bore the signs of Cistercian simplicity and poverty. A large school was under the care of the Fathers, who taught agriculture as well as literature. We resolved to assist at the midnight office, and nothing to my heart was ever more impressive than the simple chaunt, the three notes, forever alternating from side to side from the two choirs, in which the protracted office was sung, especially considering the recollection of those long rows of white-robed monks. The slow, sweet accents, with long interpause, of that never varying yet never tiring monotony of rise and fall, under which the rapidly varying sense of the psalmody advanced, in which also, without variation of a note, the lessons, responses, the antiphons, even the gospel was sung, seemed to express the acquirement of an unchangeable patience and peace in the soul, which the voices of that tranquil choir of mortal men seemed to shadow, in the sense of an ever-varying sentiment, in the tone in which that sense was chanted, an unchanging eternity. One seemed to have realised, in a word, that sentence of St. Augustine: 'Join thyself to Eternity and thou shalt find rest.'

Next day we parted with the courteous and hospitable Abbot, and proceeded through the beautiful scenery by the Blackwater until we reached the hospitable roof of Father Fogarty, the parish priest of beautiful Lismore, a friend of the Bishop and of the Australian Mission. But, habituated as we were to tropical climates, the chill of that night watch in the monastic choir had sunk into our very bones. And though we were near the end of a bright July, we begged of Father Fogarty, as the greatest charity he could do us, to make a good roaring fire. And highly amused he was, as he piled wood upon burning wood, and watched our pale faces and shivering frames, until a good dinner combined with glowing flames put us to rights. And yet that Cistercian choir clings to memory, recalling men dead to the world, but alive to God.

At Clonmel we saw the excellent Dean Burke, always so careful of the prisoners who came from its gaol to New South Wales. Making part of our way in an open car across the bogs, every now and then we came upon groups of men, all alive to the General Elections then going on. The country was then enjoying the first fruits of the Emancipation Act. But the Bishop talked of nothing but New South Wales, and the advantage of immigration thither to steady men. At Kilkenny, as we were walking from the Black Monastery, as it was called, the old Dominican Convent, still in Dominican hands, we met John O'Connell and the Mayor in the street, and they gave us a beautiful specimen of that freedom of election which had been won at so much cost. John O'Connell was the Catholic candidate, and they told us they had got all their former electors safely locked up in farms with plenty of whiskey to amuse them, the object being to secure them from being tampered with by the enemy, and to be able to conduct them under the conduct of true friends to the poll. They asked us to go and address them, as it would cheer them up in their confinement, but we, of course, declined with as much politeness as we could muster.

At Cork, Father Mathew[2] not only gave us his heartiest welcome but became our guide through the city, which gave us an opportunity of witnessing his wonderful influence and popularity as the Apostle of Temperance. On first meeting he started back and said: 'I expected to meet a venerable man with a white head, and not a man of your age. I have printed 20,000 copies of your sermon on drunkenness. You are entitled to a silver medal.' And he gave me one.

The Temperance Movement was at its height. The house of Father Mathew was turned into an office for temperance purposes. He had three secretaries constantly engaged. He told us that he had spent £1,600 in aiding temperance bands alone, and that the medals he had given away and his extensive correspondence were sources of great expense to him. His work involved a complete system of administration. He conducted us to the celebrated educational convent of the Ursulines at Blackrock, of which he was the temporal father, and we spent a pleasant day there. When, however, in the course of conversation the nuns proposed to sing the spiritual song beginning, 'When reflection recalls the sad hours I have squandered', a graceful offer as it was composed in that convent, the Bishop, with tears in his eyes, begged it might not be sung. This puzzled the nuns until it was explained to them that it had so often been sung at Downside as a most touching thing under early and happy associations, and that the repetition of it under circumstances so far asunder from those simple times would be too overpowering to his feelings. Then the nuns appreciated the compliment thus unintentionally given to the power of that pathetic composition. I remember well, how, sitting with the other boys round the fire soon after my arrival at Downside, Father Wassal came in from Bonham and Dr. Polding asked him to sing it for us, and sang with his remarkable voice. It thrilled through me as I think no words set to music ever did before. But then it was so completely suited to my then condition of soul.

One of our chief objects in visiting Cork was to see Father England, brother of the Bishop of South Carolina, the man who had done more than any other on this side of the world for the convicts embarked for Australia. He was chaplain to the convict establishment at the Cove of Cork, and a man of more indefatigable zeal and untiring charity there could not be. We knew when a convict ship arrived from Cork that half our work was done. He heard every man's confession, gave books to all who could read, and letters to all who deserved particular attention. We were disappointed in not finding him − he had recently died. We saw his sister, the Superioress of the first Convent of the Presentation, founded by Miss Nagle[3] herself. We went to visit an emigrant ship preparing to start for Sydney, and the emigrants were delighted to have a few words and a blessing from their future Bishop.

We dined also with Bishop Murphy and saw, of course, his great collection of books, the work of his life, which covered every wall of his house from kitchen to attic, passages and stairways included. He teased Father Mathew in his pompous way about his temperance movement, towards which we were given to understand that he was never very cordial, and the want of hearty co-operation from his Bishop was obviously an element amidst the good Father's trials. As we walked through the Cork market place, the old women were wakened up at the sight of Father Mathew, and how they did bejewel and bedarling as he shied off into a side street from their over-whelming clamours. He had brought the blessing of sobriety to a number of these poor women.

We went by coach from Cork to Killarney and, stopping to change horses at an intermediate town, a large group of electioneering men, armed with shillelaghs, came up to the coach and asked if there were any Tories there. A foolish young Englishman answered from the top of the coach: 'I'm a Tory.' In an instant two men climbed to the top of the coach and pulled him down into the middle of the group, and every stick was quivering over him for a blow.

I quickly cried out to the Bishop, who was at the other side from what was going on: 'Get out your cross, jump down, or they will kill the man.' I pushed the coach door open and shouted to the men: 'Stop! Here is the Catholic Archbishop of Sydney, a great friend of Irishmen, who wants to speak to you.' They stopped, listened to the Bishop, gave three cheers for him, and let the man go. Pale and trembling he came up to the Bishop, and asked if he might know to whom he was indebted for his life. The Bishop gave him a stern rebuke for his folly, and said to him: 'You little know what a terrible history goes into the ears of these poor people with that hated word *Tory*.'

We sailed over the Lakes of Killarney with the usual enthusiasm, and witnessed some exciting election scenes, which the temperance movement saved from degradation. All was good natured and good humoured.

On our return to England we separated, each on our own way. Some letters passed between us on my proposed appointment to the Bishopric of Hobart Town, against which I was as averse as ever; and even more so because I felt that, good priest as he was, as Father Therry had been placed as Vicar-General in Van Dieman's Land, I should have the same difficulties to meet there as I had on my first arrival in Sydney, owing to his want of management in temporal affairs.

Having nothing whatever in the meantime to do, I told the Bishop that I thought of going to the Tyrol to pay a visit to the Adolorata and the Ecstatica, respecting whom Lord Shrewsbury's[4] pamphlet had recently appeared; adding that I hoped to gain some valuable spiritual impression from the visit. But I received a letter from the Bishop in reply which somewhat surprised me, as he told me that our relations were at an end. As a matter of course I wrote to Dr. Barber, then Provincial of the South, and to Dr. Brown, then Vicar-Apostolic of Wales, as they were two of the three, Dr. Polding being the third, who had originally advised me to go out as Vicar-General to New South Wales. I told them the contents of the letter I had received. And without more ado I wrote to the Secretary for the Colonies informing him of my retirement from the Colony, and settled my account for salary with the Colonial Agent. I then went at once to my monastery, and wrote to the President-General to inform him what I had done, and to await his directions. Dr. Marsh was again in office as General, and he wrote me a very kind letter, saying that I should be glad of some rest at Downside after my many labours.

Father Wilson was then the Prior. He gave me some teaching in the school and, amongst other work of the kind, the spiritual instruction of a class of boys whom I found very restless and inclined to be troublesome at their spiritual reading. Surprised at this in a College where propriety of conduct had always been so marked, I asked them to tell me plainly what was the reason of it. They said they had for some time had St. Francis de Sales' book on the Love of God for their reading book, and that it was hard and dry for them to understand. I found that these lads of between twelve and fourteen years had had to wade through the disquisitions on the mental and moral faculties and, as it was all metaphysics to them, I did not wonder at their restless and petulant behaviour, so got their book changed for another. But in returning to my monastery I myself learnt a great lesson. Having been in authority and accustomed to be concerned with affairs on a large scale ever since my ordination, at first I found everything so flat and unexciting that when directed by my Prior to do something simple or another, I used to feel my heart jump up against the command; and looking down, as it were, on these curious motions of the lower nature, I used to say to myself:

'Holo! What does that mean?' I then learnt the difficulty that attends the retiring from the habit of active authority in the vigour of life, which without this experience I should not have anticipated.

After a short time thus spent, I received directions from the President-General to put myself under the Provincial of the South and to take in hand the mission of Coventry. The Reverend Bernard Paillet, who had been recently ordained, had been recently appointed to it, but he was very nervous about the responsibility of the missionary life and at Cheltenham, on the way to Coventry, his nervous attack increased and deprived him of his sight. I was therefore requested to take his place. On my arrival on an evening after dark in Coventry, I found the mission under the care of a young girl and in a most desolate condition. The mission had been for some time under the care of Father Stephen Barber, who had been repeatedly in an asylum, and he, a good weak man, did nothing but say his prayers, on which he was engaged continually. He was utterly incapable of looking after the people or doing anything for them beyond saying Mass. Father Pope, who had been there before him during the time of his infirmities before he died, had exerted himself to the utmost, had infused a spirit of piety into the little flock, but the administration, if it can be called administration, of Father Barber had left the people to scatter, and many souls had gone from the Church altogether. Those who had remained faithful had got into bad odour with the Provincial, who told them they were constantly writing complaints to Bishop Walsh, which were forwarded to him. I found them, however, to be good, simple people only anxious to have the mission restored and I did my best to put them right with my Superior. Four of the leading men were sergeants of the recruiting staff, all in the habit of attending their duties regularly.

I found the chapel very small, in a very naked condition, and though not so many years built, the walls were cracked through, and exhibited considerable rents. As to the little bit of a house, there was scarcely space for anything in its little rooms but for myself and a small table. And one of the bedrooms, the one afterwards assigned to Mother Margaret, was cracked in the wall from top to bottom.

Excepting one very respectable farmer, and Mr. Hansom[5], the only member of the congregation who kept a servant, they were almost all of the decent class of weavers or watchmakers, and were truly devoted to the Church. The furnishing of the chapel was very poor, nor had I ever saved money that I might put it right; but there was sufficient endowment for the support of the priest and this enabled me to direct the people's contributions to the good of the mission and support of the school. The only good thing about the place was the schoolroom, built by Father Cockshoot. There was a schoolmaster, Mr Walsh, a very good old man, and not a bad schoolmaster, but there was no schoolmistress. Mrs Amherst, of Kenilworth, whose husband had been recently buried in the Coventry chapel, took a kind interest in the mission, and helped me materially in my first beginnings. My dear mother also sent me a supply of house linen, etc. I soon obtained an assistant in Father Clarkson, and the work went on.

For a time I had my sister Rebecca, afterwards Mrs. Vincent Chalmer, living with me. I hoped she would be able to give me a good deal of assistance in looking after the poor, but she was a good deal of an invalid. The example of her piety, and her looking after the house was all the advantage I gained, and after a while she left me. I will not go into further detail on the Coventry Mission, as I have done so in my memoranda on Mother Margaret.

Notes

1   Mss.2. spells this Mellerai. This famous house of Cistercians of the Strict Observance (Trappists) was, at that time, a new foundation, having been made by Irish monks returning from Melleray in France. The house had been officially consecrated as an Abbey in 1838. In 1954 it established a daughter house in Kopua in New Zealand. A foundation from another Irish Cistercian Monastery was made round the same time in Tarawarra, Victoria, Australia.

2   Theobald Mathew (1790–1856), was the great Apostle of Temperance in mid-nineteenth century Ireland, England and America. He is said to have given the total abstinence pledge to over seven million people. When Ullathorne met him he was starting this anti-drink crusade after twenty-five years of fruitful social work in Cork. He was also, at the time, Provincial of the Capuchin Order of Ireland.

3   Nano (Honoria) Nagle (1728–1784), foundress of the Presentation Order, formed to educate the poor of Cork and which blossomed into a world-wide institution.

4   John Talbot (1791–1852), Sixteenth Earl of Shrewsbury. Ullathorne gives an account of his visit to the Adolorata in the following chapter.

5   Charles Hansom, Architect and Town Surveyor of Coventry.

Chapter Thirty-Seven

Further Travels to Italy

Meanwhile, Bishop Polding had reached Rome, had given in his report of the Australian Mission in which I did not even find my name mentioned, a fact which did not surprise me, or give me the least idea that it meant anything personal. It was simply a result of a mental habit. With the aid of Father Nicholson, an Irish Carmelite, afterwards Bishop of Corfu, he also brought forward his plan and petition for an Australian hierarchy. This proposition was warmly received, and the Bishop rose into high favour.

I received a letter from the Bishop informing me that in consequence of my strong objections to Hobart Town, on the score of Father Therry, and the necessity it would involve of a new conflict with him in his advancing years, I had been nominated for Adelaide. Now, besides my strong objection to accept the Episcopacy at all, Adelaide had never had a single priest and at that time could not support a priest with all the Catholic resources of the Colony put together.

On receiving this communication I went to Loughborough and made a retreat of eight days under Father Pagnani. The conclusion to which I came at the end of it was to decline Episcopacy in every shape. I therefore returned to my mission and, considering the matter settled, I opened anew the correspondence with Mrs. Amherst, which had been suspended by this incident, with a view of obtaining the services of Mother Margaret, then in Belgium.

A week or so after her arrival, as I have elsewhere stated, I received a second letter from Bishop Polding, now become Archbishop of Sydney, complaining of my delay, and requesting me to accept the nomination. I then went off to Rome for the purpose of getting the point settled in the negative, and on my arrival there presented a memorial to that effect to Propaganda. The memorial succeeded. I was freed from the appointment to Adelaide, the Reverend Francis Murphy was appointed, and I was set free to return to my mission.

During my stay in Rome I became acquainted with Father Nicholson who told me he had been much pressed by the Archbishop to go out as his Vicar-General. He asked me, smiling: 'Suppose Dr. Gregory were to differ with me, how would things go on?' I told him that Dr. Gregory was a young man who hitherto had not exercised any influence upon the business of the diocese, although an intimate friend of the Archbishop's, and that I did not think that any serious inconvenience would arise from that quarter. But the Father declined the invitation and from subsequent knowledge I must doubt if Father Nicholson would have suited as Vicar-General. His qualities were of another order. The Archbishop and he were both sensitive men by nature, and would have come together in matured life with different habits of viewing things.

At my farewell audience with Gregory XVI, who then looked aged and infirm but full of dignity, His Holiness told me that the Archbishop much regretted that he could not have me as one of his suffragans but I felt perfectly satisfied that I had done right in declining. It was only at a later period I found out that Father Nicholson, at that time all influential with Cardinal Franzoni, Prefect of Propaganda, had advised His Eminence to keep me in view for an English Vicarate. Father Nicholson after that kept up a correspondence with me, but had I known that he had given such a recommendation, I should not have been disposed to continue it. However, his advice explains a letter that I received from His Eminence in the following year, in which he announced that a See had been constituted at Perth, in Western Australia and offering me the appointment, adding, however, that if I was not inclined to accept it, he wished me to recommend some suitable person for that appointment. As that diocese was most suitable for a mission to the blacks, I recommended Father Brady, who had a long experience in the Island of Bourbon[1] among the negroes, was an excellent missionary, and had great attraction for the aboriginal population. He was appointed but later on the Archbishop called on the Spanish Benedictines to establish a mission to the blacks in that quarter.[2] The Queen of Spain took an interest in the work and sent them out in a frigate. One of them was appointed Bishop. The two Bishops did not pull well together, probably from want of sufficient defining of their respective jurisdictions, and Dr. Brady retired. But the mission to the blacks has been a great success.

On my departure from Rome I was asked by Dr. Grant, of the Scotch College, if I would travel with an elderly lady, Mrs. Hutchinson, of Edinburgh, for her protection. Mrs. Hutchinson, the widow of Colonel Hutchinson, had been, before her conversion, a leader and sort of centre to the Irvingites[3] at Edinburgh; but after her conversion had become the chief founder of St. Margaret's Convent, in whose interests she was now in Rome. I consented to travel with her, and the more readily as she wished to go by the Tyrol, and to visit the Adolorata and Ecstatica[4], then exciting a great deal of attention. At Assisi we stayed two days, and I was deeply interested in all that was associated with St. Francis and St. Clare. The mountains and plains of that austere region breathed of the heroic poverty and ecstatic detachment of those two representatives of the ardours of Divine Love. We stayed at the hospitium of the Portiunculum, and were entirely under Franciscan influence. The old King of Bavaria[5] was at Assisi at the same time.

Thence we made our way by the Umbrian chain to Cortona. At Perugia I had a letter to the Abbot of the celebrated Benedictine monastery and, as I could not remain there as a guest, having a lady under charge, the Abbot kindly put his carriage at our disposal, and sent a Father to be our guide. At the hotel we met the celebrated Mrs. Gray, who opened the English mind to the ancient Etruscan remains, and found her full of enthusiasm with her discoveries.

In the still loftier placed city of Cortona, after visiting the shrine of St. Margaret, I made special inquiries regarding the Ecstatica of Sansovina, of whom the Earl of Shrewsbury wrote in the second edition of his book. The Bishop was absent but I was given to understand that he had given it no especial countenance, except to allow her daily Mass and Communion in the house. A grave canon with whom I conversed was inclined to use discouraging language: he thought it a case of catalepsy. But the Franciscan Fathers of St. Margaret's assured me that it was a remarkable case, and well worth a visit. We resolved to go to Sansovina, and one of the canons kindly gave me an introduction to the Archpriest who was the director of the person in question.

Like Cortona, Sansovina was situated on very high ground, and we had to get oxen to help our horses up the steep ascent. At the rude inn I asked the servant girl if many strangers visited the place. She said: 'Until lately, very few; but now a great many.' I asked why they came. She answered: '*A cosa di questa ragazza.*' (Because of this lass.) And she added: '*Un gran Principe di Londra e venuto.*' This was Lord Shrewsbury. The peasantry of Italy generally imagined in those days that England was somewhere in London. After I was Bishop of Birmingham, a Bishop asked me in the Papal sacristy of the Vatican: '*Monsignor, sta questo Birmingham in Londra o in Scozzia?*' And when I assured him that it was in the very centre of England, he still wished to know whether this Birmingham was in England or in America. Geography in those days was not a strong point, even with learned Italians.

In the evening we called on the Archpriest, who struck me as having a great resemblance to the famous O'Connell both in size and figure, as it had also struck Bishop, afterwards Cardinal, Wiseman as he told me at a later time. He received us very kindly, and said he would gladly give us an opportunity of observing what was most remarkable in the young person under his care, if we attended the Mass next morning, which he should say in her room. I then asked for a private interview with him, and asked him to tell me candidly what were his own observations of the case, as far as he could properly communicate them. He told me that he had made it a rule never to volunteer any remark, but that he would frankly answer any questions. In reply to mine, the Archpriest sketched her history and that of her poor parents, and how her infirmities had come upon her after great solicitude in attending her mother in an illness. Did she take much food? She lived on the air, water and a little lettuce. Was she supposed to have the stigmata? She had the sense, but not the manifestation of them. She had prayed much that they might not appear. She also had peculiar relations with the Ecstatica of the Tyrol, Maria Möerl, knowing much of what passed with her. What were the chief singularities that distinguished her? These I might observe for myself at the Mass next morning. I wished him good evening, thanking him for his kind attentions, and one of his curates showed us through the town. He was not very communicative on the subject which chiefly interested us, but prudently referred me to the Archpriest. Yet he warmly defended the innocence and purity of her character, despite the stories about her being deluded or a deceiver.

Next morning, early, we went to the house and were shown up to the small bedroom. Besides ourselves there were two poor women, pilgrims from Loretto, in their pilgrim hats with their staves and cockle-shell stitched on their capes. The Archpriest, with another to assist, was preparing to begin Mass at an altar by the wall facing the bed. On the bed lay the poor girl robed in a long, white, cotton dress, covered with a sheet. Beside her sat on one side her sister, on the other another female relative.[6] I at once observed that her head was large and that her nervous system was dominant over her muscular force in an unusual degree. I was in altogether a critical spirit of mind and put myself in the position on my knees where I should best be able to observe what occurred, not knowing what that was to be, for I had no special recollection of what Lord Shrewsbury had stated in his book. At the Offertory she rose up to her feet as you would raise a statue, without apparent effort to use the bed with her arms as a fulcrum to start from, and after a minute of prayer her arms expanded, she gradually descended to her reclining position, and the two attendants drew the sheet over her. What struck me chiefly besides her recollected appearance was the way in which she slowly descended into the horizontal position without the muscles of the back collapsing at the angle at which ordinarily they cease to sustain the frame; and I resolved to watch this more closely, if the opportunity again presented itself. She rose and prayed, and again descended, at the Elevation. Again, before Communion. And I observed that her descending again did imply a force of some kind in the dorsal muscles that continued to sustain until she reached her recumbent position, or nearly so, so that her descent was quite gentle.

After her Communion she rose three times, but now it was no longer towards the altar but in the direction to where I was kneeling. This awakened suspicion and I thought: 'What is the meaning of this? Is she showing herself?' But I was afterwards told that when the Holy Eucharist was no longer on the altar she turned towards the Blessed Sacrament in the public church. On one of the occasions when she rose, the curate kneeling by me said: 'Blow towards her!' I did so and she waved to and fro upon her toes like a reed shaken by the wind, apparently quite unconscious of any external action. Every time she rose she stood thus elevated upon her toes, and expanded her arms in the act of rising, as she closed them to her sides in the act of descending. The number of times she rose after her Communion marked, we were told, the number of her special prayers, one being for those present, as she had been requested beforehand.

So soon as the Archpriest was unvested, I went up and whispered: 'May I now speak to her, and that in private?' The Archpriest said: 'Certainly.' And all cleared out of the room. I went up to her and said with some severity of voice: 'All this is very dangerous for your soul. I cannot imagine the depth of humility that is necessary for your security. To be looked at every day, to be talked about by thousands of tongues as something strange and wonderful, to be attacked by others as a hypocrite, really all this is very perilous for your soul.'

She replied, and her voice was very low, almost a whisper, yet swift in reply: 'Gladly would I be walled up from all mankind, but this is permitted me for my greater confusion.'

'But,' I said in substance, 'do not, as I hear, many people come to look at you, to ask your prayers, and to consult you just as if you were someone inspired? And is not this very dangerous for a sensitive young woman like you?'

She kept very tranquil under the attack and, with a tear trickling, she said: 'The more reason have I that all the world should pray for me. But I speak when my confessor commands me to do so.'

I then asked her one or two spiritual questions bearing on my own habits and surroundings, to which she replied briefly, devoutly and appositely, and so, requesting her prayers, I left her. I kept my impressions to myself beyond general remarks. But those impressions were that whilst she was a really pious girl, in a high-wrought nervous condition, perhaps the exterior phenomena which I had witnessed were capable of a natural solution. I have heard nothing whatever respecting her since that time. And now it occurs to me as somewhat strange that in my various journeys to Rome I never thought of making any further inquiry respecting her subsequent history.

At Florence, among other acquaintance we met the Misses O'Farrell, sisters to the Governor of Malta, and Father Nicholson, the Carmelite, who was on a visit to them. They invited us to join them in a visit to the church which contained the incorrupt body of St. Mary Magdalen of Pazzi, of which they had been promised a private inspection. It was commonly exposed only on her festival, but the fact that it was going to be exposed got wind and we found the large church so crammed with people that it was with considerable difficulty that we reached the high altar under which it lay.

On our return from the church the Misses O'Farrell heard of a remarkable case of sanctity in suffering, and after some inquiry we entered a decent-looking house and ascended to the second storey. There we found an aged mother bound by her infirmities to an armchair, and her daughter, aged about thirty-five, upon a bed, whilst a young woman attended upon them both. We were cautioned not to go suddenly near the bed, lest we should cause a shock to the sufferer. Whilst the ladies talked to the mother, I slowly approached the daughter, whose sufferings were such as I had never in my life witnessed. We were told that her legs were literally turned up upon her back, and that upon them she lay. The expression upon her features of patient suffering was indescribable. Her head and every limb shook and thrilled, whilst her lips moved in prayer. I slowly drew near the foot of the bed, the eyes of the sufferer caught mine and she startled all over. I calmly raised a finger towards heaven, she raised her eyes in the same direction and then, as if reassured, her lips continued in prayer. Her whole frame seemed to be tortured as with a fire running through her nerves. The mother had told us that her daughter had prayed long for the gift of suffering, and that she had been in this state of suffering for seven years and that she had seen such fruits of holiness in her daughter from her afflictions that she, too, had prayed, as her daughter had prayed before her, for the gift of suffering; that sometime after she also had lost the use of her limbs and was now tied to her chair; that the neighbours and many good people were very kind to her, and that the little girl whom we saw about had been provided for them and served them very affectionately. A good priest, she added, had been exceedingly kind to them, had obtained the privilege of an altar in their room, where he said Mass for them every day; 'and this (she said) has rewarded us for all our sufferings.'

The good priest had also taken an interest in obtaining relics for them, and if we opened the folding doors that closed in the altar we should see them. Opening the doors we were surprised at the extraordinary number of relics that covered the back of the walls, the sides of the altar, and the back of the folding doors, like swarms of bees. I never saw so many authenticated relics together before. This spectacle of devout and patient suffering impressed me far more deeply than what I had seen in Sansovina, although suffering was not absent in that case.

We went on to Bologna, and from there by the mail towards Mantua, but when we arrived on the Austrian frontier at Mollia Gonsaraga, the Commissary of Police, after examining our passports, declared that the lady could proceed no further. 'Why?' I asked. He declined to give a reason. The place was but a village. We were travelling by the postal courier. There was neither hotel in the place nor vehicle to be had. I stepped down, took the commissary aside, and asked him: 'If you were in my place, in charge of this lady, what would you do?'

He replied: 'I think the best thing you can do is to leave the lady here and go to Mantua yourself and see the First Commissary of Police.'

'Are you a married man?' I asked.

'Yes,' he said, 'and live with my family in that house.'

'Then you will take charge of this lady until I return?'

He promised to do so and was very civil. He gave me a letter. I left Mrs. Hutchinson in company with his wife and went on to Mantua with the courier. Arriving there, after some search, at midnight I found the First Commissary supping at the hotel. After reading the letter I presented he said: 'If the expense is no consideration, send a carriage for the lady, but stay here yourself and I will see whether she will go on or not.' I did so, and Mrs. Hutchinson arrived under care of the Commissary with whom I had left her. It soon appeared that she was under his surveillance. He was a respectable man, and showed himself really inclined to be of service to us, so I made a friend of him, and invited him to dine with us. On visiting the First Commissary at his office, he looked at her passport, cast his eye over Mrs. Hutchinson, and said: 'This lady cannot go on.'

'Why?' I asked. He was not at liberty to say. 'What then,' I asked, 'is to be done?' He offered to arrange my passport that I might return in her company. But how was I to obtain her luggage, which had been taken possession of by the Custom House? Guided by the officer from Mollia Gonsaraga I made my way to the Custom House, leaving Mrs. Hutchinson at the hotel, no doubt still under surveillance. But she was calm though troubled, not knowing a word of Italian, and unable to understand the cause, which was a great mystery to me.

I found three officials at the Custom House, all of whom were ready to speak together, and all positive that it was a grave case, that there was some great difficulty, and that the matter required time. I was referred to the police office. On our way we met a tall, genteel-looking young man, and my friend whispered to me that if I could secure his influence all would come right. He introduced me but I found him stiff and formal, and he put difficulties in the way that I could not comprehend: but he let it escape that it was *una cosa politica*, I immediately took out my notebook and recorded the words, with their date. Seeing, however, that neither I nor my friend from Mollia Gonsaraga could produce any impression, I hinted to him to drop behind and leave us together. I then began to talk to him freely as we walked along, told him I had recently come from the other end of the world, and expanded upon those wonders I had seen, which are always so attractive to untravelled Italians. He warmed up and got quite interested, and ended by saying that if I and the lady with the Commissary were ready at six o'clock in the morning, when the return courier arrived, he would take care that all should be right for our departure.

On our arrival next morning at the office, Mrs. Hutchinson's luggage was produced, thoroughly searched, and a long protocol produced which we, the commissary and the courier, had to sign, and then we received our passports, with a note upon mine which had further consequences. We engaged a carriage to take us back, and on leaving the Commissary at Mollia Gonsagara, I thanked him for all his kindness and presented him with a couple of sovereigns, saying to him: 'Tell the First Commissary that this is only the opening of the game, he will hear more of it later on.' On arrival at the gate of Palma the police, after inspecting the passports, declared the lady could not enter the city.

'Why?' I asked.

'Because it is recorded on your passport that you are returning because she is not allowed to enter the Austrian territory.'

'But this,' I said, 'is not Austrian territory.'

'True,' he replied, 'but the lady's passport is not visaed for return.'

'Where is the Chief of Police?' I asked.

'He is absent and will not be home till late tonight.'

'Where is the lady to stay meanwhile?' I asked.

'Here,' he replied. It was in one of the towers of the gate, without even a roof that I could see.

'You have our passports,' I said, 'and we can't move without them.' I then called to the coachman: 'Drive as fast as you can to the Eagle Hotel.' Off we went, and two police after us. We reached the hotel in time to put Mrs. Hutchinson in a private room before the police came up. I met them at the door and told them they could watch the exits as much as they liked but, on the word of an Englishman, if they attempted to annoy the lady it would be at their peril. Late at night we saw the chief of Police. He was a thorough gentleman. He said there was undoubtedly some great mistake, but that when the Austrians began to *finesse* there was no end of it. He thought it would be best to give us both new passports to Florence where we could see our own Ambassador.

On arriving at Florence our Ambassador, Lord Holland, explained the whole affair at once. He said that as Mrs. Hutchinson had given the name of Mrs. Colonel Hutchinson, after the Scotch fashion, they had mistaken her for the Mrs. Colonel Hutchinson of the Irish family who had assisted the escape of Lavallete from prison in 1817, although she had been dead seven years. He himself, he added, was on the long list of prohibited persons, in consequence of his father's sympathy with Napoleon, until he was made Ambassador at Florence. He advised us to take boat at Leghorn to Genoa.

We found Genoa in a high state of festivity celebrating the coming of age of the son and heir of King Charles Albert,[7] and witnessed the illumination of the port. It was the most striking thing of the kind that I ever saw. As evening drew on, in company with Mr. Bodenham, we took boat, but finding the water a little in commotion, and ourselves too low down for a good view, we got on board an English ship. All the shipping was drawn out in two lines, making a lane between them a mile long, overarched with cordage and flags. Beyond the shipping was a floating island, on which was a garden and a pavilion. The broad bay was covered with boats, each having a lantern at the top of its mast in the form and colour of a tulip. Thus the bay looked like a bed of tulips wavering in the wind. The signal frigate outside the port fired a signal, and there came down the lane of water between the ships a royal barge in form of a huge swan, the silver oars moving it majestically along from beneath the wings of the sailing bird. Conspicuous upon it was the King, Charles Albert, the tallest man in his dominions, surrounded by his family and followed in other barges by the Court. They landed on the floating island and the illuminations began, signal after signal, first the fireworks exhibited in every variety on the quay, then the chief palaces and villas on the amphitheatre of hills with their boscage came out in light, then the lighthouse with its huge basis of rock appeared covered with flame, then an eruption as of a volcano burst out on the furthermost promontory, and finally, amidst music, Milan Cathedral arose in light in all its proportions and details upon the water.

We joined a steamer in the early morning that had come from Civita Vecchia on its way to Marseilles, and there found Archbishop Polding fast asleep on the deck, with Dr. Gregory standing beside him, and got the last news from him of Australian affairs in Rome.

On our arrival in London I drew up a statement of our treatment at Mantua, which Mrs. Hutchinson sent to her brother, one of the Scottish Lords of Session. He submitted it to Lord Aberdeen, the Minister of Foreign Affairs, who opened a correspondence with Prince Metternich on the subject. The Prince sent an ample apology, assuring Lord Aberdeen that the officials at Mantua had been severely rebuked; yet, he added, they could not be altogether blamed, as the lady was so very much like the Mrs. Hutchinson in question, forgetting, if he ever knew, that she had been dead seven years. My travelling companion, however, Scotswomanlike, wrote to ask for her expenses, but Lord Aberdeen replied that really as an ample apology had been made it would be inconvenient to pursue the matter further. However, one good resulted, that all the postscribed names of English persons were expunged from the list.

Notes

1   i.e. Reunion Island in the Indian Ocean, 110 miles SW of Mauritius. It was renamed in 1848.
2   New Norcia, in Western Australia, some 80 miles north of Perth.
3   A name commonly given to the Catholic Apostolic Church, growing partly out of the teachings of Edward Irving (1792–1834), a one-time Presbyterian minister who taught that the gifts of prophecy, tongues, healing, miracles etc were meant for all who in later times should have the living faith. He was expelled from the ministry of the Church of Scotland but was accorded only an inferior rank in the sect which he had helped to found. It was a full hierarchy of apostles, prophets, evangelists, pastors and teachers. Henry Drummond (1786–1860) was appointed the first 'Apostle' in 1832 and a full college of twelve 'Apostles' met in 1835 in anticipation of the 'Second

Advent'. The sect drew extensively on Catholic, Orthodox and Anglican liturgical sources and was heavily ritualistic, making use of vestments, candles, holy oils and incense. The last 'Apostle' died in 1901 and no ordination has since been possible. The sect is currently without sacramental life. It now exists mostly in the United States.

4   Ullathorne's visit to the Adolorata is described in this chapter. He and Mrs. Hutchinson never got to the Tyrol to see the Ecstatica, Marie Möerl because of the troubles at the border also described. Maria Möerl (1812–1868), spent her life at Kaltern, Tyrol. At the age of twenty she became an ecstatic, and ecstasy was her habitual condition for the remaining thirty-five years of her life. She emerged from it only at the command of the Franciscan who was her director, and to attend to the affairs of her house, which sheltered a large family. Her ordinary attitude was one of kneeling on her bed with hands crossed on her breast, and her expression of countenance deeply impressed spectators. At twenty-two, she received the stigmata. On Thursday evening and Friday these stigmata shed very clear blood, drop by drop, becoming dry on other days. Thousands of persons saw her, among them Wiseman and Lord Shrewsbury, who wrote a defence of the ecstatic in his letters published by *The Morning Herald* and *The Tablet*.

5   Ludwig I of Barvaria who was, in fact, only in his mid-fifties at the time. He died in 1868 when Ullathorne was writing the first draft of his autobiography.

6   The later manuscript has, 'On one side sat her mother, on the other a female relative.'

7   Victor Emmanuel of Savoy (1820–1878). He succeeded to the throne of Piedmont-Sardinia on the abdication of his father, Charles Albert, following the defeat by the Austrians sustained at Novaro (1849). He was Victor Emmanuel II of Sardinia, later first King of a united Italy.

Chapter Thirty-Eight

Return to Coventry

Some time before I left Coventry for Rome Mrs. Amherst, of Kenilworth, had strongly recommended to my attention a person then residing at Bruges, whom she described as very religious, and possessing remarkable powers, and as distinguished for her wisdom as her charity; and who, she thought, would be of great value to the mission of Coventry. This was the celebrated Mother Margaret Hallahan. I begged Mrs. Amherst to do her best to secure her services, for she was the very person I stood in need of. She accepted the invitation, and when she was introduced to me by Mrs. Amherst I was much struck, not only by her remarkable figure, but still more by her great modesty, intelligence and vigour. At her own suggestion she made a spiritual retreat in preparation for the work before her, and then I appointed her to teach the girls' school.[1] But very soon afterwards I had to make the journey to Rome, and left her to make her own way. On my return I was gratified to find that Sister Margaret, as she was already called by the people, had gathered a hundred girls into the school, had found out all the sick and distressed people of the congregation, and was taking great care of them, and had already associated several respectable young women with her, who were devoted to her and her works of charity. But for an ample account of her zealous and most fruitful labours I must refer to the well-known *Life of Mother Margaret Hallahan.*[2]

Soon after I was honoured with the visit of two distinguished prelates. Archbishop Polding had appointed to meet Monseigneur de Forbin-Janson, a Prince in his own right as well as a bishop[3], at my poor cottage where I gave them the best hospitality I could. Their object in meeting was to visit the Earl of Derby at his country mansion, to plead for the release of the Canadian prisoners transported to New South Wales for their part in the Canadian insurrection. They were all respectable men, farmers or farmers' sons, of French descent; their main object was to protect the property of the Church. They were kept aloof from the criminal convicts, placed at a Government farm, and had conducted themselves with great propriety. Some time after, they obtained their release.

I did my best to entertain a man so distinguished as Mgr. de Forbin-Janson, but I could not help remarking that the good Archbishop (it was simply his idiosyncrasy) introduced me as *Monsieur le Curé*, and all day I was *Monsieur le Curé*, nor was there the slightest allusion ever made to the fact that their host had ever stood in any particular relationship with Archbishop Polding, beyond that of being *Monsieur Le Curé* of Coventry. Of course, I let the illustrious French Prince and Bishop depart under that impression.

As I found the Archbishop in difficulties as to whom to recommend for the Bishopric of Hobart Town, I took the opportunity strongly to recommend Father Willson, of Nottingham, to his attention, pointing out his remarkable qualities and singular fitness for that penal settlement. He was consequently recommended to the Holy See, was appointed, and ultimately placed under obedience to accept the office.

With Father Willson I was intimately acquainted. He told me he had not become a priest except by command of Bishop Milner, he himself only aspiring to become a lay-brother of a religious house, nor would he become a Bishop except under obedience. He had taken a great interest in the Australian Mission on my first visit to England in 1837 and 1838. I had often visited him, had seen his great influence, and the way in which he worked his mission. I paid him a visit whilst he was building the Cathedral of St. Barnabas, and observed his skill in matters of business.

On that occasion he expressed a great desire to know the nature of the Institute of the Fathers of Charity, founded by the celebrated Rosmini, who had recently established their headquarters at Loughborough. On that hint I went over to visit them, and told Dr. Pagani, then their Superior, that I had visited their Founder in Turin with the view of proposing a filiation in Australia, but had missed finding him, and that I had heard adverse remarks, and wished therefore to know the real nature of their Institute. Dr. Pagani said that I was the first person to make inquiries of them, and that he would be glad to give me the fullest information. He put the Rule into my hands, and also the Meditations in manuscript which their Founder had drawn up for the retreats of his disciples. I was struck with a certain originality in the Rule, and with a singular freshness in the Meditations; and I spent the greatest part of two days and nights making extracts from them; and was able to give an account of their system to Father Willson. Later on I made a spiritual retreat at Loughborough, under Dr. Gentili,[4] and we had much conversation, not only about the English Mission, but especially on the great importance of beginning a series of missions or retreats to the people under the approval of the Bishops. I found him quite prepared for such a work and, as I was then publishing a volume of sermons with prefaces, in the general preface I introduced the subject. This led Dean Gaffney, of Maynooth, to write to me recommending me to begin the work, and offering to pick out from the College young and duly qualified men to assist me. But I already had my engagements under obedience. Being invited by Mr. de Lisle to preach at the blessing of the Calvary erected by him on the Grace Dieu Rocks, I again met Dr. Gentili, and we renewed the subject of preaching Missions. Soon after he was invited by Father Willson to make a beginning at Nottingham, and not long after, in 1845, he and Father Furlong gave the great mission at Coventry which I have described in the Appendix to his Life.[5]

Before Bishop Willson consented to be consecrated it was arranged that the Archbishop of Sydney should meet him at my house, for the purpose of settling certain affairs, in which I was requested to arbitrate between them should it become needful. After a certain amount of discussion it was settled that Father Therry was to be at once recalled to Sydney, to leave clear ground for the first Bishop of Hobart Town, and that a certain portion of the money recently received from the Propagation of the Faith for the whole of the Australian Colonies was to be left in bank in Bishop Willson's account, to enable him to provide for his See. These points, and some minor details, being settled it was arranged that the Archbishop should consecrate his first Suffragan at St. Chad's Cathedral, Birmingham, which took place the day before he sailed for Sydney. I was invited to attend, and to read the Briefs as Bishop Willson's secretary, and a large body of Bishops and clergy were present on the occasion, the laity filling the body of the Cathedral.

But neither was Father Therry withdrawn from Van Dieman's Land, nor did the Bishop find any money left for him in the bank. This was the beginning of painful misunderstandings between the two prelates, and Father Therry's follies kept the Church in abeyance for many years at Hobart Town.

There is a passage in the life of Mother Margaret Halahan in which she takes credit for having prevented my return to Australia with Bishop Willson, through the prayers of the people. This seems the proper place in which to tell the whole of that story.

After the consecration of Bishop Willson was completed and I was assisting at his unvesting in the sacristy, I said to him: 'Now that the mitre is on your head, and not on mine, I have no objection to go out and help you.'

He looked up at me and said: 'Are you in earnest?'

I replied: 'As long as I am safe from the mitre, with leave of superiors, I am indifferent where I am sent.'

He said: 'I shall certainly write to your President-General.'

About a week after I received a letter from Dr. Barber, then President-General, saying that he had received an application from Bishop Willson for my services, and asking my own mind on the subject. I replied that my sole object on leaving Australia was to avoid the office of Bishop but that, exempt from that peril, I was completely indifferent as to where I was placed, subject to my Superior's approval. Dr. Barber wrote in reply that he felt I might, with my experience of the Colonies, be very useful to the new Bishop; that Coventry was now on a fair footing to go on and that, if the Bishop renewed his application, he would feel it his duty to let me go with him. I then told Mother Margaret that I expected to be summoned to return with Bishop Willson to Australia. Her reply was: 'No, you will not. The Blessed Virgin will take care of that.' Having her assembly of pious people for the Rosary that night, she sent messages through them to the houses of the Catholics, requesting them to watch during the whole of that night, and to pray especially for her intention. After that I heard not a word more from Dr. Barber or from Bishop Willson. I did my best to assist him in his preparations, and bade him farewell, but not a word of explanation escaped from his lips.

After he had visited the Archbishop of Sydney he wrote me a letter in which, among other things, he said: 'The next time I see you I shall have to go down on my knees.' The Bishop came to England to lay the condition of Norfolk Island before the Government, soon after my consecration to the Western District. We met at Prior Park, where we dined together. Talking by ourselves after dinner I asked him: 'Why did you write to me that, when you saw me, you would have to go on your knees?'

He started up, burst into tears, and said: 'I will go on my knees directly.'

'No,' I said, 'I will not allow it. But what did it mean?'

He then told me that he was just going to write for me to Dr. Barber when he suddenly reflected: 'Why is this man here? He began the work in Australia and ought to be there. There may be something wrong.' And knowing that I was intimate with Dr. Gentili he went over to Loughborough to consult him on the subject. They could neither of them explain the mystery, and the Dr. said: 'You had better not risk it.' 'But,' concluded the Bishop, 'I had not been in Sydney two days before I saw through the whole of what you must have gone through; and I only wonder that it did not kill you.'

Notes

1   Dr. Ullathorne's first impressions of Mother Margaret are expressed in a letter written to Bishop Brown, in Wales, dated May 8th, 1842, just before starting for Rome: 'I leave this mission: he says, 'just when it had begun to develop. I have recently received a very valuable aid in a person – a sort of Sister of Charity – from Belgium; she is English, able to teach my girls' school, visit the sick, and give instructions; and I had calculated on having two more very soon, whom I should have found no great difficulty in supporting. It would probably have been the germ of an institute. This person will remain till I return.'

Two years later January (1844), he writes to the same friend. 'Being now free from Adelaide I shall feel at liberty to work on, providing for the wants of this great population. I hope to have a third poor school in operation before long. The work that I have most before me at this moment is the commencement of a convent. I propose establishing and applying the Third Order of St. Dominic as Sisters of Charity, through the instrumentality of Sister Margaret. I am waiting to see the Provincial, and so soon as I have his concurrence I am ready to begin with four excellent persons, all thorough workers, with good, sound sense and solid devotion. Sister Margaret is invaluable. The quantity of good works and charities that pass through her hands is almost inexplicable. The manner she is spiritualising this congregation is admirable; and all this amidst a good deal of personal suffering.' (*Mother Drane's note.*)

2   *Life of Mother Margaret Hallahan* by her Religious Children (London 1869).

3   Charles Auguste Marie Joseph, Comte de Forbin-Janson (1785–1844) was in fact the second son of Count Michael Palamede de Forbin-Janson and Cornélie Henriette, Princess of Galean. He was a Knight of Malta from childhood and a soldier at sixteen. Napoleon made him Auditor of the Council of State in 1805. His family and the aristocracy looked forward to a brilliant career as a statesman for him, but he surprised all by entering

the seminary of St. Sulpice in 1808. He was ordained in 1811 and consecrated Bishop of Nancy and Toul in 1824. He was obliged to leave France
through persecution by the French Government in 1830. In 1839 Gregory
XVI sent him on a highly successful missionary tour of the United States
and Canada. It was on a visit to England shortly after his return that the
meeting with Ullathorne took place. He died unexpectedly some months
later at his family castle near Marseilles.

4   Aloysius 'Luigi' Gentili (1801–1848), was better known among the English
public at large than Newman in the 1840s. On a visit to Oxford in 1842 he
had converted Newman's Littlemore companion, William Lockhart. Newman
himself did not convert until 1845, but resigned his benefice, giving the
scandal of Lockhart's conversion as his reason. His missions and retreats
all over the country were marked by mass conversions. Even death threats
and burning him in effigy did not dampen his ardour or, apparently, lessen
his congregations. In September 1848 his Dublin mission, here mentioned,
drew vast crowds, and that in spite of the political turmoil in Ireland at
the time. His confessional was so crowded that he would sit there without a
break from the last instruction at night till Mass the following morning.
Then he was suddenly seized with a fatal fever and died after two days. He
was forty-seven years old. He is buried in Glasnevin cemetery. See *The Life
of the Rev. Aloysius Gentili LL.D., Father of Charity and Missionary
Apostolic in England*. ed by the Very Rev. Father Pagani, London 1851.

5   See Chapter 45, details of their later mission in Bristol.

Chapter Thirty-Nine

Thoughts on the Rosmini and Religious Orders

Before beginning the church at Coventry I made a brief tour in Belgium and on to Cologne with Mr. Hansom. I was then paying a good deal of attention to Gothic architecture and art, and the object of this tour was to examine some of the best specimens of mediaeval art. I was deeply interested by much that I saw, and took notes of my observations, which I still have somewhere in an old notebook.[1] Having the advantage of Mr. Hansom's powers of observation to sharpen my own I got a pretty clear impression of the aesthetic principles of the old artists, and to comprehend the fall of Art in more recent times. Northern Art, again by its very contrasts, brought out to greater appreciation the antagonism between the abstract nature of Christian and the pure animalism of Pagan Art. A study of some of the German writers, of the Schlegels[2] especially, put these appreciations on their intellectual basis and contributed to the intelligence of many things, but more especially the mystical influences of ascetic feelings upon the material elements of the Creation.

Amidst my missionary work I also found time to look into Rosmini's intellectual system, mental and moral philosophy having for many years been a favourite study.

As there once at least existed an impression on the mind of some of our leading ecclesiastics that I was a devoted follower of the philosophy of Rosmini, I think it well to leave on record what had always been my real views on that subject. From the time that I formed acquaintance with his disciples at Loughborough, I admired the Rule of the Order, as I have said, and also the Founder's system of spiritual exercises, and made more than one retreat under the Fathers. But Dr. Gentili spoke to me much about a book by their Founder, still in manuscript, called the *Cinque Piaghe*. When that book was published in Italy and I had read it, I wrote to Dr. Pagani[3] telling him that there were very grave errors in it and I believe my observations were sent to the author. This was some time before it was placed on the Index. The Fathers in their kindness sent me all the works of Rosmini as they were published. In the order of their publication I read them, and as they made a large display of books on my shelves this probably led to the impression of my being a follower of his philosophy. But though I found much to admire in those writings, in his philosophy I detected what I considered to be grave and fundamental errors which would not stand by the common teaching of the Church.

The first thing to which my attention was awakened was a doctrine in the first volume of his psychology where he describes the generation of man. He there describes the formation of the soul as being a touch of Divine light upon the *materia deposita*, upon the embryo. This description evidently left out any created spiritual substance of the soul, and the context left the meaning clear. I then wrote to Dr. Pagani and had repeated conversations with Dr. Berletti in which I asked how the spiritual substance of the soul was to be accounted for. My difficulty was sent to Rosmini himself. In reply I was told that I must wait for other books still in manuscript, the titles of which were mentioned.

I waited for one book after another but the explanation did not come. At last the volume *De Reali* appeared, and on receiving it I was told that I should find in it what I sought. But instead of finding the desired explanation, to my astonishment I found this doctrine that: 'Creation is division in God; that this was not Pantheism because Pantheism taught that all things were God.'

Soon after discovering this error, so fundamentally opposed to the teaching of the Church respecting Creation, I received a letter from a secular priest in the West of England, telling me that he had long been devoted to Rosmini's philosophy but that he had had doubts and misgivings about it for some time past, and asking me to give him my mind on the subject. In reply I wrote a long letter, telling him of the fundamental errors which I had observed in that philosophy.

Many years later on I received a letter from Cardinal Newman informing me that a letter had come to him from the then representative of the Order in Rome, asking him as a particular favour for a letter that might be a support to him in a special audience with the Sovereign Pontiff. Apprehensive that this audience might concern the writings of Rosmini, I recommended His Eminence to be cautious what he wrote, and gave him an account of the grave error to be found in his philosophy. This must have been about the time when the second examination of these works began, including the posthumous publications,[4] for about two or three years later came forth the Decree of the Holy Office condemning forty propositions contained in these works.

Of the Institute as a missionary body I have a very good opinion as well for its discipline as for its piety and zeal for souls. Rosmini's Meditations, several of which Dr. Pagani unfairly modified and published under his own name, certain of his spiritual letters and Dr. Gentili's Private Retreat, exercised a considerable influence in systematising and fixing on my mind certain clear views on the relations of the soul with God through certain eminent virtues and through the action of the Church as God's instrument and as the administrator of His divine grace. They completed for my mind a circle of ideas beginning with the Benedictine exercises of Abbot Cisneros, going on through those of St. Ignatius, and receiving a certain scientific illustration from St. Thomas' great treatise on the virtues and the theology of grace. The contribution of Rosmini to my intellectual resources on spiritual things consisted chiefly of certain distinctions, dividing between the natural and the supernatural elements in the soul, between the elements of subjection and freedom, that exists within the sphere of religious obedience, in the intimate relations between the divine virtue of justice and that of charity, and in the principles that guide the soul in her call to good works and holy undertakings, and in the clearness and force with which he expounds the Church as God's Holy Society, and the Minister of Truth of Grace, and of the body and spirit of her Divine Founder. Yet he proceeds, like St. Thomas, by the way of intellect, rather than through the path of moral and ascetic feeling.

I have always been disposed, nevertheless, to look upon the early ascetic Fathers, the Fathers of the desert, as having most thoroughly worked out the true maxims of the ascetical life, and as having reduced them to the most pithy maxims. Their life was so completely spent between themselves and God, and was so fenced in by seclusion, labour and self-denial; God and the soul was so exclusively their aim, and their grace was so abundant, their lives so simple, that they appear as the very prophets as well as the experts of the interior life.

Upon their light and experience the great ascetic rules were drawn up, and such men as St. Benedict, St. Dominic and St. Thomas expressly took them as their guide, as their doctrines are condensed in the Institutes and Conferences of Cassian, whilst Rodriguez, Alvarez de Paz, and the other chief spiritual writers of the Society of Jesus, have drawn their lights in copious streams from the same sources.

In studying the Religious Orders as spiritual schools, it has often recurred to me that whilst each has a characteristic temper and lore of its own, and a disposition to lean upon some individual quality or virtue as distinctive of its life and work, this very tendency requires a guard against its running into some correlative defect. And for want of this guard being always vigilantly observed, Religious Orders are mostly prone to deteriorate. Thus the temper of the Benedictine Order is largeness of spirit, or freedom, apt to degenerate into laxity. That of St. Francis is poverty, apt to degenerate into sordidness. That of St. Dominic is rigid law and science, apt to degenerate into the stiffness of the letter and pride of intellectual culture. That of St. Francis de Sales is spiritual sweetness, apt to degenerate into spiritual softness. That of the Carmelites is contemplation, apt to degenerate into leaving Our Lord's Life and Passion into abeyance. That of the Society of Jesus is the practical, apt to discard the contemplative spirit, and to degenerate into policy.

Moreover, whenever an Order turns aside from the special aim and scope of its founder, and takes to other employments or pursuits, its spirit evaporates in proportion, and it acquires some new spirit that is not in accordance with that of its founder.

As to the secular clergy, Our Lord's own pastoral Order, of His own divine foundation, I have thought more and more that their designation as *seculars* is a calamity for them; that it misleads the mind as to their true character as a sacred Order, to which Our Lord said: 'Ye are not of the world, as I am not of the world.' I have thought that if they had been designated as the sacred Pastoral Order, and if the theory of their sacred vocation had been drawn out and kept before them with its spiritual laws and rules, as the regular bodies have had their holy position and sacred obligations drawn out and epitomised in the formulary of their rules, it would have exercised a vast influence upon their sanctity as well as upon their spiritual influence. This has been attempted from time to time on select bodies of the clergy in individual dioceses, but the result has been to convert those bodies into new religious institutes, thus defeating the original intention of sanctifying the secular clergy.

Only a general provision emanating from the Church's authority would meet the requirement.

I give these glimpses into certain portions of my mental history rather than a record of the trains of thought and the epochs of special light that have sprung in my soul, whether from the striking out of lines of thought by dint of circumstances, contact with persons and things, or out of those courses of reading on many sciences and many expositions of human life and history, which would form a more complete biography than the mere narration of those transactions in which I have been engaged, and those events with which I have come in contact.

Father Brady had been sent, after my departure from Sydney, to commence the Mission of Western Australia. Without previous communication with his ecclesiastical Superior, he left his mission for Rome, and there presented a report on its condition, and petitioned the Holy See for its transformation into a Bishopric. He concluded his petition with a recommendation that in the appointment of a Bishop, Dr. Ullathorne should not be overlooked.

With this recommendation before him, Cardinal Franzoni wrote to me, stated the intention of appointing a Bishop of Perth, and offered it for my acceptance. But His Eminence concluded that if I should not think well to accept it, he would be glad if I would give him my opinion of Father Brady, and also of Dr.—, O.S.B. Declining the appointment for myself, I gave my frank opinion of both ecclesiastics with reference to the contemplated See of Perth; not, however, being then aware that Father Brady was negotiating without the knowledge of the Archbishop of Sydney. Somewhat to my surprise Father Brady was appointed. And as on the failure of his success the blame of the recommendation was, as I have been told, thrown upon me by Propaganda, I may as well here state the substance of what I said respecting him. In reply to the question I represented that he was a devout man and a good missioner, who had shewn a special attraction towards the aborigines, and had been successful in organising the extensive mission of Windsor, but, I added, He was educated in France, and passed much of his early missionary life in the Isle of Bourbon, and when I first met with him in London, he spoke the English language very imperfectly, and I doubt if he can write or speak any language sufficiently well to enable him to secure the respect of the Governor and officials of the colony, a matter of very considerable importance for a colonial Bishop.

I have no hesitation in saying that the Archbishop ought to have been consulted before this Bishopric was cut off from his own, and that in saying all the good I was able of Father Brady as a missioner, I never dreamed of my words being construed into a recommendation to Episcopacy,[5] and I apprehend that the veritable cause of his appointment was the influence of his presence at Rome, and of his report.

Bishop Brady has withdrawn from his See for a long time, and now resides in Ireland. The See itself was divided into two, although the European population is very small, and two Spanish Benedictines were appointed, the one as Administrator of Perth, the other to a second See, chiefly devoted to the Aborigines. This arrangement led to conflicts, that have ended in the resignation of Bishop Terra of Perth, who has retired into Spain. Bishop Salvador, who still remains, has published a history of the mission.

In the first General Chapter of the English Benedictines, held after my return, the assembled Fathers were pleased to vote me the title *Predicator generalis ob merita* which gave me a seat for life in the general Council of the Congregation. But in consequence of my nomination to Episcopacy before the succeeding Chapter, I never sat in that assembly.

Notes

1   In a letter written at the time he says, 'How I should like to grind the noses off the faces of the men who are changing so many of the Gothic fronts of the old houses into modern flat ones.'

2   The German brothers, Karl Wilhelm Friedrich (1772–1829) and August Wilhelm (1767–1845), von Schlegel, late eighteenth and early nineteenth century writers on aesthetics who were known as the Messias of the Romantic School.

3   John Baptist Pagani (1806–1860) later succeeded Rosmini as Second General of the Institute of Charity.

4   Rosmini died in 1855, having unhesitatingly accepted the Church's decision that all his works be dismissed (*esse dimittenda*).

5   This sits uncomfortably with Dr Ullathorne's assessment, originally included in Mother Drane's version of 1891, on page 244 above.

Chapter Forty

Coventry Church

The congregation at Coventry began rapidly to increase, the little chapel was excessively crowded and it became necessary to think seriously of building a church in its place. As its position was by no means central I examined various situations in more central positions, but could find none that were purchaseable that would not have involved the removal of buildings that would have made the ground very costly. There was ample space in the garden attached to the old missionary premises and I therefore resolved, with the approval of the Provincial, to build the church in the old position. Mr. Charles Hansom was a young Catholic architect the Town Surveyor of Coventry, but he was more acquainted with the Greek and Palladian than with the Gothic styles. However, we put our heads together, made a study of the Gothic, visited and measured the old Catholic churches in several counties, and finally fixed on the lancet style of the thirteenth century for the nave, which I proposed should be developed into the Early Decorated for the chancel and later chapels. But the funds had to be raised for the work, and after establishing a weekly collection in the congregation I went forth and solicited alms over the most populous parts of England. This was a new experience and one that taught me many useful things. Happily I received a large contribution from Mr. Charles Eyre, of Bruges, an old friend of Mother Margaret Hallahan's, which helped us much. I had left a considerable library in Sydney, this, I thought, ought not to be removed from a country where books of that valuable kind were scarce. I therefore proposed to the Archbishop of Sydney to leave them there on condition of receiving £150 to buy a set of the Fathers. But that sum went to the building account.

The nave was built first with the tower, and was constructed with unusual solidity for the time.[1] Our great difficulty was to find a sculptor for architectural sculpture was, at that time, a lost art that was only beginning to be revived under the celebrated Welby Pugin *sic*. However, we found a farmer's boy who, though untutored, had a genius for that kind of art, and with the help of casts with which we provided him, he succeeded tolerably well. It was in the early time of transition from the old chapels to churches; St Chad's and the church at Derby were alone completed, and no one of the later generations can realise the shifts to which we were put for funds, as well as for builders to realise our designs. But when Pugin examined the plans, and afterwards the completed structure, he not only commended its solidity, but considered it to be a pure revival of the style of the thirteenth century. The nave was first completed with the chancel arch bricked up and then, with a temporary altar, we took possession of it. We had now a great deal more space which soon filled and, at the evening services, became closely packed, every standing space being filled as well as the seats.

At those evening services I adopted the method of the Fathers, and gave expositions of large portions of books of Holy Scripture. I gave lectures on the beginning of Genesis, and explained the Creation: this drew a number of Freethinkers as well as others. I explained the Epistles of St. Paul to the Romans and to the Galatians: this drew a considerable number of Dissenters. I took the history of the Patriarchs, and this awakened general interest. But though I gave out the text of Scripture part by part as I advanced, I was not so tied to the text as not to expatiate freely on any point of doctrine or moral teaching that the text suggested, after the manner of the Fathers.

I found not only that this method was effective in drawing full congregations, but that it led to many conversions. And I have no hesitation in saying that, for evening lectures, whoever is versed in the Holy Scriptures and in the manners and customs of the Holy Land, will find this method one of the most effective that can be adopted. It was the method of the Church for twelve hundred years. But here let me tell an anecdote. After I was removed to the See of Birmingham, I adopted much the same method of Scriptural instruction in the Lenten evening lectures at the Cathedral. Some, however, of the reverend clergy did not relish this revived method of instruction, though the people delighted in it. As there was not a little twittering among them about it, I resolved to put an end to it. So on ascending the pulpit on Sunday evening I said to the congregation: 'You, my brethren, who are of the opinion that your Bishop should instruct you according to his own judgement, and not according to the judgement of other persons, please hold up your hands.' A thousand hands were lifted up and I heard of no more objections.

Sometimes curious cases would occur. For instance, a girl who had lost her mother became a pious convert in the school, but her father was a complete infidel. He came with her to church sometimes, but there was no getting him to say a prayer. He was a working man, who had dabbled in the ologies. He talked to me about his love and worship of nature, and the four elements. 'Elements?' I asked. 'What elements?'

'The four elements,' he replied.

'You a chemist,' I answered, 'and talk of the four elements. Come to the church next Sunday, and hear what I shall say to you.' He came, and I took for my text 'From invisible things all things visible were created.' I went into the subject of invisible causes; from that I passed to the one Supreme Cause and so to Creation and Providence, and illustrated my theme by showing how all visible and material things were convertible into visible elements by the application of science, when they were more the objects of science than in their concrete forms. After the instruction the man came to me in the sacristy and said: 'Sir, I shall be ever grateful to you. You have proved me to be a fool.'

'Just what I wanted you to know,' I said. 'It is the first step to your becoming wise. Now you must begin to say your prayers.'

He did so but a fortnight afterwards there was a violent knocking at the door at midnight. I went down and found the same man there in a state of vehement excitement. He said: 'Feel my heart.' It was beating like a hammer. I got him inside, soothed and tranquillised him, and then he said: 'I can't pray; I have no belief.' I told him to go home and rest, and come to me next day. He was quieter then and I asked him: 'Have you more confidence in my knowledge than in yours?'

'I have,' he said.

'Well, on my knowledge begin again and say your prayers with your daughter, and come to me for instructions.' He did so and became a steady Christian.

Another opportunity for instruction arose in the schoolroom. After Mother Margaret arrived, she had a devotional little altar placed in the girls' school, and placed a triptych upon it in which she enshrined her favourite little statue of the Blessed Virgin. Three nights in the week she got a number of girls and women together, and they sung the Litany of Loreto, and said the Rosary. The number of persons drawn to this devotion increased until the girls' school had to be opened into the boys' school, and the two rooms became crowded with men as well as women. Strangers came in numbers, and as the weekly collections for building the church were paid there every Monday night, I went to the school and after the devotions were ended and the collections received I sat down and gave a familiar sort of fireside talk. At one time I took the people in imagination to Rome, and described to them the churches and devotions. At another I got them to the Holy Land, and described the holy places. Now we entered into the Catholic Antiquities of Coventry, and its old religious customs; then some sketches of voyages and travels were given. At another time it was the picturesque life of a saint, or a series of anecdotes, or the invention of a parable or two. On these familiar talks the ears of the people hung with attention, and the place was generally crowded. Then the young women devoted to Mother Margaret would ask this or that woman, when they saw her to be a stranger and interested, if she would like to speak to Mother Margaret. This led to interviews after the rest had gone away, when a few pithy words would often lead to conversions. Sometimes men also asked friends they had brought to come and have a word with me. What then passed in the schoolrooms got talked about in the town, and in the ribbon factories, which drew other persons to come and listen.

After the church was completed it drew numbers of people of all classes to see it when unoccupied. It was a new thing to see a Catholic church, with all its Catholic appointments, just like the old churches as they were furnished in the Middle Ages; and I had a person there to let me know when there were several visitors. I then went in and explained to them both the church and all its symbolism, with which the congregation was made thoroughly acquainted. This sometimes led to interesting conversations on the Catholic religion, and catechisms were accepted.

In instructing converts, I never brought them into classes; I observed that this made them shy, and that they preferred coming alone. I found also that by instructing them one by one it was easier to adapt even a shorter instruction to their individual states of mind and several characters. But I had a remedy for those briefer times of instruction, which I found very valuable. If the neophyte was a man, I introduced him to some Catholic man of the same class on whom I could rely; if a woman, she was introduced to some devout Catholic woman. These I appointed as sponsors; they had them by them in church, taught them Catholic customs and manners, answered their questions and made them acquainted with other Catholics so that they did not come into the church as isolated persons.

Those were happy days. The growing congregation was united like a family. I had all sorts of help including, after the church was built, two Reverend Fathers, instead of one. We said Mass at Kenilworth also on Sundays and festivals, which was the beginning of that mission. We had a lending library in the school, and books were given out and received each Sunday afternoon, when many people spent their time about the enclosure round the church, to which they were devoted. At the time when I was called from Coventry to other work we were receiving converts at the rate of a hundred a year.

Before the chancel could be begun it was necessary to pull the house down, and I rented a house of considerable size in an adjoining street. My reason for this was that Mother Margaret and I had already planned the beginning of a Religious Community of Dominican Tertiaries, and this required a series of rooms and a chapel for their use; and it became expedient to place the other clergy in other lodgings. This was not done without the formal approval both of the Provincial and of the Bishop. The novitiate was begun, and was conducted under my general directions. Mother Margaret, who was already a professed Tertiary, managing the details of observance, and infusing her vigorous religious spirit into the novices, who already began their active works of charity as part of their formation.

When the chancel was completed and the partition wall removed, the people, on their entering the church on the following Sunday, were struck with wonder and admiration at the scene presented to them. The deep sanctuary, the large east window, rich in colour with its saints and tracery; the light rood screen with its rood loft, holy rood, and impressive figures; the beautiful lateral arches opening into parclosed

chapels, to the expenses of which they had specially contributed; the high altar, richly decorated; and the stalls for
the clergy and the choir — these things filled them with delight
and rewarded them for all their sacrifices. For the first time in
their lives they saw a real Catholic church and never tired of
being taught what, in all its details, it symbolically expressed
to their senses. It was consecrated by Bishop, afterwards Cardinal, Wiseman in the year 1845, and on the following day all
the Bishops of England assisted at the solemn opening which
was attended by many of the Catholic gentry of that and
neighbouring counties. In the afternoon a great entertainment
was given to the Bishops and the visitors in the old Catholic
Guild Hall, which was filled with guests.

On that occasion I first put on the full Benedictine habit,
and in that costume received those who came to the opening,
and put them in their places. But the habit had been unknown
in England since the time of Queen Mary, and some of those
who came to the opening did not relish its appearance. About
that time I was invited to preach at the opening of the Church
of St. Edmund, Liverpool, but when I replied that, as a
Benedictine, I always preached in the habit of the Order,
I received a reply from the venerable Father at the head
of that church that 'another preacher would be provided.'
On being asked to preach at the old Sardinian Chapel in
London, I went up to the pulpit in the habit of my Order as
a matter of course, but on returning to the sacristy I encountered a sharp rebuke from the senior priest who was warmly
indignant. Much of the old timidity of the persecuting days
was still to be found in England, but in the colonies we had
learned greater freedom. Cardinal Wiseman was also teaching
the English Catholics to bring forth all our religious practices
openly and without disguise.

Notes
1   The foundation stone of Coventry Church was laid on May 29th, 1843.

Chapter Forty-One

Consecration as a Vicar-Apostolic

Bishop Baines of the Western District of England died suddenly in July 1843, the night after he had officiated at the opening of St. Mary's Church, Bristol. And I was informed at a later time by Dr. Grant, then secretary to Cardinal Acton, that Propaganda proposed to Gregory XVI, that Bishop Brown of the Welsh District should be transferred to the Western District, and that I should be appointed to succeed Bishop Brown in Wales. This was confirmed by a letter received by Bishop Brown at the time, in which he asked me whether, in the event of my being appointed to succeed him, I would take to the house which he was about to engage for his residence at Chepstow. In my reply I said that I thought it very unlikely that I should be appointed, and even more unlikely that I should accept, but as he had put a definite question I ought not to leave him without a definite answer. That my opinion had always been that a Vicar-Apostolic should live in the principal town or city of his district, where he could exercise most influence, be surrounded by a body of clergy, and perform the episcopal functions in the most becoming way. Chepstow would not, therefore, be a place that I should choose for a residence.

But when this proposal was carried to the Sovereign Pontiff, His Holiness immediately replied, *'No, no! Questo Monsignor Baggs.'*

Dr. Baggs was Rector of the English College in Rome, was well known to the Pope and a favourite. He was appointed to the Western District and I escaped for the time. But only for a time. He wore down rapidly under the trials of the Vicariate and especially through the troubles and opposition he met with from the Superiors of the College of Prior Park, who were also the trustees of Bishop Baines' will, as I learnt from those in his confidence as well as from letters which he entrusted to a priest to be delivered to his successor, he contemplated resigning his Vicariate. He died in October 1845, about a month after the opening of the Coventry Church.

Rumours soon reached me that I should again be put on the list of recommendations for the Western or the Welsh District, for the latter in the event of Bishop Brown being removed to the Eastern. I also received a letter from Bishop Brown which provoked me at the time. In that letter the Bishop said that some disadvantageous impressions had been made on the mind of a Vicar-Apostolic on the occasion of opening the Coventry church, that he had noticed in me an independence of spirit, a want of sufficient attention to the distinguished guests who assembled on that occasion, and something forward in my stepping up on a bench when called upon to speak at the dinner in the Town Hall. I say this letter provoked me, because in the church I had entirely devoted myself to arranging for the convenience of those who attended the church on that occasion. For the first time in recent ages I put on the full Benedictine habit, intending henceforth to wear it always in the church and house, and I took my position along with the second priest, at the bottom of the church, for the purpose of conducting all who entered to their seats, and of looking after the general accommodation.

As to the forwardness in the Town Hall, I, of course, felt some enthusiasm for the Coventry Mission and the new church, and probably gave it expression, and as I occupied a place in the middle of the hall, and not at the top table, which was left to the Bishops and more distinguished guests, and as the hall was crowded, I felt I could neither see, nor be seen in speaking, unless I got a little higher than the floor, so I naturally enough stepped on the bench where I had been seated.

In deference, then, to Dr. Brown, my old master and *confrère*, I wrote a reply to his letter with the sole object of giving him such explanations as might remove impressions from his individual mind. I also said something in reply to one of his remarks with the object of removing any notion of my being inspired with any absurd hauteur, adding that my sympathies were not easily brought out except among the poor people with whom my missionary life was bound up. Not long after this I received a letter from my dear old friend Father Heptonstall, in which he expressed his regret that I had written this letter of explanation to Bishop Brown, adding that my letter was very likely to transfer me from the Order to the Episcopate. This communication opened my eyes, and I saw that the Bishops had had my name under discussion and, knowing that one most excellent Bishop had been the intimate friend of Bishop Baines, and that he deeply sympathised with what was called the Prior Park party, I at once understood how the remarks upon me had arisen.

After some months more had elapsed, I received a letter from Cardinal Acton, in which His Eminence informed me of my nomination by the Holy See to the Western District. He pressed me to accept upon the consideration that in these days, and especially in England, the Episcopate was more of a burden than an honour.

I had no friend to whom I could communicate this sudden communication except Mother Margaret. I went to her in the school, where she was teaching, and putting down the young child she had upon her knee, she came into the house and at once said: 'I see by the look in your eyes that you are made a Bishop.'

Although she felt it was a great crisis for her and her little community, as well as for myself, yet she thought only of me; for she knew well that it was a summons from the only work for which I felt any attraction. I told her I should lose no time in going to my Religious Superior, and that until I had heard his remarks I should hold my mind in complete suspense. Accordingly I went by the next train to Stanbrook where Dr. Barber, the President-General of the Benedictines, resided. To him, after he had read Cardinal Acton's letter, I stated some of my difficulties. I knew it was no use touching on those more interior difficulties connected with the *nolo episcopari*, because observation had taught me that such objections are always construed on a contrary sense. But I put forward the defects in my education, my want of scholarship, owing to the rapidity with which I passed through the schools at Downside, and my reluctance to be lifted into a circle in which I knew I should not feel myself free in mind and completely at home. As to the difficulty of managing a difficult ecclesiastical party, to say the truth, having had some experience of the kind, it was not that which troubled me so much. Being in the vigour of life, presumptious as it may have been, I did not much shrink from facing things of that kind. Dr. Barber spoke to me with the affection of one who had long been my spiritual father, and with something of the authority which such a position gives. He represented to me the unsettled state of the Western Vicariate, the prolonged evils that had resulted from it, and the need there was of someone experienced in human affairs, detached from party, cool and decisive in temper, to meet the emergency. He spoke frankly and warmly, and as I said that nothing but our[1] obedience would induce me to accept, he said that as far as he could, he gave me that obedience. I then knelt and asked his blessing for the last time, but he said; 'No, henceforth I must ask your blessing.'

Soon after my return to Coventry the venerable Bishop Walsh paid me a visit. He not only urged me to accept, but was very kind and affectionate in the advice he offered as to the steps to be first taken. I wrote to Cardinal Acton and expressed my willingness to do my best to carry out the intentions of the Holy See. I then went to Ratcliffe College to prepare for consecration by a retreat under the direction of Dr. Pagani. Bishop Wiseman kindly presented me with his copy of the Bishop of Bellay's *Practice of a New Bishop*, and with that, and Barbosa's[2] chapters on spiritual qualities required of a Bishop, I endeavoured to penetrate into the conditions of soul demanded of one who is called to that sublime office and responsibility.

My reflections and the conversations I had with Dr. Pagani, who combined Italian with English experiences, led me to consider the English Vicariates and the actual condition of things in England as but provisional and transitional. The share I had in promoting the Australian hierarchy naturally induced me to reflect on the want of a similar organisation for our own country. I saw that the first step towards that must be the establishing something like a centre from which to organise an ecclesiastical government. Something of the kind had already been done in the Midland District, and I resolved to take such a position as that I could have something of a body of clergy round me, with and through whom I might be able to multiply ecclesiastical force and discipline. Those views took strong possession of my mind.

But experience subsequently taught me how difficult it is to establish anything homogeneous in a diocese without the aid of an ecclesiastical seminary, exclusively devoted to the formation of the purely ecclesiastical spirit; and how many counteracting elements are apt to spring up where a diocese is constituted of a clergy drawn from a number of quarters and animated by very different and even conflicting traditions as to what the exigencies of discipline require of them.

My consecration as Bishop of Hetalonia, appointed Vicar-Apostolic to the Western District, took place at Coventry on Sunday, June 21st, 1846, the same day on which Pius IX was crowned as Sovereign Pontiff. All the bishops then in England were good enough to attend. Bishop Briggs was the consecrating Bishop, and Bishops Griffiths and Wareing were the assistants. Bishop Wiseman preached the sermon, Dr. Newman and his brethren, recently received into the Church and but just arrived at Oscott, honoured me with their presence. Mr Lucas,[3] who was present, devoted a considerable portion of the next week's *Tablet* to the day's function. How glad I should be to be able to revive the sense in all its fullness that flowed in upon me, as the mitre was placed by the three Bishops on my head. My friends observed that at that moment my face underwent an extraordinary change, and assumed a singular expression. It seemed to me as if I had in that moment a great uplook into the Heaven above, and that authority came down thence into my soul, and power with authority. It was a feeling and a view that came upon me, such as I never had before or since, that I could realise as I did at that moment in which the consecration was completed. Nothing subdues one's soul, and softens down its hard and stiff egotism into the responsive sense of dependence on God and His operations, like the greater sacramental gifts, in the moment of their descent into the soul.

After his consecration a Bishop ought surely to be let retire into three days of silence, as the Benedictine does after his profession, that he might enter into his grace, as his grace has entered into him. And it is a trying thing to have immediately to entertain his brother Bishops, clergy and friends, as necessarily had to be done that day by going to an hotel.

I shall never forget the extreme kindness with which the Bishops welcomed me amongst their number, and especially how very encouraging and fraternal were the words addressed to me in private by Bishop Griffiths. He had one of the most humble, modest and episcopal hearts that I ever knew, and he knew well the value of fraternal sympathy and encouragement on the part of an old, to a young, Bishop.

Bishop Walsh asked me in his gentle, smiling way if I knew what a Bishop was, and on requesting his light on the subject, he said: '*Episcopus est homo epistolis scribendis et querelis audiendis damnatus.*' ('He is a man condemned to writing letters and hearing grievances.')

Although freed at my appointment from the Coventry Mission, I had yet to provide for the future of my little Dominican community. On an understanding with Bishop Walsh, they were to rejoin me at Bristol so soon as I could provide accommodation for them. Meanwhile they remained at the house at Coventry.

I had next the trying task of parting with that good and pious flock which I loved so well, and who had been so great a consolation to me. I knew them all so well, with all their little histories, and many of them I had received into the Church, and seldom have Pastor and Flock understood each other better than we did. But few of them gave me real trouble, and they were so much of one class, the industrious weavers and watchmakers, that they were like one family.

They presented me with a beautiful chalice for which they had subscribed £40, and it was offered me at an open-air meeting outside the Church, amidst many tears. They had requested Father Aylward, the Dominican, to come over from Woodchester,[4] to speak for them on the occasion; and I promised that I would always use the chalice at my daily Mass, which would remind me of them, and this promise I have kept now for two and twenty years.[5]

It was long a pleasure for me whenever I have gone to Coventry to look from the pulpit on the old faces; but alas! how many of them have disappeared. Those whom death spared have been scattered by the loss of the Coventry trade, after going through years of suffering and destitution.

When I reflect on the frequent external causes which came to interfere with the work of that mission, and to threaten removal before it came, that I had three times to change my residence; to pull down the old chapel and house; to build first the body of the church, then the chancel and a large house, to go over the country soliciting aid for these buildings; to enlarge the school; and also to train the religious Sisters, it almost surprises me to think how much was done for the mission. But in that work I had the aid of a second, and afterwards of a third, priest. I also had the invaluable aid of Mother Margaret, whose influence over the people was a spiritual power that was always growing. My four years and a half at Coventry were the happiest and most fruitful years of my life, and I left it with extreme regret.

Notes

1   The Benedictine vow of obedience.
2   Augustino Barbosa (1589–1649). Portuguese Canonist, briefly Bishop of Ugento in Italy, noted for his piety and extraordinary memory. He could memorize whole books at one reading. His work referred to here is doubtless *Pastoralis Sollicitudinis, sive de Officio et Potestate Episcopi Tripartita Descriptio*. Rome, 1621.
3   Frederick Lucas (1812–1855), M.P. and journalist. Brought up as a member of the Society of Friends he came under the influence of Thomas Chisholm Anstey (1816–73), and converted to Rome in 1839. In 1840 he started the weekly Catholic paper *The Tablet* which is still the foremost mouthpiece for Catholic thought in Britain. He was M.P. for County Meath.
4   Mss. 1. reads Woodchester, which is in Gloucestershire. Mss. 2. says Hinckley, which is in Warwickshire. It is of little moment.
5   This from Mss. 1. Mss. 2. reads: ... a promise I kept for forty years.

Chapter Forty-Two

Vicar-Apostolic for the Western District

Of the state of things in the Western District I was but too well aware. Mr., now Bishop, Vaughan came to Coventry by the advice of Father, afterwards Bishop, Hendren, and explained to us the state of the College of Prior Park. From Dr. Gentili, who had long been a professor there, I also heard much. And although after hearing various statements, I still held my judgement suspended, and my mind open to hear the other side. I was prepared for difficulties.

Dr. Brindle was President of the College and also Vicar-General, and I continued him in these offices provisionally, and until I had time to examine into the requirements of the District. I had also written to him to say that though I should first proceed to Prior Park, which had been the residence both of Bishop Baines and Bishop Baggs, and should remain there a month for the purpose of shewing my interest in the establishment, yet my intention was to fix my residence in Bristol.

My motive in selecting Bristol was that it was the most populous city in the District, that it appeared to me the most suitable centre for a Diocese, that there was room amidst its population for a considerable religious expansion, and that Bath was already occupied by my brethren the Benedictines. I felt that as a Bishop it was my duty to place myself in a special manner at the head of the secular clergy, who had no other superior, to gradually form a staff of picked men around me, to have such a church in my own hands as would serve the purpose of a cathedral, to provide for the multiplication of missions in Bristol, and to get one or two active religious communities at work there and, in short, to devote my first and last energies to forming a missionary centre for the entire District. The policy of Bishop Baines had been to form a great collegiate establishment. In that undertaking he had absorbed the whole resources of the District, and it had proved a failure in itself, as it had also embroiled the whole District, and divided it into two parties, which had then stood in bitter antagonism.

The College was at a low ebb for pupils, whilst it was embarrassed with very heavy debts and was at the mercy of the tradesmen to whom it owed heavy bills. One lady had £20,000, her whole fortune, invested in it, yet could scarcely get enough of interest from it on which to live in the most economical way. Often, instead of money, she only received very painful letters. Another lady had invested £7,000 and she could get no interest at all, and the replies to her letters, which I saw, were even offensive. Nearly £8,000 had been taken possession of that had been left to Tiverton by a French priest, the result of his labour, self-denial and management of his life, and in return for this scarcely enough money could be got to keep up the mission. And this put the trustees of that property in a very discontented state. The attempt made by Bishop Baines to get possession of the property of the flourishing Benedictine convent at Cannington had ended, first by the convent being taken from under the Bishop's jurisdiction, and next in their removal to the Central District.

The very servants of the College had all their wages for a number of years invested in it. In fact, they got but little except for fees for shewing the house. The housekeeper had £500 invested, the butler and housemaid had theirs in proportion. So that the establishment was tied to its servants as well as to its tradesmen. And as to the tradesmen, butcher, fishmonger and grocer, as large sums were owing to them, they did what they liked in providing the College, their bills being from three to five hundred each.

Dr. Brindle himself had a sum of money invested on which he claimed compound interest, raising it from £5,000 to £6,000.

Such was the material condition of Prior Park, with a school at the time which did little more than meet its own expenses. But there was a traditional spirit in its managers and friends which was satisfied with no other idea than that the chief function of the Bishop was to provide resources for its maintenance, compared with which the missionary work of the Diocese seemed altogether a secondary consideration.

The heads of Prior Park and their principal supporters were either the ex-Benedictines who had abandoned the Benedictine Priory of Ampleforth to aid Bishop Baines in founding Prior Park, or the pupils they had taken from there, and several of whom had become priests. Of course, the nomination of a Benedictine could not be acceptable to them, and there can be no doubt, indeed I saw written proof of it at the time, that they had hoped for the nomination of Dr. Brindle himself, and Dr. Brindle, in a letter to a lady, had expressed the probability of his nomination.

The fact of my being Benedictine was not all. I was a member of the Priory of St. Gregory's, Downside, situated in the District, which had so severe a conflict for its very existence with Bishop Baines and his advisers, and which had been long under Interdict in consequence, until the intervention of the Holy See had restored that Priory and College to its normal state. I must say, however, that nothing could exceed the delicacy with which the Fathers of that Priory acted. Whilst thoroughly wishing me well, and anxious to see the District restored to unity and peace, they did not ask of me, or at all expect from me any special notice or patronage, but whilst their feelings were of the kindest, they left me to pursue a completely independent course; not seeking to influence my mind or my acts in any manner whatsoever. The Prior Park influence was not all concentrated in the College. Certain of its elements were scattered here and there in the District.

My first night in the Western District I passed at Bath at Mr. Robert Tichborne's, Mr., afterwards Archbishop, English having accompanied me from Coventry. The next morning, after saying Mass at his residence, I went up in Cappa Magna in Mr. Tichborne's carriage accompanied by Father Cooper of Bath and the Reverend Mr. Vaughan to Prior Park, where I had a public reception according to the ritual. I addressed a few words to the assembled clergy and laity in chapel, and met a large party at dinner.

The next day I began to feel what a lonely being I was at Prior Park. Dr. Brindle kept a sort of state in the central mansion which was truly palatial. I had assigned to me a bedroom and a small sitting-room, and was informed when Dr. Brindle was about to dine. Although Dr. Brindle was the General President, he exercised no practical influence over the establishment. Mr. Vaughan was President of St.

Paul's College, which contained but a few students, Mr., now Bishop, Clifford, then a cleric, was Prefect, and Canon Rossi and Reverend Mr. Woollet were professors. In St. Peter's College, Mr. Parfitt was President, Mr. Broderick, in minor orders, was Prefect, Mr. Shepherd, a cleric, and Mr. Kavanagh, a layman, were teachers. Of this body Messrs. Vaughan and Parfitt were the only ones who gave their cordial allegiance to me, and from them alone could I learn anything of the real state of things.

There were also at Prior Park, teaching the classics, Messrs. Neve, Collins, Estcourt and Capes. Mr. Capes resided with his family at the little house called the Priory. These were all recent converts, and very anxious for a better state of things in the establishment, for which they looked to the new Bishop. Mr. Northcote and Mr. Healy Thompson were residing in Bath, but had not yet taken any share in the work of the College.

For myself, as far as Dr. Brindle and his adherents were concerned, I was a solemn stranger, solemnly treated. After a day or two I found it best to join the priests table in the common refectory. Dr. Brindle continued in his solitary state. He said Mass in the great chapel at a certain hour wearing his purple soutane and train, and his Doctor's ring, breakfasted, wrote a few letters, and then walked down to Bath to the Reading Room and to visit a few friends. He returned by four to dine alone, unless he had guests, the dinner being rather formal, and with a certain display of plate. If I had occasion to speak with him the matter was arranged by a formal message, through his valet. Perhaps the following anecdote will illustrate the state of things as well as anything else. I told Mr. Parfitt that I had not a single provision in my room for locking up a private paper. He said he had a bureau in his room which he would send me and the keys belonging to it. Mr. Parfitt was superintending its transit, and as it crossed the great hall the housekeeper came and asked where it was going.

Mr. Parfitt said: 'To the Bishop's room.'

Upon which she said: 'Nothing can be moved in this establishment without Dr. Brindle's approval.'

Upon hearing this I sent for Dr. Brindle and spoke to him plainly upon this strange treatment.

Prior Park exhibited a strong example of what I have remarked in a less degree in some other places, the evil of resting securely upon the credit and character of magnificent buildings and palatial surroundings. It was the weakness of the Jews rebuked by Jeremias. They too often measured the grandeur of their religion by the magnificence of their temple. 'Thus said the Lord of Hosts, the God of Israel; make your ways and your doings good, and I will dwell with you in this place. Trust not in lying words saying: The Temple of the Lord, the Temple of the Lord, it is the Temple of the Lord. For if you order well your ways and doings,' etc.

Prior Park was a palace, and was built for a palace, and its occupants were proud of its stately structure and beautiful scenery. It gave them a sort of elation that warped the judgement. It was a show for the inhabitants and visitors of Bath twice a week, and this function of the establishment wedded its Superiors to the keeping up of a costly style of embellishment. I tried but failed to induce the giving it up as a bi-weekly exhibition. In this respect it was the chief emolument of the servants, who got but little of their wages. When it came to a question of turning pictures and plates into capital to pay off pressing debts, the exhibition feeling was one of the strongest motives of opposition.

When buildings and surroundings are plain and simple, men feel they must rely on themselves and that their work and character constitutes the establishment. But when the material encasement is resplendent it is too often allowed to supply for the internal deficiencies of its living inhabitants. It is the old story of the plain person outstripping the Beauty because she has only her mind and heart to rely upon.

I have been more then once complimented by able and distinguished foreign prelates on the magnificence of Oscott, but in private I said to them: 'This is all very well for a College for the education of our nobility and gentry, but tell me, is it the style of thing you would choose for the training of your clergy?' They turned grave and replied: 'Ah, that is altogether another question.'

I speak of German as well as French Bishops, and of men experienced in the training of youth to the ministry. I quote these remarks in no disparagement of Oscott, for it is wonderful considering the predominance of the lay element in that establishment, what good priests it has sent forth, and how good a spirit has been maintained there; but it comes in to illustrate a principle. Unfortunately Prior Park was stamped all over, inside and out, with a secular tone. The only cross

visible upon the outside of that vast range of building was
the one put up by the Protestant Bishop Warburton upon the
gable of the chapel, when he possessed it, as the heir to its
wealthy founder whose daughter he married. Inside, the statue
of a saint, even of the Blessed Virgin, was not to be found. Mr.
Vaughan told me that when he was appointed President of St.
Paul's he put up a statue of the Blessed Virgin, and that one of
the Superiors came up and said: 'Let us have no Romanizing
here. Take it away!'

Dr. Gentili, who with Dr. Pagani and several others of the
Rosminians taught there and guided the spirituals for a considerable time, in Dr. Baines' time, used to speak to me long and
ardently, and with sad exclamations, upon the minimised tone
of things that prevailed in his days. And I have been told by
secular priests who were students in his time that he would go
about the house in distress of mind, saying he verily believed
that 'the devil was in the place'. I have heard an amusing story
from eyewitnesses of his having set the boys to pull down the
statues of the pagan gods that adorned the frieze of the cor-
ridors leading from the central mansion to the wings, then
converted into the two Colleges. The College of St. Peter's
was originally a pavilion, consisting of rooms from billiards,
smoking, etc. That of St. Paul's was originally the stables and
their appurtenances. The whole had been constructed for its
wealthy proprietor, the patron of Pope, Fielding and other literary men, by an Italian architect on the model of a first class
palace. Dr. Baines had converted these wings at great cost into
two Colleges, but the vice of adapting an original construction
for other purposes rendered the two Colleges inconvenient for
any purposes. The central mansion was reserved for the episcopal residence, and when burned down it was reconstructed
with greater splendour but less accommodation, the great
central hall being carried up to the roof, and occupying more
than a third of its entire space.

But to return to Dr. Gentili, he had got a rope around Hercules, and the boys were put to the other end of it, and he
directed them: 'When I say the third time, "Come down, you
great monster," all of you pull together!'

He had given the signal once, and twice, when Dr. Baines
put his head out the window and stopped the destruction.

It is a literal fact that after the great flight of steps were
constructed up to the portico, a feature which spoiled the
architect's design, and pulled down the elevation of the whole

façade to the eye, these pagan gods were taken down from their elevated position, manipulated with canvas and plaster, and made to represent two rows of saints, standing on the two sides of this broad flight of steps; and that Hercules with a tiara, a plaster cope and a triple cross in his hand in place of his concealed club, did duty for St. Gregory the Great. But they were afterwards restored to their original forms and places.

The word *minimise* has been a good deal abused for controversial purposes of late, but it correctly represents that spirit in which Prior Park was ordered and guided. It was of a piece with Dr. Baines' Pastoral against devotion to the Sacred Heart which he stigmatised as being 'in bad taste'. I have in my possession a copy of Pope Gregory XVI's correspondence with the Bishop on that subject, sent by His Holiness' direction to my predecessor, Bishop Walsh. And when Mr. Beste was putting out his injudicious vindications of Bishop Baines, had he gone a little further I should certainly have published that correspondence as well as to vindicate the conduct of the Pope as of my predecessor Bishop Walsh. Happily for the reputation of his subject, Mr. Beste stopped in time. In that correspondence, nothing can exceed the paternal kindness and forbearance of the Pope, whilst the replies to his letters are offensive, sarcastic and filled with the spirit of retort. At last the Pope rose in his dignity, declared that he had corresponded privately with the Bishop solely with the hope of bringing him to a better spirit, and to save him from humiliation, but as this had failed he must not leave Rome until he had signed the document that would be put before him. Cardinal Barnabo, when once driving me in his carriage to the Vatican told me that he, then a young prelate, engaged in the Penitentiary,[1] had drawn up that document by the Pope's directions.

Notes

1   The Sacred Penitentiary is one of the three tribunals of the Roman Curia, the other two being the Sacred Roman Rota and the Apostolic Signatura.

Chapter Forty-Three

Tackling the Prior Park Problem

This brief history of painful things has not been introduced here gratuitously. It was necessary for understanding the traditional spirit which I was called upon to encounter. Dr. Gentili used often to say that Prior Park had not yet had all the scourging requisite for the changing of its spirit, and whatever might be the value of the prophecy, the event responded. For my part, I certainly went to the District with an earnest desire to do whatever I could to remove its difficulties, and to put it, if possible, in a state of prosperity, and if I failed to do anything for it, it was simply, as will appear, owing to the opposition, the dead passive resistance, put by its Superiors against all action on my part.

On arriving in the District I found no fund of any kind, not even a shilling, remaining for the maintenance of the Bishop. Bishop Collingridge's savings, who had proceeded Bishop Baines, and which had amounted to somewhere about six thousand pounds if not seven, were all absorbed in Prior Park. It was the bottomless pit, receiving everything and returning nothing. From this diversion of all funds that could be gathered anywhere the missions were languishing, and widespread discontent prevailed. The few gentry of the District, if only on this score, were all discontented with Prior Park and its managers.

I had never saved money. I was, and always have been, satisfied with meeting my expenses, whilst I always avoided the contracting of personal debts.

On my appointment Father Scott, then Provincial of the South, very considerately offered me the loan of £100 to meet my first expenses, and that I repaid in the course of two years. On my arrival in the District I found a letter from Sir Edward Doughty, offering me his friendship, and enclosing a cheque for £50 as his first annual subscription towards my personal expenses. And a little later on, the Reverend Mr. Vaughan wrote to another gentleman of the District who very kindly made up an annual subscription to the amount, including Sir Edward Doughty's, of about £150 a year.

At this time Archbishop Polding arrived from Australia, and immediately on his arrival he wrote me a letter expressing his grievous disappointment at having arrived so late, just after my consecration, as he had come to Europe with the intention of soliciting my nomination as his coadjutor in Sydney. His Grace was present at the exhibition which took place a few days after, when the colleges broke up for the vacation, and my solitude became a solitude indeed. But though I had promised to reside for the first month at Prior Park, and though I kept that promise, I did not slumber there. I began to look into Bristol and Clifton. I visited sundry missions and convents. I took, in short, a survey of the District, dropping down here and there, and hearing all I could learn of the state of things.

I also went to assist at the consecration and opening of Mr. Hornyold's church at Blackmore Park, and consecrated an altar. I had had something to say in the designing of that beautiful church, the nave of which is an adaptation of the one at Skelton near York, designed by the architect of the transept of York Minster. And the porch at Blackmore, one of the most beautiful of modern designs, was planned by Mr. Hansom[1] at my suggestion, being developed from the door at Skelton, which is only a thickening of the wall to secure well-recessed jambs. The stone for that church was brought from the Hazlewood quarries, from which York Minster was built, its hardness and fineness securing sharp and enduring lines. I had also suggested the adoption of the decorated style in the chancel, so to express in the transition from the plainer lancet of the nave into the more floriated and lightsome, the passage from the secular to the more sacred and mystical portion of the building. It was thus I thought that the different styles might be combined with more significative effect, now that we possess them all. The expressiveness of York Minster itself very much results from historic development rather than original design.

But my inward mind was all this time occupied with the future of Prior Park. Amongst other persons, I consulted with

Father, afterwards Bishop, Hendren, a man of much learning and of solid principles, and who had the interest of the District at heart. The Franciscan convent of Taunton where he was director and the Salesian convent at Westbury were thoroughly devoted to the episcopal authority and gave me all the aid and co-operation they could in meeting the first temporal difficulties.

During the vacation, then, I resolved to make some modification in the staff at Prior Park, and that not merely for the purpose of asserting the Episcopal authority and prove it a reality, but with a view to the gradual modification of its elements, and to render it more efficient as well as loyal. I removed Mr. Shattock to Tiverton and put in Mr. Kenny from Poole as Procurator, and I sent Mr. Woollet to Poole in place of Mr. Kenny. I invited Mr. Northcote to the College as Prefect of Studies and Mr. Healy Thompson as professor. As there was no communication between the two Colleges except through the kitchen departments I had a new door made at St. Paul's College for the purpose of avoiding this grave inconvenience. This act tested the spirit of the Superiors. It was wonderful how reluctant and lingering was the disposition against this order, assented to in words, neglected in execution until the last pressure was applied.

I presided at the meetings of the Superiors and the professors to arrange the course of studies for the coming year and it was settled upon.

I then rented and took possession of a residence in King Square, Bristol, and left Prior Park. Before doing so, however, I asked Dr. Brindle for the papers and records of my predecessors, Bishops Baines and Baggs. He told me there were none. 'What,' I asked, 'neither accounts nor correspondence?' He replied none whatever. I had been told by various persons after my consecration that I should never see Dr. Baines' papers. As to Dr. Baggs, he was not likely to trust them to Dr. Brindle, although from a sort of necessity he had continued him as Vicar-General as he held everything in his hands from Dr. Baines' times, and had his name in a good many deeds, besides being the legal heir of, and with, Mr. Shattock the legal proprietor of Prior Park. I believe that Dr. Baines' papers were destroyed. Yet after I and my successor Dr. Hendren had left, in Dr. Burgess' time, a small book was produced containing notes of Dr. Baines' administration. All that was delivered to me was a quantity of papers bound in folios containing the correspondence of Bishop Walmesley, Bishop Collingridge and a few early papers of Bishop Baines.

As the studies were commencing at Prior Park, difficulties began to appear. Resistance to the new arrangements began to show themselves. It became obvious, nor was I unprepared for it, that the Brindle party would have no way but their own. I therefore took a decisive course. I proposed that either Dr. Brindle and the other legal trustees should manage the College, and be responsible for it, in which case I could not consider it as the seminary for training ecclesiastics, but only as a lay college, nor could I devote the funds of the District obtainable through episcopal influence to it; though I must of necessity retain the right of canonical visitation; or I, myself, would undertake to carry it on, in which case my authority must be paramount in all its direction and management. Dr. Brindle and his colleagues took the first alternative and at once began to order things on the old traditions. The result of this was that on September 9th Messrs. Neve and Collins came over to me at Bristol to ask whether the College was under me or under Dr. Brindle, and I explained to them in a few words that it was under Dr. Brindle, who had chosen that of two alternatives. But when on the morning following this interview, Dr. Brindle met the priests and professors to make his arrangements, the Rev. Messrs. Vaughan, Parfitt and Kenny, as well as Messrs. Northcote, Neve, Capes and Collins, resigned their posts.

Dr. Brindle at once addressed a letter to me, stating what had occurred, begging me to go over, and exclaiming at the end of his note: 'Is this to be the end of poor Prior Park?'

I went over without delay. It was a critical moment just as studies ought to be commencing. I plainly pointed out to him that it was a necessary consequence of the course he had adopted, but that if he gave over the establishment into my hands, I was still ready to take it up with all its difficulties. But he stood obstinately to his own notions, and there was no remedy. He obtained the aid of Dr. Rooker from Bishop Brown of Wales, and asked to have Mr. Shattock again, who was restored to his place of Procurator and made head of St. Peter's College. This gentleman said on his return that 'they had killed two bishops and were likely to kill a third,' and the saying got about. I took care that my retort should get about also – 'That I had been in the habit of killing difficulties that attempted to kill me.' As Dr. Rooker, a clever teacher, was one of the ex-Benedictines, and Mr. Shattock also one of those who had migrated from Ampleforth, the old leaven was now stronger than ever. They had also two outposts in two other of the ex-Benedictines party, Mr. Burgess, who still remained in the Welsh District, and did all he could to draw Bishop Brown into their interest, keeping up an active correspondence with the disaffected College, and Dr. Metcalf at Trenchard Street, Bristol.

Misled by their statements, Bishop Brown himself now began to interfere with me, and although he was more quiet, I knew that he kept up an active correspondence with good Bishop Briggs, the senior Vicar-Apostolic and ancient friend of Bishop Baines. Dr. Briggs I contrived to see, and explained to him the real state of things, and he appeared satisfied. With Dr. Brown I had much greater difficulty. He had claims on the funds of the District, having formerly belonged to the Western Vicariate. Returning in his company and that of Archbishop Polding from Alton Towers, after the opening of the Cheadle Church, the Archbishop had uttered some words about my rights in the property of Prior Park, which Dr. Brown hastily interpreted as signifying that I excluded his claims. On this he warmed, not only that night, but still more next morning, still harping upon the idea that I wished to exclude him from all his rights. I was very quiet, called his attention to the fact that I said nothing, and adding that as I knew the real state of things it was impossible for me to open my mouth, or commit myself to any statement. But he claimed the right to advise me, on the plea of having been my former Superior, and on that of having exerted himself to obtain my nomination. I could only reply that I really did not thank him for this last service, however well intentioned. And that, in my episcopal office, independence of all but the Holy See was essential to success. The subject was continued in a correspondence, and hints given of my proceedings with respect to Prior Park which showed me how much he had been misled as to facts. But I resolutely planted my foot on the verge of my District and resisted all interference from without. The Bishop then wrote to Cardinal Acton complaining that I did not look to him for advice, to which Cardinal Acton replied by pointing out the independence of one Vicar-Apostolic of another.

I had reason to fear that as soon as it became known to the creditors that the Bishop was not responsible for the establishment, there might be an execution put into the house, and

I wished to secure all I could that had belonged to the District prior to the existence of the College. I therefore sent Mr. Estcourt, who had been appointed my secretary, with a note to ask Dr. Brindle for Bishop Collingridge's books. These, with some reluctance, were given up. I also wrote for a set of the Bishop's vestments for my private chapel. Dr. Brindle sent me a lot of cotton velvet vestments, which were unrubrical, and which I could not use. I then wrote to request that the vestments and church plate which had belonged to Bishop Baines before Prior Park came into his hands, and which of right came to his successor, should be given over to me. This was refused on the score that they were the legal proprietors of all that Dr. Baines had left; and were responsible for the debts inherited from him. Now, my chief object was to save sacred things from being seized for debts for which they certainly were not liable, and having existed as a possession of the District before the College. But to all my representations. I received nothing but the shortest replies, indicating dead resistance. In vain also did I apply for an account of the temporal condition of Prior Park, of its debts and liabilities. There was but one resource left in my hands. I was resolved to make a visitation of the establishment, and visitations in form were not at that time in vogue amongst us in England, unless amongst religious bodies. I accordingly sent notice of my intention, and fixed a day and hour for its commencement. I took with me the Reverend Mr. O'Farrell and another priest whose name I do not recall, but I was particular to avoid taking anyone who had been concerned in any party matter or who might be considered as obnoxious to the managers of Prior Park.

On our arrival it was raining and Dr. Brindle expressed his regret that the Blessed Sacrament was not in the Great Chapel, but at St. Peter's College, to which I could not pass for the rain; and proposed to have it brought over to the Great Chapel for me. I burst into an expression of surprise at this proposal, saying: 'It is I who had come to visit the Blessed Sacrament, not to receive the visit.' And I went over to St. Peter's Chapel. This was a specimen sample of the spirit of the place.

The vestments, church plate and other ecclesiastical furniture was produced at my call, examined and its history inquired into, when it clearly came out that the most costly

part of it had been presented to Bishop Baines before Prior
Park was bought, and belonged to his episcopal outfit. Still
they maintained that as they were the universal legatees of
Dr. Baines, it belonged to them and to Prior Park. When
the large chapel, in which the public Sunday services for the
whole College were celebrated, came to be examined, I found
it was the custom to bring the Blessed Sacrament on a Sunday
afternoon from St. Peter's Chapel in a private way, through
that College, along the corridor, and along the passage of the
kitchen departments, and so up a private staircase into the
chapel, where it was deposited on a credence table by the
wall covered with a veil, until wanted for Benediction after
Vespers. This was done to avoid deforming the symmetry of
the altar and its furniture, consisting of large candlesticks and
a cross in the centre of the same pattern in the base and the
shaft as the candlesticks. There was no lamp in the chapel.
Examining the superaltar a little closely, I had it opened, and
found a little square door in it that was almost invisible, but
which presented a little keyhole. It must be recollected that
Dr. Brindle had told me on arriving that morning that the
Blessed Sacrament was not reserved in that chapel. It was the
altar at which he said his daily Mass, and the one at which I
had said Mass the month I was at Prior Park. And certainly
there was no sign ever given of a consciousness that the Blessed
Sacrament was there. At my suggestion Mr. Bonomi searched
and found the key of this almost invisible door in the sacristy.
It was opened, and behold, inside the step of the superaltar
was a very small ciborium, as black as ink, and in it the Blessed
Sacrament which everyone seemed to have forgotten. I wrote
out an order, that a tabernacle should be placed on the altar
and a lamp suspended before it; and that the bringing of the
Blessed Sacrament from St. Peter's on Sundays and festivals
for giving Benediction should cease. Dr. Brindle said they had
a tabernacle and lamp and it should be done.

I next called for an account of the property, its assets
and liabilities, and I quoted the canons showing the right
a Bishop had to this information. Mr. Shattock, the Procurator, was the chief spokesman to this proposal. He said
they did not deny that what I had said was the law of the
Church, but they stood on the law of the land. In short
they declined, even though I allowed them more time in
case they were not prepared. I told them I should be satisfied with receiving the statement in writing at a later time,

if they would mention how long would be required. But they stood to their refusal. I then gave a written copy of the directions I had laid down for the Blessed Sacrament and retired.

Notes

1   Mother Drane identifies him as Charles Hansom, of Coventry, mentioned above, rather than the more famous Joseph Aloysius Hansom, his elder brother, also refered to.

Chapter Forty-Four

The Case of Prior Park at Rome

I saw there was nothing left but to proceed without delay to Rome, to lay the state of things before the Holy See, and to ask that His Holiness would appoint a Commission to enquire, and to report the result to Propaganda, and then to obtain instructions from the Sovereign Pontiff as to what any future proceedings should be. I had already transferred the Vicar-Generalship from Dr. Brindle to Mr. Hendren. And I left for Rome without delay, at the end of January 1847.[1] So soon as Dr. Brindle heard of this step he wrote me a letter, which reached me in France, offering to do what I required if I would return. But it was now too late. I could not trust to vague promises, after what had passed, and I proceeded on my way to Rome.

My letters to Mother Margaret, which must be at Stone, and which were written in the intimacy of spiritual friendship, will be the only vivid recollection remaining on paper of this and other visits to Rome.

Cardinal Franzoni was still head of Propaganda and Monsignor Barnabo was secretary. On being presented by the latter to Pius IX, I gave His Holiness a brief sketch of the subject on which I had come, and he asked me what I proposed doing with Prior Park. To this I replied that it was such a gulf[2] to the District and, I believed, so encumbered with debt that perhaps the best thing to do with it would be to give it up to the creditors; but that what I asked was the appointment by apostolic authority of a commission of enquiry. To this His Holiness replied: 'Very well'. I then illustrated the case by comparing it with that of a merchant or a banker who should come to me to Confession, and admit that his liabilities were two or three times greater than his assets, and who, upon further interrogation, allowed that he did not see in what way he could meet hem. I ask him if he is willing to call together those creditors whose property he is wasting, and to make known the condition in which it stands. He declines; and I am compelled to refuse him absolution.

I presented a memoir on the question to Propaganda, and pointed out how my authority was set at defiance, and solicited the nomination of a Commission.

Meanwhile an agent arrived to represent the trustees. This person, Signor Martini, was an Italian layman, an emigrant on account of political affairs from the Austrian dominions in Italy. He lived at Bath and had been employed as Italian teacher in the Colleges during the previous years. Of course he knew nothing about the College affairs beyond other externs, but he had a glib Italian tongue. Dr. Rooker had devoted some private money of his own to providing for the expenses of his agent. I was asked by Propaganda to meet this person and see if anything could be accommodated. Of course I declined doing so. I represented that this person was a layman, a man who had fled from his country, an extern to the College, a person who knew nothing of its affairs, a person who came on the part of those who were in a position of disobedience, and who had brought no letter to me, and of whose delegation I had received no notice. With this reply Propaganda was satisfied. Archbishop Nicholson was then at Rome. I asked him what he would have done in like circumstances. He said: 'If all the Cardinals had asked me I should have declined.' I asked a Roman Prelate. He replied in the same sense. However, this good man, who has since repeatedly expressed to me his regret for having taken such a commission, was very active. He exhibited both to the Pope and to Propaganda an engraving of Prior Park, not as it was, but as it was contemplated to be, with an additional story upon it, spoke with warm Italian eloquence upon the wrong of destroying so magnificent an institution, taking as usual the walls as a symbol of their contents; represented me as a Benedictine, and consequently prejudiced against those who had left the Order, and as wedded to Gothic architecture, consequently inimical to Italian models. These representations given with Italian tact failed not to produce for the time a certain influence upon Italian minds, nor did I think it became me to take the least notice of them.

I was asked at Propaganda whom I would recommend for the Commission, and I pointed out Bishops Griffiths and Sharples as men versed in financial matters. I then said that

I should think it desirable that the third should be a priest and one who was on friendly terms with Dr. Brindle, as that would give him the advantage of a friend in court, and would facilitate his making any private representations that he might think desirable. I then mentioned Dr. Cox as having the double advantage of being the Head of a College, and of being Dr. Brindle's friend. A Commission consisting of these three persons was accordingly appointed to investigate and to report to the Holy See. So soon as I had got the document, I returned to England as rapidly as possible. At my parting interview with the Sovereign Pontiff I briefly explained my ideas with respect to the future organisation and development of the District. He asked me how I proposed to find resources for their accomplishment. I answered that I had no resource but the Divine Providence, of whose work I had seen beautiful examples in my short day. Then His Holiness seized my two hands and said with ardour: '*Si, si, la Providenza, la Providenza!*'

The Commission sat for nearly a week at Prior Park, but though I sat with it, I confined my action to furnishing information. I laid before it my correspondence with Dr. Brindle, which produced a painful impression, especially on the mind of Bishop Griffiths. He wished to question Dr. Brindle upon it, on which I proposed to retire, to leave both parties at more freedom. The Commission resisted this, but I maintained that it was only proper delicacy, and I did retire. After some explanations had passed, Dr. Griffiths, as presiding, as was afterwards repeated to me, spoke to Dr. Brindle with episcopal plainness. He said: 'Dr. Brindle, until I read this correspondence, I did not know you. Here is resistance to your Bishop in every line. As your Bishop gradually and justly grows displeased with you, you show no sense of it, and his words are like balls fired at a woolsack, they drop dead and without effect, from your passive resistance to his voice.'

When this was over, and I returned, I was asked to give facts as proof of my having been disobeyed. I then gave the history of the visitation, handed over my copy of the directions I had drawn up for the proper decorum of what concerned the Blessed Sacrament, etc., and asked for the Commission to call for the copy which I had given to Dr. Brindle. I then requested them to go and see with their own eyes, whether my injunctions had or had not been complied with. 'The Reverend Sacristan,' I said, 'will accompany you, perhaps the President also, and I will remain here until you return.'

They went, came back, and Dr. Sharples said: 'Not a single thing has been done. Everything is as you found it.'

Then began the investigation into the financial state of the establishment. Mr. King, the Catholic solicitor of Bath, who had a heavy mortgage upon it, and was a warm friend of Dr. Brindle and his associates, was called in to aid, and to give information. The best obtainable valuators were engaged for each species of property. Prior Park as a marketable property was considered as most available for a money return, if the great building was taken down, as it was too large, too near Bath and had not sufficient land for a wealthy resident, being besides in other respects unsuited.

Its construction and situation equally unfitted it for any public institution, as well as its great extent, and want of concentration. The house, then, was of no marketable value, but if pulled down, the land might be gradually sold for villa residences. But then it would cost more to take down that building, and dispose of its stone as a quarry, than it would to quarry the same quantity of stone from the ground behind it on the same estate. Such was the opinion of the best judges of house and landed property. Mr. English, the best salesman of pictures and furniture in the West of England, valued everything in his line, and undertook to get a considerable sum for the paintings. And although there was a great reluctance on the part of the College to give them up, as it would so much alter the character of the place as a show house, yet the Commission insisted that they ought to be sold, to meet the pressing debts, and deliver the College out of the hands of the tradesmen. If I recollect right, Mr. English was confident of obtaining four or five thousand pounds for them. The catalogue was published and the sale attempted, but they went so low that the sale was stopped, and very little money obtained. This was a sort of test of the fancy valuation put on other parts of the property. However, at the time, they made out their assets to be some twenty-five or twenty-six thousand pounds, which the Commission did not themselves think would fetch in the market much above twenty thousand pounds, whilst the liabilities, including Dr. Brindle's claims, arouse to sixty thousand pounds or not much short of it.

A report on the state of things was drawn up for presentation to Propaganda. But though the Commission certified in detail to the material condition of the establishment, they did not think it expedient to recommend any course of action for meeting further difficulties, or guiding the future policy as to its management.

At the annual Episcopal Meeting in Low Week, it was decided that Bishops Wiseman and Sharples should proceed to Rome to make certain representations, and to propose the establishment of the Hierarchy, and Bishop Sharples undertook to present to Propaganda the report of the Prior Park Commission. But this Bishop was already a great sufferer from that destroying disease, diabetes, which had already impaired his energies, and which ultimately took him off. He presented the report, but did little more. No very decisive action was taken by the Holy See on the subject. Some two thousand pounds were realised by sales, chiefly from pictures, and Prior Park went struggling on in its own way much as before.

Notes

1   'All this should be changed to 1848, as it is a mistake to put it as occurring in 1847.' (Ullathorne's own note on Mss.1 written in the handwriting more characteristic of Mss.2.)

2   This word is indecipherable in the manuscript. I have followed Sir Shane Leslie's use of the world 'gulf' although if this is correct Ullathorne has spelt it 'gulph', as was often done. Even so it is a strange word to use with the preposition 'to'.

Chapter Forty-Five

Work from Bristol

Meanwhile I had begun to work at Bristol. Mother Margaret and Sister Osburg had come to me at my residence in King's Square, and the other two sisters were kindly received at the convent at Westbury, until I could provide a place for them. Mr. Vaughan and Mr. Estcourt were also with me, and they searched all Bristol over for a place for their convent, and finally they succeeded in obtaining a house in Queen Square. They then began to teach the school at St. Mary's, under Father O'Farrell, and to visit the sick and poor.

I removed Mr. Metcalf from the old Trenchard Street chapel, finding the great inconvenience of having one who was of the Prior Park party so close to me, and placed Mr. Vaughan there in his stead, but Mr. Metcalf declined the mission I offered him, and went to the Yorkshire District where, soon after, he died of the Irish fever, in the performance of his missionary duty at Leeds. Soon after Dr. Gentili and Mr. Furlong were invited to give a mission at Trenchard Street, and thus began the spiritual movement in Bristol. It was the first ever given in the Western District, and it exercised a great influence upon the Catholic population.

My earnest desire was to build a new church in Bristol which might serve as a cathedral, to which I might attach my residence, and which might serve as a centre for the District. Messrs. Vaughan and Estcourt searched in all directions for a site for the purpose, but all in vain. Mr. Vaughan then suggested the consideration of repurchasing the ruin of the great church begun by Father Edgworth at Clifton. This property had cost Father Edgworth a very large sum of money, had ruined him with debt, and he was compelled to fly the country. It was taken possession of by Newport Bank, and had stood a useless ruin for many years, and a disgrace to the Catholic body. It consisted of the site of the present convent, then furnished as a small chapel and house, rented and occupied as a mission for Clifton, and the vast substructures now occupied as schools, and of the walls of the present church standing without any side windows up to within two feet of their present height, and a colonnade of six huge columns raised to half their height in front.

Through Mr. Philip Jones, one of the chief proprietors of the bank, the whole property was bought for £3,000, including a mortgage held upon it by Mrs. Riddell. Of this sum the Dominican Sisters paid £1,000 for the convent portion. The rest I took for the sum of £2,000. Mr. Markland came about that time to reside at Clifton, which was the commencement of an influx of Catholic residents. He gave me £100 towards commencing operations. It was the opinion of architects and builders that the ruin could not have been roofed, the span being so large, and the walls so thin for carrying the requisite beams. Before I purchased the property a notion had been entertained of securing it for a public market, but the roofing seemed to be a difficulty in the way.

This point, however, I had considered before making the purchase. It would have cost £10,000 to have finished it according to the original plan. It was a question whether in that case the walls could have been raised high enough to get in the contemplated windows. As it stood, except two windows at the entrance end, it was altogether blind and dark.

I sent for Mr. Hansom, told him he must put his architectural reputation into his pocket, and simply follow my directions, and that I was determined to make a Cathedral of it at a cost of £2,000. I directed him to raise the walls round to a level of about two feet above their natural height, and then to put in two rows of columns, not of stone, for they would have to come on the crown of the crypt vaultings, but of wood, to be made stouter to the eye by casings. As for their foundation, I said, there is none, and we must run two beams the whole length upon the crown of the vaulting, like the keels of two ships, joint the separate pieces together upon the supporting sub-walls, mortice them into the end walls, and then step the wooden pillars upon them. Having raised these pillars, cased them and expanded the tops into capitals at the height of the walls, we next raised wooden semicircular arches above them so as to receive an open roof. This would give us the requisite height, and enable the building to carry a roof.

We thus succeeded at a small cost of converting the ruin into the present Cathedral of Clifton.

We thus succeeded in defeating the prognostics of the architects, in provoking the world at large by the odd character of the building, and in establishing a centre for the Diocese.[1] The Bishop's house was subsequently raised by Bishop Hendren, and the cut stone used in that structure was quarried out of the enormous pillars that stood in front. As to the windows they were cut out of the walls as they stood. But this was not the completion of my plan. I intended to have built a large sanctuary and sacristy at the entrance end, covering the whole building, at a later period, and to make the entrance from the transept on the opposite side to the convent. It is this which explains the structure as then completed, the present altar end being intended to be ultimately the end opposite the altars and chapels. Thus completed, it would have made a large and effective cathedral. I constructed a chancel large enough for a chapter, having always before my mind the hope of seeing the Hierarchy established in England, as I had seen it done in Australia. Whilst this work was going on, I took possession of the house built for a convent, with Mr. Vaughan and Mr. Estcourt. This I did for the purpose of carrying on the Clifton Mission and preparing the way for the Dominican community, then in Queen Square, Bristol. After a short time, I rented a house on the other side of the church, in Meridian Place, and then the Sisters took possession of their little convent and began to form the schools of Clifton in the crypts under the church. Mother Margaret began to construct the convent as it at present stands, and enlarged and raised its chapel, so as to make it an entirely new building. For originally it was low and small, with its cells over the body of the chapel.

Bristol had its two churches close to each other. I made a careful study of the whole city, and mapped it out into four missionary districts, with the intention of ultimately expanding the two missions into four. With this view the land was bought in Pennywell Lane, and a school commenced there. And now, at this time, the four missions then contemplated have been realised under the administration of Bishop Clifford.

As all common funds of the District had been sunk into Prior Park, there were neither resources for the education of priests, nor for administrative purposes, nor for the mainte-nance of the Bishop. I organised two annual collections in all the churches for the forming of an administrative fund. I did my best also to cultivate the religious spirit in the convents. I gave a spiritual retreat to the nuns at Taunton, who were always very faithful co-operators, and in consequence of the want of confessors, I had frequently to act either as ordinary or extraordinary confessor at Westbury. This excellent community was also full of zeal for the advancement of religion in the District. There was one, and only one, of the old convents that did not respond, as I could have wished, to my solicitude. But that was owing to their having a chaplain of the Prior Park school rather than to anything else, and I am unwilling to enter into acts here which have since been regretted, but which compelled me at the time to act with firmness. Unfortunately, the want of experienced clergy for the guidance of communities did not allow me to take the decisive step from the first which my judgement pointed out, and which would have put matters right at once.

Although in the course of my brief Vicariate in the West I traversed the greater part of it, and opened two churches, yet there was so much to be done at Bristol and Clifton, and resources of all kinds were so limited, that I was compelled to limit my chief energies for the time to the works that were going on.

I did my utmost to induce the Redemptorist Fathers to establish a mission in that part of Bristol called Bedminster, and the Belgian Provincial came over to examine it, but they shrunk from the undertaking. A difficulty arose with another Religious institute that is too instructive to be passed over, if past experience is to be of any use to future rulers in the Church. Dr. Brindle had informed me that a certain mission had been established and its church raised by a secular priest, a man of great zeal, piety and self-denial, that the mission had been made over by my predecessor to a Religious institute whose chief Superior was a foreign Bishop, and that to prevent the possibility of its alienation it was important that the Vicar-Apostolic's name should be joined in the title deeds with those of the Fathers who held it. This seemed to me to be both just and prudent advice. I proposed it. The Fathers declined entering into the question. I saw the foreign Bishop, appealed to his good sense as a Bishop to direct my having that security against the possibility of alienating what was really the property of the mission. He also held on to a passive course. What was the result? It turned out that these

Fathers had actually pledged this property to a Liverpool merchant for a loan of money with which to purchase a property in a Northern District. And the property, church included, which I had thus striven to make secure from alienation, was sold by the merchant when Bishop Errington was Bishop, and had to be repurchased by him. It subsequently turned out that the English Superior of the institute, himself a foreigner, had actually persuaded the Bishop, foreign Superior, to whom I had applied, that two females of the mission had misled me by false representations, although I had never seen or communicated with those said persons in my life, and at the very time that these representations were made, the property had been secretly pledged, unknown to the ecclesiastical authority of the District. When the affair became public, so ashamed was the Provincial here spoken of, that he fled the country. I was then in Birmingham, but his brethren actually entreated me to ask the episcopal Superior to send him back. Of course, I declined interfering.

This was a period when a number of new Religious institutes of religious men were being introduced into England, and their inexperience being as great as their zeal, in their earlier years they committed grave errors, as well as did much good. They formed hasty judgements of the English clergy, and spread those judgements by their correspondence abroad, and especially in Rome. They formed equally hasty judgements upon their own work, and thus misled their correspondents upon a second point.

It may be taken as almost a rule in the English Mission that wherever a new mission is begun with energy, there are always a certain number of persons to be found in and about the locality who are predisposed for conversion, and a considerable number more who are attracted for a time, but fall off again, unconverted, after curiosity has been satisfied. This state of things generally lasts for two or three years, and then it comes to the same hard plodding as in the old missions where progress is only marked by progress of time.

A striking example of what I have said occurred in the Western District during the short time that I was placed over it. A Religious community from abroad had been placed in one of its remote missions by my predecessor, Bishop Baggs. For a time they seemed to be doing wonders. They sent the most flaming accounts of their progress to the Continent, and from time to time to our own Catholic newspapers. They introduced a convent of nuns of a different institute from their own into the mission. Of their progress great things were also heard. In vain did I advise the Religious Superior of the mission to be more moderate in these statements, and assure him that by keeping his progress quiet he would best save himself from vigorous combinations[2] of the Protestant communities, to check his influence amongst the people. A good deal of money was obtained from the Congregation of the Propagation of the Faith. At last the Secretary of the Congregation sent me one of the flaming statements, about the mission, sent for publication in the *Annals*, asking me whether it would not be more prudent to keep such documents private than to print them. Of course I coincided with this opinion, and the document was not published. Soon after came the usual lull, and the reaction, and the usual plodding, and then these Fathers left the place in disgust and planted themselves in another Vicariate. They completely stripped the place, pulling up the very flower-roots which a lady had planted for them in their garden, and taking them away with them. Nor was this all, without a word to the Bishop, under whose jurisdiction they were, and without his knowledge they took away the nuns also, and uncanonically planted them in the Vicariate, and near themselves in the new mission to which they betook themselves.

Being called off myself, soon after, by very important affairs, and then transferred to the Central District, I had no opportunity of putting this affair to rights, but I did let those nuns know that until they had their leave of transfer from my successor they were in an uncanonical position.

By this time Dr. Gentili and his companion, Father Furlong, had been giving retreats, or missions, to the congregations all over the country, and kindled a new spirit in many places. He had expressed to me the wish of trying the experiment of carrying on one of these missions in some suitable place for a whole month together. For it was found that the first week or so did little more than benefit those who, from the good habit of attending their religious duties required it the least, whilst those who required a great deal of time, both for instruction and for being solidly prepared for the Sacraments, and for being settled in a new course of life, were not catered for. Moreover, he felt that time was needed for giving a complete body of systematic instruction adapted to the several classes that make up a congregation as well as to the children, and also to the Protestants who presented themselves first as hearers only, then as converts under instruction. I therefore resolved to give this illustrious missioner the opportunity he sought, and a month's mission was settled to be given at St. Mary's, Bristol.

It was very successful, but excessively laborious and exhausting to the missioners. As there was no house attached to the mission, Dr. Gentili would live and sleep in the sacristies, that he might lose no time and might continue the work early and late. The mission took place at a period when all Europe was harassed with revolutions, when thrones were falling on all sides, and when Charles Albert of Savoy began his conflict with Austria, and the Sovereign Pontiff was surrounded with those perils which ultimately led to the Roman republic. These things preyed much on Dr. Gentili's mind and increased the exhaustion brought on him by his excessive labours. I saw him frequently, and he told me much of what was passing in his mind. I saw that he felt the necessity of relief by communication, and I consequently encouraged him by exchange of thought. He said much about his English experience and very much regretted his earlier and less informed judgement upon the English clergy. He especially regretted having written so much to Rome which subsequent knowledge had corrected in his mind. He told me that the many missions he had given convinced him that the English priests knew best how to manage the English mind and to make their work secure by avoiding that haste, precipitancy and public excitement which defeated itself by awakening the adversary to vigilance and to counteracting efforts. He hoped, he said, to do justice to the English clergy, to their steady, silent, prudent labours and their self-denial, in letters to be written when he got a little leisure for the purpose.

But alas! he did not live to fulfil his intentions. By the close of the mission, which went on even to the end of the month with but little flagging, he and his reverend companion were completely exhausted. Their Provincial, Dr. Pagani, came to Bristol to see them, and to him I strongly represented the absolute need there was of at once giving a period of repose to men whose lives were so valuable. 'Without it,' I said, 'you may be sure they cannot last.' And I represented that Dr. Gentili was in a state of feebleness which required immediate attention. Mother Margaret who, with her Sisters, had aided in the mission amongst the women and girls in the schoolrooms, made a similar representation. Dr. Pagnini felt it deeply. But they had engaged to go direct and without delay to give a course of missions in Dublin, and Dr. Pagnini could only promise that they should have repose after those missions were over.

What they did in Dublin, and how Dr. Gentili died there in the midst of his labours, is a matter of history. However great a grief his death was to me, however great a loss to the English mission, his death did not surprise me, for he was half dead from mental and bodily exhaustion before he began his work in Dublin, and the toil and excitement which came upon him with the rush of that fervid people to his discourses and his confessional was too much for his mortality.

Not to dwell longer upon the details of my work in the Western District, which did not last two years, and during which I was twice called to Rome, I now come back to the most important and eventful of those labours which mark the track of my episcopal life. But this will need some preface.

Notes

1   This in anticipation of the re-establishment of the Hierarchy.
2   This is obscure, but it is Leslie's reading and I can offer no better.

Chapter Forty-Six

Agitation to Restore the Hierarchy

For a considerable time past there had been discontent amongst the clergy with the government by Vicars-Apostolic. They felt the want of a voice in the nomination of their Prelates, and still more did they feel the need for fixed law both to settle the relations between Bishops and clergy on a sure and firm footing, and to regulate the administration of ecclesiastical affairs. On the other hand, the Vicars-Apostolic were harassed with many difficult ties. They found themselves presiding over the state of things that had outgrown the provisions for their government furnished by Benedict XIV in his *Apostolicum Ministerium* of 1753. They felt the absolute need of a code of laws, drawn up from local experience and in which the clergy might have a voice, with which the clergy might be imbued. There were not infrequent appeals by the clergy from the Vicars-Apostolic to Rome, and though the Vicars-Apostolic were generally found to have been right in the substance of their acts yet this did not content the clergy as, unacquainted with the principles of ecclesiastical law and guided mainly in their judgements by the principles of the British Constitution, they were not unfrequently impressed with the notion that the Vicars-Apostolic were favoured at their expense.

Still, the acts of the Vicars-Apostolic were often guided by their own subjective sense of right and wrong rather than by any precise and accurate law and, more than the clergy, they felt the want of fixed rule and a written law to which both they and the clergy could appeal. Synods could not be held, the Prelates had no local head other than by claim of seniority, they had no canonical council, and the clergy had not their properly graduated positions or any voice in the nomination of their ecclesiastical superiors. Again, there was a strong feeling throughout the English Catholic body that, as compared with other churches, and even with much younger churches than their own, with those of North America and of Australia, which had already got their Hierarchies, we were left behind in a provisional, exceptional and anomalous condition, which was as much a reproach as it was an inconvenience.

In the Apostolic Letter constituting the Hierarchy it is stated that many petitions had come from England in favour of its establishment. From the days of Mr. Pitt, English statesmen had repeatedly expressed their wish to see the Catholic Bishops in England made Bishops in Ordinary, as being more conformable to the principles of the British Constitution than vicars of the Pope. In the Report of the Episcopal Meeting held in London in 1845 I find Bishop Griffiths proposing to petition the Holy See 'for the restoration of the Hierarchy so far as changing the Vicars-Apostolic into Titular Bishops of England.' The Bishops assembled agreed to this proposition, and Bishops Wiseman and Baggs were requested to draw up a statement of the reasons for, and the difficulties against, the change to Ordinary Bishops for transmission to Rome.

At the Annual Meeting of 1847, the first at which I assisted, it was found that confusion had reached its height. Certain laymen, and especially Mr. Anstey and Mr. Hamilton, both comparatively recent converts, had made grave representations to Propaganda, as unjust as they were unfounded, against the venerable Bishop Griffiths, and had become very active in thwarting the councils of the Vicars-Apostolic with respect to obtaining legal provisions for the security of our ecclesiastical property. I refer especially to Mr. Romilly's Bill for settling Catholic Trusts, on which advice was sought from Rome, and which through the intervention of these mischievous men was set aside through the silence of Propaganda, passing over our letters altogether. Of this Hamilton had told me something when at Rome in the previous year, and I was also able to report the unjust charges laid against Bishop Griffiths.

With all these facts before them the Bishops resolved to request Bishops Wiseman and Sharples, the Coadjutors of the Central and Lancashire Districts, to proceed to Rome, as well to explain on the part of the Vicars-Apostolic as to feel their way towards obtaining a Hierarchy. In conversing with Cardinal, then Monsignor, Barnabo, Secretary of Propaganda, and while representing the serious embarrassments in which the Vicars-Apostolic were placed, Mgr. Barnabo said: 'You will always have these troubles and questions until you ask for the Hierarchy. Ask for it, and I will support you.'

The two Coadjutors made their petition accordingly. In reply they received a document drawn up some time before by Cardinal Acton in which it was argued that the English could not safely be trusted in that position of greater independence implied in the constitution of Ordinary Bishops, for as much as their whole history betrayed the spirit of faction, division and resistance to the Holy See. Bishop Sharples replied to this document in Rome, and Bishop Wiseman wrote in reply from Fano. It was triumphantly responded amongst other statements that no people could exhibit greater sufferings or more numerous deaths incurred for no other reason than their adherence to the Holy See than the English Catholics.

The Revolution was then making rapid progress in Italy as in other countries; the relations between Austria and Italy were becoming serious. Bishop Wiseman was requested to return to England without delay with a special commission of a political character to the British Government, and Bishop Sharples, already suffering severely from the disease which ultimately took him off, returned also. Still the question of the Hierarchy had been mooted, and the Vicars-Apostolic received a letter from the Holy See requesting them to meet as early as practicable for the purpose of drawing up a scheme for dividing the eight Vicariates into at least twelve Bishoprics. The Episcopal Meeting was held in November of the same year 1847. Bishop Griffiths had departed from this life and Bishop Wiseman was now the Vicar-Apostolic of the London District.

In drawing up a scheme for the Hierarchy it was thought desirable that, as far as practicable, the portions of the country which had the fewest Catholic resources should be attached to those which had more, so that one might be aided by the other. The result of the discussion was to propose a division of the eight Districts into twelve Dioceses as follows:

The Western District to be divided into two Dioceses, viz:

1. The Diocese of Plymouth, including Cornwall, Devonshire and Dorsetshire.

2. Clifton, to include Somersetshire, Gloucestershire and Wiltshire.

3. A Diocese to include Oxfordshire, Buckinghamshire, Berkshire, Isle of Wight and Channel Islands.

4. Middlesex, Hertfordshire, Essex, Surrey, Kent and Sussex.

The titles for these two Dioceses were left unsettled for special reasons.

5. See of Nottingham to include Nottinghamshire, Lincolnshire, Rutlandshire and Derbyshire.

7.[1] See of Shrewsbury to include Shropshire, Cheshire and North Wales and the Isle of Man.

8. See of Newport to include Herefordshire, Monmouthshire and South Wales.

9. See of Birmingham to include Warwickshire, Staffordshire, Worcestershire and Leicestershire.

10. See of Liverpool to comprise Lancashire.

11. See of Leeds comprising Yorkshire.

12. See of Newcastle to comprise the existing Northern District.

Anticipating that the new order of things was soon to take place, the Bishops thought it desirable to have the aid and experience of Dr. Grant[2], then Rector of the English College in Rome, and agent to the Vicars-Apostolic, to aid in drawing up the documents. And accordingly Bishop Wiseman was requested to write to Rome and ask leave for him to come to England, and that Dr. Errington might take his place in Rome during his absence.

It was left as usual to the Vicar-Apostolic in London to transmit the result of our consultations to the Holy See, and during my negotiations at Rome in the following year I supposed that this scheme was before the Holy See but, to my utter surprise, when on my return I met the Bishops at Salford, Bishop Wiseman in reply to a question from me admitted that it had never been sent.[3] And as we heard no more about the proposal of Dr. Grant's coming to England, Dr. Grant himself wrote to the Bishops previously to the next spring's meeting, proposing in his diffidence that some competent person should be sent to Rome either to aid him or to supersede him as episcopal agent whilst negotiations of so much importance were going on.

At the Episcopal Meeting commenced in London on May 2nd, 1848, we were requested by the Holy See to present three names to Rome for a Coadjutor to Bishop Walsh in the Central District and also names for a successor to Bishop Riddell deceased, in the Northern District. The representations made at Rome by various discontented priests against the Vicars-Apostolic, the machinations of Messrs. Anstey and Hamilton, and their supporters, and other circumstances very harassing to the Episcopal Government of the Catholics in this country, awakened the most serious reflections, and it was thought desirable that some priest of standing and capacity should be sent to Rome as bearer of a memorial to the Holy See upon these difficulties, and as extraordinary agent for the purpose of pressing on the question of the Hierarchy, as well as of rectifying the erroneous statements that had found a hearing there. Bishop Wareing suggested Dr. Husenbeth as a person well qualified to act for us. He was invited to come to London. But on presenting himself, that reverend gentleman gave personal reasons against his undertaking so grave a task that perfectly satisfied the Bishops that he was entitled to be excused from undertaking this delicate task. One grave reason was his state of health.

The Bishops had therefore to cast about for someone else, when Bishop Brown of the Western District suggested that a Bishop would be the best envoy, and that I should be invited to undertake the work. As all the other Bishops promptly united in this request, I put myself at the service of my brethren, who immediately subscribed the funds requisite for my expenses. I was to present a Memorial signed by all the Bishops to the Sovereign Pontiff, expository to the sentiments of the Bishops respecting the serious difficulties they experienced from the constant representations made by the discontented in England at Rome; to endeavour to obtain the early appointment of a new Vicar-Apostolic in the North, and a Coadjutor for the Central District; and to press on the affair of the Hierarchy.

Making a few arrangements at Clifton, and leaving Father Hendren as my Vicar-General in my absence, a few days after the Episcopal Meeting closing I started for Rome. At Paris I met with Archbishop Nicholson, who was also on his way to Rome on altogether a different embassy. He was the bearer of a letter from Lord Clarendon, then Lord-Lieutenant of Ireland, to the Sovereign Pontiff, offering certain guarantees for the security of Catholic education in the colleges then being established in Ireland, and since called the godless colleges, and asking whether any further guarantees were required.

But the Archbishop stopped so long in Paris that another agent, a priest, was sent in his place, with another copy of Lord Clarendon's letter. Meanwhile Archbishop McHale and Bishop O'Higgins of Ardagh reached Rome on the part of those who were opposed to all negotiation or concession, and with Dr. Cullen in co-operation with them, who was then President of the College of Propaganda, they proceeded to make the most vigorous representations. On the other hand, when Archbishop Nicholson at last arrived he, and the emissary sent later on his side, in consequence of his retarding amongst his friends in Paris, came into conflict as to which was the veritable representative of Lord Clarendon and of Archbishop Murray.

It so happened that each of these emissaries had shewn me his papers, and each appealed to me against the other. It was, however, no business of mine to be more than a passive observer of this triple conflict, and all I did was to stand amazed at seeing my friend Nicholson first taking up an embassy of this delicacy, he having his See in Corfu, and being a Carmelite Friar to boot, and then lingering amongst his friends for weeks in Paris when the cause into which he so heartily entered was pressed for time, and his adversaries were on the wing. The result of the joint representations of Archbishop McHale, Bishop O'Higgins, and Dr. Cullen were that no answer was given to Lord Clarendon's letter. This policy was no doubt dictated by the wisdom of the Holy See yet I could never understand it. For it appeared to me that a counter-proposition might have been sent, proposing that the colleges intended for Catholics should be exclusively under Catholic management, and exclusively taught by Catholic professors. It was probably the first time in modern days that a high official of the British Government had, so to speak, gone on his knees to the Pope, and whilst all the requirements of courtesy would thus have been met, the promoters of this educational scheme would at the same time have been thrown on the defensive, or have been put on the wrong side in the negotiation, while the principles of the Holy See would have been thoroughly asserted. Lord Clarendon's letter was courteous, proposed that certain professorships should be Catholic, and asked whether any further guarantees were required by the Holy See, and was clearly open to a reply asserting the whole principle of separate education. I may have been misinformed as to the absolute silence of the Holy See, though I was told it in Rome, but this was also the general impression both in England and Ireland. And it is certain that the Government considered itself insulted, that Lord Clarendon was embittered, and that this affair, occurring some two years previous to the promulgation of the hierarchy, had its influence upon the excitement awakened by that measure. And not only this affair of the treatment of Lord Clarendon's measure, but the treatment of Mr. Romilly's Catholic Trust Bill, on which the

English Bishops had asked the guidance of Rome, but on which, through the machinations of Messrs. Anstey, Hamilton and Co., no answer was vouchsafed to the English Bishops. And Mr. Romilly, disgusted at having no Catholic support, let the Bill drop, though that would have put our Catholic church property and our chantries on a secure footing, especially with such modifications in the details of the Bill as we might have obtained in committee. In the year 1854, when Cardinal Wiseman was in Rome on the subject of another Trust Bill, beset with greater difficulties, as he subsequently informed the Bishops, he pointed out how we had been left without guidance, and were consequently reduced to silence, during the agitation of Mr. Romilly's more satisfactory Bill, and Cardinal Barnabo admitted frankly that they had been completely misled.

Notes

1   There is no No. 6 in this list. In the event the diocese of Northampton may have been envisaged as comprising, Northamptonshire, Norfolk, Suffolk, Cambridgeshire, Huntingdonshire and Bedfordshire.
2   Thomas Grant (1816–1870) Rector of the English College and first Bishop of Southwark.
3   See below, Chapter 48, pages 321–322.

Chapter Forty-Seven

Revolution in Paris

It was whilst I was in Paris on my way to Rome in May, 1848, that the attempt was made to establish the Red Republic,[1] and I was an eyewitness of most of the chief scenes of that attempt. The Republic established after the overthrow of King Louis Philippe was still on foot, under its three heads, and its Constituent Assembly: but Committees of the Red Republican school were seething here and there with truculent fellows keeping sentry at the doors, red-capped, red-sashed, the very scum of the populace. The day before the attempt they conducted a funeral procession of men who had died of their wounds received at the barricades in the first conflict. The whole affair was obviously a scene got up to move the populace. After the two hearses followed a number of wounded men, bandaged, and crawling along, and then came the wives or children of the dead or wounded, the procession being flanked by Red Republicans in their ordinary clothes, but with red sashes, and some of them with red caps, carrying their muskets with fixed bayonets, as a guard of honour. They were all of a piece, a dirty, ghastly procession, and in sepulchral tones they called upon all persons to take off their hats, as they slowly passed through the streets.

The next morning I was taking an early walk when, crossing the *Place de Carrousel*, I saw a group of some twenty men in blue blouses with a tall well-made man in their centre, evidently the commander of the group, a man of respectable as well as of a commanding appearance, head and shoulders above the rest, wearing also a blue blouse over his suit of black broadcloth. They at once recalled to my mind St. Real's description of the appearance and bearing of the conspirators of Venice before their outbreak. They walked on with rapid steps, with minds bent up and concentrated, with eyes bent forward and downwards, and they tightly grasped the bludgeons with which every one of them was armed. I stood gazing at them, astonished that not one of the many passers across the great Palace Square seemed to take any special notice of them, that the sentries of the National Guard and the police seemed to take no special note of this strange group. As to the regular army it had been removed by the Republican Committee from the city to the suburbs. I was myself quite certain that these men were proceeding to some rendezvous in contemplation of some desperate act, and that in connection with the Red Republican exhibition of the previous day.

Some hours later, I think about eleven o'clock, I was passing in company with Dr. Nicholson in a hired carriage past the doors of the Legislative Assembly, when we saw those very men, accompanied by others of the like description, forcing their way into the Legislative Assembly. Alarm was at once raised, and an officer seized our horse's head, turned us round, and directed us to proceed back over the bridge. We did so, and on reaching the *Place de la Concorde* I got out, leaving my companion, who was of a nervous type, to go on his way, being myself curious to see what would come next.

The drums were beating the reveille all over Paris, and regiments of *Gardes Mobiles*, the latter consisting of the *gamins* of Paris, and with no other military costume than their native rags, though completely armed and regimented, came marching into the *Place de la Concorde* and around the Legislative Chambers until, in little more than an hour, there were 100,000 men concentrated under arms. Placed on the high ground above the place, I saw all that passed.

Beneath me the General commanding the National Guard dismounted, came in front of a regiment, waved his sword, said a few words; when cries arose from the regiment that were bitter with indignation. The men rushed from the front rank upon him, and tore off his epaulettes. In the next morning's papers I learned that he had ordered them to ground arms and unfix bayonets; and that they had proclaimed him a traitor and renounced his command. He was in the conspiracy.

That evening I dined with a party with the Miss O'Farrells in the *Rue de Rivoli*. As Paris was in a great state of excitement, when the rest of the party had retired, I stayed for the protection of the ladies in case of any emergency, until late at night. A few doors from them was a house occupied by Sobrière and his gang of conspirators. A considerable force concentrated here, and the police entered Sobrière's house to arrest him and his companions. But for some time he was not to be found, until at last they pulled him down by the legs from inside the chimney. The ladies and myself watched what was going on in the streets from the windows. The National Guards exhibited their bourgeois qualities to perfection. They sang the first lines of *Mourir pour la Patrie*, and other such rhapsodies *pour encourager*, never getting beyond the second line, from defect, it seemed, of memory; and they talked in short, hurried sentences with one another as they marched in very wavering lines. One regiment had a soft, lusty man at its head, with whom a man of the streets tried to enter into controversy, asking what all this meant. To which the weary marching man replied, obviously annoyed yet incapable of resisting the spirit of colloquy: *'C'est assez qu'il y a quelque chose.'* Then turning to his men, he said: *'Ne repondez pas.'* But his questioner was tenacious and a group was gathering round him. But suddenly a pistol was fired in the colonnade just by the house from which we were looking, when the regiment, apparently without orders, halted, faced round to the colonnade and levelled their muskets. I then requested the ladies to retire into the back room, which they did very reluctantly, wishing still to see the fun. The men soon, however, recovered arms, faced to their first position, and marched on. At last we heard cries of: *'Vive la ligne.'* And looking out, saw a regiment of the regular cavalry advancing amidst the cheers of the people. It was obvious that the bulk of the population did not want the Red Republic.

That night it was ordered that the windows should be illuminated to furnish light to the streets for military operations. There was apprehension also lest the city should be set on fire. But the night passed over quietly, the chief conspirators being already under arrest at the *Hôtel de Ville*. Next morning I went out early. The troops of the line were bivouacked in the streets, and a strong force of cavalry guarded the approaches to the *Place de la Concorde* and the Legislative Assembly, blocking all approach to them. A few hours later was a great concentration of the National Guard around the *Hôtel de Ville*, and I saw the prisoners carried off accompanied by a strong force to Vincennes. It was amusing to see the bourgeois soldiery carrying their bread-loaves and sometimes their sausages on their bayonets, where they roasted and fried in the sun, and were likely, when eaten, to get a good deal of help to get them down from the casks of *vivandières*, who were on great force on the occasion. One poor girl who I observed in her regimentals halting along with a lame leg and with difficulty keeping her place. The citizen forces were in high glee at their bloodless victory.

I went on the same evening towards Marseilles, and at every town we came to the officials with tricoloured badges across their breasts were vigilant in inspecting passports, and inspecting the features of travellers.

Note

1   On May 15th a mob invaded the Chamber of the Constituent Assembly, decreed its dissolution, and declared war against the Kings of Europe. The situation was saved by the timely appearance of the National Guard.

Chapter Forty-Eight

Plans and Plots in Rome

Arrived at Rome, I took up my quarters in the English College where I had the advantage of being nearer the Propaganda and the residences of the Cardinals than in my old quarters in the Benedictine monastery in Trastevere, and where I had the still greater advantage of being in constant communication with Dr. Grant, the agent of the Vicars-Apostolic. Dr. Grant had been secretary to Cardinal Acton, and had great experience in the management of business in the Roman Congregations. I had forgotten to say in its proper place that when in Paris I called upon Monsignor Fornari, the Papal Nuncio. To him I spoke on the subject of my delegation to Rome and I showed him the document addressed by the English Bishops to the Sovereign Pontiff. He entered into its subject with warm interest, and pointed to two passages in it, on which he advised me to insist very strongly. He also requested me to take a packet of despatches from him to the Cardinal Secretary of State, which I took care to deliver immediately on arrival.

On the following day, May 27th, I had my first interview with Cardinal Franzoni, the Prefect of Propaganda. His Eminence received me with great courtesy and kindness. He had wished to see me, he said, and to converse on many things face to face. We had a long but desultory conversation, during which I had to vindicate various steps taken in England by Vicars-Apostolic which had been erroneously presented at Rome. There were at that time no less than three cases pending at Rome between priests and Bishops. McDonnell versus Bishop Wiseman, who had written very offensive pamphlets against that distinguished Prelate. Mr. McDonnell on his removal from Clifton had asked my leave to go to Rome not, he declared, on any business, but simply as an act of

319

piety, and for a little recreation. Yet being there, where he still was on my arrival, he told me he had addressed a letter to the Pope, in which he had informed His Holiness that Bishop Wiseman had taught heresy, and that Bishop Walsh had not treated him honestly. Then there was Mr. Hearne at Rome carrying on an appeal against Bishop Brown of Lancashire, about whose case I had been entrusted with papers, and felt it my duty to do what I could in defence of the Bishop; and moreover there was the appeal of Mr. Frank Trappes against the same Bishop. On all these subjects I had to enter at length in this interview with Cardinal Franzoni. These very appeals and the agitation they were causing, constituted a strong argument for the necessity of a more regular order in our ecclesiastical administration.

But it was to Mgr. Barnabò, the energetic Secretary of Propaganda, that I chiefly looked for carrying through the question of the Hierarchy. On the same day I had an interview with him in company with Dr. Grant, and henceforth my narrative will be chiefly drawn from the notes which I requested Dr. Grant to take of the interviews he had at previous times with this Prelate and with various eminent personages, or from my own notes taken at the time whenever Dr. Grant was not present.

Mgr. Barnabò at once plunged into the question. He said that the Hierarchy had been chiefly delayed by the question of a proper person for Archbishop, and by the difficulty about the succession of the property held by the Bishops under their actual titles. The first difficulty might be met by our presenting a memorial suggesting how London, where Bishop Wiseman was acting as pro or provisional Vicar, was to be filled up; and how, in the event of Bishop Walsh being placed there with Bishop Wiseman for his Coadjutor, a Bishop was to be found for the Central District.

Both the British Prelates and the Holy See considered it of great importance that the Vicariates should be filled up before the Hierarchy was constituted, and there were, in fact, three Vicariates vacant, or in question. The Northern District was actually vacant, the London District was occupied provisionally by Bishop Wiseman, and as the Holy See contemplated moving Bishop Walsh to London in view of the Archbishopric, this would leave the Central District vacant.

Mgr. Barnabò further said that the letters from England left the impression that Bishop Walsh had been gained over to offer his resignation of the contemplated Archiepiscopal See of Westminster. His Holiness had appointed a special Congregation of seven Cardinals for the question of the Hierarchy, and Mgr. Barnabò promised to have the Congregation assembled early in June, provided I would at once suggest a plan for arranging the choice of Bishops for London and the Central District, the plan to avoid touching the sensibility of the Bishops about seeing a younger Bishop placed over them, as Archbishop, and at the same time allowing Dr. Wiseman to remain in London as Coadjutor, in case of Bishop Walsh being appointed there.

The Vicariate of the Northern District was to be treated as a separate and independent question.

Mgr. Barnabò also said that the plan of division or erection of new Sees was meant by the Cardinals to be referred to the Bishops after they should become *Bishops*, but he recommended that, as I had come with full powers on this subject of division as well as upon others (I had presented a document expressive of this delegation), I should prepare a Memorial on the subject of the division, or redistribution of the Vicariates into Sees, to be considered by the Cardinals, if they seemed inclined to enter into the question at once.

It may seem strange that the Right Rev. Secretary should speak as if they were still unprovided with the Bishop's views as to the division of the Vicariates into Sees, since at the instance of the Sacred Congregation the Bishops had met in November of the previous year, especially for the purpose of devising a plan of redistribution, and since they actually did devise such a plan; but the fact is that, though this plan was completed and left with Bishop Wiseman in London, as well as a letter containing the arguments for and against the division of Southwark from London as a separate See, on my return from Rome, at the meeting of the Bishops at Manchester, the Bishop admitted in reply to my question that he had never sent them.[1] I was very much surprised when I heard this, for through the whole negotiation I had supposed that the plan drawn up in London was all the time in the possession of Propaganda. I might have divined the contrary had I closely considered Mgr. Barnabò's remarks about their intention of consulting the Bishops on the division, and his suggestion that I should draw up a plan, coupled with the fact that the plan drawn up in London was never once alluded to by Propaganda during the whole course of the negotiation; but somehow it never entered my head to imagine otherwise than that the plan must have been sent, as it was left in Dr. Wiseman's hands for the purpose of being sent, as also the letter respecting the division or not of London from Southwark had been left, with the signatures of the Bishops attached to it. I can only conjecture the cause of their not having been sent: Bishop Wiseman was very strongly opposed to every idea of separating Southwark from London.

I made no mention at Propaganda of the general Memorial which the Bishops had signed for presentation to the Pope, as I had not yet had my interview with His Holiness, but I briefly urged some of its contents as from myself as an argument for the Hierarchy.

On the day following this interview I had a long conversation with Dr. Grant on the history of events preceding my arrival. He told me that when the Bishops had been required to write their several and separate views on the best mode of meeting the difficulty in the transition from Vicars-Apostolic to Ordinary Bishops with respect to the transition of property, Bishop Wiseman had sent a summary of the Bishop's letters, upon which, for their own justification, Propaganda had requested the transmission of the original letters. They had only arrived on April 15th, 1848, and this had delayed the advancement of the question of the Hierarchy, as the subject had to enter into the Apostolic Brief.

Quite recently Dr. Grant informed me that Mgr. Palma, then *Minutante*[2] for England, had asked Dr. Newman, then studying at Propaganda, for a brief historical sketch to aid him in drawing up the preface of the Brief and that this was in 1847, but Dr. Newman pleaded his absence from documents and referred him to Dr. Grant, who accordingly supplied him with the requisite materials. These facts tend to prove that when Rome took up the case it was thoroughly in earnest, and that the delays arose from want of adequate information, rather than from any indisposition to proceed.

In consequence of the conversation with Mgr. Barnabò, I drew up a memorial in English which Dr. Grant put into Italian, in which I represented:

1. That of the three names presented for the Northern Vicariate the Bishops had fixed their attention on the Rev. Mr. Hogarth, a man of energy, who had evinced a very marked capacity for business, and who had been Vicar-General to two

Bishops in succession, and was at present Administrator of the District.

2. With respect to filling up the London District, in view of the future Archbishopric, the Holy See expresses its desire to nominate Bishop Walsh, Vicar-Apostolic of the Central District, as first Archbishop. He is a man, I said, venerable for his virtues as for his years, is respected and beloved by his colleagues and celebrated for the great and many works he has accomplished for the service of religion during the one-and-twenty years of his Episcopate.

But the difficulty presents itself that with years come infirmities, and these leave him but little inclination to take up a burden to which he considers his remaining strength unequal. And the fact is to be considered that Bishop Walsh has even expressed the wish to have permission to retire from the cares of Episcopacy, and to pass what of life remains to him in tranquillity and retirement.

In favour of Bishop Walsh's nomination, then, there stood his distinguished merits, his being the head of the Episcopate by seniority, the Bishops always having maintained a deference towards their senior Prelate not only in their assemblies, but in all their relations with each other, and with the Holy See. Hence the Bishops would find in the nomination of Bishop Walsh but the continuance and complement of a position of superiority which they already respected in him, and that the susceptibility to which even the most exalted are liable would not arise from his appointment. Again, those who for many years have borne with him the heat and burden of the day, in cultivating the Lord's vineyard, would see, not without pleasure, their Apostolic labours crowned in him by the head of the Church.

On the other side must be considered his age, his infirmities, the operations to which he has had to submit, which render him no longer capable of prolonged attention to business. These things have given rise to the remark which has reached Propaganda that his nomination would not be satisfactory in so far as this — 'that he must mainly govern through another, and that it would be found more expedient to nominate another at once to the Metropolitan See.'

If, then, the Sacred Congregation decides upon nominating Bishop Walsh Metropolitan, there can be no doubt but that he will at once and immediately require a coadjutor. For if, in the year 1840, when of fewer years and less infirm, this aid

was granted him, much more in his heavier burden in a new
See, but partially known to him, will the want of a Coadjutor
be pressingly felt.

3. The selection of the new Archbishop or, in the event of
Bishop Walsh's promotion, that of his coadjutor, must in
good measure be guarded by the actual state of the Archiepiscopal Diocese, and by the local circumstances of London.
This city is important in a Catholic point of view, as well for
the vast and uncounted number of Catholics who inhabit it,
as for the rank and respectability of many, who either ordinarily or for many months of the year reside there, and for the
resources both spiritual and temporal it offers. Here are to be
found all that are most distinguished in talent, in science and
in dignity, in Court and in Parliament. Here, also, is the centre
of all those efforts, which the Protestants put forth, both
for the maintaining of their errors and for the maintaining
of their establishments, and for the founding of Protestant
Bishoprics, not only in the Colonies, but also in Asia and
even in the kingdoms of Europe. Unhappily, it must also
be added that here, also, are to be found all those moral
evils, which result from the great wealth and the extremest
poverty commingled, and from the close assemblage of so
vast a population.

In nominating Bishop Wiseman as the pro-Vicar of London,
the Holy See has already pointed him out as the fittest person
for the government of that Diocese. Bishop Wiseman has
already sought out the most obscure and populous quarters of
London for the formation of new missions for the poor, and
the good work so commenced is extending itself to more fortunate classes. To found the churches required for those missions will, of necessity, require one having influence over the
wealthy, that the necessary means may not be wanting. Again,
the converts present an important class in the present day,
through the virtue of talents and wealth to be found amongst
them, and their influence over their Protestant friends and
relatives. And Bishop Wiseman, in that kindness which he
has always shewn them, and the efforts he has made to aid
them, is in a position extensively and effectually to influence
their good dispositions to be useful to the Church. By his controversial writings, and the conversions wrought through his
zeal, he has shewn his capacity to sustain that contest which
must be waged throughout England, but especially in London,
against Anglicanism and Sects of Error. In short he is at the

head of Catholic literature in England, which of late has done so much service to religion.

I then pointed out that if Bishop Walsh was appointed Archbishop, the nomination of Bishop Wiseman as his coadjutor was the only way of avoiding his removal from a position in which the Holy See had already placed him as pro-Vicar of London, and that a man of his personal merits and qualifications could not be removed altogether without its being interpreted as a censure upon him, which would prove an impediment to his usefulness in another position.

But if appointed coadjutor, I suggested that it should be 'with future succession', otherwise the spirit of party and opposition now existing would continue, and other inconveniences would arise during the remainder of the new Archbishop's life.

4. With respect to appointing a successor in the Central District, of the three ecclesiastics recommended by the Bishops to the Holy See, the Reverend John Moore, whose qualifications the Bishops had described, was warmly recommended by Bishop Walsh himself, as well as by Bishop Wareing, and also by Bishop Wiseman who, as belonging to the Central District had the fullest opportunity of knowing his merits, and in whose recommendations all the other Bishops concurred.

5. Finally, for reasons alleged, I recommended in this Memorial that all the Vicariates be filled up before the Brief of Hierarchy was promulgated.

After preparing this Memorial, which in my collection is called Document A, I proceeded to draw up a second Memorial upon the proposed increase of Dioceses, which is called Document B.

In this Memorial I stated that the chief difficulties that presented themselves to the minds of the Bishops on the question of increasing the number of Dioceses were:

1. That of finding an adequate maintenance for the Bishops.

2. That of at once finding the requisite number of suitable persons for the office.

As to the first of these difficulties some Bishops, even now, have no fixed or certain income of any kind, and are altogether dependent on voluntary offerings. Some have a small fixed income, but quite inadequate. No more than two, if even more than one, possesses a maintenance sufficient without further free-will offerings. Several are so poor as to have seriously to reflect on the expenses of even requisite journeys in their District.

The result of subdivision would be to diminish the actual means of subsistence, as well by subdivision of any small income now possessed by some Bishops as by diminishing the number of supporters in any given district through further limitation of subjects.

A parallel difficulty will be that of providing for poor missions and the planting of new ones with diminished resources. In some Districts all missions are very poor. In all, there are certain missions, those commencing especially, that depend on what the Bishop can raise from the whole District in aid of them.

A Bishop of a wealthier District can commence new missions even without great local assistance, where a poorer one cannot make the first move unless some wealthy person comes forward, and even then it generally requires additional aid from the Bishop.

Until recently local efforts were aided by the Bishop sending a priest to solicit alms all over England, but in consequence of the number of applications of this kind, and the increased demands upon each locality, for its own purposes, and for general collections in aid of the episcopal administration, this system is exhausted and has become barren. It was always attended by many inconveniences. And the increased demands that must result from a further increase of Bishops, each urging on new works to the utmost, will entirely destroy this resource, already small and precarious.

With respect to the difficulty of at once finding a sufficient number of properly qualified persons for the Episcopal Office, it is to be noted that many Bishops have been made of recent years for England and the Colonies, in proportion to the body of clergy. Great losses have been sustained by pestilence amongst the most valuable priests; whilst a very large proportion of our clergy are young and inexperienced or natives of other countries.

If, on the other hand these difficulties can be surmounted, there can be no doubt but that a great impulse would be given to religion by multiplying the centres of episcopal energy and influence by a more effectual government of the remote portions of our present extensive Districts.

Three plans for increasing the Episcopate appear to present themselves:

1. That of a considerable increase at once against which the difficulties advanced above have to be considered.

2. That of providing an actual plan to be filled up by gradual increase, which if I understand correctly, has been done in America. In this case the Bishops who anticipate a future division of their Sees will have to guard against the temptation of organising their resources upon their own future portion of territory, and thus increasing the difficulties of the new future Bishop in the remainder.

3. That of nominating a small increase for the present, leaving further increase to be guided by future exigencies. In which case the new Diocese will have to be arranged with reference to the number of Catholics and their resources, if we consider the temporal question, or with reference to extent of territory if we consider the question of efficient government.

To this exposition I added that, being cognisant of the sentiments of all and each of the Bishops respecting the contemplated subdivision of the Districts into Dioceses, and being commissioned by them to answer such further questions as the Sacred Congregation might propose, I awaited the further commands of their Eminences.

I further suggested that perhaps the most expedient course might be to fill the vacant Vicariates, to change their titles into those of ordinaries, and after their new position had become consolidated, the Bishops in their first Provincial Synod might be called upon to propose the names of those most capable of filling the new Dioceses upon such plan and on such principles as the Sacred Congregation might prescribe.

I next expressed the ardent desire which the Vicars-Apostolic, clergy and laity in England entertained of seeing the Church in England established upon the firm and solid basis of the Hierarchy, pointed out the fruits of it already visible in our Colonies and amongst the descendants of the British Isles in America, and urged that it would end many disputes and controversies that then agitated us, putting an end to parties that only existed on one condition of doubt, uncertainty and expectation deferred, and put an end to that democratic tone to which things were tending and which enfeebled the spirit as well as the principle of obedience. I further pointed out that this new internal strength would give us a new force against our many adversaries.

Finally I observed that Vicars-Apostolic were not forgetful of the claims of the clergy or disposed to neglect them, but wished to see them possessed of every privilege that peace, discipline and the welfare of the Church might require or permit. During the last two Episcopal Meetings this subject had engaged the most serious attention. Fully instructed in the views of my brethren on the subject, I wanted to know whether the Sacred Congregation thought that this subject should occupy the attention of the First Provincial Synod or whether their Eminences thought it best for me to expound the views of the Bishops for the present consideration of the Congregation; whether, in short, their Eminences thought it well to furnish the Bishops with the principles to guide them in legislating on the subject or thought it better to provide this legislation themselves.

These two Memorials, Italianised by Dr. Grant, were presented to Mgr. Barnabò on June 2nd. Dr. Grant was with me, and we obtained his permission to prepare another paper on the expediency of taking up some of the old titles. He promised to look over the papers already in hand and to say if we were to amend or lengthen any of them. He also gave us the impression produced on him by several conversations with the Pope and some of the Cardinals that the plan for placing both Dr. Wiseman and Dr. Walsh in London was very welcome to them, as overcoming all difficulties. It was plain that the letters from England had thrown Propaganda into great doubt about the extent of Dr. Walsh's infirmities (physical) or his desire to resign Westminster being in earnest.

He said that the Pope had desired him to hold the Congregation *subito*, at once, and he added that it would be had during the month of June.

We afterwards saw Cardinal Franzoni and recommended expedition to him, and we had a similar message conveyed to Cardinal Altieri.

Cardinal Franzoni intimated that it would be impossible to unite the two titles of Ordinary Bishop and Vicar-Apostolic, as suggested by some persons, for a way out of certain difficulties.

Notes

1   See above Chapter 46, page 311.
2   The *Minutanti* (literally those who take the minutes) are officials of the secretariates of Propaganda occupied with the subordinate affairs of certain regions.

Chapter Forty-Nine

The Great Affair in Progress

I must here introduce an episode which had some little influence on the great affair in progress. I have said that the Reverend Mr. McDonnell was in Rome. On leaving England after receiving my commendatory letters he had addressed me in one of his last letters. Always courteous and measuring his speech with great propriety when face to face, like some other men I have known, he could not resist being sharp and offensive with his pen when writing to a Superior. On my arrival in Rome I required a retraction of this letter, and reminded him that, if he had a real complaint, he was now in Rome and could bring his case before our common Superior. To this letter he at once replied by requesting me to consider whatever he had written to me as withdrawn and held for not written, and this as an act of dutiful submission. I at once sent a letter by a messenger expressing my content, and stating that if he would call I would give him back his letters. This moved him, and especially the promptitude with which I had removed all suspense from his mind, as I heard from certain friends of his.

When he called, I took the opportunity of assuring him how solicitous the Bishops were to consider the position and provide for the privileges of the clergy in the coming Hierarchy, in proof of which I read him the passage I had just been writing to Propaganda on the subject in Document B as above quoted. No sooner, however, had he heard this than he went to his lodgings and penned a letter to the Cardinals of Propaganda in which, as a missioner of thirty years standing, he earnestly obtested[1] the Sacred Congregation not to grant the state of Ordinaries to the Vicars-Apostolic before the missionary priests received the rights of parish priests and were made fixed, 'as was customary before the present generation of Vicars-Apostolic,' lest, if it were not granted, 'the

329

last state of the clergy should be worse than the first.' This
singular letter was dated June 6th. This and his previous letter
to the Pope, charging Bishop Wiseman with heresy and Bishop
Walsh with injustice, roused a deep indignation.

Mr. Trappes' case had been for some time decided against
him. A preliminary decision had been given against Mr.
Hearne. I had brought out more papers from the Vicar-
Apostolic of Lancashire on that subject. I saw him and he
listened to me with much respect and deference, and was
inclined to come to terms and leave Rome. Poor man, in
defending a priest from assassins he had received a severe
wound. The state of things in Rome was very troubled. Assas-
sinations were not infrequent, and my friend the Bishop of
Natchez almost immediately after his arrival in Rome was
attacked by a band of ruffians, with a view of causing alarm,
and with difficulty escaped into a shop in the Corso. The war
between Charles Albert of Savoy and Austria was on foot and
Rome was kept in constant agitation with the view of enlisting
men for the war, and in the hope of forcing the Pope to join
against the Austrians.

June 3rd. I requested Dr. Grant to ascertain from Mgr.
Barnabò if Mr. McDonnell had put any case before Propaganda. He replied that there was nothing pending at Propaganda, but that Mr. McDonnell had written several papers
to the Pope, and that His Holiness wished to know who
he was. Dr. Grant also gave in my Memorial, Document
C, on the subject of retaining some few old titles of English
Catholic Sees.

In this Memorial I stated that an opinion was growing
in England that it was expedient to retain some ancient
titles, especially where the city was the most populous and
important of the Diocese. In last year's discussion the Bishops
had thought it best to avoid the ancient titles, as well to
avoid Protestant susceptibility as to avoid the liabilities of
the Emancipation Act of 1829. Some, however, were inclined
to change that view, and certain reasons presented themselves
that deserved to be weighed.

1. To abandon them altogether would be construed into a
tacit admission of the validity of Protestant Orders and succession or, at least, as being an act of respectful consideration
towards the Hierarchy of the Protestant Establishment. But
this would be to sustain and continue a deception and delusion
which of late years has been used for keeping many people

from entering the Church. There is a Party which teaches that the Church has never condemned the Anglican Establishment, or 'Church', and that the latter is a living branch of the Church Catholic, and that she has the apostolic succession. If then we avoid all the titles held by our ancient Bishops, even when there are evident reasons for taking them, and that in all cases we shall give force to the notion that the Holy See dares not touch a sister church (and one on equality with that of Rome, to use their expressions) and that Rome thus confesses the Apostolicity of their ministers and their Communion. The importance of avoiding this impression, especially as entertained by the Puseyites, has appeared a strong reason to some of the Bishops.

Were the Holy See to act with open and manifest independence of all that is external to the Church, as would be evident in principle, by taking one or two names, at least from ancient Sees, now usurped by Protestants, the argument now put forth by Protestants could no longer be upheld. Delusion would cease on this point, and the power of the Holy See would become more manifest, and its acts could not be interpreted into signs of timidity.

2. The Government could only contravene this step where an express law stood against resuming titles. The law of 1829 is the one generally cited as what the Government might enforce. But in the 23rd page of his *Treatise on the Penal Laws*, Mr. Anstey observes that whoever shall without legal authority assume the name and title of Archbishop of any Province, Bishop of any Bishopric or Dean of any Deanery in England or in Ireland shall pay for each act £100; this law is limited to the case of assuming the title, whether in speech or writing. And it would seem that even with respect to a person assuming such title, it will be very difficult to obtain a verdict where the individual does not use the title literally of Archbishop or Bishop in conjunction with the local title – for example, that of York. Difficult would it be for the courts in such case to enforce a new penal law which is of strict interpretation.

[I give the substance of Mr. Anstey's passage, not his exact words, and from the Italian translation of the original.]

It appears then that:

1. The law only affects certain titles when used in a certain manner.

2. In Ireland Bishops use their titles when identical with those of Protestants without the Government interfering.

3. Public opinion in England is opposed to any positive Act of Government against liberty of conscience.

4. In the Colonies Bishops have taken titles already used by Protestants.

5. By express Acts Government has acknowledged the existence of the Irish Episcopate, and though the titles have not been acknowledged, yet by a regulation recently issued by the Lord Lieutenant they are to be addressed by the title of Archbishop and Bishop respectively, and to have precedence before lay Barons.

I then suggested Bristol in place of Plymouth for a title:

1. Because it is the most important city of the Western District, having four missions and two active convents.

2. Because it is the Bishop's residence.

3. Because he is building a cathedral there.

4. Because the Anglican Bishop is called Gloucester and Bristol, and by leaving out Gloucester the law is avoided.

In like manner St. David's (Menevia) might be taken in place of Newport.

1. Because the Vicar-Apostolic of Wales is impressed with the importance of taking some old titles for the reasons alleged.

2. Because the law is limited to England, and being penal would be limited to England as not mentioning Wales.

3. Because the Welsh are devoted to the memory of St. David, one of their most famous Bishops, and are tenaciously attached to whatever is ancient and associated with the times before their subjugation to England.

4. Because this is the old title nearest the residence of the Bishop.

Such is the substance of the Memorial on the titles. The day on which it was presented Mgr. Barnabò gave into Dr. Grant's hands a copy of the Rules of a new institute for religious women which had been put before Propaganda for approval, requesting him to inform me that he wished me to write my opinion upon them and to consider the formal communication through Dr. Grant as equivalent to a written request from him. Accordingly I examined the Rules and drew up a document in which I pointed out what I conceived to be the canonical defects in the Rule that required to be supplied. For various reasons the approval of the Rule was delayed.

June 5th. On this day I had my audience of the Pope and presented the joint Memorial of the Bishops, which in my papers is Document D. This document, drawn up by Bishop Wiseman and signed by all the Bishops, set forth, after suitable preface, the difficulties encountered by the Bishops from a certain faction that was also influencing certain of the clergy:

Letter to His Holiness Pope Pius IX

In a country where a Bishop is without those external accessories that uphold him in a Catholic country; where he is poor and laborious as any simple missionary; where he has alone and unaided to administer, to regulate and to meet the needs of all; where instead of finding a support from the State and the laws, he has to encounter the keen adversaries of his spiritual authority, it is of the utmost importance that the one and only force that is left to him should be kept in its vigour from all efforts to weaken or destroy it. As vicars of the Holy See, entrusted with the government of a not insignificant part of the Church, and that in a difficult position and in difficult times, we have every need of a kind and paternal protection in face[2] of our clergy and people from the Holy See, and of finding in the exalted and unwavering firmness of the supreme authority, of which we are the feeble representatives, a secure refuge and a resolute support in our conflict with the factions and the disturbers of good order, and we should not for a single moment be left open to any contrary opposition. But the partisans to whom we refer would not have it so believed, but industriously spread their rumours to the contrary. They delight to insinuate into the souls of the faithful, and especially of the clergy, that the Vicars-Apostolic enjoy but small credit at Rome, that the Holy See is weary with the complaints and appeals that are daily brought against them, and that Propaganda is favourably inclined towards whoever promote these appeals, and receives them graciously. Such sayings are certainly false, and yet they are repeated on the authority of those who declare they speak from experience.

During the last and present year certain priests have appealed to the Sacred Congregation against their Vicars-Apostolic, and these, according to their own account, have not hesitated in their petitions to utter the grossest insults not only against their Ordinaries but against all the Vicars-Apostolic, calling them oppressors, tyrants and still worse names. And yet, if we are to believe them, they have been treated with consideration, and have suffered no reproach for their boldness. And because the Holy See has mercifully endeavoured to avoid any extreme rigour in its decisions, first by their letters and then by their talk, wherever they have gone they have sung their own victory and proclaimed the total discomforture of the Episcopal authority. And how this has afflicted the good amongst the clergy and given triumph to those who were less well disposed! For the cases to which we refer are public and notorious, so that many of the clergy well know the character of those who figure in them, and see in it but a conflict between the Episcopal authority and its defamation. Neither in writing or otherwise can we adequately describe the scandal and injury arising to the Catholic religion from the cases which have given occasion for these appeals. But if your Holiness would deign to appoint impartial persons to examine into these cases on the spot, full conviction would be given of the motives that have led to this step.

And what is the result? We grieve, Holy Father, to say it, but we feel the Episcopal Authority is enfeebled in our hands, that we fear to put forth any vigorous exercise of it, even in the most urgent cases. From Rome we know that there are persons who write to those who already have appeals, instigating them to come forward with new charges against the Bishops, and promising them a good reception, and assuring them that the more there are the more they will prevail. So that some of us, who have to deal with some troublesome,[3] shall we say scandalous, priest, dare not touch him lest he instantly go and increase the number of appellants against the arbitrary tyranny of the Bishops!!!

Another circumstance has added to these inconveniences. There are not wanting in Rome persons belonging to these kingdoms who delight in giving their hands to, and in assisting and supporting, whoever comes there with a hostile spirit against the Bishops of England. These persons, whose piety and virtue we call not in question, support with the influence derived from long residence in Rome every cause that is taken up, and the evil is increased for sometimes, being seculars, they have less right to intrude themselves into ecclesiastical affairs.

Such, Holy Father, are the bitter griefs we have thought it our duty to lay at the foot of the one Supreme Authority of the Church and the Vicar of Christ. We have spoken with effusion of heart, knowing well to whom we address our words, to one who cannot but listen with fatherly affection to even the least of his sons, to one who estimates frankness above all eloquence, and who fully appreciates that loyalty of heart of those who are addressing him. And that we may have our recourse with greater earnestness under this circumstance to the more than paternal goodness of Your Holiness, we have resolved amongst ourselves that one of our number, the Vicar-Apostolic of the Western District, should come in person to the feet of Your Holiness, there to express our unviolable attachment to the Holy See, and to treat with all solicitude on the affairs of this Church; but especially to renew those fervent prayers and instances we have already made for the restoration of the Hierarchy in England, and to supplicate your Holiness, as we fervently do, that you would deign to bring what has been so felicitously begun to a happy conclusion for the good of this nation, upon which, and upon ourselves and the flocks committed to us, prostrate at your feet, we implore your Apostolic Benediction.

This Memorial was dated May 12th, 1848.

On my entering the Presence with the Memorial for presentation His Holiness at once said that he entertained a great esteem for the Vicars-Apostolic of England, and rising, he removed some papers from the seat and asked me to be seated by his side. After kneeling for the benediction and to give the homage, I replied that I was happy to hear this from the lips of His Holiness, for in consequence of certain letters and statement made by certain clergy who had causes in Rome, and of certain laymen also, an impression that the Vicars-Apostolic had sunk in the esteem of the Holy See had been spread to England. The Pope gave a negative shrug of his shoulders and the motion of the head. His Holiness then observed that the English Minister of State had complained of remarks said in English and Irish newspapers to have been uttered by him. He added that sentiments uttered in audience in his cabinet were not truly stated, that these newspaper statements were not true, and that it was wrong to repeat his private remarks to the public. To this I strongly assented. I then began to speak of the earnest and great desire of the Vicars-Apostolic to see the English Hierarchy restored, and dwelt on the serious inconveniences resulting from our state of suspense. His Holiness said that he hoped to issue his Bull soon; that one cause of delay had been the difficulties raised in England on certain temporal questions affecting us, which demanded prudence; that the state of the times was another cause to be taken into consideration, that he could not give himself to these matters so fully as if all things with him were in a state of tranquillity, for political events demanded urgent attention.

Finally His Holiness said that he trusted that before I left Rome I should see the Bull of the Hierarchy promulgated.

Notes

1   This word, meaning among other things 'to beseech', is underlined in the original and Leslie italicised it.
2   'Turbulent priest' has been deleted in the manuscript and 'troublesome' substituted.

Chapter Fifty

Still in Rome – June 1848

June 9th. Dr. Grant said Mgr. Barnabò was highly indignant at Mr. McDonnell's letter, just received, in which he petitioned that the clergy should have a perpetual right to their missions before the Hierarchy was granted. The letter, Document E, was given to him to convey to me and I wrote a reply to it. Mgr. Barnabò said that on the previous day he had endeavoured to arrange the day for the Congregation. But the day of the Congregation was not yet mentioned. Mgr. Mobile, the *Minutante*, also told Dr. Grant that he thought, to save time, the papers would not be printed, but only reported on verbally.

June 14th. I had an interview with Cardinal Franzoni. I do not recollect all its import, having no notes of the conversation, but the subject of the Bishop's Memorial to the Pope came up. It had to be sent to Propaganda, and with it an instruction from His Holiness that statements were not to be received against the English Vicars-Apostolic without their being informed of what was said, especially when they came from the laity. Instruction had also been given that the question of the Hierarchy had to be proceeded with, with as little delay as possible, for which purpose all business not of pressing importance was to give way to it. This was afterwards ascertained still more accurately from Mgr. Palma, for many years the *Minutante* for England, a man deeply versed in all that regarded the English-speaking countries.

On the same day I saw Mgr. Barnabò and delivered in my reply to Mr. McDonnell's letter, which is Document F. He was still indignant about this letter, and asked me if the writer was a tall man, with long whiskers, who bent his head up and back, first on one side, then on the other, imitating the motion.

I said: 'Yes, that is the person.'

He said that Propaganda had received a petition from him and several letters and that a number of other letters written in the same spirit had come from England. This appeared to me to justify the Memorial which the Bishops had addressed to the Pope. But I kept my reflection to myself, for Mgr. Barnabò had been anything but pleased with that document, and with its effects upon the Pope's mind, and had said to me that it was the fault of the Bishops in not sending reports on their Districts. I asked if the remark applied to me and he said, 'No'. He also dwelt a good deal on the carelessness which had let the *Statuta proposita* get out, and of the inconveniences which the Holy See had experienced owing to the publishing of private communications as well in England as in Ireland. He then asked me if I had well considered the character of Mr. McDonnell before reinstating him, as he might give me trouble. I replied that he had good points about him, that I was not afraid of the task of encouraging him and that, if not employed, he might harass Bishops Wiseman and Walsh by new publications. I then told him how he had nevertheless abused my confidence in taking advantage of what I had shewn him from my Memorial, as to the disposition of the Bishops to provide for bettering the position of the clergy, and taking that advantage in writing this letter. At this Mgr. Barnabò laughed heartily.

I then told him what the Pope had said about his hope that I should see the Bull published before I left Rome, whereupon he said: 'Yes. The Pope has told me so; and the Congregation will be held in six days.' I then asked whether it would be proper for me to wait on the Cardinals composing it. He replied that this was not customary, where the Congregation was special, but only when it was a general Congregation. He then became very communicative and entered into the past history of the question. He said that when the question was first mooted in 1840, the authority of Cardinal Acton had induced the Cardinals to double the numbers of Vicars-Apostolic; but that Bishops Wiseman and Sharples had removed the impression created by Cardinal Acton's views. That the question was proceeding when the letters of the Vicars-Apostolic on certain temporal questions had arrived and stopped the whole proceeding. That at first he had thought that nothing further could be done than simply to change the Vicars-Apostolic into Titular Bishops, and so leave the rest to be developed by force of circumstances, and that then it was to be hoped that an increase of Bishops, the constitution of Chapters, the privileges of the clergy, etc., would all evolve themselves and follow, and the English Church would be gradually established upon the Roman model.

I also gave in on this occasion a Memorial, the object of which was to solicit that, in transferring the Bishops from their Sees *in partibus* to Sees in England, the same faculties and privileges should be continued which were already enjoyed by them as Vicars-Apostolic. Mgr. Barnabò glanced over it and said that it would be a matter of course as England, like all countries under non-Catholic sovereigns, would continue to be under Propaganda.

June 25th. On this day I sent in Document G, the object of which was to shew that the title of Plymouth would be very inconvenient for the existing Western District, from its remoteness at one extremity of the District, and to suggest that if Bristol was considered an inexpedient title to adopt, that of Clifton would be the most suitable. It stood to Bristol as Westminster to London, etc.

On the same day Cardinal Ostini sent for Dr. Grant and asked for some explanation of the titles to be given the Bishops, and about the difficulties arising from the Emancipation Act of 1829. To meet a certain difficulty he thought that the name of Bishop might be reconciled with that of Vicar-Apostolic by saying, for example, Bishop of Birmingham and Vicar-Apostolic of the Central District; but he did not think that both titles could be given simply.

The special Congregation consisted of Cardinal Franzoni, Prefect of Propaganda, together with Cardinals Ostini, Castrucane, Altieri, Vizzardelli, Orioli and Mai, with Mgr. Barnabò as Secretary. As it was not etiquette for me to call upon the Cardinals engaged in the special Congregation unless asked for, Dr. Grant took the precaution with my approval to call upon each one then in Rome, to ask if he wished to see me. Cardinal Vizzardelli had no questions to ask. Cardinal Altieri spoke a few words, had no occasion to see me then although he expressed a wish to see me before leaving Rome. Cardinal Orioli had forgotten the Congregation was the next day, but would look over the papers in time, and his observations were chiefly that the rights of the clergy could be better determined in the Synods than by the Holy See.

In the evening I called upon Cardinal Franzoni, but as there was a little circle of visitors round him, little was said about the

principal business. But the Cardinal said a few words about
the qualifications of Dr. Weedall for a Bishopric. On a later
day Mgr. Barnabò asked about Dr. Weedall, and said that
Mr. Tempest had suggested his name.

The same evening Cardinal Ostini again sent for Dr. Grant,
and discussed at length the subject of adding the title of
Vicar-Apostolic. But the conclusion was against it, and it was
concluded instead that the draft of a paragraph be inserted
in the Brief, instead, of which the Cardinal suggested the substance. On his return home we conversed upon this suggestion
and accepted it, and Dr. Grant drew it up from memory and
it was sent in. This, in my papers, is Document H.

It was sent in the next morning, and is in substance incorporated in the Brief of the Hierarchy. It says that:

'In granting to the Bishops the title and full jurisdiction
according to the Canons, the Holy See intends to do a kindness
to the Catholics of England by giving to their Pastors a greater
consideration and more perfect dignity without wishing to
deprive them of any advantages which they at present possess,
and therefore it is assumed that the Catholics, emulating the
piety of their ancestors, will increase the temporal means by
which they are to do good.

June 26th The Congregation was held.

June 27th. In obedience to Mgr. Barnabò's request, communicated the day previous, after the Congregation was held,
I went to Propaganda, asking Dr. Grant to accompany me.
Mgr. Barnabò said that the Cardinals had discussed all the
subjects of the Hierarchy with great care, and that they were
so anxious to bring them to a conclusion that they had desired
him to summon me to the Congregation during the course of
the discussion. But as it was uncertain whether I could be
found at the moment, they requested to have me consulted
privately as soon as possible. Hence the summons for this
morning. He begged that it should be kept strictly secret, so
as to prevent McDonnell having sent a new letter to the Pope
within the last day or two. He stated that the Pope was anxious
to know the result as soon as possible. And the Sacred Congregation wished me, in virtue of the delegation given me by
all the Bishops, to state at once what was to be thought on
the following points:

1. The Cardinals were of opinion that St. David's (Menevia)
was to be at once chosen for Wales, as not being included

in the law of 1829. They further thought that in order to remove every pretext from Protestants, it was desirable that all the Sees should be old ones. Is this practicable? And if the Bishops are so poor, how are they to pay the fine of £100 for each offence? But the Cardinals were much struck by the opinion in Anstey's *Penal Laws* of the futile nature of the prohibition clause and by the ease by which it could be evaded.

2. They wished to divide England at once into at least twelve Sees, and I was requested to suggest the places for the Sees and, if possible, also their boundaries; the Cardinals considering that it would be difficult to obtain the concurrence of the Bishops to a suitable division later. Moreover, the Cardinals considered that the two leading objections (want of Bishops and want of money) were not sufficient to delay this division, especially as the first might be obviated by leaving the new Sees for a time under the care of other Bishops. Their attention was principally directed (I do not know by whom) to London; and they found that the south side of the Thames had been under a different Bishop from the north side, and that as far back as the time of Innocent III, 1215. The Archbishop of Canterbury, to whom the north side belonged, had built a residence at Lambeth[1], which is still the dwelling place of the Archbishops. The Congregation had observed that on the south side there would be the important towns Brighton, Southampton, Winchester, The Isle of Wight and the Channel Islands.

I must here observe that it is obvious the Cardinals had no plan of division of boundaries before them, a plain proof that the one drawn up for the twelve Sees in the Episcopal Meeting of November, 1847, had never been sent to Rome.

3. Mgr. Barnabò continued: he said that he had seen the Pope since the sitting of the Congregation, who expressed himself gratified at the general plan proposed for England. Mr. McDonnell had presented himself at Propaganda before his departure, and had asked for answers to his letters as he was going away. Mgr. Barnabò replied that no answer could be given until the Cardinals had decided on the English affairs before them. Mr. McDonnell said: 'But I am going away.' To which the Right Rev. Secretary replied: 'You can go.' He told me that the absurd letter addressed to the Pope had given great offence.

During the sitting of the Congregation I had sent in a letter to be delivered immediately to the Secretary with an extract from a letter just received from England, in which these words occurred: 'Dr. Walsh is certainly dying. It is thought the nuns of Princethorpe who were nursing him, will have to bury him.'

On reading this to the Cardinals, Mgr. Barnabò told me that they were resolved to make him Archbishop. They said: 'Whether he be living or dead he shall be the first Archbishop of Westminster.'

The Bishops were to be asked to draw up a plan without delay for raising the condition of the clergy. He said that the Cardinals wished me to state further who would be a fitting Bishop for the Central District. They considered that the circumstances of Oxford required a man of imposing learning and they did not believe that such could be found in Mr. Moore, who had been represented by the Bishops as in point of learning a *mediocris*. Dr. Newsham they had declined for the Central District as being deaf, and they wished me to state whether it would be better to transfer another Bishop, or to choose a priest. But, he added, looking steadfastly at me, the Cardinals wish you to be transferred to the Central District. They are quite aware of your attachment to your present District, but if you will sacrifice that attachment to the general interest of England, the difficulty will be at an end.

This announcement took me by surprise. Objections sprung up in my mind at once. But I felt that it would be unwise to urge them or to give any definite reply on the spur of the moment. I therefore kept silent. As we were retiring Mgr. Barnabò took Dr. Grant aside and pressed this point on his attention.

In the course of the day I drew up a statement against the proposal of removing me to the Central District. I had considered in my own mind, first, that it was my business to carry out the instructions of the Bishops as expressed in their joint deliberations at their meetings and, secondly, as regarded individual Districts, as the Vicars-Apostolic of those Districts had severally expressed them to me. Bishop Walsh individually and the Bishops generally had recommended Mr. Moore for Coadjutor to Bishop Walsh.

It was only at a later period that in reading Barbosa's work, *De Officio et Potestate Episcopi*, I discovered the error of the Vicars-Apostolic in the term they had used in drawing up the character and qualifications of Mr. Moore for the information of the Holy See. The Cardinals had attached the technical sense to the word *mediocris* as applied to the science, whilst the Bishops meant more than that technical sense of the word conveyed. They were not, when they wrote the word, aware of its technical sense. Barbosa tells us there are three graduated terms used with respect to the science required in a Bishop. These are *scientia eminens*, *scientia sufficiens* and *scientia mediocris*. The *scientia eminens* is when a man has the knowledge requisite for his office in his head; the *scientia sufficiens* is when he has it not in his head but knows where to find it; and the *scientia mediocris* is when he neither has it in his head nor knows where to find it. The Bishops in using the word *mediocris* intended to express moderate learning, and they ought to have used the word *sufficiens*, which would have truly expressed the case. But this technical sense of the word I did not then understand.

But the mere misapplication of this word would not, I think, have decided the case, had it not been for hostile letters written from England, and that to an unfair excess against the ecclesiastic in question. He had loyally stood by his Bishop in his difficulties. He had also been successful in attracting and receiving members of the Puseyite party. But it was reported of him, by whom I did not ascertain, that he had read a work of Dr. Pusey's from the pulpit in Birmingham. I afterwards ascertained that this had only consisted in reading passages for a controversial purpose, as one would have presupposed. But this was not all.

One day in conversing with Cardinal Franzoni, I happened to correct his pronunciation of an English name. This induced him to produce a letter for the purpose of asking the pronunciation of one or two other names. And, looking at the names written in the letter over his shoulder, I saw it was a letter written in part against Mr. Moore, and could pretty well conclude from whom it came. Obviously, to use a prison phrase, there was 'a down on him'. Good Bishop Walsh, again, wrote to me and urged me to do my utmost to get Mr. Moore appointed as his Coadjutor, but this letter dated June 26th did not reach me until all was settled. Still, knowing his wish, I did my best to second it.

Notes

1   The geography is here confused. Lambeth is south of the Thames and it was, indeed, the *south* bank which had never been under episcopal jurisidication other than that of the Bishop of London.

Chapter Fifty-One

Negotiations Continue

After I had returned from Propaganda on that eventful day, I felt all the difficulty of my position; I wrote a letter to Mgr. Barnabò in which I represented the difficulties of the plan for removing me. I told him plainly that I had not that scholarship which was supposed, that I had gone late to college after a life on the sea, and had been passed rapidly through my courses. I represented that, whereas the Western District had always been under regular Bishops, the Central had been always under seculars. I urged other reasons, and begged that the whole question should be reconsidered.

The following day (June 28th) I had another interview with Mgr. Barnabò, this time entirely between ourselves. I entered into the difficulties into which I felt myself thrown, on account of the Cardinals having put aside the names recommended for the Central District. I detailed whatever I had heard from Bishop Walsh, and from the other Bishops respecting the three ecclesiastics whose names had been recommended, and also gave the reasons alleged at the Episcopal Meeting why others of higher qualifications or greater maturity could not be given. I especially dwelt upon the fact of the number of ecclesiastics who had been drawn from that District for the Episcopal office. I then put forth the names of two ecclesiastics of other districts for consideration, in case it should still be resolved to put aside the names already before Propaganda, suggesting further inquiry, however, as my long absence from England had left me not very intimate with the clergy beyond my own District.

I further raised the question how far it might be considered a reflection on the District to bring its Bishop from another quarter. But Mgr. Barnabò repeated that the Cardinals felt that if I would sacrifice my attachment to my District for the

344

general good, the difficulty was at an end. He then detailed the particular reasons alleged by the Cardinals, and the remarks which they had made, but of which I have kept no record. Seeing there was no chance left for the nomination of Mr. Moore, I then put forth Dr. Grant as a suitable person, assigning my reasons for his appointment, whilst I stated what I conceived the lesser reasons against, which ought not to stand in the way. I then gave Mgr. Barnabò the letter I had written on the subject. He read it there and then. It contained my conscientious difficulties. He said he did not think the reasons alleged viable, and reasoned against them in detail. He concluded by asking me whom I could recommend for the Western District. He would read my letter, as I wished it, to the Cardinals, but did not think it could alter their views, and he would treat it as a private paper afterwards.

At the same interview Mgr. Barnabò told me that Mr. Tempest had said that the Bishops were unwilling to recommend some men of learning for the Episcopate because they held views different from their own; but that in consequence of the Memorial addressed by the Bishops to the Pope, his observations and suggestions had been put aside. This busy layman was very assiduous in suggesting names and schemes. He had actually, with the help of an Italian priest who had been in England, drawn up a plan of his own for sixteen Bishoprics in England, and had presented it to Propaganda. It was put into my hands by Mgr. Barnabò, and I wrote a critique upon it.

On June 30th Mr. Tempest called on me. He had ascertained, he said, that the Hierarchy was to be established and the number of Bishops to be increased. He promised to give me a copy of a paper drawn up by a priest and presented to Propaganda about the division of the Vicariates into Sees. This of course was the joint product of Tempest and Dr. Melia. Mr. Tempest said that the information about the Southwark side had been furnished by Dr. Cullen.

On June 27th Mgr. Barnabò had said that this had been done at the request of Propaganda. Mr. Tempest put forth the name of Reverend Mr. Wilkinson of Liverpool as that of one fit for a Bishopric. This communication proved more and more the activity of lay interference with our ecclesiastical affairs. I took the opportunity to dwell on those subjects on which I knew Mr. Tempest to have strong prejudices, and explained that in these matters the Bishops had been misunderstood and misrepresented, for example, their supposed feelings about the regulars.

He, of course, fished all he could for information of what was passing, but I abstained from communicating information, alleging the secrecy enjoined by Propaganda.

I never could understand the secret of this good man's influence, which, however, began to dwindle after this period, and ultimately came to nothing. He was a pious enthusiast without judgement, and was always looking after *mirabilia*. He was a great believer in the shepherd girl in the Pontine Marshes, Catherine of Spezzia, who was set up as a prophetess and worker of miracles, and afterwards was discovered to be an imposter. I have in my possession a long document sent by him to an English convent, containing a wonderful history of a nun written by a confessor whom she deceived and whose imposition respecting the having the stigmata was so ingeniously discovered by the General of the Carmelites. There was nothing extravagant and out of the way in the religious world which he did not lay hold of, and about which he did not write enthusiastic letters to a convent in which he had a sister. At last it was observed at Rome that, though a married man, he was leading this meddling life in Rome apart from his wife, and was told that his duty was to rejoin her. He went to Rome recently and there died suddenly.

June 30th. The Four Memorials, or Documents, I, J, K, L, were sent to Propaganda.

Document I enlarged upon the method best suited to meet certain difficulties with respect to the succession of Ordinary Bishops to Vicars-Apostolic, in the wording of the Apostolic Brief granting the Hierarchy, and was in fact a reinforcing of Document H.

Document J. Before delivering this document I again explained to Cardinal Franzoni my reasons against going to the Central District, but finding they made no impression, I gave in the document. It was a reply to the request that I would name someone to succeed me in the Western District. In that paper I stated that the only person of the District whom I could recommend was my Vicar-General, the Rev. W. Hendren of the Order of St. Francis. I pointed him out as a man experienced in both the missionary and religious life, having been long a missioner in Wales, and now for some time

Confessor to the Franciscan Nuns at Taunton. Distinguished in almost every kind of learning, he had shewn much prudence in his advice as well as in acting, during the two years he had been Vicar-General. Well known and much respected, he was a man distinguished by his gravity. But, I added, it is to be regretted that from time to time he suffers much from gout. In recommending this ecclesiastic I had more than one thing to consider. I had to select, from a very limited number of ecclesiastics, one who was learned, the Cardinals having declared that they would not recommend for Bishops men who had not this qualification. I had to avoid those who were of the Prior Park party. And I had to keep in mind that the Western District had always had Vicars-Apostolic from the Benedictine or Franciscan Orders.

Document K. This important Memorial embodied a plan for the distribution of the eight English Vicariates into twelve Dioceses. In drawing it up, as stated in my preface, regard was had to local circumstances, to the sentiments expressed by the English Bishops in their meetings, and the future expansion of religion.

The territorial distribution recommended in this document was accepted and incorporated in the Brief of the Hierarchy. I had intended to attach Oxfordshire to the London Diocese, but Mgr. Barnabò said that they particularly wished to attach Oxfordshire to Birmingham. Lancashire would most probably have been proposed to have been divided into two Sees but for letters I received from its Vicar-Apostolic, urging that the times were difficult, that it would be difficult to maintain two Bishops, and that he could reach any part of his District in two hours. At his earnest request, then, I did not propose this division.

London was divided by the Thames, and Southwark appointed a See at the instance of Propaganda which, as we have seen, had the subject already before it.

The names which I proposed for the twelve Sees, after deliberating with Dr. Grant, will be found some of them different from what was ultimately adopted.

I proposed London for the Archiepiscopal See, afterwards changed for Westminster. Bristol, which I proposed originally, was changed for Clifton; and Newcastle, which I proposed, was changed for Hexham, though at a later period Newcastle was added as an additional title to Hexham. York, which I named for a Bishopric, as this did not legally clash with the

Protestant Archiepiscopal title, was changed to Beverley. The other titles were promulgated as originally proposed, except that that of Newport was added to St. David's or Menevia. The cause of these changes I will explain in due time.

The document was accompanied with a map exhibiting the eight districts, and the proposed twelve Sees marked in different colours, with the situation of each title indicated.

The document concluded with the following remarks: In proposing this plan of division, regulated on the principles pointed out by the Sacred Congregation, the undersigned cannot but observe that the Holy See is proposing to renew our Church as it existed in its earlier period. In the celebrated Synod of Arles three British Bishops assisted, and amongst the first to sign the Acts was the Bishop of London. But what is more striking in the parallel is the fact that the Apostle of our Country, Pope St. Gregory the Great, in a letter to St. Augustine, contemplated erecting London into an Archiepiscopal See, contemplating the time when York might be made a second Archbishopric with its twelve Suffragans. The Pope's words to St. Augustine are these: 'And, in regard that the new church of the English is through the goodness of the Lord, and your labours, brought to the Grace of God, we grant you the use of the Pallium, only for use in the solemnisation of the Mass; so that you in as many places ordain twelve Bishops who shall be subject to your jurisdiction, so that the Bishop of London shall, for the future, be always consecrated by his own Synod, and that he receive the honour of the Pallium from this Holy and Apostolic See which I, by the Grace of God, now serve. But we will have you send to the City of York such a Bishop as you think fit to ordain; yet so, that if that city, with the places adjoining, shall receive the Word of God that Bishop shall also ordain twelve Bishops and enjoy the honour of a Metropolitan. For we design, if we live, by the help of God, to bestow on him also the Pallium.'

To this Memorial was added Document L which was a reasoned exposition upon each of the twelve titles proposed, extending to eleven folio pages.

July 1st. Dr. Grant saw Mgr. Barnabò, who desired that copies of all the Memorials should be made out so that each Cardinal might have one.

July 4th. The copies, as requested, were sent in.

July 5th. Dr. Grant saw Mgr. Barnabò, who desired him to inform me that Mgr. Vespasiani (the *minutante*) had been instructed to prepare the papers speedily for the Congregation, and especially those that bore on the Brief of the Hierarchy.

July 7th. I had now received Bishop Walsh's letter, before alluded to. He says he is very ill, and incapable of letter-writing. He entreats me to do all I can to get Mr. Moore appointed immediately, commending him for his 'piety, zeal, energy, amiable manners and learning,' as the proper person for Coadjutor. I took a translation of this letter at once to Propaganda. And I then pointed out to Mgr. Barnabò in the fullest detail, as I find noted at the time by Dr. Grant, the difficulties that would attend the removal of Bishop Walsh from the Central District as well as Bishop Wiseman to London. Whereupon Mgr. Barnabò told me in the strictest confidence, and not to be repeated, the whole motive which had actuated the Cardinals in their decision, in order to show me that nothing which I could state had been left unnoticed or unconsidered by them. He engaged to lay Bishop Walsh's letter (Document M) before the Cardinals.

He also stated that the only cause of delay was that the substance of the Bull was being prepared, and that the substance of the Constitution of Benedict XIV was being incorporated as *principes provisiores*, to prevent any possibility of misunderstanding, especially with reference to Regulars, and that no uncertainty might arise out of the change as to the actual powers of the Bishops in relation to the changes to be effected in their titles. Mgr. Barnabò also told me that he would give me due information when the Congregation of Cardinals would take place, that I might be at Propaganda in readiness to give information on the spot, and to save time.

He also gave me Dr. Melia's paper of which Mr. Tempest had spoken, giving a plan for eighteen Sees, requesting me to keep it strictly private. This is Document N.

July 10th. I sent in Document O, being the observations on Document N.

July 16th. On His Eminence's invitation I went with Dr. Grant to Cardinal Ostini's consultation, preparatory to the Congregation. There I also met Mgr. Ferrari, the sub-secretary for extraordinary ecclesiastical affairs, and later on came in Mgr. Corboli, just returned from a special delegation to Austria.[1] Several points relating to the points to be discussed in the Congregation were entered upon, and I was surprised at the accurate knowledge which Mgr. Corboli showed respecting the Hierarchy of Australia. I had put forward what I conceived a case in point from the condition of the Australian Church, which he upset in a moment by his knowledge of events more recent than I was possessed of.

July 17th. The Congregation was held. I was called into the Congregation. All the Cardinals of the Congregation were there except Cardinals Orioli and Altieri. There had been a considerable desire to have Cardinal Mai present, on account of his skill in solving difficulties. And he came in for the occasion from Frascati, where he had been intently engaged on the Vatican Codex of the Scriptures. As it was quite unprecedented for a Bishop to be present at a Congregation of Cardinals, there was an instant's hesitation as I stood awaiting Their Eminences' orders, but Cardinal Franzoni, from the top of the table where he presided, arose and invited me to take a seat at the table by his side.

Cardinal Mai complimented me on the suggestion embodied in what I have given as Document K, as very suitable for its purpose. But in reality the merit of the suggestion belonged to Cardinal Ostini. The chief point on which the Cardinals wished to hear me respected the titles. They were particularly anxious to avoid any conflict with the English Law. On this subject I spoke, replying to the questions raised one after another. And when it came to the vote, the most learned Canonist amongst the Cardinals shook his head and demurred. Here, then, was the one and only difficulty. The great authority of that Cardinal, the one who drew up the body of the Brief, suspended further proceedings for the time. At a sign given me I withdrew.

July 18th. Mgr. Barnabò gave me the result of the previous day's Congregation. He said that it was fully decided that Bishop Walsh should be translated to London with a view to becoming its first Archbishop; and that I was to be removed to Birmingham, and Mr. Hendren to be made Vicar-Apostolic of the Western District, which I could announce to him. With respect to the Hierarchy, the only difficulty that remained to hinder its promulgation was the question of titles, and the Cardinals wished that each Bishop should write to Propaganda his opinion respecting his own, or such as in the re-division would come out of his district. On hearing this I at once proposed to go myself to England to put the Bishops in possession of all that had passed, as they would then more clearly understand the point of difficulty before writing their opinions. There would be an assembly of the Bishops at Manchester, at the opening of the Salford Cathedral, and I should be able to arrive in time to meet them when assembled together. I should be able, also, to explain what had passed with respect to the new appointments, so as to prevent misconceptions on that subject. This proposal Mgr. Barnabò thoroughly approved, and as he had to report the result of the Congregation to the Sovereign Pontiff he would put the proposal before His Holiness, and ask for a farewell audience for me.

July 19th. Dr. Grant saw Mgr. Barnabò and offered his own suggestions, before the determinations of the Congregations were taken to the Pope, amongst which was a recommendation that the new appointments might be made in the simplest way to save time, and that the nominations of Bishop Walsh and myself should be preceptive.

July 20th. Dr. Grant took the precaution of giving a correct list of proper names for the new appointments to prevent any errors in the documents, and also solicited faculties for the new Vicars-Apostolic. He also obtained from the Archives an authentic copy of the Oath as taken by the English Bishops at their consecration.

The same evening Dr. Grant and myself were walking near the Sciarra Palace when we accidentally met Mgr. Barnabò, who said that the Pope had approved everything, and had sent to Bishop Walsh and to myself a *sacratissimo precepto*, a command under obedience to accept our appointments. I was to take from the Pope a present of a gold chalice for St. George's Cathedral, Southwark, which was soon to be opened, and was to have my audience on Sunday.

I have no note of what passed at the audience. All I recollect is that the Pope was very kind in his expressions towards the English Bishops, to whom I was to convey his sentiments, and the desire to establish them in the Hierarchy with as little delay as possible.

I ought not to close the history of this important negotiation without dwelling upon the great services rendered to the cause by Dr. Grant. His readiness of resource, his practical knowledge of Roman business, his acquaintance with the Cardinals, his intimacy with Mgr. Palma, whose long and intimate experience in English ecclesiastical affairs gave him great weight in Propaganda, and his promptitude in making himself useful on every occasion, the advantage I had also in discussing every point with him before drawing up the documents, which gave me advantages to which I attribute much of that success which attended the negotiation.

Note

1   The word *Austria* is unmistakable in the manuscript though it would appear from what follows that may have been *Australia* was what was meant.

Chapter Fifty-Two

Revolution in Rome and a Bishop for Birmingham

It was whilst I was in Rome that Mgr. Palma was made secretary of Latin Briefs, which transferred him from Propaganda to the Quirinal, where the Pope then resided, and Mgr. Vespasiani took his place as *minutante* for the English-speaking Churches. Mgr. Palma's appointment was universally applauded as a recognition of the merits and services of a most deserving man. It was he who drew up the Brief *Numeris Apostolici* in 1840, which increased the English Vicars-Apostolic from four to eight. He it was who, at a still earlier period, had carried out the instructions of Cardinal Gonsalvi and of Gregory XVI, when Prefects of Propaganda, respecting English Catholic affairs. He was the means of providing a chaplain and confessor for Napoleon I at St. Helena. He prepared the celebrated Bull *Multa Praeclara* for the settlement of Indian affairs, and the Brief re-establishing the Partriarchate of Jerusalem. And the historical introduction with which the Brief restoring our Hierarchy opens was his work. His well-known lectures on Ecclesiastical History were revised by Dr. Grant. And it was at his suggestion that Cardinal Wiseman wrote his article in the *Dublin Review* in vindication of Pope Boniface VIII. He was a man who carried his learning and experience with such an absence of all pretension and had so warm a heart, and manners so simple, and spoke with such a *bonhomie*, that it was delightful to converse with him. He was shot dead through the window of the Quirinal, whilst quieting the alarms of his aged mother, when the Pope's palace was attacked by the rebellious populace soon after I left Rome.

During my stay there, Rome was in a very uneasy state, and it was wonderful to witness the calmness with which the ecclesiastical affairs of the world were proceeded with amidst so

354 *The Devil is a Jackass*

many local perturbations and solicitudes. The clubs, or *cicoli* as they were called, were the centres of plots and conspiracies. The National Guards were their instruments, and consisting of tradesmen and mechanics of Rome, they were passing their lives in idleness, dissipation and intrigue. Even the very youth, mere children, were enrolled in a military corps of their own, equipped and armed, and sharing all the agitations of the period. They drummed and marched, and exercised as much as their elders. Nothing distressed the Pope more than this corruption of the youth of the city. The revolutionary Press was absolutely wild in its legends of the prowess of Charles Emmanuel of Savoy and his army, at the very time that he was being beaten at all points. They routed and slew the Austrian Army so often that the wonder was how they still found fresh Austrians to rout and to slay. The hawkers of these papers were even heard saying to one another that it was no use going on, for the people no longer believed their lies, or would buy the papers that contained them.

Numbers of young men were enlisted for the Northern Army, who went off to the war believing in their simplicity that they were going to fight for the Pope and for the Faith. And I heard much of the wailings of the pious mothers and of honest and loyal fathers at this seduction of their sons. There were perpetual marchings and drillings, and demonstrations before the Pope's palace of the National Guards, accompanied by that youthful corps called the *Esperanza di Roma*. As the corps of National Guards were enrolled, one after another, they went begging from house to house for money to buy uniforms, accoutrements and their favourite helmets of the old Roman shape.

Reminiscences of the ancient republic were everywhere affected. Nothing could take place without some military demonstration or other. When Cardinal Altieri drove to the opening of the Legislative Assembly he was preceded by all the regiments of the National Guard. I was proceeding to an audience of the Pope, and was delayed an hour or more on the way, the streets were so blocked up, and I got a sharp rebuke in the antechamber for being so very late after my appointment, until I got out an explanation of the cause of delay. The Pope himself said, not to me but to another from whom I heard it, that 'the reins were dragging in the mud'.

Every new concession led to a new demonstration, and increased the voracity of the populace for change. Priests were more than once assassinated in open day, and in the midst of the city, to increase the alarm and intimidation.

At last a great body of these armed men marched off to the war and Rome for a time seemed more tranquil, yet only seemed so, for the conspiracy was every day making progress. And when I proceeded to the diligence to make my start for Civita Vecchia, accompanied by Dr. Grant and several of the students, I was so struck with the sullen and concentrated demeanour of many of the people whom we passed that I took Dr. Grant aside, told him I was sure that something of a most serious nature was going to take place, and that very soon, and urged him to get the students away to the country house as soon as possible. That night the false news of a great victory over the Austrians was spread, and the conspirators forced their way into the churches and rang the bells. The real fact was that Marshal Radetski had cut the Piedmontese Army in two, and had virtually finished the war. But it was the beginning of the revolution in Rome. Soon after, Count de Rossi, the Pope's Minister of State, was assassinated, Mgr. Palma was shot, and the Pope fled to Gaeta.

The Jesuit Fathers had quitted Rome before I arrived there, and the venerable Father Glover was concealed in the house of Mr. Englefield, where I met him more than once. I remember I was to have visited the convent founded by St. Dominic, which was just opposite Mr. Englefield's house, but the nuns sent me a message through Mrs. Englefield that, in consequence of the state of Rome, they durst not open their doors.

Arrived at Genoa, I found the city in a state of excitement. Military orderlies were riding to and fro, and carriages and other vehicles, filled with families, were pouring into the city from the country. I found a great crowd assembled in the square before the Post Office and, asking an *Abbate* what this silent, anxious crowd signified, he said they were waiting for news from the Army. Soon after the courier drove up, and the swaying and murmuring of this crowd of all classes shewed that their excitement had got to its highest pitch. A window was thrown up, and an official read out a short despatch. It simply described the position where the Army stood, and said that two pieces of artillery had been actively employed. It was obvious there was nothing satisfactory to tell. The crowd dispersed in sad silence. Nobody in Genoa seemed inclined to talk much. There was the sense of disaster everywhere.

I succeeded in reaching Manchester the evening before the opening of the cathedral at Salford, and found the Bishops there assembled. Mr., now Bishop, Turner, then Vicar-General, was much disappointed that Lancashire was not to be divided into two Dioceses, and Bishop Sharples, then Coadjutor, expressed himself still more strongly on the subject. I could only allege the instructions of the Vicar-Apostolic on the subject, which I had put forth to speak for themselves. Bishop Wiseman did not like the separation of Southwark from London. This, however, was the act of the Holy See itself, which had had all the arguments, pro and con, before it. And I had acted on the instructions of Propaganda on this subject.

On the afternoon of the following day, in an assembly of the Bishops, I explained all that had been done, and delivered the instruction that each Bishop should write to Rome his own sentiments concerning the titles in which he was interested, his own and any other, that might be subdivided from his Vicariate.

The question of the division of Lancashire into two Dioceses was brought up, and the clergy of that portion which now forms the Diocese of Salford addressed the petition to the assembled Bishops, strongly but respectfully advocating the division.

After a little dissatisfaction expressed by this or that Bishop on points of detail, a cheerful view of the whole subject was manifested, and Bishop Wiseman, though he did not like the boundaries given to the London Diocese, spoke in warm and loyal language for accepting with gratitude all that had been accomplished. He said that it was natural for individual Bishops to take partial views of what especially affected themselves, but that it was a great measure, carefully considered by the Holy See, and no doubt wiser in all its arrangements and provisions than we in the first moment of looking at it through the lights of our individual interests could completely realise. He then proposed that a letter should be addressed to the Sovereign Pontiff expressive of our acceptance of the arrangements made and of our gratitude, recommending at the same time that Lancashire should be divided into two Dioceses. That another letter should be addressed to the Congregation of Propaganda, and that each Bishop should communicate his individual views respecting the title of his See. These letters were unanimously signed. Bishop Wiseman next proposed that a vote of thanks should be given to me for my services in the negotiation at Rome, and when the Bishops had concurred in this proposition, in thanking them, I drew attention to the services of Dr. Grant.

The Briefs for Bishop Walsh's translation and my own and for the new Vicars-Apostolic of the North and of the West arrived soon after, when my connection with the Western Vicariate ceased. In acknowledging the document to Cardinal Franzoni, I briefly stated what had passed in the Salford meeting, stated that my private opinion had always been in favour of the division of Lancashire, but that I had represented the views of its Vicar-Apostolic. Finding, however, that the Coadjutor, the Vicar-General and the clergy were so strongly expressed in favour of the division, I had no doubt but that the Holy See would take the proposal of division into favourable consideration. This was done and the twelve first proposed became thirteen Sees. A few words added to the Brief of the Hierarchy was all that was required to give effect to this decision.

I consecrated Bishop Hendren at St. Mary's on the Quay, Bristol, the present pro-Cathedral at Clifton not being yet ready for service, and Bishop Wiseman preached on the occasion. He had never met Bishop Hendren before and expressed himself to me as much struck by his ecclesiastical gravity and the extent and solidity of his information.

In leaving Clifton for Birmingham, it was with painful regret that I parted with those of the clergy and with those convents that had so zealously and loyally stood by me and supported me in the difficult position in which I had there stood. My plans for Bristol and Clifton were coming into practical shape, and I regretted much the leaving them unfinished. The community of my own Dominican children, who had followed me from Coventry, and whom I cherished with so special a care, were now expanding in numbers as in discipline and in their works, and these also I must leave behind; promising, however, to establish a filiation of them in my new jurisdiction, so soon as I could see my way to it. My last act was to commend them to the care and kindness of Bishop Hendren. My faithful friend and co-operator, Mr. Estcourt, accompanied me to Birmingham.

On arriving there I was received by the main body of the clergy of the District in St. Chad's Cathedral; Dr. Newman and the Oratorian Fathers who had recently taken possession of old Oscott were also present. The clergy dined with me, and Dr. Weedle addressed me in their name in a beautiful discourse, in which his loyalty and that of his brethren, the clergy, to the one appointed over them by the Holy See was cordially expressed, cordially received and, what is much more, that loyalty was realised to the letter. For the first time in my agitated life I found myself placed in a peaceful jurisdiction, over a united clergy, conspicuous for their devotion to the episcopal authority. And my difficulties in my new responsibility were not so much of a moral as of a material character. To my dismay I soon discovered that the administration was involved in a huge gulf of debt; of debt to such an extent that had I known the state of things beforehand, I verily believe that I should have struggled still more, and to my very utmost effort, against my translation. Good Bishop Walsh explained to me the state of things as well as he could, but he kept no regular accounts, and scarcely any documents. Accounts had been entered by Mr. Searle so long as Bishop Wiseman had had the administration. But the whole temporal administration both of missions and college was in a state of collapse, and all the funds, or nearly so, were exhausted.

I saw but one way possible of saving the District, and that was an odious one, yet there was no remedy. I resolved to let the clergy know the real state of affairs, and to get their consent to a general reduction of incomes, until things were in a better condition. The funds for church education were all sunk or spent, and I resolved to establish a new fund through contributions and collections. But it was impossible to obtain that sympathy, confidence and aid which I required from the laity, without making them, in some degree, partakers in the difficulties in which I was placed, and this I did in a series of financial pastorals. Mr. Estcourt took the tracing of the funds and their management in hand under my direction, and it was through his persevering assiduity that the state of things was, after a length of time, cleared and set in order.

I ought not to omit recording the great edification and the loyal co-operation that I received from Mr. Moore from the moment I entered the District. He had gone through a very humiliating trial, which had no other effect than to draw out the solid qualities of his character, and to confirm whatever Bishop Walsh had said of his piety and energy. Soon after my arrival, I had to place him as President over St. Mary's College, Oscott. Dr. Weedle I called from Leamington to preside over the Cathedral mission and act as Vicar-General; but his habits had been too long moulded for the vigorous work required in this post, and he took the mission and convent duty at St. Mary's, Handsworth, and Mr. Jeffries took his place at St. Chad's.

It is not my intention to carry this narrative into the administration of the Central District, or of the Birmingham Diocese. But it would be incomplete without giving an insight into the further history of the negotiations that led to the promulgation of the Hierarchy.

Chapter Fifty-Three

The Hierarchy Restored to England

The Pope was absent from Rome from November, 1848, to April, 1850, and no Congregations were assembled for a considerable portion of that time. From April 30th to June 30th, 1850, there was nothing but cannonading and martial law under the Republic, and Mgr. Barnabò was living with the Armenian Fathers under the protection of the Turkish flag. After order was restored Mgr. Vespasiani, the *Minutante* for England, was sent on a mission to Malta and the case of the Hierarchy was deferred until his return in April 1850. Meanwhile there had been no new materials added to the case except that the wishes of the Bishops respecting their titles had been ascertained in the course of the summer of 1849, and the division of the Lancashire District into two Sees had been recommended. Mgr. Vespasiani prepared the new matter after his return, and they were discussed by the Cardinals in June, 1850.

Finally Mgr. Barnabò asked Dr. Grant to make out a short petition, reciting how matters then stood in order that the Cardinals might come to their final act upon a definite request and statement, holding the place of a *ponenza*.[1] In doing this Dr. Grant quoted a passage from a letter to him from the Earl of Surrey to the effect that whenever the Hierarchy was granted it should be 'a word and a blow'. The Cardinals completed their work and the Brief was prepared.

On July 9th Bishop Wiseman addressed to me a letter on some business which he concluded with these words: 'In a few days I will write to you *ut frater studiosissimus*'. As this was a style he had never used before, and a style frequently used by Cardinals, I at once wrote to him to say that I was confident from his slip of the pen that he had received the Cardinal's Hat, which I knew was in contemplation for him. To this he replied by return of post in the following terms:

'When I concluded my last letter I certainly did not intend to convey the meaning Your Lordship has drawn, though as soon as written it struck me the last words might bear the construction.

The rumour is now so public here (how it got out I know not) that I feel almost justified in acknowledging its truth. To those who speak to me, I am obliged to content myself with not denying it; and I have written to Rome to say that the matter is now as good as public.

This being the case I can assure Your Lordship that I have been in a state of unnatural constraint from not being able to write to my brethren on a matter in which naturally I should have wished to consult with them.

I have written to Rome as much as one may write for himself, but in vain; and I fear my total separation from England in about a month is decided. What I have felt and what I feel is known to God alone. I dare not act in any way that would oppose His Holy Will, but to leave the work that is going on now here is to me the heaviest trial that has ever befallen me. Your Lordship will see that I cannot act upon this matter otherwise than as a rumour which I do not contradict. Whether anything should be done I feel unable to judge; for I ought to hold myself, if possible, indifferent. I propose being at Birmingham, *en passant*, early after the 21st.'

A passage in this letter bears obvious allusion to the regrets I had expressed to the new Cardinal on the prospect of losing his services and his leading in England. At the time specified in his letter Cardinal Wiseman called on me in Birmingham. In the course of our conversation he said that in the course of a fortnight he expected to quit these shores forever, as the Holy Father had stated that he would provide his successor in London. He then added that for certain reasons which he alleged he thought it probable that I might be his successor, and having this feeling he wished to give me his ideas, if I would allow him, of the London District. At once, upon this, I frankly told him my reasons why I considered myself unfit for that post, and spoke in detail as I saw and felt. After this interview the Cardinal told those who accompanied him that he did not think that any of those of whom rumour spoke would go to London; and I have no doubt but that he had completely bent his mind on returning to England if he could accomplish it.

The venerable Bishop Walsh had departed this life in the previous year and the new Cardinal had succeeded him as Vicar-Apostolic. On his arrival in Rome Cardinal Wiseman, as I have been informed by Cardinal Barnabo, represented that his services were still required in London.

A Canadian Suplician, the Abbé Quiblier, also drew up and presented an argument to shew the importance to the interests of the Church of keeping Cardinal Wiseman in England, and the Pope was much struck by it. It is also said that the politicians, apprehensive lest the new Cardinal's influence in their line should counteract that of Cardinal Antonelli, threw their weight into the same scale. Later on the impression grew in Rome that Cardinal Wiseman, with his habits and constitution, could not have plodded at the labour of the Roman Congregations, but though he himself might not have had much apprehension I do not think that this was a point that at all entered into the consideration at the time, or would have influenced it had it been started.

It was decided that His Eminence should return to England, and only one difficulty remained for solution. For a Cardinal to be a Vicar-Apostolic was without precedent, and to make such a precedent was considered inexpedient. The difficulty was solved by promulgating the already prepared Brief of the Hierarchy and making Cardinal Wiseman the first Archbishop of Westminster.

How the Hierarchy was promulgated and what agitation followed[2] is well known, but what led to this excitement is not perhaps so well understood. When present at the deliberation of the Sacred Congregation I had given Their Eminences the most solemn assurance that no English law would be violated in the promulgation of the Hierarchy as then planned, and the fact that no law could be found by the Crown lawyers to meet the case, as admitted by the necessity of passing a new law after the fact to meet the case,[3] proved that I was right. This I told Lord John Russell in my letter to him, printed in *The Times* newspaper.

On my return to England it was generally reported that the Hierarchy had been then established, and the statement appeared in some newspapers. Still there was no excitement. How then was the excitement actually brought about? It came about in this manner.

When Bishop Wiseman was sent from Rome with a special mission to the English Government in 1846, he sent before him a letter addressed to *The Times* expounding the policy involved in his mission. The Pope was then extremely popular in England and the letter was well received. The result, however, of that mission was the sending of Lord Minto to Rome as a sort of non-official envoy from England. Intended to be a support to the Pope, he became an embarrassment, leaguing himself with the party of revolution. When the same Bishop Wiseman was made Cardinal and First Archbishop of Westminster, His Eminence had the impression that an announcement of these facts would also be acceptable in England. And accordingly a letter was addressed from Rome to *The Times* under his inspiration, which, as the Cardinal himself subsequently told me, *The Times* kept for three days unpublished before its managers decided as to what course they should adopt. They finally resolved to raise the country, and it must be remembered that the letter arrived at the most vacant time of the year in politics. Accordingly they no sooner published the letter than they began to set the country in flame against its contents. Soon after, a copy of the Brief of the Hierarchy got into the French *Univers. The Times* seized upon it at once, and worked upon its contents with all its power. It is a positive fact that this Brief thus got into *The Times* several weeks before a single copy of it reached England by way of promulgation. Then came Cardinal Wiseman's Pastoral from the Flaminian Gate.[4], the last thing wanted to raise the flame of excitement to fever heat.

More than once *The Times* had put the question whether no statesman could be found to turn this 'political capital' to use, and Lord John Russell now fell into the snare and published his letter to the Bishop of Durham without consulting any of his colleagues in office. That the Queen got excited by the unguarded language of the Pastoral appears probable, and was said at the time; that the Cardinal wrote it never dreaming of the excited state of the country and of the use *The Times* was prepared to make of it was quite certain. The error was in the Vicar-General's giving publication under circumstances wholly different from those contemplated by its eminent author.

Coupled with these documents there were other things which tended to make the members of the administration sore. There was still a vivid remembrance of the rebuff received by Lord Clarendon, the Lord Lieutenant of Ireland, when his letter to the Sovereign Pontiff about the Irish Colleges was allowed to drop unanswered. There was still remembrance of the way in which Mr. Romilly's bill for settling our Catholic property had been treated. There were the troubles and controversies connected with Lord Minto's mission to Rome. He had been sent by Lord John Russell, who was his own father-in-law, and was sent on the Pope's invitation through Cardinal Wiseman. True, he had acted a disloyal part to the Pope, but Lord John had been badgered about it, and this did not sweeten his testy temper. Then Cardinal Wiseman, instead of coming direct to England, went direct to Vienna, was entertained by the young Emperor, and it was just after the affair of the brutal treatment of one of the Emperor's generals in a London brewery, which had caused irritation on the side of Austria. And the Cardinal wrote a letter with something of the tone of patronage to Lord John from Vienna, at least so the letter announcing his return as Cardinal to England was interpreted. This last combination of circumstances led to the inference, however untrue in itself, that they were going to have a Cardinal devoted to Austrian influences in London.

After all the solicitude exhibited by the Roman Cardinals in discussing the Hierarchy, the subsequent policy demanded in its promulgation undoubtedly was that it should have been done as quietly and as much within our own circle as possible. Unhappily the opposite course was adopted, which defeated all the precautions that had inspired the Roman Congregation and the Pope.

The first weight of the controversy on the part of the Church fell upon me. I saw the expediency of issuing a joint declaration from the Bishops, drew one up, and got the signatures and approval of all the Bishops except that of Bishop Briggs, and he being the senior Bishop I did not feel justified in acting in any joint manifesto without his co-operation. He simply wrote back that, 'We ought to hold ourselves in our silent dignity'. The fact was, as I afterwards found out, that he did not see any paper until the second day after its appearance and, in fact, knew little of what was passing. At last he also took alarm, and wrote me a letter suggesting that Dr. Newman ought to be invited to write, and laid down the style in which he ought to write. As in duty bound, I shewed the letter to Dr. Newman who could only give a silent shrug, as I expected.

When at last Cardinal Wiseman's Pastoral appeared in *The Times*, and the Durham letter of Lord John followed, I went up to London, prepared to go on the Continent to meet the Cardinal and consult with him what was to be done.

I saw his Vicar-General who said that so many messages had been sent to the Cardinal, and such urgent ones, that he was sure to be here soon. But what was wanted, and what the lawyers in Westminster Hall were calling for, was a pamphlet on our side. The world wanted to know what we had to say in reply. I told him I would return to Birmingham and have one out by the end of the week.

I asked him: 'How could you have published that Pastoral? You must have known that Cardinal Wiseman never contemplated the state of things amidst which it was destined to appear; and that, had he known what was going on, he would not have written in that style.'

He said: 'I am young and inexperienced, and in my perplexity did not know what to do, so I thought it best to obey the injunction within it, that it should be read in the churches on the Sunday following its arrival.'

I asked him why, in an affair of such importance which involved our common interests, he had not taken the advice of some of the senior Bishops before doing so. He said he had not thought of that.

I returned to Birmingham and began the pamphlet. Mr. Estcourt got together the passages from Lord John Russell's former parliamentary speeches in which he had assumed the principles upon which the Hierarchy had been established, the similar passages in Lord Lyndhurst's speeches, etc. I wrote a letter for the Cardinal that might reach his hands on his arrival, telling him what I was doing, informing him how Lord John had gone against all his antecedent maxims, etc.

On the Cardinal's arrival, two days after, his Vicar-General wrote to me, informing me that the Cardinal himself wished to write, and asking me if I would give him my materials, and come up to London to explain them. This I accordingly did, and His Eminence, from materials chiefly gathered up by Mr. Estcourt and myself, published his famous appeal.

It must be said that when once the Cardinal was on the scene he fought his battle manfully. His appeal and the Birmingham public meeting stayed the flood and turned the tide. The address which I had prepared, to be issued with the signatures of all the Bishops, was turned to another use, and published as the declaration of the Catholic clergy and laity of Birmingham, and after having been adopted by them at a general meeting, being proposed by Dr. Newman.

A few anecdotes, omitted in their proper place, may conclude the subject of the Hierarchy. Cardinal Wiseman, in his *Reminiscences of Four Popes*, tells us that Gregory XVI had expressed his willingness to restore the Hierarchy under certain contingencies, and at the very time marked by him the arrangements for its restoration commenced.

When Bishops Wiseman and Sharples put in their petition and reply to Cardinal Acton's paper, on the petition coming before Pius IX, His Holiness declined giving any opinion upon it, until he had offered the Holy Sacrifice three times, and after the first and second Mass he spoke with uncertainty on the subject. After the third Mass he said: '*Adesso sono tranquillo.*' (Now I feel tranquil on the subject.)

Cardinal, then Mgr., Barnabò inherited the papers of Cardinal Polidori, and it was amongst these that he found Cardinal Acton's paper against conceding the Hierarchy to England, the paper which Drs. Wiseman and Sharples answered in 1847. Dr. Grant says that Cardinal Acton's words to him always were: 'Everybody in England, Bishops and Regulars, tries for the Hierarchy in the hope that his own power will become greater thereby, and will be disappointed in this hope.' His chief objection was that England would be less attached to the Holy See under the Hierarchy.

The Five Sees left in administration under the existing Bishops in 1850 were filled up in June, 1851, and as the Ecclesiastical Titles Bill was then under discussion in Parliament, it was thought advisable to allow them to be consecrated before it became law. The Bishops of Clifton, Plymouth, Shrewsbury and Salford received power to be consecrated under a decree of Propaganda without waiting for the arrival of the Briefs. The fifth Bishop, Dr. Grant of Southwark, was consecrated at Rome.

Cardinal Vizzardelli drew up the Brief for constituting the Chapters, as well as that of the Hierarchy.

All the Bishops met in London in November, 1851, and agreed upon the petitions preparatory to the first Synod, which are embodied in the Rescripts of April, 1852, printed in the Appendix to the first Provincial Synod.

The clause in the Apostolic Brief of the Hierarchy taking away and abrogating all peculiar constitutions and privileges as well as customs, had in view, amongst other objections, the complete suppression of the English Chapter. The history of this singular corporation, as given in Dodd's *History*,[5] was laid before the Holy See. It was established by Bishop Bishop[6] with Apostolic authority and had continued by appointing its own members; and strange to say, its members claimed to possess the ecclesiastical jurisdiction in England, and whilst as missioners its members obeyed the Vicars-Apostolic, they had a sort of crypto-doctrine that the Vicars-Apostolic were interlopers, and that the right of nominating Bishops rested with them. I have seen a correspondence between the late Mr. Jones of London and Dr. Kirk, in which Mr. Jones maintained these doctrines in vehement language. Cardinal Vizzardelli declared that this English Chapter was invalid from the beginning, and the most elementary knowledge of the subject would have proved it to be so. The moment, however, that the Brief appeared this so-called Chapter surrendered its pretensions.[7]

It was after producing the passage from Mr. Anstey's *Penal Laws* in 1848 that Mgr. Barnabò said: 'We had long wished to see the Hierarchy restored, but we were unwilling to do anything opposed to your laws, but as Mr. Anstey shews that the law does not forbid the erecting of Sees in towns where no Protestant Sees exist, we can go on without hesitation.'

The Church in England ought never to forget the debt of gratitude it owes to Cardinal Barnabò, through whose zeal and energy this great measure was achieved. How actively, faithfully and perseveringly His Eminence has laboured from the Year 1847 to the present time, 1868, in preparing all subjects respecting England, its Hierarchy and its Synods for the consideration of the Sovereign Pontiff, is well known to all the Bishops.

The conducting of the first Provincial Synod was the masterpiece of Cardinal Wiseman. He it was who drew up the decrees, except the Constitutions for the cathedral Chapters which were committed to Bishop Grant. The unity and harmony which pervaded that Chapter is one of the most delightful reminiscences of my episcopal life. Certainly no one but Cardinal Wiseman, who concentrated his whole capacious mind upon it in one of his happiest periods could have brought it to so successful an issue; or have given to it so great an amount of Ecclesiastical splendour. And there the rule and precedent was established for the conducting of our future Synods.

With the completion of the Hierarchal Order I conclude these reminiscences, uncertain whether at a future period I may resume and continue them or not.

Notes

1   Papers officially 'placed' with a Sacred Congregation, the word being more commonly used with reference to beatifications and canonizations.

2   By the time Cardinal Wiseman reached England in November 1850 the fanatical fury of the agitation caused by the so-called 'Papal aggression' was at its height. Every article printed by *The Times* on the subject was more bitter then its predecessor; the premier's famous letter to the Bishop of Durham, inveighing against the Pope's action as 'insolent and insidious' fanned the flame; Queen Victoria showed her sympathy with the agitation in her reply to an address from the Anglican Bishops; riotous public meetings, and the burning in effigy of Pope, Cardinals and prelates kept the whole country in a state of ferment for several weeks; and Wiseman in his progress through London was frequently hooted, and stones thrown at the windows of his carriage. Nothing daunted he instantly set about the composition of his masterly, *Appeal to the reason and Good Feeling of the English People on the Subject of the Catholic Hierarchy*, a pamphlet of some thirty pages addressed to the people themselves rather than to the educated minority who in the writer's view had so grossly and inexcusably misled them. The cogency and ability of the appeal was frankly recognised by the English Press, and the political enemies of the government were not slow to point out the inconsistency of its dealings with the Catholics of England and Ireland.

3   *The Ecclesiastical Titles Bill*, make the assumption by Catholics of Episcopal titles in the United Kingdom a penal offence. It was introduced into Parliament early in 1851 and became law on 1 August; but it was a dead letter from the first, as Gladstone had the courage and prescience to declare that it would be. Its provisions were never enforced, and it was repealed during Gladstone's first premiership twenty years later.

4   On 29th Sept., 1850, the Papal Brief re-establishing the Hierarchy in England had been issued.

    On 30th Sept., 1850, Nicholas Wiseman was named a Cardinal.

    On 7th Oct., 1850, Cardinal Wiseman announced the new Hierarchy to English Catholics in his Pastoral sent *From the Flaminian Gate*.

    These events all took place in Rome and, of course, it took time for the Pastoral officially to reach London.

5   Charles Dodd (Ullathorne gives it a single 'd') was the pen name of Hugh Tootell (1671–1743), a Lancashire born cleric who was educated at Douay. He wrote his *Church History of England from 1500 to 1688* over a twenty year period at Harvington Hall in Worcestershire. It was published in three folio volumes between 1737 and 1742 at Wolverhampton. It says something of the times that Brussels appears on the title page. He appears to have entertained a marked prejudice against the Jesuits, however on his deathbed he expressed his desire to die in peace with them.

6   William Bishop (1553–1624), First Vicar-Apostolic in Episcopal orders after the old Hierarchy died out in the reign of Elizabeth I.

7   In 1623 Bishop Bishop 'instituted a Chapter of twenty-four canons, who were to assume jurisdiction whenever there should be for any reason no Vicar-Apostolic, which happened at one time for thirty years. His right to make such an institution has often been questioned, but during the period referred to, Rome recognised their jurisdiction. On the restoration of the Hierarchy in 1850, when Diocesan Chapters were erected, the 'Old Chapter' did not dissolve, but changed its name, and as the 'Old Brotherhood of the Secular Clergy' it exists today, a lasting memorial to the first Vicar-Apostolic.

Appendix
A SPIRITUAL MAN

A SERMON

Preached in St. Chad's Cathedral, Birmingham,

(March 26, 1889)

AT THE SOLEMN REQUIEM FOR THE

Most Rev.

WILLIAM BERNARD ULLATHORNE, O.S.B.,

ARCHBISHOP OF CABASA

AND

FIRST BISHOP OF BIRMINGHAM

BY THE

Rt. Rev. JOHN CUTHBERT HEDLEY, O.S.B.

BISHOP OF NEWPORT AND MENEVIA.

BURNS & OATS, (Ltd.), LONDON AND NEW YORK

A Spiritual Man

And the Spirit of the Lord shall rest upon him. He shall not judge according to the sight of the eyes, nor reprove according to the hearing of the ears. He shall judge with justice, and shall reprove with equity; and faith shall be the girdle of his reins.
— Isa. xi. 1–3.

These sacred words were spoken of One greater than man. Yet they may rightly used to describe a follower of that great Master. If the Master has sent His Spirit — if He went up to the heavens and was taken from mortal sight for the very purpose that His Spirit — that is Himself, the very God — might more effectively be with us and remain with us, it must be true of many men, as the world rolls on, that the Spirit of the Lord rests upon them.

Today we have to speak of such a man. The world is nothing to him now. He can speak to us no longer, nor we to him. The great gulf has been passed, and we see the well-known face no more. His spirit's outward tabernacle — itself no longer the same — is all that is left to our senses; in a few hours it too must be laid in the ground. In this solemn hour, then, when the sense of his passing is strong upon us, when Nature, God's minister, with gentle and mournful touch, begins to blot his features out, when the outward vesture of his immortal spirit fittingly rests for a few silent and pleading hours before an earthly altar of the living God, let us venture to commune together, you, my friends, and I, who unworthily stand here and fix before our inward gaze the real man — the man who will never die. For good or for evil, no man ever dies. His personality persists, his soul lives on, his consciousness is not interrupted, he carries as a vesture the merits and the evil of his life. It is right that man should never judge the dead.

371

But today we can say much more than that. Let those venerated remains be lifted high with solemn pomp, let the lights burn, let the dirge and requiem resound! Your hearts are full of prayer for his expiation; but you are prepared also to reverence the memory of a bishop, to thank God for a priest, to rejoice in the thought of a great teacher, and gently to sorrow for a father and a friend.

It would be impossible to give from this place a biography of William Bernard Ullathorne, of the Holy Order of St. Benedict, Archbishop of Cabasa, and the first Bishop of Birmingham; and happily it is altogether unnecessary. There are few Catholics, whether priests or laity, who read at all, who have not to some extent followed the interesting and chequered life of a man who, in some respects, was a great man, and who was remarkable alike in character, in mental power, and in action. The few data I shall find it useful to give will be rather to illustrate his spirit than to present his history.

Born on the seventh of May, 1806, at Pocklington, a small Yorkshire town, not far from York, he was in his eighty-third year when, in the early afternoon of the feast of St. Benedict, God's messenger, Death, came to his bedside at Oscott, to end his sufferings and to lead him over the threshold of life eternal. Of these eighty-three years, sixty-five had been spent in the religious habit of the Order of St. Benedict. It was on St. Gregory's Day, 1824, at St. Gregory's Monastery of Downside, that he was asked, as we have all been asked, what it was he sought, and that he answered, as the confessors before him and their humble imitators after him have answered, 'If it please God and you, I desire to save my soul among you, under the rule of the Blessed Father St. Benedict.' A life so long and so full is a life with a beginning, a middle, and an end: a preparation, a culmination, and a sunset. Let us first see what his preparation was.

There are three masters for every novice. I speak of all beginners who range themselves on God's side and begin to live and to learn. Their life is their learning, and their learning is almost their entire life. Their masters are men, things, and God; the voice of teachers, their environment, and the Holy Spirit. Perhaps Bishop Ullathorne learnt little from men, at any time of his life. There were teachers at Downside at that time, of whom he said, that he learned the elements of mental philosophy which stood its ground amid all the multifarious reading of his after-life. There was one name especially to whom he confessed his obligations as an exact and learned exponent of divinity and morality. He was too thorough a man not to understand that one cannot learn without docility and humility. It was a lesson he was never weary of repeating in his retreats and on other occasions. Therefore, when he went to the monastery, young and eager, after some experience of the roughness of the world, it was to submit himself; and I have heard him say that he found among his Benedictine superiors, together with a simplicity at which even a young man was tempted sometimes to smile, a spirituality, a traditional method of direction, and a self-sacrifice which satisfied and captivated his spirit.

Then he had books. There are few men who during their whole life have read more persistently. He was as far as possible from being a book-worm. But there are minds which feed and grow on books. There are characters to whom books are not so much information as development. Other men read for facts, for views, for the interest of the panorama which the printed page unfolds; they read to use their reading, they read for curiosity, they read that they may for an hour forget their troubles. But the former read chiefly in order to recognise and make sure of their own thoughts. For men of this order of mind have a serious strain of thought, which goes to the root of things; active thought, with a keen point, which pierces through disguises, tears away coverings, and strives after the principles of the wise man and the views of the philosopher. And as human reason is in every man a created participation of the Divine Intelligence, it follows that the sound philosophical thinkers of every age think alike. The great thoughts of humanity are few. They are few, but they are powerful, like the powers of nature which make up the moving universe. Yet, like them, they are infinite in variety; for although the sun and the air, the earth and the element of water, almost exhaust this creation, yet not twice does the sun rise alike, not twice does the forest sway the same way to the winds, not twice the waves in their ceaseless motion dash in the same curves upon the rock.

Those who remember Bishop Ullathorne in his youth recall the figure of a student bowed over the folio of a Father of the Church. He read Augustine and Origen, Ambrose and Tertullian, Chrysostom and his own St. Bernard; he was borne to them because he found the thoughts that were his own thoughts. He had thoughts – thoughts about God and nature, the soul and eternity, Christ's love, and man's endurance. They were the thoughts which suited his temperament. In him, it is true, in those early days — and as he would have said, all his life — those grand ideas were rudimentary, unconnected, half unrecognised, like the sphinxes of ancient civilizations, almost buried in the heaped-up desert sand. But in the Fathers they stood out clear and distinct. As he read he saw what his ideas meant, what his speculations led to. He grew confident and full of heart when he beheld his own faint outlines stand so firm and bright in the page of St. Ambrose. He rose, as an eagle rises slowly above the mountain ridges, when Augustine carried him up to serenest heights of speculation, and the universe and its fate were seen spread out below in continents and rivers rolling seas. He loved to find the sternness of his spirit and the tenderness of his spirit — for he had both — formulated in pathetic severity and self-denying sweetness in the letters and homilies of St. Bernard. Many a time did those constant readings bear fruit in the practical utterances of his life. Every priest, and many of his flock, know how habitually his words came out with the unmistakable brand upon them of some ancient doctor; and he has left it on record that in preaching to the convicts of New South Wales on the darkest sins of human nature he was never so effective as when he was almost literally translating from the Fathers.

Then Bishop Ullathorne was a man who did not learn from human voices alone, living or dead. He was not a mere thinker; he was keen for work from the very beginning. He stepped boldly into business when it concerned him. He had the greatest belief in using his hands. On ship board — and he passed many a month of his life there, whether in his early sailor days, or as a missionary travelling to and from the Antipodes — he learned to do everything, and he practised himself in habits of quickness, readiness and endurance. But it was in more apostolic and priestly matters that his early life prepared him most. I pass over his novitiate. During his young monastic life he had that training which is derived from the teaching of boys — a discipline which in every man who is worth training develops two invaluable powers, the control of temper and the secret of holding the attention of others.

But when, in the twenty-seventh year of his age, he was sent as a missionary to New South Wales, it was then that every faculty of his mind and body began to be stimulated to the utmost. He had to seek out sinful men and women, and to induce the most degraded of convicts to turn to God. He had to preach, to pray, to labour, to travel. He had to deal with Government officials, and make public protest against deep-seated and terrible abuses. He had to conciliate his own priests and fellow-workers. He had to take up the cause of the Faith in speeches and publications. Whatever Bishop Ullathorne had read, whatever he had studied or learnt, there can be no doubt that his strength and characteristic force, both in doing and enduring, came largely from these Australian days. In all this history there is nothing so full of interest, of energy, of generous self-sacrifice, as the record of the years during which he laid the foundations of that great Australian church. When he landed at Port Jackson there were no more than half-a-dozen priests, besides himself, in all that continent. Before he died he saw a hierarchy of twenty-eight bishops, the guides and leaders of a numerous clergy and people, as strongly Catholic as any flock in the world.

But how can we calculate or estimate that teaching of the Holy Spirit which was going on during these years of his preparation? Naturally, such discipline of the soul is hidden within the soul itself. A man does not talk about his prayer and his self-restraint. The education of his spirit is generally a secret, even to himself. There are signs, however, which can be read; and we can gather that in spite of the immense activity of those early days, he was training himself in great ideals. There is an interval between his return from New South Wales and his appointment to an English bishopric – the period, that is to say, which he spent as a missionary priest in Coventry. Of these days we have one or two glimpses. In 1842 he refused the bishopric of Adelaide. I possess a letter in which he gives at great length his reasons for declining a post so hard and ungrateful. They are of purely historical interest. Adelaide is a very different See now – forty-seven years after. But the proposal stirred him strangely. He says, 'I have written to the Provincial to ask to go for a week and make a retreat before making my answer.' – (Easter Monday, 1842.) The climate, he goes on to say, would most certainly break him down, not to speak of the peculiar and enormous difficulties of the position. He did not like to refuse; a month or two later he writes, 'I only want to do what is right; but what can I do, or what ought I to do? My mind is brooding, despite of me, and my detestable pride makes me miserable enough; my health is affected, and thus reacts upon my mind. What can I, or ought I to do? All I want is to do right, but I am groping in the dark.' – (Ascension, 1842.) Here is the curtain lifted for a moment from the struggles of a human heart, studying to walk right before his God, and taking refuge in humility and prayer.

The cloud passed by and he was left at Coventry. Then we find him throwing his whole heart into his mission work. 'What might be done by men full of discipline, energy, and self-abnegation!' – he writes (January 30th, 1844) – 'Would not any one whom God should call to such a work do more as a monk even than as a bishop? After I had given out my ideas on the want of Apostolic men in the preface to the *Sermons*, I received a long and warm letter from a Professor of Maynooth, since a bishop, urging me to take up the task, and offering to select me ten or twelve picked young men to aid the undertaking in every way.' – (ibid.) These were his aspirations and his ideals – and he 'thought it good' (I again quote his words in 1844) 'to write and speak of these things, and the more the better, as it might hasten the Apostolic hour.'

His dream was that perhaps it might one day be given to him to inspire one or two fellow-priests with his own generosity and thoroughness. He lived to do the work from a higher place and over a far wider field. But it is touching now, half a century afterwards, to disinter these relics of a youth that began to give itself wholly to God and to learn the secret of Jesus.

And now years must be passed over. We have seen something of his preparation. Let us try to understand a little his real work. I have ventured to apply to him the words that were spoken of his Master: 'There shall rest upon him the Spirit of the Lord.' I have thought that there was no way to describe him better than to say he was a *spiritual man*. St. Paul says, 'now we have received not the spirit of this world, but the spirit which is of God' (1 Cor. ii. 12.) And this is the sense in which the Apostle uses the word spiritual three verses lower down – 'The spiritual man judgeth all things'; that is, the really spiritual man hath a measure and a test to judge of everything in heaven and on earth. For the presence of the Spirit of God in the heart of God's saints is a greater manifestation of God than God's creation is.

To be truly 'spiritual,' is to a human being more than was the stirring of power to the new-made earth, when the Spirit in primordial days moved on the face of the waters. It is in

St. Paul chiefly that we read the character of this heavenly Spirit, the value of this heavenly wisdom. He compares it with every other kind of wisdom and every other spirit. It is a nobler Spirit than the spirit of the material world; for though the world is wonderful, and beautiful, and admirable, yet the universe revealed to the Spirit is grander and more lovely still. The heights and the depths of grace, the sunshine of Divine presence, the beauty and variety of the Church, the clear horizon of the everlasting hills – these are the world of the Spirit.

It is nobler than the wisdom of sense; for sense is short-sighted, and sense can only take in what time and mortality present; but the Spirit knows the glorious past, and grasps the bewildering future; the Spirit sees and hears the unembodied realities which are round about us everywhere. It is infinitely more precious than the wisdom of the flesh; for the flesh aims low, loves to lie in earthly sunshine, and dreads the arrows aimed by mortal hands; but the Spirit is straitened, and is trod upon, and is bruised, and is put to death, and yet lives, and grows, and rejoices. For in truth, the wisdom of the Spirit is the wisdom not of man, but of God Himself – a new creation, a glorifying of the creature, a radiance born of no earthly sun, but the sun which was lifted up on Calvary. It is a mighty Spirit, for nothing on earth can quench it, and everything must be one day beneath its feet. It is a sweet Spirit, a kind and gentle Spirit, for it recognises its Creator's loving touch in every man and in every created thing. It is a true Spirit, not knowing how to lie, without fiction and without guile, simple and straight; for it has only one object for all its aim and all its striving, and that object is the God whom man must finally possess, for whom his heart was made, and whom his heart must have, or be forever desolate.

No one who knew William Bernard Ullathorne will fail to recognise his features here. He was a Christian, and a Catholic, and a religious, and a priest. Many virtues go to the making of a good man in every one of these respects. But there are good men who strike one chiefly as being spiritually wise. There are men who, in the spiritual field as others in the arena of this world, think our ends, organise means and plan results; who try what is false and reject it; who are clearly conscious whither they are going, and whither other people ought to go. They reflect on the problems of the world out of sight;

they solve questions by spiritual principles; and as they clear their own path through the tangle and peril of existence, so they become fitted and apt to guide other men. I judge from his books, from his letters, from his dealings with soul, from his views of human life and human suffering. He was a spiritual man.

To give an idea of his spiritual life during the last forty years – the years of his work and force – I will quote a letter which has never been published. It was written as far back as 1853. It is in many respects an interesting letter, for it was written when he was in Warwick gaol, detained there on account of his legal liability for the failure of a bank. It presents a singularly vivid sketch of his directness of view and his unconventionality. The letter reads as if he were translating his own meditations.

I find that in a gaol as in a convent everything helps recollection. Indeed, it is the world without that takes us from attention to God within. If we will only look away from our own subjective existence and look straight towards our Lord, who is always with us, even when we are not with Him, we shall find all places alike. For God is our true place. The real bane of our life is that low inward living on our own personal feelings, always and at all times searching the agreeable and shunning the disagreeable ones. Sifting them in the sieve of our self-love. Coiling ourselves up in our cherished sentiments and sensations, as the snail coils up his poor viscera within his shell. Never fairly throwing ourselves out openly and faithfully to Our Lord. How can He operate on such materials kept closed within the sensitive coil of nature by such a will?

An earnest look at the soul into our Divine Lord's presence, an earnest listening to His few and simple words of infinite life and power, an earnest surrender of all our interior tendencies and feelings to His tranquil attraction – this is to find ourselves with our Lord and His eternal years at each moment of existence.

After an hour thus introverted not into our own sense, but into our Lord's heart, of Whose emotions, as the Man-God, the Psalms are the written exposition, return to yourselves, and the light which has been gathering and warming all the time will reveal layer beneath layer of pride and nothingness within the habitual life, of which the soul dreamed not. Then arises wonder upon wonder at the mystery of such an existence as ours, and at the goodness of God. And adoration, with the beginning of a true perception of the facts how God is all and we nothing, except as He operates divinely on our nothingness, and that by adhering with our will to Him and His operations we alone begin to live true life.

My brethren, these are the words of a spiritual man. They were written thirty-six years before he died. They are a programme of his life. How many of you have heard echoes of those words? – you, his clergy, as he sat with his pastoral staff in his hand in his Chair in this cathedral Church; you, seminarists, in his familiar conferences; the religious women of his diocese at their *grilles*; men and women of every rank in private and touching letters; his flock at large in those broad and graphic pastoral letters with which you are familiar; nay, all English-speaking Catholics in these wise and grave books, so truly spiritual, which he was happily spared to give to the world.

I cannot give – perhaps no one could give – details of his hours of prayer and contemplation. He was a man who never spoke directly of his own devotional exercises. But I can give you three facts. First, his life was a retired and unworldly life; therefore he had abundant time for interior prayer. He moved about, it is true, from mission to mission, from convent to convent, as a bishop must; he appeared at the openings of churches, and at the funerals of his clergy; he was seen from time to time in the houses of some of those devoted laity who mourn his loss as deeply as any of us. But even on his journeys he lived a reserved and unworldly life; idle conversation, frivolous amusement, even the innocent recreation of walks or games – these things were not according to his spirit. He read much, but not light reading. Therefore, in spite of the task of administration, his time was free for the daily sacrifice of prayer, and his heart was never out of tune with worship, with union, with compunction.

Next, we know how intensely his intellect (to say no more) realised the necessity of interior prayer. One reads that in the three last great books of his life. Now a man who was seen to live much in society and to be occupied with earthly business might be suspected to preach what he did not practise. Not so a man who lived in reserve, detachment, and ascetic severity.

Then, thirdly, he must have prayed, because he was self-restrained, and because he was patient. No one who knew him can doubt that self-mastery and silent patience grew upon him as his life went on. Now this is a sure proof of habitual communing with God, and with our Blessed Saviour in His Passion. Therefore I believe that that room he occupied for so long – that quiet room amid the dinginess and noise of Birmingham, where his books stood round him, and his papers lay about – was a cell and shrine of meditation. I believe that the dimly-lighted oratory where our Lord's real presence dwelt was to him truly the house of God and the Gate of Heaven; the chamber where God was as a Friend who speaks and is spoken to; the threshold of that invisible world, which his servant ever strove to enter, ever strove to live in. I believe there was not a sanctuary in the diocese, whether of devout convent or of poor mission, where his spirit has not poured itself forth, at silent evening or in early morning, in ardent, deep, and true, and lengthened prayer.

His spiritual character displayed itself externally in every branch of his duties, in all the details of his office. It was very marked in his dealings with his clergy. I am speaking in the presence of that clergy of the diocese of Birmingham, whom he loved so well, and of whom he was so justly proud. They know his ways and methods better than any extern. But I venture to think they will agree with me that he was a wise, firm, and kind Superior. I think they would say, if they were asked, that his wisdom was spiritual wisdom, his firmness founded on the fear of God, and his kindness not the kindness which kills, but which builds up to our Lord. His manner, no doubt, had its drawbacks, as it had its advantages. He was always a little difficult of approach, unless he himself took the initiative; it was the effect of his determination to be genuine and straight. But I will dare boldly to assert that no man has ever seen him speak, or act, or command, or reprove, in temper, in self-assertion, or in bitterness. He was never small, nor mean, nor selfish. Those who came in contact with him felt that they had met a real man, rooted and founded in unmistakable solid earth – a man who might rebuff you, but would never pass you false coin. When he did speak freely he was copious in speech. All his life he was ready to write, whether on public matters or to his friends; and he would talk, sometimes subtly, sometimes learnedly, sometimes playfully, with a fluency and force which many here can bear witness to.

It was certainly his beloved clergy who were nearest to his heart. It was they who gave him the opportunity of carrying out the longing aspirations of his early years. His whole Episcopate was one effort to 'hasten the Apostolic hour.' His method, it seems to me, may be described in one word. He aimed at spiritualising the hearts of his priests, rather than drilling their steps. He was not a man for many rules or many questions. If he could make a young heart realise its God – if he could touch a priest with the mission and the message of his Lord – if he could get a labourer in the vineyard to listen to the love which speaks from the Cross – he was satisfied. The rest would come. His ecclesiastical discourses, his synodical addresses, and his numerous letters will form a body of spiritual teaching for priests of which this diocese may well be proud. And indeed, this great Midland diocese, which has listened to Milner and to Wiseman, has been emphatically built up to our Lord by Bishop Ullathorne. His organisation, his careful administration of temporalities, his seminary, his synods, his visitations, and his books have left upon it the impress of his mind; nay, not of his mind so much, but of that Spirit of God who deigned to possess his heart and his intelligence.

In speaking of his pastoral work, it would be wrong not to allude to his labours for religious women. But no more than an allusion can here be made. His grand object in all that he said and wrote for them was this: that the religious life of women, which is so holy and so fruitful, might be established by solid and prudent rule; that law might exclude whims and fancies; that principle might prevail, and not personality; and that the women consecrated to God might walk at peace in the large and airy cloister of knowledge, rational obedience, and theological direction. There are no hearts that will mourn for him or pray for him today so faithfully as those dear and cherished nuns, from the contemplative of the Perpetual Adoration to the Sister of Mercy who 'goes about doing good,' to whom the very choicest fruits of his spirit were given, even to the end. It was naturally in communication with interior souls, who had renounced the world and the flesh, that his own spiritual wisdom flowed so freely. His religious have, therefore, the truest picture of his character – his character, not as it came from nature, but as it was shaped, chastened and lifted up by the work of the Holy Spirit. They could tell the world more than I can. They could tell what they have learnt from him. To them he was what he wanted *them* to be. 'God alone!' was his device, formulated, perhaps, though not first conceived, in the humble presbytery at Coventry, where St. Thomas and St. Bernard were his only intimate friends, amidst his ceaseless toil for the poor work-people and their poor children. 'Nothing created between me and my God!' was his prayer; uttered many a time in the lonely solitudes of the vast ocean. 'Truth is Humility, and humility is only Truth,' was his philosophy, learned from the luminous words of an ancient solitary, who had found it out amid the sands of the Nile valley, to hand it down to one who often said that his ideal of life was his monastic cell.

Perhaps I ought to give some sketch of his public life; but it would be impossible here, and it is all sufficiently written elsewhere. In England he was Bishop, first at Clifton and then here in Birmingham, where he lived for forty years. In Catholic matters he was ever at his post; whether it was to negotiate the restoration of the Catholic Hierarchy or to stem the tide of the 'Papal Aggression' fury, which Birmingham to its credit was the first community to shake off, or to 'unravel' the sophistical declamation of statesmen against the Church, or to point out errors in books and periodicals, his pen was ready. Solid, large, learned, and picturesque, his style had a rugged force; it was the verbal utterance of genuine thought and honest ideas. Willingly, too, would I dwell, did opportunity allow, on his gift of counsel, his life-long devotion to the Holy See and to the hierarchy of his own country. It was his way, in his numerous dealings with the Sovereign Pontiff and with the Roman Congregations, to take the greatest possible pains in the preparations of every document he set before them. For this purpose he constantly read widely in Canon Law and in general theology, and he devoted all the power of his acute mind to the orderly exposition of every principle and of every fact which bore upon the case in hand. It was therefore recognised that he was a counsellor who might be relied upon. There are those here present who know how Rome trusted him, how his brethren in the hierarchy valued his learning and experience, how many delicate negotiations in every part of the country were committed to him, and how many pilgrims used to come to Birmingham to ask his advice. In public matters, political, civic, or social, not pertaining to his office, he rarely took part. This city of Birmingham hardly knew him by sight, but men did know him somehow; and this attendance here today of his Worship the Mayor and of other representative men may be taken as a sign that Birmingham is not ashamed of a man to whom a Newman thought fit to point when he wished to give to the world an example of a thorough and straightforward Englishman.

For many years Bishop Ullathorne had suffered more or less continual bodily pain. The life of a bishop is indeed one of constant mental suffering; but of that he discovered little, even to his friends. I have one letter, written in 1856 – that is thirty years before he resigned his pastoral staff – in which he speaks thus to an intimate friend: 'It has been my misery ever since I had a mitre to deal with troubles. And if it had not been for the good moral state of the clergy of this diocese, I do not know how I could have gone through with it ... Nothing but the inward fear that it would be a cowardly running away from the Will of God has kept me from secretly departing the diocese, and burying myself in some lonely place in a remote country, like the old hermits, and there labouring for my daily bread. I am, and I was, quite aware that this was a temptation, and it had gone; but it will show you how much that administration of this diocese has been a pressure upon me – on me, whose ideal of a happy life is that of a monk in his monastery.'

But besides this weight of a bishop's solitude, his Lord and Master was to send him that which would draw him yet nearer to Himself. Suffering may harden the heart which has to encounter it. But suffering, accepted, embraced, taken to the open heart which has studied the sufferings of Jesus – such suffering elevates the desires, purifies the passions, intensifies love, and gives Divine charity a certain hue and character of the charity of the Sacred Heart itself. He learnt all this in many a week of solitary pain. And those who were nearest to him during his late severe and prolonged sickness, will tell you that he has written nothing in his books on Patience and on Union with God which he did not illustrate in his own carrying of the Cross of his Saviour; and moreover, that the spiritual principles of a lifetime, when the last strain was put upon them, grew into habits and instincts of nature itself; that his fine character discovered new depths, as the valleys are revealed when the sun gets low, and that a transformation seemed to be beginning which was only to be contemplated before the throne of the God whom he had chosen from his youth.

We must pray for his soul; for there are very few who do not need the expiating fires of Purgatory. We must think of him in the Holy Sacrifice; we must ask Most Holy Mary to plead lovingly for the servant who wrote so well on her Immaculate Conception; we must beg St. Benedict, who brought him by his own special prerogative a happy death, to intercede for him. Let not this be forgotten. In other ways, forgotten he cannot be. A career has begun and has grown, as a seed grows into a tree, and today the noble tree has gone down, as all mortal things must. But the world of the mind and of the spirit knows no such things as failure and decay. As the slow years and the mighty waters have in days gone by fashioned the hills which stand unmoved while the world lasts, so the turmoil of human strife and the fire of the Spirit have shaped and perfected a spiritual man; and whatever monument we build to his memory, his soul lives on forever, and his name will be cherished by his children's children for many a generation yet to come.

*The tomb of the Most Reverend William Bernard Ullathorne, O.S.B.,
Archbishop of Cabasa and First Bishop of Birmingham in St. Dominic's
Convent, Stone, Staffordshire.*